B[illegible] and Hungary

PICTOR INTERNATIONAL

Jó napot kívánok!
Üdvözöljük Magyarországon!

Hello!
Welcome to Hungary!

Travel Publications

Hannay House, 39 Clarendon Road
Watford, Herts WD17 1JA, UK
☎ 01923 205 240 - Fax 01923 205 241
www.ViaMichelin.com
TheGreenGuide-uk@uk.michelin.com

Manufacture française des pneumatiques Michelin
Société en commandite par actions au capital de 304 000 000 EUR
Place des Carmes-Déchaux – 63 Clermont-Ferrand (France)
R.C.S. Clermont-Fd B 855 200 507

Dépôt légal mars 2000 – ISBN 2-06-154201-8 – ISSN 0763-1383
Printed in France 05-02/1.2

Typesetting: Le Sanglier, Charleville-Mézières
Printing: I.M.E., Baume-les-Dames
Binding: I.M.E., Baume-les-Dames

Cover design: Carré Noir, Paris 17e arr.

THE GREEN GUIDE
Spirit of Discovery

Leisure time spent with The Green Guide is also a time for refreshing your spirit, enjoying yourself, and taking advantage of our selection of fine restaurants, hotels and other places for relaxing: immerse yourself in the local culture, discover new horizons, experience the local lifestyle. The Green Guide opens the door for you.

Each year our writers go touring: visiting the sights, devising the driving tours, identifying the highlights, selecting the most attractive hotels and restaurants, checking the routes for the maps and plans.

Each title is compiled with great care, giving you the benefit of regular revisions and Michelin's first-hand knowledge. The Green Guide responds to changing circumstances and takes account of its readers' suggestions; all comments are welcome.

Share with us our enthusiasm for travel, which has led us to discover over 60 destinations in France and other countries. Like us, let yourself be guided by the desire to explore, which is the best motive for travel: the spirit of discovery.

Contents

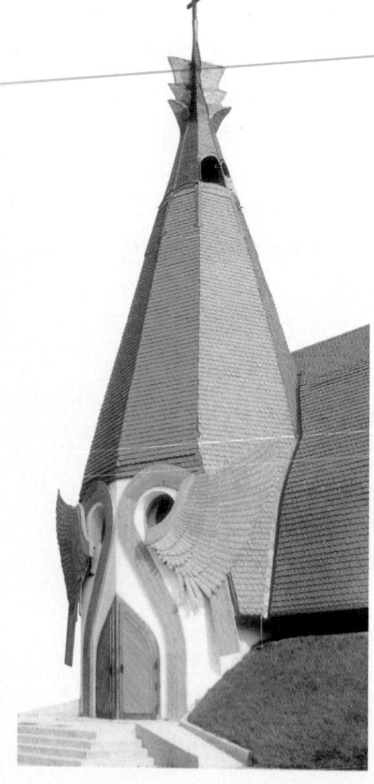

I. Galos

Siófok Lutheran Church

MAGYAR KÉPEK Kft

Herend porcelain

Sights 74

Admission times and charges 266

Index 277

R. Mattes

Water games

MAGYAR KÉPEK Kft

Budapest – Liberty Bridge

Maps

MAPS AND ROAD ATLASES FOR USE WITH THE GUIDE

Michelin map 925 Hungary

– a road and tourist map, scale 1:400 000, showing the road and motorway network, roads and motorway distances and the administrative boundaries of the provinces, with an index to locate the names of the places indicated.

and to get to Hungary:

Michelin map 970 Europe

– a road and tourist map, scale 1:3 000 000 showing the principal roads and motorways, towns or exceptional tourist locations and relief, with an index to locate the principal place names.

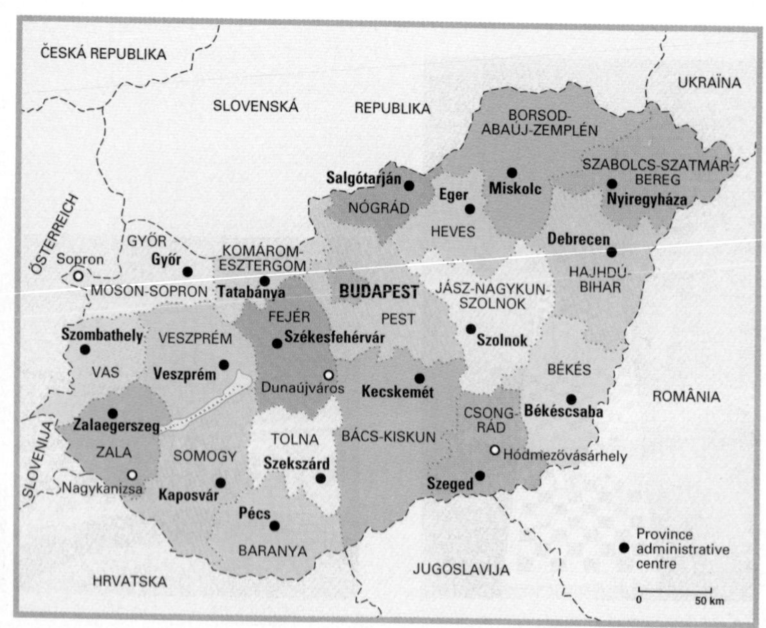

Europe road and tourist atlases 136 and 130

– n° 136: spiral-bound atlas (Western Europe, scale 1:1 000 000, Eastern Europe, scale 1:3 000 000) containing road information, a mileage chart, 74 town and urban districts, a climate map, with an index of towns and other place names indicated for easy location.

– n° 130: bound atlas (same scales).

In addition to these maps and atlases, our web site – www.ViaMichelin.com – enables you to work out detailed itineraries with travelling times, as well as offering a number of other services.

THEME MAPS

TOWN MAPS

MAPS OF DRIVING TOURS DESCRIBED

M. Guillot/MICHELIN

Budapest – Walk along the Duna korzó

Using this guide

This guide contains a wealth of information. You can find:

● **Thematic maps**: on principal sights, driving tours (the essential sights for a short trip), places to visit (how to choose your main destination according to accommodation and the surroundings) and on public transport in Budapest, found on the inside back cover of the guide.

● **Practical information:** useful addresses, accommodation, sports activities, admission times for visiting sights presented in alphabetical order (indicated by a blue clock in the "Sights" section), dates of festivals etc.

● **an Introduction:** to learn more about the country before you leave or while you are travelling – the countryside, history, traditions, food and drink, art and the country as it is at the present time.

● **Sights**: towns and interesting sights are presented in alphabetical order. The smaller places are indicated as excursions from larger towns or areas. Hungarian names have been used as far as possible in the guide to enable you to locate them more easily when you are on the spot.

For certain places (Baja, Balaton, Budapest, Bugac-Puszta, Bükk, Csongrád, Debrecen, Eger, Esztergom, Gyöngyös, Győr, Hévíz, Hollókő, Hortobágy-Puszta, Kalocsa, Kaposvár, Kecskemét, Keszthely, Komárom, Kőszeg, Mátra, Miskolc, Nagycenk, Nyíregyháza, Pannonhalma, Pápa, Pécs, Sárospatak, Sopron, Szeged, Székesfehérvár, Szentendre, Szolnok, Tapolca, Tata, Tihany, Tisza-tó, Tokaj, Visegrád), a choice of hotels and restaurants with addresses is indicated by a blue band, marked "Travellers' addresses". The clock sign ⓥ following some of the sights indicates that they feature in the Admission times and charges section in the last part of the guide.

● an **Index** at the end of the guide: to locate the description of a monument, information on a famous person from the region or an interesting boxed text as quickly as possible.

We greatly appreciate comments and suggestions from our readers. Please write to us at Michelin Travel Publications, Hannay House, 39 Clarendon Road, Watford WD17 1JA website at our website: www.ViaMichelin.com

Have a pleasant journey.

J.-Ch. Gérard/MICHELIN

In the Hortobágy region

Key

	Sight	Seaside Resort	Winter Sports Resort	Spa
Highly recommended	★★★			
Recommended	★★			
Interesting	★			

Tourism

	Admission Times and Charges listed at the end of the guide		Visit if time permits
	Sightseeing route with departure point indicated	AZ B	Map co-ordinates locating sights
	Ecclesiastical building		Tourist information
	Synagogue – Mosque		Historic house, castle – Ruins
	Building (with main entrance)		Dam – Factory or power station
	Statue, small building		Fort – Cave
	Wayside cross		Prehistoric site
	Fountain		Viewing table – View
	Fortified walls – Tower – Gate		Miscellaneous sight

Recreation

	Racecourse		Waymarked footpath
	Skating rink		Outdoor leisure park/centre
	Outdoor, indoor swimming pool		Theme/Amusement park
	Marina, moorings		Wildlife/Safari park, zoo
	Mountain refuge hut		Gardens, park, arboretum
	Overhead cable-car		Aviary, bird sanctuary
	Tourist or steam railway		

Additional symbols

	Motorway (unclassified)		Post office – Telephone centre
	Junction: complete, limited		Covered market
	Pedestrian street		Barracks
	Unsuitable for traffic, street subject to restrictions		Swing bridge
	Steps – Footpath		Quarry – Mine
	Railway – Coach station	B F	Ferry (river and lake crossings)
	Funicular – Rack-railway		Ferry services: Passengers and cars
	Tram – Metro, Underground		Foot passengers only
Bert (R.)...	Main shopping street	3	Access route number common to MICHELIN maps and town plans

Abbreviations and special symbols

C	Chamber of commerce (Kereskedelmi kamara)	**POL.**	Police station (Rendőrség)
H	Town hall (Városháza)	**T**	Theatre (Színház)
J	Law courts (Bíróság)	**U**	University (Egyetem)
M	Museum (Múzeum)		Carriage rides (Városnézés hintón)
P	Province administrative centre (Megyeháza)		Vineyard (Borvidèk)

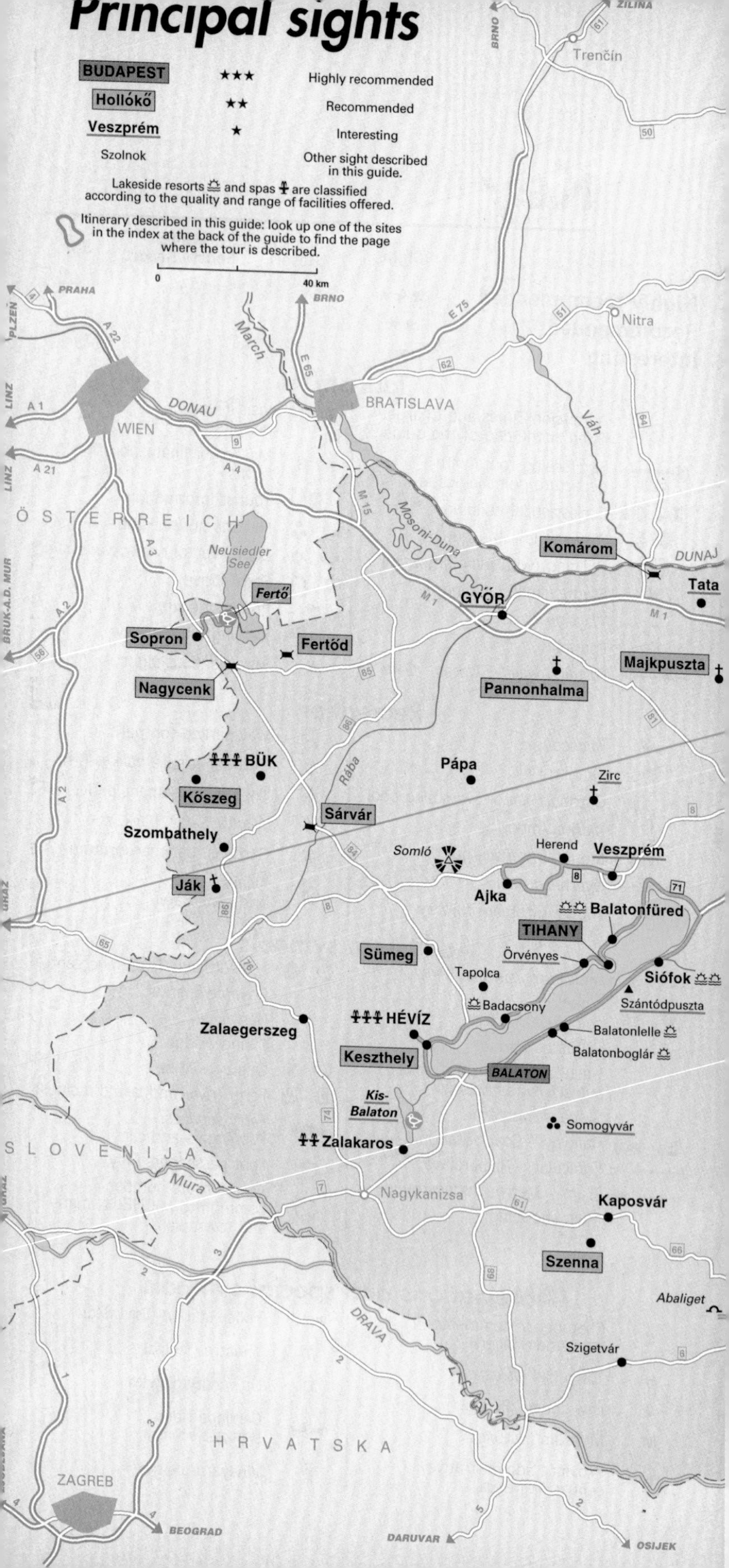

Principal sights
BUDAPEST ★★★ Highly recommended
Hollókő ★★ Recommended
Veszprém ★ Interesting
Szolnok Other sight described in this guide.
Lakeside resorts and spas are classified according to the quality and range of facilities offered.
Itinerary described in this guide: look up one of the sites in the index at the back of the guide to find the page where the tour is described.
0
40 km
ZILINA
BRNO
Trenčín
PRAHA
PLZEŇ
BRNO
March
E 65
E 75
Nitra
A 22
WIEN
DONAU
BRATISLAVA
Váh
LINZ
A 1
A 21
A 4
M 15
Mosoni-Duna
ÖSTERREICH
Neusiedler See
A 3
BRUK-A.D. MUR
A 2
Fertő
Sopron
Fertőd
Nagycenk
GYŐR
M 1
Komárom
DUNAJ
Tata
Majkpuszta
Pannonhalma
BÜK
Kőszeg
Rába
Pápa
Zirc
Sárvár
Szombathely
Somló
Herend
Veszprém
Ják
Ajka
GRAZ
Balatonfüred
TIHANY
Sümeg
Örvényes
Tapolca
Siófok
Szántódpuszta
Badacsony
HÉVÍZ
Zalaegerszeg
Balatonlelle
Keszthely
Balatonboglár
BALATON
Kis-Balaton
Somogyvár
Zalakaros
SLOVENIJA
Mura
Nagykanizsa
Kaposvár
Szenna
Abaliget
DRAVA
Szigetvár
HRVATSKA
ZAGREB
BEOGRAD
DARUVAR
OSIJEK

Driving tours, places to sta

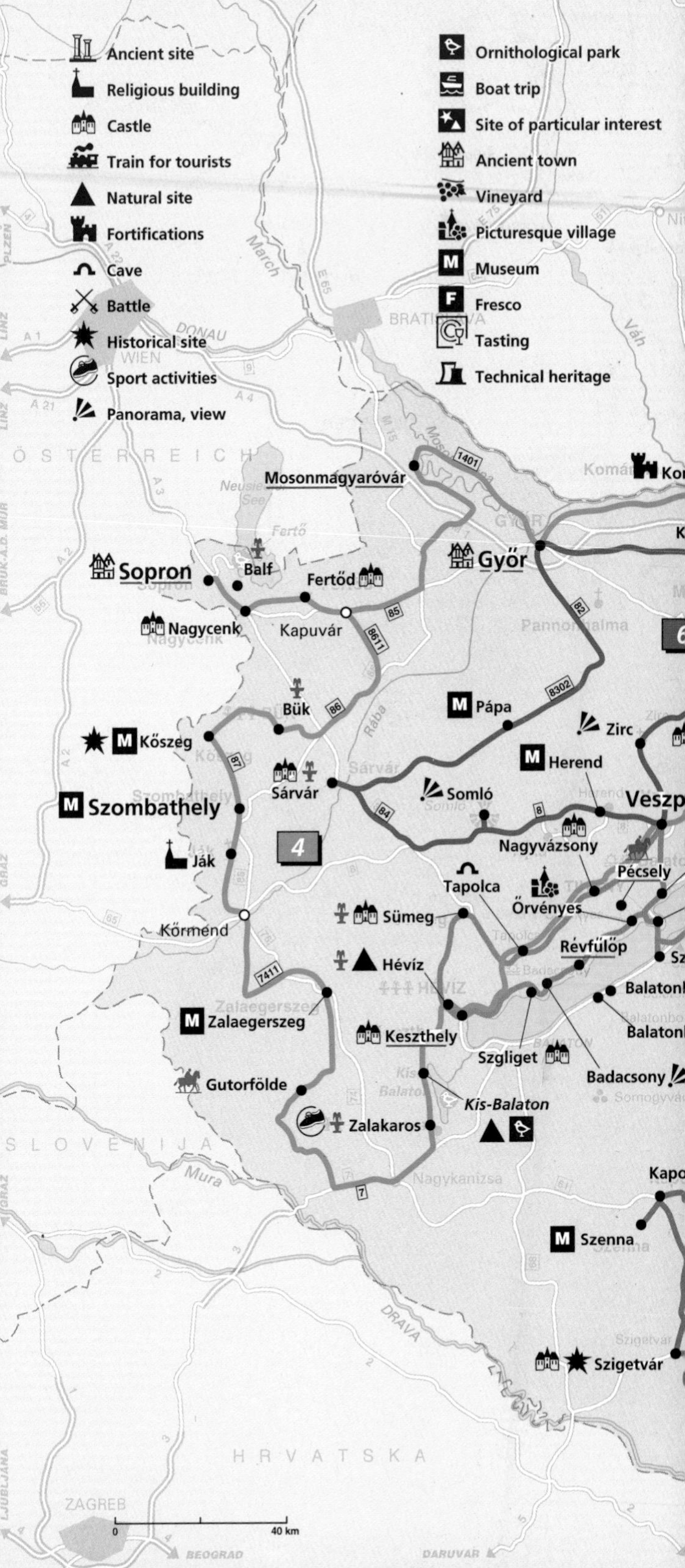

Ancient site
Religious building
Castle
Train for tourists
Natural site
Fortifications
Cave
Battle
Historical site
Sport activities
Panorama, view
Ornithological park
Boat trip
Site of particular interest
Ancient town
Vineyard
Picturesque village
Museum
Fresco
Tasting
Technical heritage
ÖSTERREICH
WIEN
BRATISLAVA
Mosonmagyaróvár
Győr
Sopron
Balf
Fertőd
Nagycenk
Kapuvár
Bük
Kőszeg
Sárvár
Pápa
Zirc
Herend
Somló
Veszp
Szombathely
Ják
Nagyvázsony
Pécsely
Tapolca
Örvényes
Sümeg
Körmend
Révfülöp
Hévíz
Zalaegerszeg
Keszthely
Szgliget
Badacsony
Gutorfölde
Kis-Balaton
Zalakaros
SLOVENIJA
Szenna
Szigetvár
HRVATSKA
ZAGREB
40 km

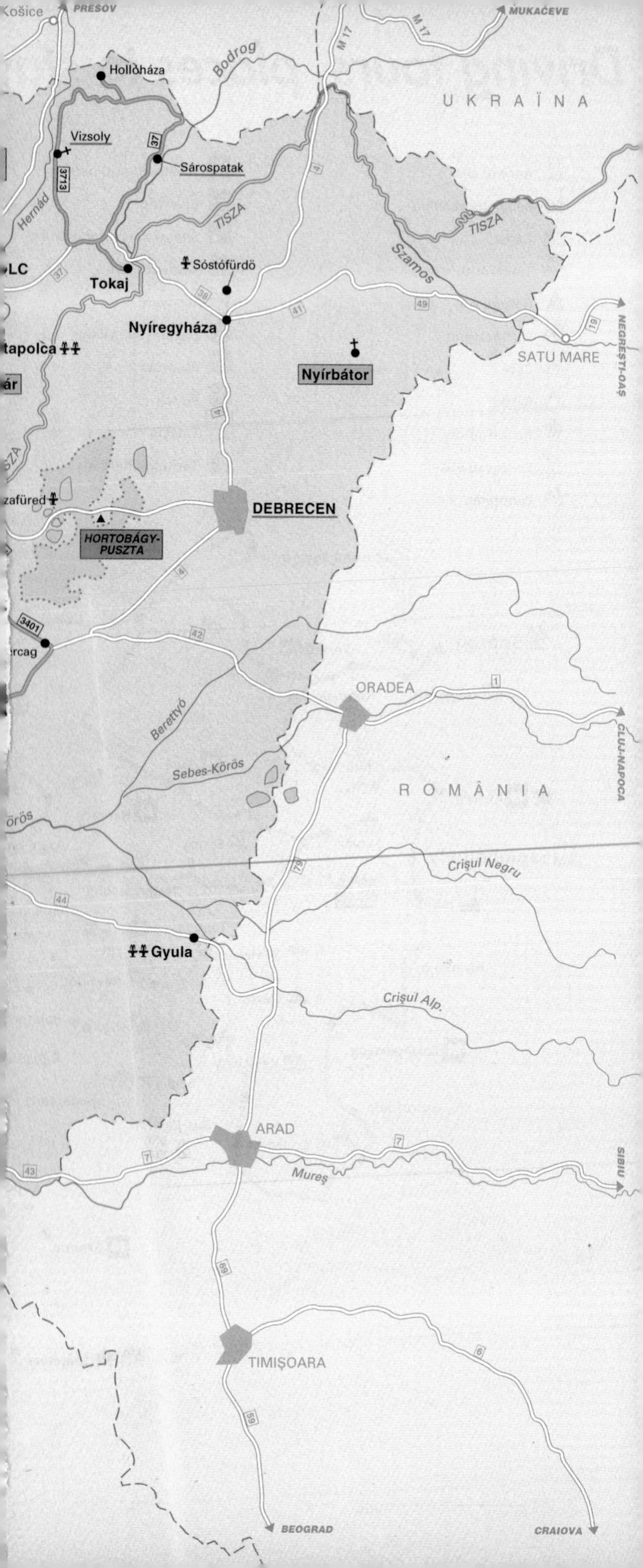
Košice
PRESOV
MUKAČEVE
M 17
M 17
Hollóháza
Bodrog
U K R A Ï N A
Vizsoly
37
3713
Sárospatak
Hernád
TISZA
4
TISZA
Szamos
Sóstófürdö
Tokaj
37
36
41
49
Nyíregyháza
19
NEGREȘTI-OAȘ
SATU MARE
Nyírbátor
4
DEBRECEN
HORTOBÁGY-PUSZTA
4
3401
42
ORADEA
1
CLUJ-NAPOCA
Berettyó
Sebes-Körös
R O M Â N I A
79
Crişul Negru
44
Gyula
Crişul Alp.
ARAD
7
7
43
Mureş
SIBIU
69
TIMIŞOARA
6
59
BEOGRAD
CRAIOVA

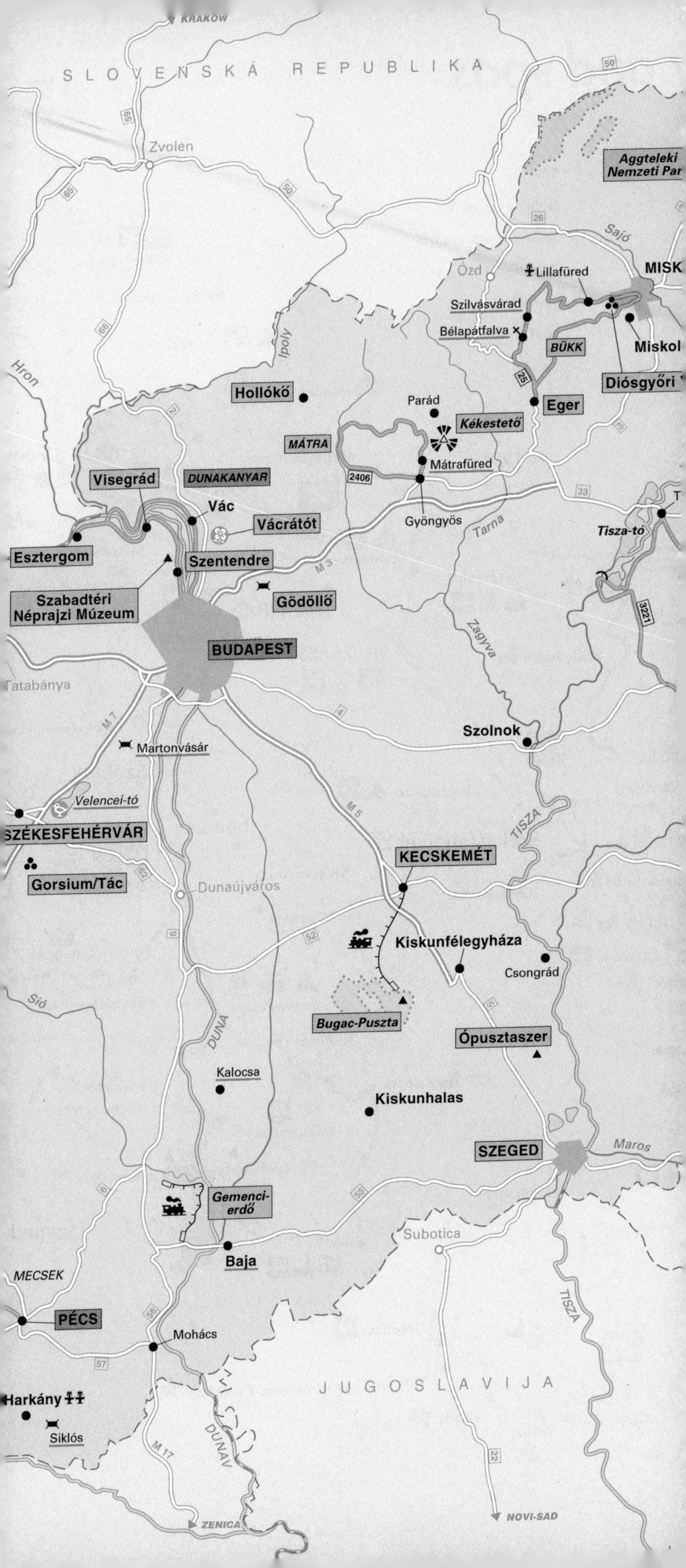
KRAKOW
SLOVENSKÁ REPUBLIKA
Zvolen
Aggteleki Nemzeti Par
Sajó
Ózd
Lillafüred
MISK
Szilvásvárad
Bélapátfalva
BÜKK
Miskol
Diósgyőri
Hron
Ipoly
Hollókő
Parád
Eger
Kékestető
MÁTRA
Mátrafüred
2406
Visegrád
DUNAKANYAR
Vác
Vácrátót
Gyöngyös
Tarna
Tisza-tó
Esztergom
Szentendre
M 3
Gödöllő
Szabadtéri Néprajzi Múzeum
Zagyva
3221
BUDAPEST
Tatabánya
M 7
Martonvásár
Szolnok
Velencei-tó
M 5
SZÉKESFEHÉRVÁR
TISZA
Gorsium/Tác
KECSKEMÉT
Dunaújváros
Kiskunfélegyháza
Csongrád
Sió
DUNA
Bugac-Puszta
Ópusztaszer
Kalocsa
Kiskunhalas
SZEGED
Maros
Gemenci-erdő
Subotica
Baja
MECSEK
PÉCS
TISZA
Mohács
JUGOSLAVIJA
Harkány
Siklós
M 17
DUNAV
ZENICA
NOVI-SAD

y and spas

Spa
Holiday resort
Winter sports resort
Traditional place to stay
Horse riding
Golf

Aggteleki Nemzeti Park
Szilvásvárad
Bélapátfalva
Lillafüred
Bükk
Felsőtárkány
Hollókő
Parád
Recsk
Sirok
Eger
Mátraszentimre
Galyatető
Kékestető
Visegrád
Szentendrei Sziget
Hatvan
Mátraháza
Szentendre
Gyöngyös
Esztergom
Tata
Gödöllő
Jászberény
Majkpuszta
BUDAPEST
Törökszentmiklós
Szolnok
Várpalota
Velencei-tó
Székesfehérvár
Lajosmizse
Kecskemét
Balatonfüred
Gorsium
Kerekegyháza
Fülöpháza
Tihany
Siófok
Csongrád
Bugac-Puszta
Kiskunfélegyháza
Kiskőrös
Szentes
Bugac
Kalocsa
Ópusztaszer
Kiskunhalas
Kunfehértó
Pusztamérges
Szekszárd
Bonyhád
Szeged
Baja
Pécs
Mohács
Mohácsi Történelmi Emlékhely
Harkány
Villany
Siklós

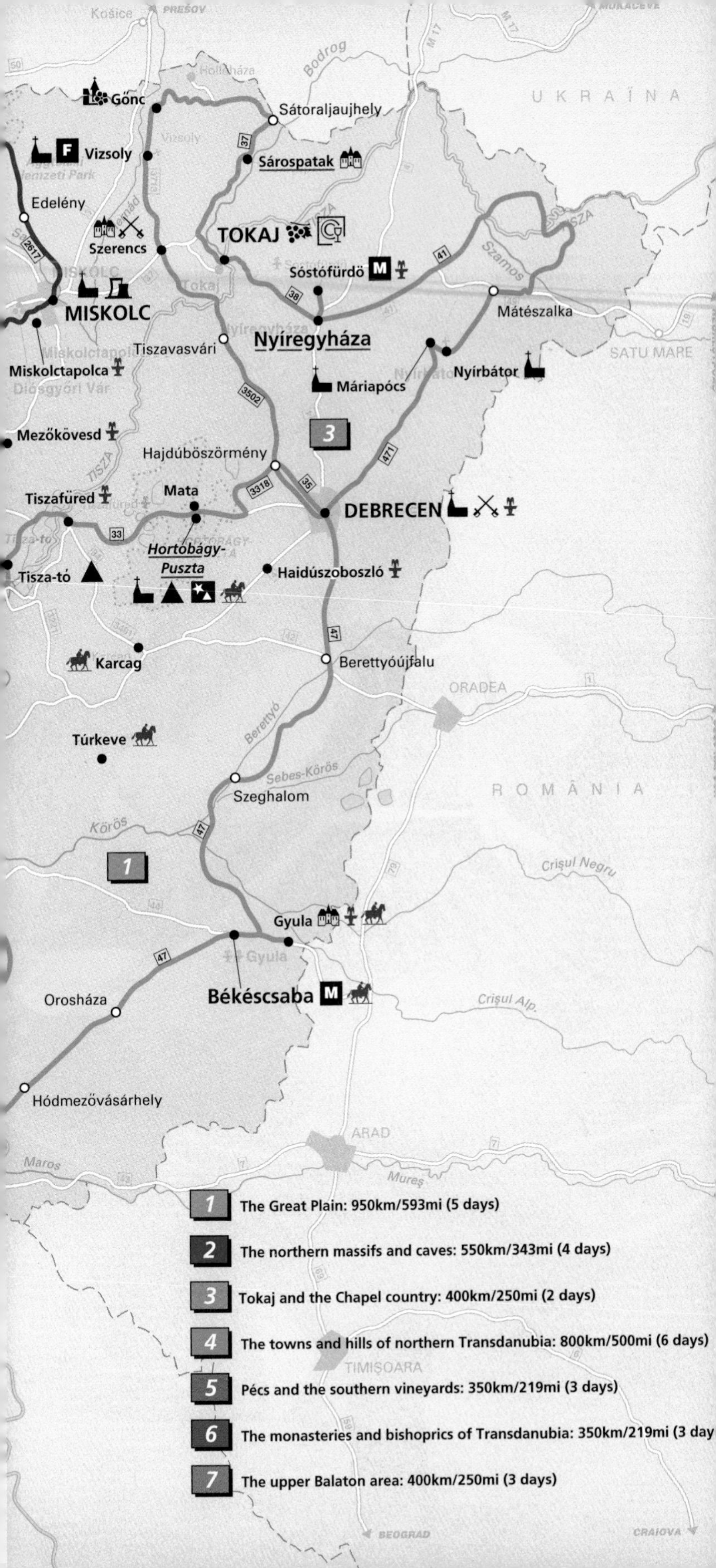

1 The Great Plain: 950km/593mi (5 days)

2 The northern massifs and caves: 550km/343mi (4 days)

3 Tokaj and the Chapel country: 400km/250mi (2 days)

4 The towns and hills of northern Transdanubia: 800km/500mi (6 days)

5 Pécs and the southern vineyards: 350km/219mi (3 days)

6 The monasteries and bishoprics of Transdanubia: 350km/219mi (3 day

7 The upper Balaton area: 400km/250mi (3 days)

Folk group at Tihany

Ph. Roy/HOA QUI

Practical information

Organising your trip

USEFUL ADDRESSES

Hungarian Tourist Office – www.hungarytourism.hu

United Kingdom – 46 Eaton Place, London SW1X 8AL. ☎ 020 7823 1032, Fax 020 7823 1459, htlondon@btinternet.com

USA – 150 East 58th Street, 33rd Floor, New York, NY 10155-3398. ☎ 1-212 355 0240, Fax 1-212 207 4103, htnewyork@hungarytourism.hu

Websites

Tourist information – www.hungarytourism.hu (in English, German and Hungarian). www.budapestinfo.hu

Accommodation – www.travelport.hu and www.budapest.nethotels.hu

General cultural information – www.kulturinfo.hu

Cultural programmes in Budapest – www.festival.city.hu

Tourist information by telephone

Telephoning Hungary from abroad – 00 + 36 (country code) + town code + number of the person to whom you wish to speak
☎ 00 36 60 55 00 44 information in English or German
☎ 00 36 1 438 80 80 information in English or German

Hungarian Embassy or Consulate

United Kingdom – Hungarian Embassy, 35 Eaton Place, London SW1X 8BY. ☎ 020 7235 5218. www.huemblon.org.uk
Consulate and Visa Section, 35b Eaton Place, London SW1X 8BY. ☎ 020 7235 2664, 4462.

Specialist travel agents

The following companies specialise in visits to Hungary and can provide information on group trips, individual trips, accommodation in hotels or in private homes etc.

East Europe Travel Centre, 5th Floor, Oxford Circus House, 245 Oxford Street, London W1D 2LX. ☎ 020 7851 4370, Fax 020 7851 4360, travel@wainternational.co.uk

Fregata Travel, 83 Whitechapel High Street, London E1 7QX. ☎ 020 7375 3187, Fax 020 7247 7884, mastertours@commodore.co.uk

For spas only:

Thermalia Travel, 12 New College Parade, Finchley Road, Swiss Cottage, London NW3 5EP. ☎ 020 7483 1898 / 7586 7725, Fax 020 7722 7218, thermalia@bigfoot.com

Travel books about Hungary can be bought from most bookshops and from the **Travel Bookshop**, 13 Blenheim Crescent, London W11 2EE. ☎ 020 7229 5260, Fax 243 1552, post@thetravelbookshop.co.uk

Hungarian food and crafts can be obtained in London from Harrods and Selfridges.

Entry formalities

Identity documents – For nationals of the UK, Ireland, New Zealand, USA and Canada, only a passport is required. Nationals of Australia must have a passport and a visa.

Documents for motoring – All vehicle drivers must have a national driving licence. If they are driving their own vehicles, they must also have the registration document and an international insurance certificate (green card).

Medical insurance – As Hungary is not a member of the European Union, it is advisable to take out medical insurance.

Animals – Animals cannot be taken into Hungary without a vaccination certificate.

TRAVELLING TO HUNGARY

By car

To choose the itinerary between your departure point and destination, use:

– **www.ViaMichelin.com**: this Internet site (certain services available on subscription only) helps you to choose itineraries and calculate distances and motorway toll fees. It also provides accommodation and other tourist information and replies to any questions you may have. In short, it is a mine of information to help you prepare your trip in the best possible way.
– **Michelin map n° 970 Europe** (scale 1:3 000 000) indicates the motorways, main-roads and B-roads. It also has an index of place names included.
– **Michelin map n° 925 Hungary** (scale 1:400 000).
– **Michelin Europe, spiral or bound road and tourist atlas** (West Europe, scale 1:1 000 000, East Europe, scale 1:3 000 000) contains road information, a mileage chart, 74 town and urban district maps, a climate map and an index of towns and other place names indicated for easy location.

By rail

Budapest is linked by rail, directly or with changes, to 15 European capital cities. From London (Waterloo International) via the Channel Tunnel and Paris (arriving at the Gare du Nord and departing from the Gare de l'Est).

Eurostar, UK ☎ 020 7928 5163

National Rail Enquiries ☎ 08457 48 49 50

By air

The only international airport is near Budapest (Ferihegy 1 and 2) and is served by the major international airlines. Since Hungary is not a member of the European Union, the Duty Free zone is open to members of the EU.
British Airways, UK ☎ 08457 79 99 77.
British Midland, UK ☎ 0870 240 7034
MALÉV, Hungarian Airlines: www.malev.hu
MALÉV, 1st Floor, 22-25a Sackville Street, London, W1S 3DR, UK. ☎ 020 7439 0577, Fax 020 7734 8116, london@malev.hu
MALÉV, Fifth Avenue, Rockefeller Center 630, Suite 1900, New York, USA. ☎ 1 800 223 6884 (tollfree), ☎ 1 212 757 6480, Fax 1 212 459 0675, info@hungarianairlines.com
MALÉV, 175 Bloor Street East, Toronto, Canada. ☎ 1 416 944 0093/94, Fax 1 416 944 0095, toronto@malev.hu
MALÉV, 403 George Street, Sydney, Australia. ☎ 61 2 9244 2111, Fax 61 2 9290 3306, wassyd@worldaviation.com.au
MALÉV, 310 King Street, Melbourne, Australia. ☎ 61 3 9920 3860, Fax 61 3 9920 3880, wasmel@worldaviation.com.au
MALÉV, 217 George Street, Brisbane, Australia. ☎ 61 7 3407 7188, Fax 61 7 3407 7149.
MALÉV, 249-251 Pulteney Street, Adelaide, Australia. ☎ 61 8 8306 8411, Fax 61 8 8306 8439.
MALÉV, 250 St George's Terrace, Perth, Australia. ☎ 61 8 9229 9212, Fax 61 8 9229 9399.
MALÉV, Trustbank Building 6th Floor, 229 Queen Street, Auckland, New Zealand. ☎ 64 9 379 4455, Fax 64 9 377 5648.

By coach

For information on international travel by coach, apply to:

Eurolines, 52 Grosvenor Gardens, Victoria, London SW1W OAU. ☎ 020 7730 8235, Fax 020 7730 8721.

By hovercraft

From April to October, it is possible to go to Budapest via the Danube by hovercraft, leaving from Vienna (Austria) with a stop at Bratislava (Slovakia). In high season, there are two departures a day: Vienna 8am and 1pm, Bratislava 9.20am and 2.20pm, arrival at Budapest at 1.30pm and 6.30pm.

In the land of the Magyars

Also see the pages on Budapest in the Sights section.

DRIVING IN HUNGARY

Speed limits – Be careful as checks are frequent:
- built-up area: 50 kph/31mph
- single lane roads: 90kph/56mph, with trailer 70kph/44mph
- dual carriageways: 110kph/68mph, with trailer 70ph/44mph
- motorways: 130kph/81mph, with trailer 80kph/50mph

Motorways – There are four motorways in Hungary:
- **M 1**: Budapest-Györ-Hegyeshalom (toll on the Győr-Hegyeshalom section, Austrian border)
- **M 3**: Budapest-Gyöngyös-Füzesabony

To drive on the M 1 and the M 3, you need a road tax disc (available in fuel stations). It costs 1 400Ft for 9 days.
- **M 5**: Budapest-Kecskemét-Kiskunfélegyháza (toll: 2 450Ft)
- **M 7**: Budapest-Balatonvilágos

To the south of Budapest, there is a four-lane carriageway road, the **M 10**, which avoids the capital and links the M 1, M 7 and M 5 motorways.

Fuel – There are no problems with availability of fuel. Service stations are frequent and may be self-service. The Hungarian company, MOL shares the market with the European or American multinationals (BP, ARAL, ESSO, SHELL, TOTAL etc).
- Super: *szuper*
- Unleaded super: *szuper ólommentes*
- Diesel: *diesel*
- Fill it up please: *tele kérem*

Road signs and markings – On the whole they conform to European standards.

Safety belts – Obligatory in the front and back of vehicles.

Children – Children under 12 years of age must be seated at the rear of the vehicle. Babies and very young children must travel in a child's seat in the back of the vehicle.

Lights – All vehicles must travel with **dipped headlights on (day and night)** outside built up areas, on all roads and motorways. Be careful, checks are frequent, even for tourists. **Motorcycles must have lights on (day and night) everywhere.**

Drink and drive – "If you drink, don't drive". Hungarian law views this seriously and the permitted percentage of alcohol when driving is **0**. Checks are frequent and foreign tourists should not expect preferential treatment. Sanctions applied can range from a simple fine (an on-the-spot fine to be paid in *forints*) to the confiscation of the driving licence.

Mobile phones – Use is prohibited when driving.

Rendőrség – This is the Hungarian name for the police and is found on all police vehicles.

GENERAL INFORMATION

Embassies

United Kingdom – H-1051 Budapest, Harmincad u. 6. ☎ 266 2888, Fax 266 0907.

Ireland – H-1054 Budapest, Szabadság tér 7-9. ☎ 302 9600.

USA – H-1054 Budapest, Szabadság tér 12. ☎ 475 4400.

Canada – H-1121 Budapest, Budakeszi út 32. ☎ 392 3360, Fax 392 3390.

Australia – Királyhágó tér 8-9, Budapest, ☎ 457 9777. www.australia.hu

New Zealand (Consulate) – H-1125 Budapest, Nógrádi utca 8. ☎ and Fax 331 49 08.

Currency, foreign exchange and payment

The Hungarian currency is the **forint** (national abbreviation: **Ft**, international abbreviation: **HUF**). Although this is now convertible in other countries, visitors should take travellers' cheques or cash: euro, pounds sterling, US/Canadian/Australian dollars etc. For information, and given the fluctuations of the forint, it is not unusual to find prices indicated in euro. This is often the case for hotel rooms.

There are foreign exchange facilities in banks, foreign exchange bureaux (cash), travel agencies and hotels (to be avoided, as the rates are not as good).

Under no circumstances should visitors change money in the street with people offering "black-market" deals at attractive rates; there is a high risk of being swindled.

Banknotes: 200, 500, 1 000, 2 000, 5 000, 10 000 and 20 000Ft.

Coins: 1, 2, 5, 10, 20, 50, 100 and 200Ft.

Credit cards such as Visa, American Express, MasterCard and Diners are accepted everywhere.

Money can also be withdrawn from automatic cash dispensers using these cards. They often have a **Bankomat** sign for easy recognition. Instructions for use are often given in several languages, in English and German in particular.

Telephone

Phone boxes take coins (10, 20, 50 and 100Ft) and cards. Cards are on sale from post offices, kiosks, tobacconists' *(Trafik)* or newsagents'. Price: 900Ft for 50 units, 1 800Ft for 120 units.

To telephone abroad – 00 + the relevant country code (44 for the United Kingdom, 1 for the US and Canada, 61 for Australia, 64 for New Zealand etc).

To telephone another town in Hungary – 06 + town code + number of the person to whom you wish to speak.

Electricity, time and opening times

Electricity supply – 220 volts.

Time – In summer, the time in Hungary is GMT + 2 and in winter it is GMT + 1, ie 1hr ahead of the United Kingdom.

Opening times – Shops are generally open from Monday to Friday from 10am to 6pm and from 9am to 1pm on Saturdays. VAT refunds *(see Budapest: Shopping)*.

Holidays

– 1 January: New Year's Day
– 15 March: National Day (anniversary of the 1848-49 revolution)
– Easter and Easter Monday
– Whitsun and Whit Monday
– 1 May: Labour Day
– 20 August: St Stephen's and Constitution Day (Stephen I, first king of Hungary)
– 23 October: Republic Day (anniversary of the October 1956 Uprising)
– 25 and 26 December: Christmas

Tourist offices

Tourinform offices will provide visitors with any information on places to visit, types of accommodation etc. The addresses of the main offices are given in the Admission times and charges section at the end of the guide.

Tourist information

Freephone numbers for foreign tourists (24-hour service)

☎ 06 80 66 00 44
☎ 06 80 55 00 44

Hungary by train

Express and InterCity trains serving the various tourist regions leave from Budapest:
– West of the country: Győr, Sopron, Veszprém, Szombathely,
– East and South: Debrecen, Nyíregyháza, Szolnok, Békéscsaba, Gyula,
– South: Kecskemét, Szeged, Kaposvár, Gyékényes, Pécs
– North: Miskolc,
– Lake Balaton: Balatonfüred, Tapolca, Siófok, Fonyód.
All province administrative centres have direct train links with the capital.

Reduced rates – Tourists can purchase 7- or 10-day go-anywhere tickets for first and second class. These tickets bear the holder's name. A day ticket is also available for unlimited travel around Lake Balaton.

Hungary by coach

The Hungarian company, **Volánbusz** (yellow coaches) has numerous lines serving large towns and resorts. From Budapest, information and reservations:

Destinations in the West – Coach station, Erzsébet tér (5th district).

Destinations in the East – Népstadion út Station (14th district).

Destinations in the Danube Bend – Árpád híd Station.

ACCOMMODATION AND RESTAURANTS

Green Guide Hotel and Restaurant addresses – Inserted in the pages describing towns and sights are the addresses of hotels and restaurants. All these establishments have been carefully selected: preference has been given to the originality of the decor, an exceptional location in the heart of a town and, in some cases, the price. Comfort, peace and quiet and high-quality food have also been included in our criteria. To enable you to discover the variety of Hungarian gastronomy, we have primarily selected restaurants offering traditional food.

Magyar Turizmus Kártya (Hungarian tourist card) – This costs around 6 000Ft. It is valid for one year and allows visitors to obtain reductions in some hotels and restaurants, on railways, Volánbusz bus lines, Mahart boats on Lake Balaton, the Budapest Card, some car rentals, taxis in Budapest etc. The card is on sale in some Volánbusz stations, fuel stations and travel agencies.

Hotels

Prices are often indicated in euro and include breakfast.
While hotels in Budapest, like many other capital cities, are expensive, you will find good, better priced hotels in the provinces. You should also try a *panzió*, a small family style hotel, often located in pleasant surroundings. In the Hortobágy, the region famous for its horses, several establishments arrange rides, which makes a stay in this area particularly attractive.
Tourinform or the tourist offices in each country provide a free catalogue called "Hotel", which gives the names and addresses of hotels and other types of accommodation by town.
On the **web**: www.miwo.hu, www.hotelinfo.hu and www.travelport.hu

Restaurants

See also the Introduction: Food and Drink.
You will always be able to find a place to eat at any time of the day, in town or in the country. There are several names given to types of restaurants:
– *étterem*: a classic restaurant with a set and an *à la carte* menu
– *csárda*: a country inn
– *büfé*: fast-food type restaurant, counter service (sandwiches, cakes, hot and cold drinks)
– *vendéglő*: grill/pub and restaurant
As soon as you are seated you will be handed a menu and the waiter will ask what you would like to drink. This is customary while you are choosing your food.
A traditional meal is usually composed of soup, a main course, dessert, a drink and coffee to finish. Often when you order coffee, you will be asked if you would like a *cappuccino* or *espresso*.

Service charge and tips

Service is not always included in the bill. In this case, add 10 to 15%. Tips are up to the customer.

Bed and breakfast

Accommodation in private homes is very popular. In the summer season you will see numerous *"Zimmer frei"* (bed & breakfast) signs around Lake Balaton or even people holding up notices of this kind.

Youth hostels

Visitors with an International Youth Hostel Association membership card can obtain price reductions in several hostels.
Request the **Ifjúsági szálláskatalógus / Hungarian youth hostels / Jugendherbergen in Ungarn brochure** from the Tourist Office. You can also contact the **Hungarian Youth Hostels Association**, 1077 Budapest, Almássy tér 6. ☎/Fax 352 1572.

Camping-caravanning

The Hungarian Tourist Office provides a **Camping Ungarn/Hungary/Hongrie/Ungheria/Magyarország** map free of charge (1:550 000) indicating the location of campsites on the front and a table listing campsites and the facilities available on the back. There is an abundance of campsites on the shores of Lake Balaton, the "Hungarian Sea".

Discovering Hungary

BUDAPEST

Budapest, the Pearl of the Danube, is in fact three towns, Buda, Óbuda and Pest, separated by a legendary river. *See the pages on the Hungarian capital in the Sights section.*

DRIVING TOURS

At the beginning of the guide, on the map on pp 13 to 15, we suggest 7 tours on different themes, all numbered and colour-coded. Depending on your interests and the time you have to spend, the tours will help you get to know Hungary. They are as follows:

- The Great Plain: 950km/593mi (5 days)
- The northern massifs and caves: 550km/343mi (4 days)
- Tokaj and the Chapel country: 400km/250mi (2 days)
- The towns and hills of northern Transdanubia: 800km/500mi (6 days)
- Pécs and the southern vineyards: 350km/219mi (3 days)
- The monasteries and bishoprics of Transdanubia: 350km/219mi (3 days)
- The upper Balaton area: 400km/250mi (3 days)

SPAS

At the beginning of the guide, the locations of the principal spas are indicated on the map of driving tours.

Hungary can be considered the great spa country. The number of hot water springs with curative properties in this part of Central Europe is quite extraordinary. Over 100 urban areas and over 400 spas are available to tourists and people taking treatment. According to current legislation, thermal waters are waters whose temperature is over 30°C/86°F. The waters are not only used in specialised balneotherapy establishments for purely medical treatment but also in swimming pools, lakes and seasonal bathing establishments more oriented towards enjoyment and relaxation.

Budapest has around 40 baths supplied with water from natural thermal springs or wells.

Gabler/MAGYAR KÉPEK Kft

Hárkany

Some date from Roman or Turkish eras and others from the early 20C. In addition to their curative properties, many of these baths are unique from an architectural point of view.

The distinctive feature of **Hévíz** *(see HÉVÍZ in the sights section)* is its hot-water lake. You can take advantage of this water both outside or in the pavilions at any time of year. It is particularly beneficial if you suffer from rheumatism or problems with your limbs. Even in the harshest winters, the water temperature never falls below 26°C/79°F and, in addition, it moves constantly and is renewed every 28 to 30hr.

Information on some of the spas and their characteristics is given below:
Balf: rheumatology, gastro-intestinal disorders; **Bük**: rheumatology, gastro-intestinal disorders; **Sárvár**: rheumatology, gynaecology, dermatology, respiratory tract, gastro-intestinal disorders; **Zalakaros**: rheumatology, gynaecology; **Harkány**: rheumatology, gynaecology; **Balatonfüred**: gynaecology, gastro-intestinal disorders; **Eger**: rheumatology; **Hajdúszoboszló**: rheumatology, gynaecology, dermatology, gastro-intestinal disorders; **Mezőkövesd-Zsórifürdő**: rheumatology; **Debrecen**: rheumatology; **Gyula**: rheumatology, gastro-intestinal disorders.

FISHING

Angling is, of course, subject to observance of prevailing national and regional regulations which specify that anglers must be in possession of a fishing ticket and a national permit. Anyone over the age of 18 can use two fishing lines, each of which may have a maximum of three hooks. Be sure to obtain information on fishing periods and catches, depending on the province. Provided the authorised sizes are respected, adults are limited to a catch of five fish per day.
Good places for fishing: Lake Velencei (carp, pikeperch, pike, bream, catfish, eel), a branch of the Danube at Ráckeve (carp, pikeperch, catfish, pike, bream), Lake Balaton (pikeperch, eel, bream, pike, carp), Lake Pécs (carp, catfish), Lake Tisza (carp, catfish, pikeperch, pike, bream).
Information: Horgászvizek Magyarországon/National Anglers Federation, Korompai utca 17, 1124 Budapest, ☎ 1/248 5127, Fax 1/248 5128. The **Fishing in Hungary** brochure is also available from Tourinform or tourist offices (in English, French, German and Hungarian).

HUNTING

Foreign hunters must send in an application to the hunting office of the region chosen, indicating the type of game to be hunted. You will need to fill in and return an application form and you will then receive an "invitation letter" and other official documents. This letter must be presented at the Hungarian Embassy in your country of residence to obtain a permit to take your own gun into Hungary.
Tourinform or the Hungarian Tourist Office has a free brochure called **Hunting in Hungary** which has the addresses of the hunting offices, classified by province.

HORSES AND HORSE-RIDING

Hungary and horses: two names which go together perfectly. While the Great Plain is the ideal place for long rides or horse shows, each province has riding centres where visitors can enjoy the sport at all levels.
Tourinform distributes a free brochure in English entitled **Riding in Hungary**. In it you will find the addresses of the principal riding centres with their facilities, level and languages spoken etc.

J.-Ch. Gérard/MICHELIN

Information can also be obtained from **The Hungarian Equestrian Tourism Association**, Ráday utca 8, 1092 Budapest, www.equi.hu
There is also a pocket map, **Lovasturizmus Magyarországon** published by Top Gráf (key in Hungarian, German and English), which indicates the places where the horse is king: various horse sports, riding tours, trips in carts, riding schools etc. The addresses of riding centres are indicated on the front.

In the Hortobágy region, the **Epona Rider Village** is a paradise for riders who can take their own horses. This centre has around 50 rooms, flats and houses with stables attached. Beginners will be delighted to learn how to ride or drive a team, and perhaps gallop off into the distant horizon. It is also a base for visiting the surrounding area. The centre can arrange hot-air balloon, cart or boat trips. Swimming pool and tennis courts for relaxation. ☎/Fax 52/369 020.

SAILING

Lake Balaton is the Hungarians' favourite holiday resort. Nautical sports predominate, especially windsurfing and sailing. Keszthely, Badacsony, Siófok and Balatonfüred are the principal harbours for these activities.

WALKING

Landscapes that have remained almost intact, plains, marshes, forests, hills and mountains: all these natural treasures are a source of enchantment to those whose idea of discovering a region or even a country is with a haversack and a good pair of walking boots. Walking enthusiasts will find over 10 000km/6 250mi of hiking trails. Most of the protected areas are open to nature lovers. The nine national parks (Aggtelek, Lake Balaton, the Bükk Mountains, Danube and Drave, Danube and Ipoly, Fertő-Hanság, Kiskunság, Körös and Maros) are ideal places. Some sectors can only be visited with a guide. Ask at the local Tourinform office for information.

In the Bükk Mountains starting from Lillafüred – Whether you want to take a short walk or a long hike through the forest, the possibilities are endless. Paths are well signposted and excellent maps are available for you to find your way in the hills and forests. Make sure you calculate your time properly and have the right equipment so that you are not taken unawares without shelter or food.

SMALL TRAINS

These small steam trains (known as nostalgia trains) allow visitors to discover two major tourist sites from another angle.

Northern shore of Lake Balaton – From Keszthely to Badacsonytomaj the trip lasts 1hr 45min. It is possible to get off at Balatonederics and combine the trip with a visit to a wine cellar (tasting). From Balatonederics, it is also possible to take a special train to the Great Plain or Puszta. The price includes a typical meal, a horse show and traditional music and dancing.

Danube Bend – From Budapest to Szob the train follows the left bank, offering various views of the legendary river. The trip takes 2hr.

For information, contact **MÁV Nostalgia**, Belgrád rakpart 26, 1056 Budapest. ☎ 1/317 1665, Fax 1/269 5242.

CYCLING

There are cycle paths in Budapest, between Budapest and Szentendre, on the north shore of Lake Velencei and near Lake Balaton. Hungary has a network of B-roads with little traffic, ideal for cycling. The Tourinform offices can arrange trips, bicycle hire, take care of transporting luggage and even make arrangements for picnics in the forest.

Tourinform distributes a free map in English, the **Bicycle Tour Map**. Roads are indicated on the front (including those prohibited or not recommended for cyclists) along with stretches of roads where cycling is possible and places with accommodation etc. There are round trips and itineraries across the country on the back of the map, to enable cyclists to discover the main sights. Also request the **Hungary by Bike** brochure which has a choice of itineraries.

The **Explore Hungary by Bicycle** brochure suggests 5-day trips covering 55-75km/34-47mi a day, 3-day trips, or one-day trips. There are also theme trips, for instance to the Sopron Hills and the Small Plain, the hills in Vas province, the Zala Hills, the Bükk Mountains, the Cherhát Hills, and the Zemplén and Tokaj-Hegyalja massif. The map on the brochure shows regions suitable for cycling, as well as the road network (motorways, A-roads and B-roads), and the main railway lines.

GOLF

Golf enthusiasts can choose from these clubs:

– **Bük** (57km/36mi from Sopron), **Birdland Golf & Country Club**, 96ha/237 acres, 18 holes, golf lessons, accommodation on the site;

– **Hencse** (25km/16mi from Kaposvár), Hencse National Golf & Country Club, 97ha/240 acres, 18 holes, golf lessons, accommodation on the site;

– **Kisoroszi** (35km/22mi from Budapest), **Budapest Golf Park & Country Club**, 66ha/163 acres, 18 holes, golf lessons, accommodation on the site;
– **Szentlőrinc** (9km/5mi from Pécs), St Lorence Golf & Country Club, 57ha/141 acres, 18 holes, golf lessons.

WHAT TO BRING BACK FROM HUNGARY

Customs regulations – The following can be taken out of Hungary without any customs duty by people over the age of 16:
– 250 cigarettes or 50 cigars or 250g of tobacco,
– 2 litres of wine and 1 litre of spirits,
– 1 litre of toilet water and 100ml of perfume,
– non-commercial goods not over 270 000Ft in value.

Arts and crafts – Kalocsa embroidery, embroidery and blouses from the Matyó region, black ceramics from Nádudvar, wood carvings, pottery, Michka jugs from Mezőcsát, cloth from Sárköz, blue cloth from Pápa, *papucs* (women's slippers) from Szeged.

Porcelain and crystal – Herend and Zsolnay porcelain, Ajka crystal.

Food products – Wine, such as the famous Tokaji Aszú, Egri Bikavér or Bull's Blood and Badacsony. Apricot brandy or barackpálinka. Foie gras and salami. Garlands of paprika, garlic or onions or ground paprika (mild or hot).

Calendar of events

1 January

Budapest .... New Year Concert at the Pest Concert Hall (Vigadó): Hungarian operettas and Viennese waltzes.

January

Budapest .... International circus festival.

February

Debrecen .... Hajdúság regional carnival.

Seventh Sunday before Easter

Mohács .... Procession of the "Busó": masks carved out of willow and painted are paraded with rattles and bells to proclaim the death of winter and the arrival of spring. Bonfire on the third day.

Second fortnight in March

Budapest, Debrecen, Eger, Gödöllő, Győr, Kaposvár, Kecskemét, Pécs, Sopron, Szentendre, Szombathely Spring festival: classical and modern music, plays, operetta, opera, folk groups, Hungarian and foreign ballet, films.

April-October

Szentendre/Open-air museum ....Festivals and traditions: folk groups, traditional crafts, religious and country festivals.

Easter Saturday

Magyarpolány .... Crucifixion and resurrection: the Passion, re-enacted by the people of the village, ends with fireworks.

Easter Saturday, Sunday and Monday

Hollókő .... Easter festival: folk art and traditions in the village, which is on the Unesco World Heritage List.

May

Salgótarján .... International Dixieland Festival.

Balatonfüred .... Festival of the unfurling of the sails on Lake Balaton.

Szentendre/Open-air museum .... Whitsuntide gathering: folk and religious traditions, arts and crafts, music and dancing.

J.-P. Garcin/PHOTONONSTOP

Folk group in Szentendre

End of May

Debrecen	International military music festival.
Tiszaújváros	International hot-air balloon competition.
Miskolc	Diósgyőr castle festival: plays, puppets, tournaments, medieval fair, banquet and music.

June

Budapest	WOMUFE (World Music Festival): music and song from all over the world.
Balatonföldvár	Földvár Festival: concerts, folk programmes, fireworks.

June-July

Győr	International cultural festival: puppets, street theatre, folk dancing and music.
Nyírbátor	International street theatre festival: masked actors on stilts.

June-August

Gödöllő	Inside the main courtyard of the royal castle, concerts, plays and horse-riding events.

July

Fertőd Castle	Esterháza festivities, Haydn festival: opera, ballet, puppet shows, plays and fireworks.
Máta	Hortobágy international horse-riding days.
Apaj	Kiskunság Shepherds and Riders Day: livestock show, games, team races, cooking competition, riders' ball.
Budapest	Jazz Jam: international jazz festival.
Miskolc..	International Dixieland Festival.
Siófok	Gold Shell International Folk Festival: Hungarian and foreign folk groups.
Eger	Eger festivities: historical show within the castle walls.
Baja	Fish soup festival: soup is prepared in over 1 000 cauldrons. Music, folk groups and fireworks.

July-August

Szeged	Open-air festival: plays, opera, concerts.

Beginning of August

Budapest/Óbudai-sziget	A week-long music festival draws young people from all over the world.

August

Mogyoród/Hungaroring	Hungarian Grand Prix: World Formula 1 championship.
Balatonfüred	Wine weeks: the wine-growing regions are represented. Folk groups, fireworks on the 20th.
Debrecen	Floral carnival: procession of floats decorated with flowers, folk groups, fireworks.
Budapest	Arts and crafts festival in the Buda castle district.

September

Szilvásvárad	Lippizaner Riding Festival and international team competition.
Budapest	International wine festival: processions, dance, auction sales, election of the Wine Queen.
Makó	International onion festival: fairs, concerts, plays, riding events, fireworks.
Kalocsa	Paprika festival, classical music, folk dances, processions.
Pécs	European festival of drinking songs: in honour of grapes and wine.

October

Békéscsaba	Csaba sausage festival.

October to mid-November

Győr	Arts festival of Baroque nostalgia: plays, music.

Further reading

Reference

Hungary and the Habsburgs 1765-1800, Éva H Balázs, Tom Wilkinson *(Central European University Press, 1997)*

The Dissolution of the Austro-Hungarian Empire 1867-1918, John W Mason *(Addison Wesley Longman Higher Education, 1996)*

A History of Modern Hungary 1867 – 1994, Jorg K Hoensch, Kim Traynor *(Addison Wesley Longman Higher Education, 1995)*

A Golden Age, Art and Society in Hungary 1896-1914, Gyöngyi Éri and Zsuzsa Jobbágyi (editors) *(Corvina/Lund Humphries 1990)*

The Habsburg Monarchy 1809-1918, AJP Taylor *(Penguin, 1964)*

The Hungarian Revolution of 1956, György Litván (editor) *(Addison Wesley Longman Higher Education, 1996)*

The Last Days, Steven Spielberg, David Cesarani *(Weidenfeld Illustrated, 1998)*

Castles Burning, Magda Denes *(Doubleday, 1997)*

Budapest, A Guide to 20C Architecture, E Heathcote *(Ellipsis, 1997)*

Revival Architecture in Hungary: Classicism and Romanticism, Anna Zádor *(Corvina/Helikon 1981)*

Art Nouveau in Hungary, Judit Szabadi *(Corvina, 1989)*

Standing in the Tempest. Painters of the Hungarian Avant-garde 1908-1930, SA Mansbach *(Santa Barbara/MIT Press 1991)*

Budapest, A Cultural Guide, Michael Jacobs *(Oxford University Press, 1998)*

General

Birds of Hungary, Gerald Gorman *(C Helm, 1996)*

A Concise History of Hungarian Music, Berice Szabolcsi *(Corvina 1974)*

Hungary at Home, Irén Ács *(Jövendő, Hungary)* photos

The Art of Hungarian Cooking, Paula Pogamy Bennett and Velma R Clark *(Hippocrene Books, New York, 1997)*

The Cuisine of Hungary, George Lang *(Penguin 1985)*

The Hungarian Cookbook, Susan Derecsky *(Harper Collins)*

The Wines and Vines of Hungary, Stephen Kirkland *(New World Publishing, Budapest)*

Literature

The Oxford History of Hungarian Literature, Lóránt Czigány *(OUP, 1984)*

Description of a Struggle: The Picador Book of East European Prose, Michael March *(Picador, 1995)*

Selected Poems 1933-80, George Faludy *(McClelland & Stewart/University of Georgia Press)* out of print

Under the Frog, Tibor Fischer *(Penguin, 1992)*

A Time of Gifts and **Between the Woods and the Water**, Patrick Leigh Fermor *(Penguin)*

The Adventures of Sinbad, Gyula Krúdy *(Central European University Press, 1998)*

The Paul Street Boys, Ferenc Molnár (1907) classic work

A Book of Memories, **The End of a Family Story**, Péter Nádas *(Jonathan Cape, 1997-9)*

Be Faithful Unto Death, Zsigmond Móricz *(Penguin)*

The Glance of Countess Hahn-Hahn, Down the Danube, Helping Verbs of the Heart, She Loves Me, Péter Esterházy *(Penguin)*

Kaddish for a Child not born, Imre Kertész, Christopher C Wilson, Katharina M Wilson *(Northwestern University Press, 1998)*

Budapest Then and Now, Imre Móra *(New World Publishing, Budapest)*

Bridge at Andau, James A Michener *(Fawcett Books, 1974)*

Czardas, Diane Pearson *(Corgi, 1977)*

Embers, Sándor Márai *(Viking/Penguin, 2002)*

Glossary

A few pronunciation rules

c = **ts** as in tsar
cs = **ch** as in chair
gy = **d** as in during
h = **h** as in hair
j = **y** as in yoga
ly = **y** as in yoga
ny = **n** as in new
s = **sh** as in ship
sz = **s** as in sun
ty = **ti** as in Katia
zs = **s** as in pleasure
á = **a** as in bar
e = **e** as in restful
é = longer, **ay** as in day
i = short **i** as in fit
í = **ee** as in bee
o = **o** as in dot
ó = **oo** as in door
ö = **er** as in driver
ő = **ir** as in first
u = short **u** as in put
ú = **oo** as in tool
ü = short **u** as in chute
ű = long, tight **u** sound, as in French 'rue'

DAYS OF THE WEEK AND MONTHS

nap	day	**május**	May
hónap	month	**péntek**	Friday
hét	week	**június**	June
január	January	**szombat**	Saturday
hétfő	Monday	**július**	July
február	February	**vasárnap**	Sunday
kedd	Tuesday	**augusztus**	August
március	March	**szeptember**	September
szerda	Wednesday	**október**	October
április	April	**november**	November
csütörtök	Thursday	**december**	December

NUMBERS

0	**nulla**	20	**húsz**
1	**egy**	30	**harminc**
2	**kettő**	40	**negyven**
3	**három**	50	**ötven**
4	**négy**	60	**hatvan**
5	**öt**	70	**hetven**
6	**hat**	80	**nyolcvan**
7	**hét**	90	**kilencven**
8	**nyolc**	100	**száz**
9	**kilenc**	1000	**ezer**
10	**tíz**		

EVERYDAY WORDS

yes	**igen**	exit	**kijárat**
no	**nem**	today	**ma**
please	**kérem**	yesterday	**tegnap**
thank you	**köszönöm**	tomorrow	**holnap**
good morning	**jó reggelt kívánok** (early in the morning) **jó napot kívánok**	pardon	**tessék**
		post office	**posta**
		post box	**postaláda**
good evening	**jó estét kívánok**	stamp	**bélyeg**
goodbye	**viszontlátásra**	police	**rendőrség**
excuse me	**elnézést**	hospital	**kórház**
okay	**jó**	doctor	**orvos**
open	**nyitva**	dentist	**fogorvos**
closed	**zárva**	chemist	**patika, gyógyszertár**
entrance	**bejárat**		

SIGHTS

apátság	abbey	**kápolna**	chapel
barlang	cave	**kastély**	castle
bazilika	basilica	**kert**	garden
dóm	cathedral	**palota**	palace
domb	hill	**piac**	market
emlékmű	monument	**rom**	ruin
erőd	fortress	**strand**	beach
erdő	forest	**temető**	cemetery
folyó	river	**templom**	church
ház	house	**tó**	lake
hegy	mountain	**vár**	fortified castle
híd	bridge		

ON THE ROAD AND IN TOWN

car park	**parkoló**
service station	**benzinkút**
super	**szuper**
high grade unleaded	**szuper ólommentes**
diesel	**diesel/dízel**
fill it up please	**tele kérem**
garage	**autójavító műhely**

FOOD

breakfast	**reggeli**	duck	**kacsa**
lunch	**ebéd**	turkey	**pulyka**
dinner	**vacsora**	goose	**liba**
menu	**étlap**	foie gras	**libamáj**
eat	**enni**	soup	**leves**
drink	**inni**	salt	**só**
plate	**tányér**	pepper	**bors**
fork	**villa**	jam	**lekvár**
knife	**kés**	butter	**vaj**
spoon	**kanál**	bread	**kenyér**
glass	**pohár**	vegetarian	**vegetáriánus**
table napkin	**szalvéta**	vegetables	**zöldség**
cup	**csésze**	beans	**bab**
the bill please	**a számlát kérem**	French beans	**zöldbab**
fish	**hal**	potatoes	**burgonya**
pike	**csuka**	mushrooms	**gomba**
pikeperch	**fogas**	cauliflower	**karfiol**
catfish	**harcsa**	sweetcorn	**kukorica**
trout	**pisztráng**	lentils	**lencse**
carp	**ponty**	tomatoes	**paradicsom**
eggs	**tojás**	asparagus	**spárga**
meat	**húsételek**	green salad	**saláta**
fried	**sült**	cheese	**saj**
grilled	**roston sült**	fruit	**gyümölcs**
roast	**sült**	apple	**alma**
lamb	**bárány (hús)**	orange	**narancs**
beef	**marha (hús)**	banana	**banán**
very rare	**alig sütve**	melon	**sárgadinnye**
rare	**félig átsütve**	watermelon	**görögdinnye**
medium rare	**közepesen átsütve**	grape	**szőlő**
well done	**jól átsütve**	peach	**őszibarack**
pork	**sertés**	pear	**körte**
ham	**sonka**	dessert	**édesség, desszert**
veal	**borjú (hús)**	cakes	**sütemények**
game	**vadételek**	sugar	**cukor**
poultry	**szárnyasok**	ice cream	**fagylalt**
chicken	**csirke**		

DRINKS/ITALOK

water	**víz**	wine	**bor**
still water	**sima víz**	red wine	**vörösbor**
mineral water	**ásványvíz**	white wine	**fehérbor**
ice cubes	**jégkocka**	bottle	**üveg**
sparkling water	**szénsavas ásványvíz**	half-bottle	**fél üveg**
fruit juice	**gyümölcslé**	cheers	**egészségére**
orange juice	**narancslé**	coffee	**kávé**
apple juice	**almalé**	tea	**tea**
tomato juice	**paradicsomital**	hot chocolate	**(meleg) kakaó**
beer	**sör**	milk	**tej**
	pohár (0.3 litres/1/2 pint)	hot	**meleg**
	korsó (0.5 litres/1 pint)	cold	**hideg**

AT THE HOTEL

hotel	**szálloda**	bathroom	**fürdőszoba**
room	**szoba**	shower	**zuhanyzó**
single room	**egyágyas szoba**	air-conditioning	**légkondicionáló**
double room	**kétágyas szoba**	key	**kulcs**
twin beds	**ikerágy**	how much?	**mennyibe kerül?**
double bed	**franciaágy**		

Lake Balaton

J.-Ch. Gérard/MICHELIN

Introduction

Hungary before and after the Treaty of Trianon

To relate Hungary's history is to recall its splendour, its times of greatness and pomp. Over the centuries, its influence was felt over a considerable part of Europe. From 1867 to the end of the First World War, in an empire shared with Austria, Hungary was a kingdom of some 20 million inhabitants living in an area of 325 000km²/125 000sq mi.
Relating Hungary's history also recalls painful and tragic moments, and visitors will hear talk of the Treaty of Trianon. This treaty, signed on **4 June 1920**, imposed severe punishment on Hungary for being on the losing side. The consequences were very serious and marked Hungary's destiny throughout the 20C.

Hungary during the First World War

Before the First World War, Hungary was part of the Austro-Hungarian Empire, ruled by Franz Josef of Habsburg, the Emperor of Austria who was also king of Hungary. Empress Elizabeth, better known by the name of Sissy, was also Queen of Hungary. In the Empire and the Kingdom (known in German as K und K, Kaiserlich und Königlich), three ministries were held jointly – foreign affairs, finance and defence – while the others were divided into two. The Empire became engaged in a conflict that was later to amplify, and was accused of sparking it off to resolve tension caused by the claims being made by the various nationalities. To be more precise, **István Tisza**, the Hungarian Prime Minister, played a direct part in activating the conflict. His agreement was needed for the Empire to be able to declare war. He hesitated for several days before giving his assent, justifiably fearing that Hungary would be broken up in the event of a defeat, because of its multi-ethnic population: Slovaks, Romanians and Croats alongside the Hungarians. To his country's misfortune, he finally gave in to Austrian pressure. In the heated emotion following the defeat, he was shot dead at the end of October 1918 by mutinous Hungarian soldiers.

The consequences of the Germano-Austrian defeat

The consequences of the defeat of the Central European empires were terrible for Hungary. Indeed, the negotiations at Versailles, the Trianon and at St-Germain were principally between the victors and not the countries that had been defeated. In November 1918, France sent a memorandum to President Wilson referring to the preliminary peace discussions with Germany, pointing out that, "regarding Austria-Hungary, the question does not even apply since this power has disappeared". In this way a great European power disappeared off the map in the name of the principle of nationalities. Many people think that we are still paying for the consequences of this enforced division today, which, notably, played a significant role in starting the 1929 crisis. Did the fragmented Empire already bear the seeds of its destruction before the Treaty of Trianon? This may be the case since it had failed to develop from an archaic dynastic system to a modern federal State system, offering political equality to the various nationalities of which it was composed. This said, although Germany was severely punished, it still retained most of its political and economic resources. Austria-Hungary was decimated, and Hungary broken into many parts.

The establishment of the Treaty and its consequences

The years following the First World War were particularly agitated in Hungary, with several changes in political leaders. Internal strife was prevalent and the Council Republic, which, in 1919, lasted for 133 days, gave rise to doubts regarding Communist contagion. The leader was Béla Kun (a prisoner of war in Russia, converted to communism) who had met Lenin in 1917 and worked for the International in Moscow. Only Austria maintained relations with the Council Republic, which initiated a generous policy of sharing and redistribution, created a **Red Army** and put men such as the composers Bartók and Kodály in charge of culture, and the philosopher, Lukács in change of public education. Since it was in open conflict with its neighbours, the Alliance between the Czechs, Romanians and South Slav peoples forced Hungary to cease fighting. On 4 August 1919, the Romanians entered Budapest and the Council Republic came to an end. Béla Kun went back to the Cominterm in Russia where he was shot on Stalin's orders in 1938.
On 16 November 1919 Admiral **Miklós Horthy**, supported by the Allies, rode into Budapest on a white horse. General elections were organised in January 1920 and took place in a climate of terror which claimed 6 000 victims. On 1 March, Admiral Horthy became the Regent of a country with no coastline (when it lost the region of Croatia, it also lost its only port, Fiume, now known as Rijeka). The government, comprised of small landowners and supporters of succession based on the principle of direct descent, signed the Treaty of Trianon on 4 June 1920.
Clemenceau's government had fallen from power several months before the signing of the Treaty that the French prime minister had drawn up with the other victors. The declared intention of its authors was to restore their rights to the oppressed nationalities of the defeated Empire. The territory formed by the Kingdom of Hungary was of particular concern. Of a total of 20 million inhabitants, less than 50% of the population was of Magyar origin, the majority being Slovaks, Romanians and Croatians. The first two of these were only entitled to hold lowly political positions but the latter had broader autonomy. At the time of the defeat, Serbs, Czechs and Romanians put pressure on the victors to divide up Hungary as far as possible. As a result, in all the disputed areas, and in order to guarantee the solidity of the new frontiers, arbitration settled against the Hungarians.
Of Hungary's surface area of 325 0000km²/125 000sq mi, 230 000km² were redistributed: Austria received 4 000km²/1 544sq mi, Romania 102 000km²/39 400sq mi, Serbia 63 000km²/24 300sq mi and the rest went to Bohemia. After the Treaty of Trianon, Hungary only retained 93 000km²/35 900sq mi (a surface area that was again reduced after the Second World War, when Hungary had to give up other territories near Bratislava in what was then Czechoslovakia). This redistribution of land without any movement of the population (two million people) changed the nationality of these people and placed them under new political authority. Hungary also lost 58% of its railway network, 43% of its arable land and 83% of its iron ore resources without any compensation. One episode in this series of historical events was the reclamation of Sopron, initially allocated to Austria, following a referendum. It is true to say that Hungarian nationalist irredentism did not foster good understanding and cooperation with the country's neighbours, and the treaty, rather than laying the foundations for future security, was perceived as a punishment by the Hungarians.
In museums with historical displays, the Treaty of Trianon is still mentioned and illustrated with a large number of maps. The Allies, and in particular Clemenceau and the French, are accused of originating all of Hungary's misfortune in the 20C.
The **Hungarian national anthem**, written in 1823 by **Ferenc Kölcsey** and set to music in 1844 by Ferenc Erkel, is still sung with fervour at every important occasion. It calls for God's protection for a people that some say is destined for misfortune:

"Take pity, Lord, on the Hungarians,
Buffeted by dangers;
Stretch a protecting arm over them,
In the sea of their torment.
Long dismembered by adversity,
Bring them years of joy.
These people have already made their atonement,
For the past and the future."

Historical table and notes

The Etelköz

1000-1500 BC	The Hungarians are found to the north of the Urals and on the western slopes of the mountains and then progressively settle on the banks of the Middle Volga, where they become semi-nomadic horsemen.
1C AD	The Romans subject the Celts and occupy Transdanubia, which they call Pannonia.
Early 2C	Aquincum (the present-day Óbuda quarter of Budapest) becomes the capital of Lower Pannonia.
5C	At the beginning of the century the Huns occupy positions left by the Romans. **Attila** unites the tribes in a vast empire before attacking the Eastern Roman Empire. Some Hungarian tribes move southwards and settle near the Black Sea.
9C	Breaking away from the Khazars, a people of Turkish origin from the lower Volga region, the Hungarians settle between the Don and the Dniestr in the area known as Etelköz, "The place between the two rivers".
896	Conquest of the Carpathian Basin by Prince **Árpád and the seven Magyar tribes.**

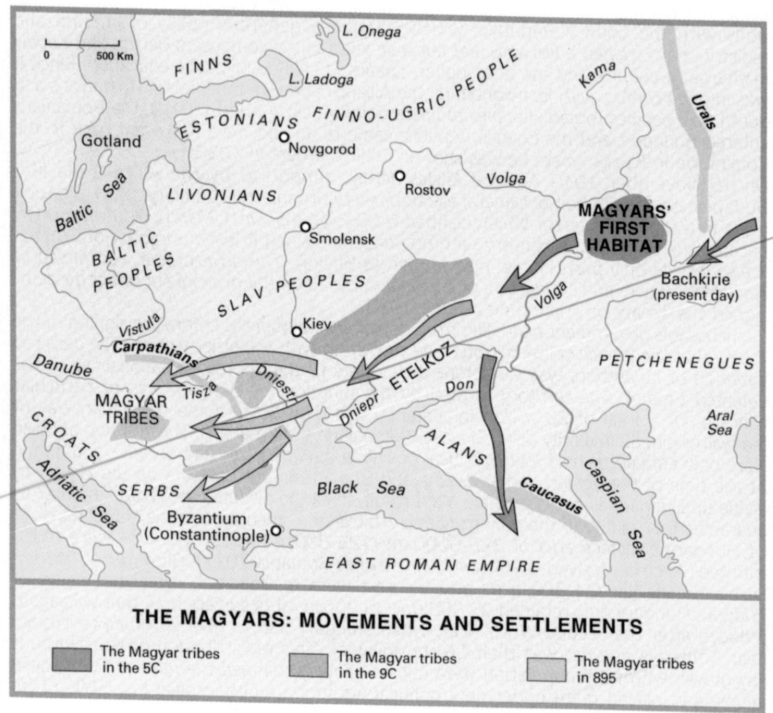

THE MAGYARS: MOVEMENTS AND SETTLEMENTS

The Árpád dynasty

902	The Hungarians destroy the Moravian Empire of Sviatopluk and Moïmir II, with the assistance of Emperor Arnulf.
10C	Magyar horsemen become notorious for their raiding and pillaging, which takes them as far as Burgundy and Aquitaine, to Naples and the shores of the Bosphorus.
955	The Hungarians are defeated at Lechfeld, near Augsburg, by the German king, Otto I the Great. Their chiefs are executed. This defeat puts an end to their raids and contributes to their settling process.
972-97	Reign of **Géza**, Árpád's great-grandson. The king is baptised and, at his request, Bruno, a monk from Saint-Gall, undertakes the conversion of the country to Christianity.
997-1038	Vajk, Géza's son, baptised István (Stephen), reigns under the name of Stephen I and continues his father's work. He is considered the real founder of the State of Hungary.
1st January 1001	Coronation of Stephen I in Esztergom Basilica.

Stephen I and the birth of the State of Hungary

Stephen I's reign, in the early Middle Ages, was of tremendous significance for Hungary. Like St Wenceslas in Bohemia 70 years earlier, he was responsible for opening up his country to Western influence by encouraging the Roman Christian faith.

Stephen was supported in his work by the French Pope, Sylvester II, who sent him a crown as a sign of sovereignty. He helped the Church to become established by founding 10 bishoprics, including Esztergom and Kalocsa. He built numerous churches and obliged all the inhabitants to go to Mass on Sundays and pay tithes to the Church.

At the same time, disregarding the traditional customs of Hungarian tribes, the king gave his country the beginnings of an administrative organisation by dividing the territory into *"comiti"* (counties), governed by a "count". The introduction of direct taxation and tolls provided the income required for this emergent State to function.

ROGER VIOLLET

Stephen I's reign was a time of tremendous change in the way of life of Hungarians. Profitable trade links were set up in all domains and the pilgrimage route from the West to the Holy Land passed through Hungary. In 1018, in fact, Stephen established his capital on this route, at Székesfehérvár. Stephen was canonised in 1083 and is remembered as a learned and extremely understanding monarch. This is attested in his *Exhortations*, which contained precepts in the art of governance, and were written for his son, the prince and heir to the throne.

1054	Schism: the final separation of the churches of Rome and Constantinople.
1077-95	After interminable quarrels over the succession, reign of László I (St Ladislas).
1095-1116	Reign of Kálmán (Coloman) the Bibliophile. During his reign, the Hungarians conquer Croatia-Slavonia, Dalmatia and the centre of Bosnia.
1141-62	Reign of Géza II. The king of France, Louis VII, and the German emperor, Conrad III, stay in Hungary during the Second Crusade.
1172-96	Reign of Béla III.

Béla III and Hungary at the end of the 12C

Béla III, a great king in both merit and stature (1.90m/6ft 6in) sought, as a ruler, to establish a balance in his relations with Byzantium (when a pupil at the Byzantine Court, he was betrothed to the Emperor's daughter) and with the West (his second wife was Margaret Capet, Louis VII's sister).

To organise his State, he modelled it on Western Europe. In 1180, he put the first chancellery in place. The royal council took shape.

During Béla III's reign, a new army was formed with "servientes". The castle commanders, *"jobagiones"*, became the landowners of the royal domain. Peasants and slaves now formed one single underclass.

Taking the Cistercian order as a foundation, Béla III revived the Church (churches were built or extended, such as Zsámbék near Budapest, Bélapátfalva, which was modelled on Fontenay, and Ják).

In 1189, at the time of the Third Crusade, Béla III received Richard the Lionheart and Frederick Barbarossa as his guests, thus bringing his reign to its apogee.

At the end of the 12C, Hungary's uniqueness became more pronounced: the kingdom had never been part of an Empire, nor a vassal State.

1217-18	András II organises a crusade. He is accompanied by the minnesingers Ruenthal and Tannhäuser.
1222	The Golden Bull grants nobles the right to oppose the king, even by the use of arms, if the king interferes with their privileges. The consequences of this charter of rights are considerable.
1241-42	Invasions by Tartars or Mongols who defeat the Hungarian army at Muhi. Béla IV is forced to settle in Trau (present-day Trogir in Croatia).
1301	With the death of András III, the Árpád dynasty comes to an end.

The wars against the Turks

1308-42	With **Charles Robert of Anjou** (Robert Károly) the reign of kings of foreign origin begins. He attacks the power of the great lords who "hold almost the entire country against him".
1357	The Ottomans settle on the opposite shore of the Bosphorus in Gallipoli, then in Adrianople.
1371	In the reign of **Louis I of Anjou** (1342-82), the Turks attack Hungary for the first time.
1387-1437	Sigismund of Luxembourg becomes King of Hungary through his marriage to the daughter of Louis I.
1396	Sigismund leads a crusade against the Turks who win a victory at Nicopolis. The news plunges the West into terror.
1444	Vladislas I is defeated by the Turks at Varna.
1453	Mehmet II seizes Constantinople.
1456	János Hunyadi, a noble from Valachia, defends Nándorfehérvár (present-day Belgrade) against the Turks. His son, Matthias is made king.
1458-90	Reign of Matthias Hunyadi, also known as **Matthias Corvinus**.
1514	Peasant revolt led by György Dózsa.
1521	The Turks seize Nándorfehérvár.
29 August 1526	Defeat at Mohács: Sultan Suleiman I, the Magnificent, crushes the troops of Louis II Jagiello, King of Hungary and Bohemia. The king dies in the battle.

Matthias Corvinus, a Renaissance prince

János Hunyadi successively served Sigismund, Vladislas Jagiello and then the child-king Ladislas of Habsburg. He placed his increasing power at the service of the fight against Islam.
On his death, even though he had held the crux of royal power in his hands, his first son was beheaded while the second, Matthias, was taken hostage by King Ladislas' advisors and taken first to Vienna and later to Prague.
Nevertheless, Matthias was elected king by the Diet in 1458, becoming the first national king of Hungary.
This man's intelligence, culture and strong character explain the 32 glorious years of his reign.
After his marriage to the Neapolitan, Beatrice of Aragon, this true Renaissance prince made Hungary a refined centre of civilisation. As a scholar had traced the origins of the Hunyadi family back to Consul Marcus Valerius Corvinus, Matthias adopted Corvinus as his family name.
Strongly supported by Pope Paul II, he took the Church's side against the Hussite kingdom, conquering Bohemia, Moravia, Lusatia and Silesia and had himself crowned King of Bohemia in Olomuc. Since the Emperor refused to acknowledge his title, Matthias took the provinces of Styria, Carinthia and part of Lower Austria including Vienna, from him.
He died in Vienna in 1490.
His work did not outlive his death, especially as the Diet chose the weak Vladislas II Jagiello to be his successor.

GIRAUDON

Battle of Mohács

The Habsburgs in Hungary

22 October 1526	Ferdinand of Austria is elected King of Bohemia in Prague.
11 November 1526	The Székesfehérvár Diet elects a national king in the person of János I Szapolyai (1526-40). Opposed by the Habsburgs, János I, supported by the Turks, sees his kingdom reduced to Transylvania.
17 December 1526	Ferdinand of Austria is elected King of Hungary at Presburg, under the name of Ferdinand I.
1541	Fifteen years after the defeat at Mohács, Ferdinand controls the north and east of Hungary (royal Hungary), Suleiman occupies the centre. Buda is under Turkish control. Szapolyai is Prince of Transylvania.
1566	Death of Suleiman I, the Magnificent, at the siege of Szigetvár.
1571	Victory of the Holy League (which includes Transylvania) over the Turks.
1591-1606	Fifteen years of war waged by the Habsburgs to drive the Turks out of Hungary and Transylvania.

Resistance to the Habsburgs

Throughout most of the 17C, Transylvania was to be the source of resistance to the Habsburgs. Three princes from three important Hungarian families were to distinguish themselves in this struggle. The first of these, **István (Stephen) Bocskai** (1605-06) rose up victoriously against Vienna, with the assistance of soldiers thirsty for battle. In 1606, the Emperor was obliged to accept Transylvania's independence, the right to worship as Protestants and to respect the nobles' privileges. A wedge was driven into the Habsburgs' centralisation policy.

Gábor Bethlen (1613-29) applied the same policy against Vienna and then, after a few concessions to the Turks, wisely developed the principality's economy. Even though the Thirty Years War was in the offing, he did not hesitate to form alliances with Protestant princes against the Habsburgs. He even managed to become master of royal Hungary before signing a Compromise with Vienna.

A third family, the **Rákóczi**, continued the implementation of Bethlen's policy, with George I Rákóczi (1630-48) and then his son, George II Rákóczi (1648-60). The latter's unfortunate adventure in Poland set Transylvania on the road to ruin. The principality's semi-independence was over.

1685	The imperial army occupies Transylvania.
1686	Liberation of Buda.
1687	The Diet declares the crown of Hungary as the rightful inheritance of the House of Austria.
1699	Peace of Karlowitz, marking the end of Turkish occupation in Hungary.
1740-90	The reigns of Maria Theresa (1740-80) and Joseph II (1780-90) introduce reforms in Hungary and see the development of cooperation between the Viennese court and Hungarian nobility.
1792-1835	With Francis II as German Emperor and King of Bohemia and Hungary under the name of Francis I, absolutism prevails in all domains.

The 1848-49 Revolution

Diet of 1825-27	The meeting of the Diet opens up the era of reform. Count István Széchenyi plays a very active role in the country's modernisation. Hungarian is declared the official language.
Diet of 1832-36	**Lajos Kossuth** stands for the 1832 Diet. He is arrested by the conservatives.
Diet of 1839	This third Diet frees political prisoners and grants non-nobles the right to own land and hold administrative positions.
1841	Kossuth starts the liberal newspaper, the *Pest Gazette*.
1843-44	The Assembly declares Hungarian to be the official language. The decision provokes opposition from national minorities.
February 1848	Revolution in Paris where the Second Republic is proclaimed.
15 March 1848	People's demonstration in Pest. A 12-point programme for the establishment of a bourgeois democracy is passed.

17 March 1848 Pressured by events, Emperor Ferdinand V appoints Count **Lajos Batthyány** to lead the government. He confirms the laws passed by the Diet: the abolition of feudalism, the constitution of a representative national assembly, freedom of the press, equality of worship and Transylvania's cession to Hungary.

September 1848 General J Jelacic's imperial army marches on the Hungarian capital. It is stopped at Székesfehérvár. General Lamberg, sent by Vienna, is killed by the crowd in Pest. Kossuth takes on the leadership of a national defence committee.

January 1849 The imperial army (Franz Josef has succeeded Ferdinand V) occupies the capital. The committee and the assembly take refuge at Debrecen.

14 April 1849 Kossuth pushes through a motion to depose the Habsburgs.

April-May 1849 The Hungarian army recaptures Pest and Buda.

August 1849 Due to the assistance requested by the Emperor from Tsar Nicholas I, the Hungarian army, now surrounded, lays down its arms. Count Batthyány and 13 generals are executed. Hungary is placed under Austrian control.

29 May 1867 After the defeat by Prussia at Sadová, the Austrian Empire seeks to appease Hungarian unrest. The Compromise institutes the Dual Monarchy.
–Hungary, Croatia and Transylvania form an independent State with its own government. This State recognises the Austrian Emperor as its head.
– The new State has a joint army, an imperial foreign policy and special financing for joint affairs.

1868 Law on nationalities: civic equality and recognition of certain cultural and religious rights.

Hungary after the First World War

1913 Government of **István Tisza**, who has already been in politics for 20 years.

1914-18 Austria-Hungary is swept into war alongside Germany and 1 million are killed in action.

31 October 1918 Bourgeois, democratic revolution and Mihály Károlyi's government.

21 March 1919 **Béla Kun's** Communist Party sets up a Council Republic which only lasts 133 days. This period will always be remembered as the era of the "red terror".

March 1920 With the assistance of the Romanian army, **Miklós Horthy**, an admiral in a country which now has no coastline, establishes himself as Regent of the Kingdom of Hungary. A reign of "white terror" is to follow.

4 June 1920 The **Treaty of Trianon**, imposed by the Allies, deprives Hungary of two-thirds of its territory and half of its population. Hungarian resentment runs high and is further stirred up by the Horthy regime which makes the treaty the principal target of its propaganda. Hitler and Mussolini are to exploit this situation.
The first anti-Semite law, introducing a *numerus clausus* in universities.

1938 Second anti-Semite law adopted, as a result of pressure exerted by Hitler's regime. It totally barred Jews from entering higher education.

27 June 1941 War is declared on the USSR.

1943 Admiral Horthy makes secret contacts with the Allies.

15 October 1944 The Arrow Cross (the Hungarian Nazis) seizes power, with the subsequent persecution and deportation of Jews. 700 000 Jews are deported, mainly to Auschwitz and Birkenau. Raoul Wallenberg, the Swedish Consul in Budapest, saves several thousand of them before his disappearance after being abducted by the Soviets.

1946 A Republic is proclaimed. Zoltán Tildy becomes President.
A new currency, the *forint* (still in place) replaces the *pengő*.

kaptál földet...
adj kenyeret!
MAGYAR KOMMUNISTA PÁRT

J.-L. Charmet/EXPLORER

Imre Nagy

1946-53 Opposition between the two blocs, the East and the West: this is the period of the Cold War. The Red Army is put into Hungary.

1948 The countries of the East form a single bloc with the USSR. The struggle against the Church begins. Cardinal Mindszenty is arrested on 26 December, charged with plotting against the State.

1949 The leader of the Communist Party, Mátyás Rákosi, becomes the head of the government. Trial of László Rajk, the Home Office Minister accused of Titoism. His former friends, including János Kádár, abandon him. He is sentenced to death and executed.

1953-55 The death of Stalin heralds a period of eased tension. **Imre Nagy**, a communist reformer becomes Prime Minister. A period of trouble follows, marked by the incessant struggle between the reformers and hardline Stalinists. Nagy is excluded from the Hungarian Workers Party in March 1955 and replaced by Mátyás Rákosi.

1956 A wind of freedom blows, particularly in intellectual circles. László Rajk is rehabilitated on 27 March. On 14 October, Nagy is reintegrated into the party.

16 June 1958 Execution of Imre Nagy in Budapest with several of his companions.

1963-88 The party, led by **János Kádár**, takes lenient measures. Kádár then undertakes economic and agricultural reforms. He is to stay in power until 1988. During these years, he so endeavours to avoid any divergence with the USSR and to maintain good relationships with the West, that he launches a plan for an international exhibition with Austria on the theme "a bridge towards the future", however it comes to nothing.

In the 1980s, the country is in the throes of economic difficulties. It survives thanks to credit facilities from the West but is heavily indebted. An economic crisis breaks out in 1987. Discontent grows. On 22 May 1988 during an extraordinary meeting of the PSOH (Communist Party), Kádár is dismissed.

The October 1956 Uprising

23 October marked the start of what is generally called the October 1956 Uprising. Among other demands, this mass uprising called for free elections, the departure of Soviet troops and freedom of the press. The political police fired into the crowd. The following day, Imre Nagy, the President of the Council, proclaimed martial law and announced that he was going to develop "national, independent socialism". The uprising spread throughout the country. A delegation arrived from Moscow, led by Mikoyan and Souslov. On 25 October, János Kádár was appointed leader of the Communist Party. The general strike became widespread. Repression was intensified. Nagy adopted the cause of the protesters.

On 1 November, Nagy announced the country's neutrality and its withdrawal from the Warsaw Pact. On 4 November, Russian tanks rolled into the capital and crushed the uprising. Kádár (who had taken refuge in the USSR) was appointed to lead a "revolutionary, worker and peasant" government. Nagy and his ministers were taken in by the Yugoslavian Embassy. The plan was to subsequently take them to Yugoslavia, with the promise of immunity. However, the Soviets arrested them and they were deported to Romania where they were sentenced to death.

1989	In Hegyeshalom, on **3 May**, the barbed wire separating Hungary and Austria is symbolically cut at the main frontier post between the two countries by the Minister for Foreign Affairs, Gyula Horn, and his Austrian counterpart. On **16 June**, Budapest holds a national funeral ceremony in memory of Imre Nagy and the 1956 victims. On 6 July, the Hungarian Supreme Court officially pronounces their rehabilitation, on the same day as the death of János Kádár. During the night of **10-11 September** around 700 000 East Germans who had come to Hungary are authorised to enter West Germany via Austria. On **23 October**, the Popular Socialist Republic of Hungary becomes the **Hungarian Republic**.
11 November 1989	The **fall of the Berlin Wall** heralds the dismemberment of the Soviet bloc.
1990	8 March: the signing of an agreement for the departure of Soviet troops before 30 June 1991. On **25 March** and **8 April**, the first free elections are held: the Democratic Forum comes to power. József Antall becomes Prime Minister. Árpád Göncz is elected President of the Republic by Parliament. In November, Hungary joins the Council of Europe.
1993	Hungary becomes an associate member of the European Union.
1994	General election won by the Socialist Party. Gyula Horn becomes Prime Minister and forms a coalition government with the League of Free Democrats.
1998	In a referendum, the Hungarians pronounce themselves in favour of their country joining NATO. The centre-right FIDESZ MPP party wins the general election. Viktor Orbán becomes Prime Minister.
13 March 1999	Hungary becomes an official member of NATO.
2000	Parliament elects Ferenc Mádl as new President of the Republic.
2001	Hungary's membership of the European Union remains a key question. An objective for 2003?

The faces of Hungary

Tucked away in the centre of Europe, Hungary lies equidistant between the Atlantic Ocean, the Urals, the Mediterranean and the Baltic Sea, stretching to the Danube Basin and sharing 2 266km/1 360mi of borders with seven States: Austria to the west, Slovakia to the north, Ukraine to the north-east, Romania to the east, and to the south, the Federal Republic of Yugoslavia, Croatia and Slovenia. Only 530km/318mi long, 270km/162mi wide and covering 90 066km²/36 026sq mi, it is easy to travel quickly from one end of Hungary to the other.

LANDSCAPE

Hungary does not really have natural borders, other than four watercourses: the Danube and the Ipoly to the north, the Dráva and the Mura to the south. The plains cover two-thirds of its territory, only 2% of which is above 400m/1 312ft in altitude.
Owing to its geographical location, Hungary is subjected to several meteorological influences. The continental climate dominates, marked by rigorous winters; the average January temperature can fall between 0°C/32°F and -10°C/14°F. In some years, it can reach -20°C/4°F and the Danube carries down large sheets of ice. Meanwhile, the average annual hours of sunshine (2 000) makes Hungary one of Central Europe's most favoured countries. It is hottest in July, with an average temperature of 23°C/73.4°F.
The average annual rainfall (500mm³/30cu in) is rather low; the country's north and south-west receive the most (800-900mm³/50-55cu in), whereas in the centre, the aridity of the Great Plain (600mm³/37cu in) gives a hint of the nearby Steppes of Eastern Europe.

The mountain chain

A mountain chain of 8 000km²/3 200sq mi runs diagonally from the north-east to the south-west, linking the last bastions of the Austrian Alps to the Carpathian Mountains. It lies in low terraces ranging from 500-800m/1 640-2 624ft. These consist of crystalline, limestone and volcanic rock in small massifs, which were broken up in the Tertiary Period, and can be roughly divided into three regions.

The Danube

Europe's second largest river after the Volga, the Danube has its source in the Black Forest and flows 2 850km/1 770mi to the Black Sea. Called the *Duna* in Hungarian, it flows across one-seventh of the country's length (428km/257mi). All Hungary's other rivers flow into it, such as the Tisza, from the Carpathians, and the Dráva. The Dráva runs alongside south Transdanubia, marking the border with Croatia for 150km/90mi. Most of the other tributaries flow into the Danube from the right: the Váli-víz, Sió and other smaller rivers.
The Danube is not deep: 3-4m/10-13ft on average and is 300-600m/984-1 968ft wide. While this great river loses very large amounts of its water to infiltration and evaporation as it crosses Hungary, it is nevertheless perfectly navigable and has been an essential connecting route since the Middle Ages between Eastern and Western Europe. In 1992 a canal was opened to link the Danube to the Main and the Rhine, creating a new river route linking the North Sea to the Black Sea.

The western hills – The massifs to the west of the Danube take on various names: the Bakony Mountains, the Vértes Hills, and the Pilis-Gerecse Hills *(see Transdanubia)*.

The Danube Bend (Dunakanyar) – After marking the border between Hungary and Slovakia for 130km/78mi in the north, the Danube cuts between the Börzsöny and Pilis hills. At the town of Esztergom it turns back in a right-angle to form the famous bend, which the Hungarians call the *Dunakanyar*, before flowing between Buda and Pest on its way south.

The northern mountains – The **Börzsöny** massif lies just before the **Cserhát Hills**, where the town of Hollókő nestles with its wooden bell-towers and whitewashed houses. Covered with oaks and beeches, the massif reaches its highest altitude in the **Mátra Mountains**, where Kékestető rises to 1 015m/3 329ft. The rough karstic landscapes of **Bükk** and **Aggtelek**, relieved by tufts of juniper, stretch to the **Zemplén** massif; they overlook the prestigious **Tokay** vineyard, whose vines grace the gentle Hegyalja slopes. In the basins separating the massifs, towns have developed around the mining of coal, bauxite and lignite. Miskolc, Hungary's third largest city, is home to the country's only iron mine, Rudabánya. Manganese, the only rare mineral, is worked at Úrkút.
The massifs of this chain are limited to the south by a great fault that has favoured the emergence of numerous hot springs.

Hungary has over 1 000 hot springs, and exploits about 100 of them. Budapest holds the world record with 128 springs supplying 30 thermal spas. As early as the Roman period, they were renowned for their medicinal properties. Bathing in thermal waters then went out of fashion, only to be revived at the end of the Middle Ages, and again under Turkish occupation. True spas catering for health treatment were built in the 18C and 19C. Today the baths are enjoying new interest, and 125 new centres have been opened within three years.
The localities with hot springs can be recognised by the prefix before their name: *füred* or *fürdő*. Among the most famous outside Budapest are Balatonfüred, Eger, Hévíz, Miskolctapolca and Parádfürdő.

The Great Plain

Delimited by the Danube and the northern massifs, the **Alföld** stretches to the borders with Romania, Serbia and Croatia, covering more than half the country (50 800km²/20 320sq mi). It is a vast Tertiary Period basin, filled during the Quaternary Period by formations created by changing seas, lakes, rivers and winds. Its highest point (182m/597ft) is to the north-east, near Debrecen; its lowest point (76m/249ft) is to the south near Szeged.

A landscape shaped by man – From north to south the Great Plain is crossed by Hungary's second longest river, the **Tisza**; its source is in the Ukraine, and it joins the Danube 1 300km/780mi further down. It is known as the "blond" river, because of the sand it carries downstream which is later swept into dunes by the wind.
In the past the Great Plain was called the *puszta*, which means "bare ground" or "desert". Indeed, its landscape suffered greatly under Turkish occupation. Devastated by Suleiman the Magnificent's Ottoman troops after the battle of Mohács in 1526, the region was not reconquered until the end of the 17C. Meanwhile, its marshy prairie was ransacked and the population decimated. The Great Plain began turning into a desert in the 19C, a period when its wild beauty was exalted by artists and poets, such as Sándor Petőfi (1823-49), who dedicated several poems to it. The dry and vibrant colours of József Tornyai's (1869-1936) paintings re-create the region's arid land, before it was cultivated.
For a century now, an informed agricultural revolution has completely changed the look of the Great Plain. The dams built in the 1960s upstream on the Tisza have made it possible to control the river's devastating flooding, while developing irrigation at the same time. Rice fields, acacias and poplars were planted as protective screens to keep the sand in place and improve the poor soil, while the extensive cultivation of cereals, fruit and vegetables was developed. As an indication of this rediscovered vitality, the plain has developed today into a chequerboard terrain of villages ringed with new houses.

The "puszta" – Nothing remains of the lonely steppe of the past except for two sanctuaries: Hortobágy National Park (80 000ha/192 000 acres) west of Debrecen, and the park at Bugac, south-west of Kecskemét (16 000ha/38 400 acres). These sandy moors, with the occasional marsh or saltwater pond, have kept their wild character.
Hortobágy Park is the largest steppe in Central Europe. **Sheep** with long twisted horns *(racka)* are still bred here in the traditional way, along with grey cattle. This ancient Hungarian breed known for its stamina serves as a gene bank for cross-breeding with others.
The herdsmen are mounted on *nóniusz* horses, and are accompanied by *puli*, black or white **sheepdogs** with long, curly-haired coats. The dove-coloured *pumi*, the white *komondor* and the brown and white *kuvasz* are other typically Hungarian breeds of dog.
The park is also home to over 230 species of **bird**: ducks, herons, bustards, great white-breasted geese.
The **Bugac** *puszta* is the most visited part of the Kiskunság Park, and is protected by Unesco as a bio-reserve.
Cars are prohibited, and the area is the domain of shepherds on horseback whose feats can be admired by visitors.

The south, Hungary's "orchard" – The extremely productive Great Plain, one of Hungary's most fertile regions, is devoted to high-yield agriculture. Between the Danube and the Tisza, the **Nagykunság** area is favoured with a loess soil, where cereals such as wheat, maize and rice flourish. **Kecskemét** is a green oasis surrounded by grapevines and apricot trees, from which the town makes its famous brandy *(barack-pálinka)*. **Szeged** to the south is the main paprika producer. In the villages this pepper is traditionally hung at the windows in the autumn, making brilliant red decorative garlands. The subsoil provides petroleum, natural gas, and geothermal energy (hothouses, urban heating).

The east bank of the Tisza – This is the **Nyírség** region, devoted to industrial plants (tobacco, wheat, sunflower and sugar beet) and vast apple orchards. Flocks of geese rest in the shade of the trees, as they do everywhere in Hungary. The breeding of pigs, ducks, turkeys and guinea fowl completes the intensive use of the land. To the north-east, **Debrecen** is Hungary's second largest city after Budapest.

PICTOR

Lake Balaton

Transdanubia

This region lying in the western part of the country between the foothills of the Alps and the Danube is known as the **Dunántúl** (32 000km²/12 800sq mi). This is where the Romans established Pannonia.

Lake Balaton – In the heart of Transdanubia, an area of plains and hills, stretches the greatest "inland sea" in Europe (595km²/238sq mi). The lake was formed after volcanic eruptions, dating back to the Tertiary Period. Some 74km/44mi long, its width fluctuates between 1.5km/1mi (at the Tihany Peninsula) to 12km/7mi. Its depth varies as well, from a few centimetres in the south to over 12m/39ft in the north near Tihany.
Only 100km/62mi from Budapest, Lake Balaton offers 256km/154mi of coastline and a particularly pleasant climate: for four months, from May to September, the water temperature is in the region of 25°C/77°F. It is Hungary's favourite holiday spot, together with Lake Velencei to the north-east (420ha/1 008 acres).
Lake Balaton is home to 42 varieties of fish, including *fogas*, a sort of pikeperch, carp, sterlet, bream and eel, which, together with barbel and catfish, are the most common fish in the country.

North of Lake Balaton – The geological relief appears as a succession of small massifs: the Pilis-Gerecse Hills, the Vértes Hills and the Bakony Mountains, of volcanic origin. The landscapes are reminiscent of Austria. **Székesfehérvár** is an old royal city, as is **Veszprém** with its many Baroque churches and houses. Grapevines and fruit trees grow on the verdant shores of Lake Balaton. The **Tihany Peninsula** is one of the prettiest places in the Lake Balaton region; covered with poplars, acacias and fields of lavender, it still has a wild atmosphere. Springs of gaseous water flow into the freshwater lake. The slightly alkaline water has made the reputation of several spas. **Hévíz**, the most famous, is west of Lake Balaton, on the edge of Europe's largest thermal lake (47 000m²/56 212sq yd).

Peasant architecture

With the settling of the Magyars in the Danube Basin, after several centuries of nomadic life, came the beginning of the fixed dwelling made of materials found on the spot. In Transdanubia wood and stone were used; in the Great Plain the long low earthen house was the traditional dwelling for a considerable time. Mud was pressed into moulds to make the walls, while the roof was made of reeds or straw. Inside, the large common room had a hearth without a chimney, and the smoke escaped freely through the roof's natural cracks and crannies. Galleries were fixed to the front of the house.
Later, as agriculture developed, summer farms were built just outside the villages. These *tanyas*, whitewashed and scattered here and there in the fields, gradually came to be permanent homes.
This heritage suffered greatly from the Ottoman invasion, from underdevelopment during the Austro-Hungarian Monarchy, then from overly rapid industrialisation. Cobwork village homes have gradually given way to modern dwellings. The remaining traditional homes are often transformed into weekend or holiday country houses. In Szentendre and Zalaegerszeg peasant homes have been rebuilt in open-air museums.

South Transdanubia – Less rugged, the southern shore of Lake Balaton includes some developed beaches, notably at **Siófok**. To the south-east, the rushes in the marshy Kis-Balaton area are a refuge for numerous species of bird. Moving down towards **Pécs**, next to the small karst massif of **Mecsek**, a Mediterranean influence can be perceived. In the hills around **Villány**, fig and almond trees mingle with grapevines, a scene reminiscent of Tuscany.
As well as its agricultural wealth, Transdanubia has a rich subsoil: natural gas, manganese, uranium, bauxite and some oil.

The Small Plain

North-west of the Bakony Mountains, the **Kisalföld** (8 403km²/3 361sq mi) is a plain formed by Tertiary and Quaternary deposits, which stretches around **Sopron** and **Lake Fertő** (322km²/129sq mi). Two-thirds of the lake is hidden by reeds; it lies on the border with Austria, where it is known as Neusiedler See – Hungary itself only possesses 23km²/9.2sq mi.
The Small Plain has a relatively mild climate, making it one of the greenest regions in Hungary. Oaks and beeches grow in the poor soil, whereas the area of intensive farming – cereals, maize, sugar beet, cattle fodder, potatoes, cows, pigs – extends as far as the Danube. Nevertheless, agriculture has had less of an impact on the landscape than in the Great Plain. Multiple crops are predominant, the farms are smaller, and the small market towns still trade farm products.
Spared by the Turkish occupation, the Small Plain has most of its medieval town architecture virtually intact, such as at **Kőszeg** and **Sopron**, and the Gothic churches and Baroque palaces at **Fertőd**, the "Hungarian Versailles". Culturally, this region remains close to Austria, from which it has only been separated since the 1921 referendum. Here, the people speak both Hungarian and German, and villages are similar on both sides of the border.

THE INHABITANTS

Demographic portrait – Hungary had a population of 10.1 million inhabitants in 1998, that is to say, an average population density of 109 inhabitants per km² (0.4sq mi). As in many other European countries over the past 20 years, the birth rate has been in constant decline.
Moreover, while 49% of all Hungarians lived in cities in 1920, today 63% are city-dwellers. Very rapid industrialisation after the World Wars called on rural manpower, without extending to immigrants.
Budapest has 2 million inhabitants, or one-fifth of the country's population. This surprisingly high concentration is easily explained. At the end of the 19C the capital saw a spectacular increase in its population, when it was the political and economic heart of a country three times bigger than it is now and in the throes of economic growth. The populations of the country's other principal cities are much lower than Budapest's: Debrecen (210 000), Miskolc (182 000), Szeged (170 000), Pécs (168 000) and Győr (130 000).

The Magyars – Historically multi-ethnic, Hungary's population was reduced by 61% following the Treaty of Trianon in 1920. Its people are now on the whole from the same ethnic origin: 97% of the inhabitants are Hungarian by extraction and speak Magyar as their mother tongue.
Because of the Treaty of Trianon which brought an end to the multi-ethnic Habsburg empire, large Hungarian minorities live today in the States surrounding Hungary: over 2 million in Romania, about 700 000 in Slovakia, 400 000 in Serbia, 200 000 in the Ukraine and some tens of thousands in Croatia and Slovenia. Moreover, with Russia, Hungary is the European country which has the most nationals living outside its territory (about 1.5 million people in Europe and in the two Americas).

The Tziganes – This ethnic group is Hungary's principal minority.
According to official statistics there were 143 000 Tziganes, or Hungarian gypsies, in 1990, but in reality they are far more numerous even if the precise number cannot be verified: from 450 000 to 800 000 individuals, or 5.2% to 7.3% of the Hungarian population.
Originally from northern India, the Tziganes came to Hungary in droves from the 15C to the 17C; their language bears a certain resemblance to Sanskrit. Despite the Communist regime's efforts at integration, they have remained something of a fringe society, living for the most part on the edges of large urban centres. In Miskolc, a north-west industrial town, they represent about 15% of the population, a figure shared with Debrecen and Nyíregyháza, to the east of the country.
Partly due to their low level of education, the Tziganes have suffered greatly from unemployment since the introduction of the market economy at the end of the 1980s.

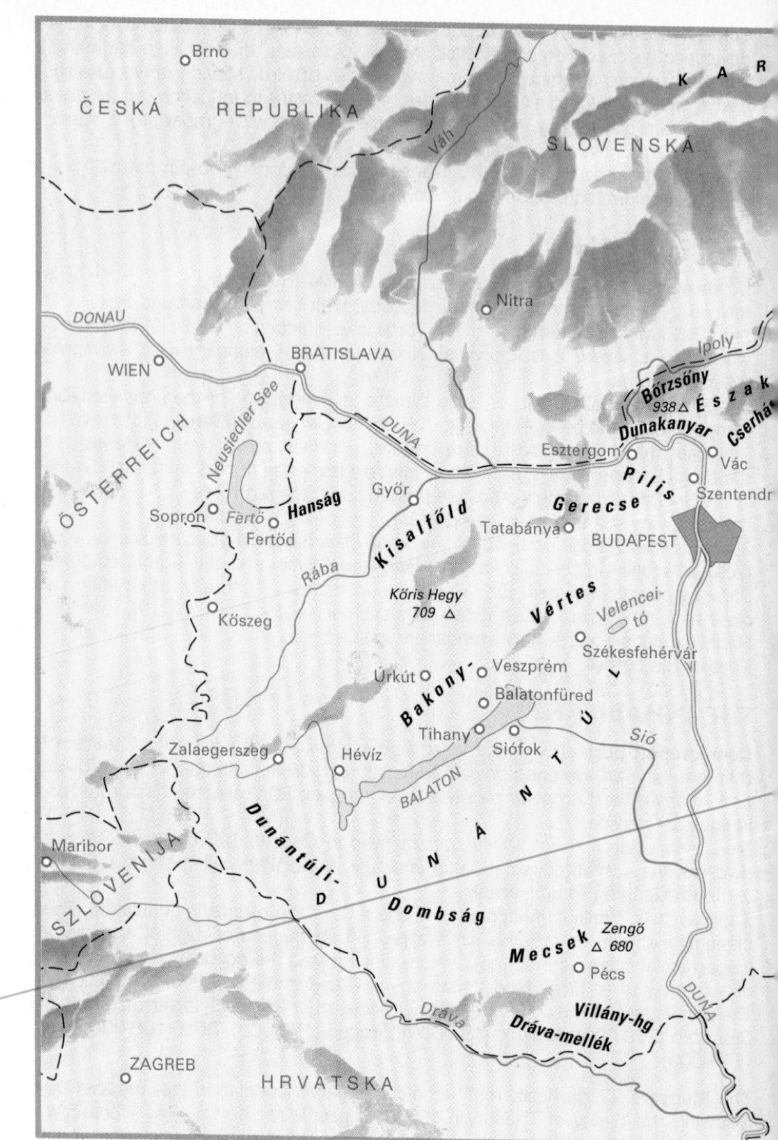

HUNGARIAN LANGUAGE

The Finno-Ugric family – Based on its origins, Hungarian stands apart from most other European languages; it has no connection with Latin, Germanic or Slav languages. Indeed, it belongs to the Finno-Ugric family, as do Estonian, Finnish and Karelian. All told there are about 15 such languages, all spoken in the Nordic countries, from western Siberia to Norway... except for Hungarian.
The melting-pot of Finno-Ugric languages was the steppe between the River Ural and the middle course of the Volga. The linguistic unity of the populations in this vast territory broke up in the middle of the first millennium, under the effect of migrations. Today, there are more differences than similarities between the languages; a Finn and an Estonian can manage to understand each other, but Hungarian is a foreign language to them.

Modern Hungarian – This bears the traces of the thousand years of contact the Magyars had with other peoples; in the Ural region, they borrowed from populations speaking an Indo-European language within the Indo-Iranian branch. Later, the Turkish and Slav peoples brought new energy to Hungarian with thousands of imported words. Moreover, elite society played an essential role in the renewal of the Hungarian lan-

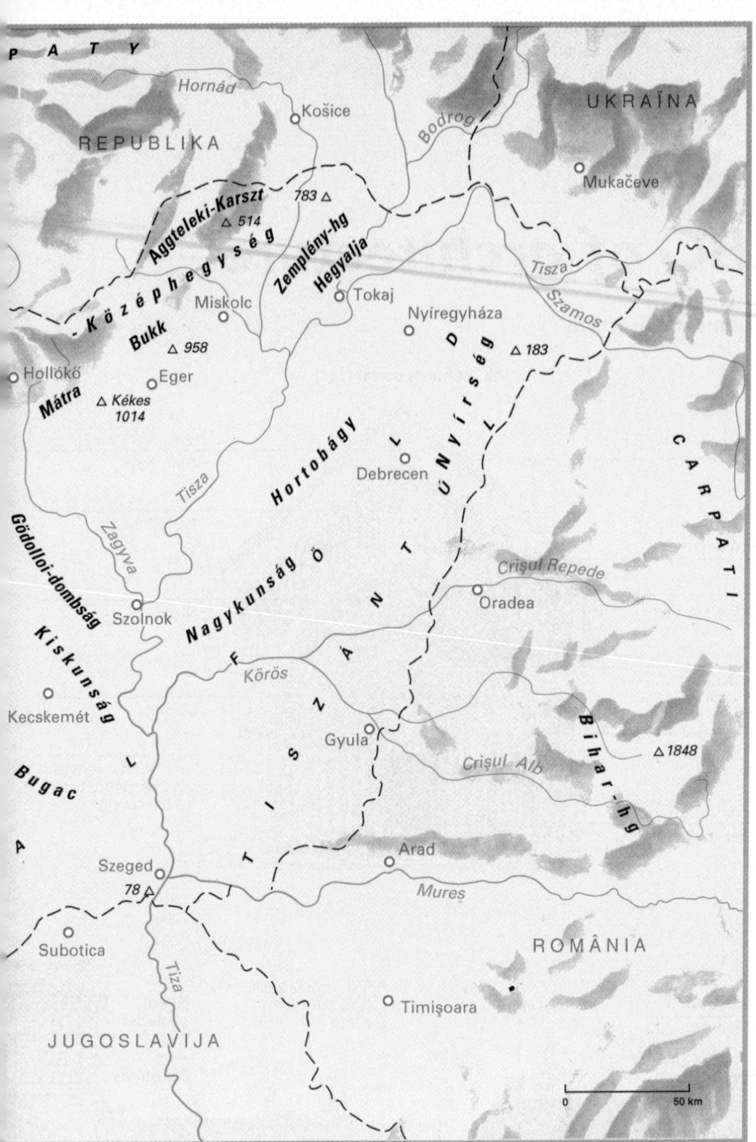

guage. The first known document containing Hungarian words is the letter founding Tihany Abbey, in 1055. This language was only actually substituted for Latin after the Renaissance, particularly in literature. In the early 19C, a passionate reform was undertaken by writer Ferenc Kazinczy, among other defenders of the language. To enrich Hungarian in abstract expressions, new terms were created, forged out of local dialects or created by analogy. In this way almost 10 000 words were integrated into the modern language.

ABC of architecture

Religious architecture

JÁK – Church portal (13C)

Pier
Twin bays
Trefoil arch
Denticular frieze
Pointed arch
Niche
Semi-circular
barrel arch
Covings
Tympanum
Arch shafts: vertical piers forming a base for the covings
Foliated scroll

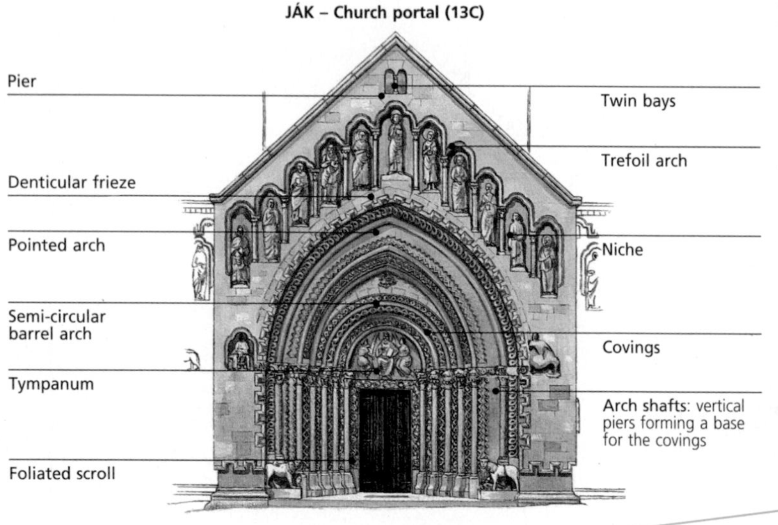

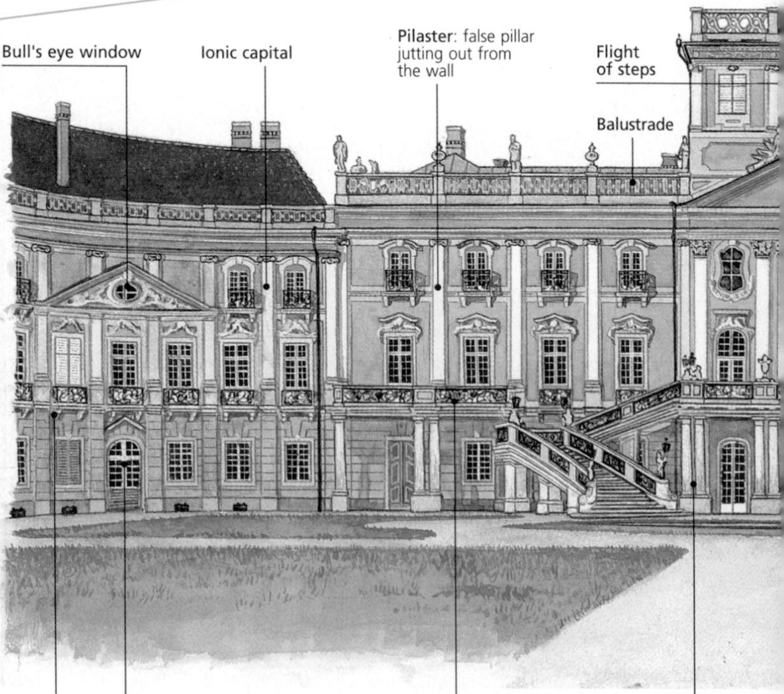

Bull's eye window
Ionic capital
Pilaster: false pillar jutting out from the wall
Flight of steps
Balustrade
Corbel
Window with semi-circular arch
Wrought-iron balcony
Double columns

ESZTERGOM – Royal Castle Chapel (12C)

Cross-ribbed vault
Groin of gothic arch
Abacus
Twin columns
Column shaft
Altar
Column base
Keystone
Gothic arch
Corinthian capital: decorated with acanthus leaves
Bay
Roll-moulding

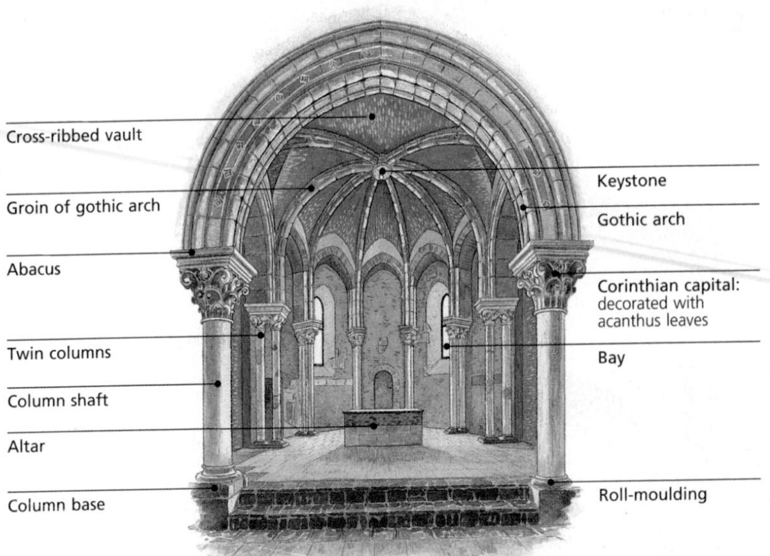

Civil architecture

FERTŐD – Former Esterhazy Castle (18C)

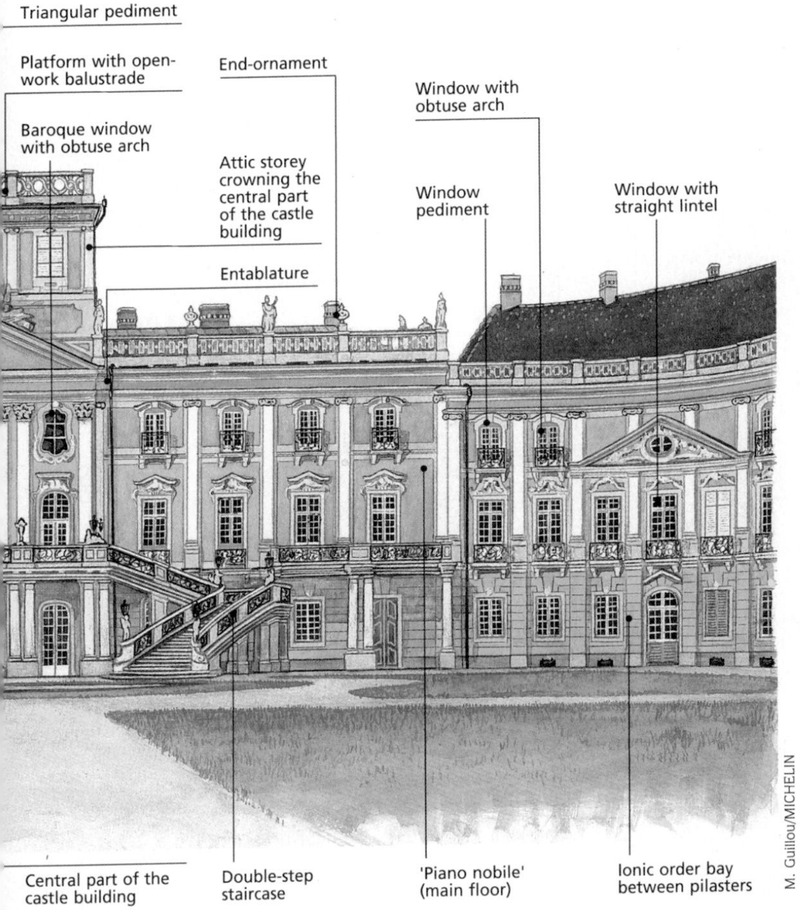

Triangular pediment
Platform with open-work balustrade
Baroque window with obtuse arch
End-ornament
Attic storey crowning the central part of the castle building
Entablature
Window with obtuse arch
Window pediment
Window with straight lintel
Central part of the castle building
Double-step staircase
'Piano nobile' (main floor)
Ionic order bay between pilasters
M. Guillou/MICHELIN

SÁROSPATAK Castle – Covered staircase (16C-17C)

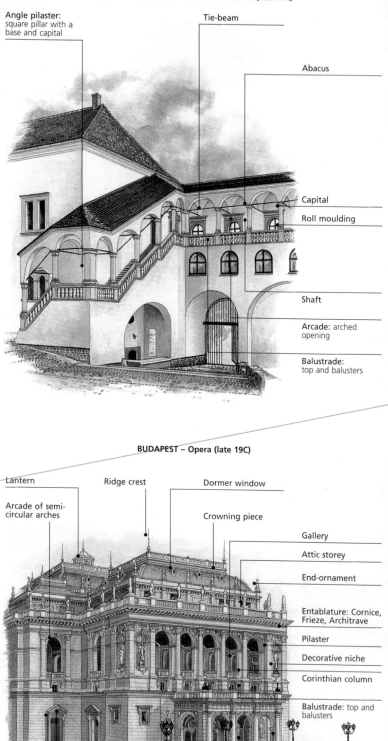

BUDAPEST – Opera (late 19C)

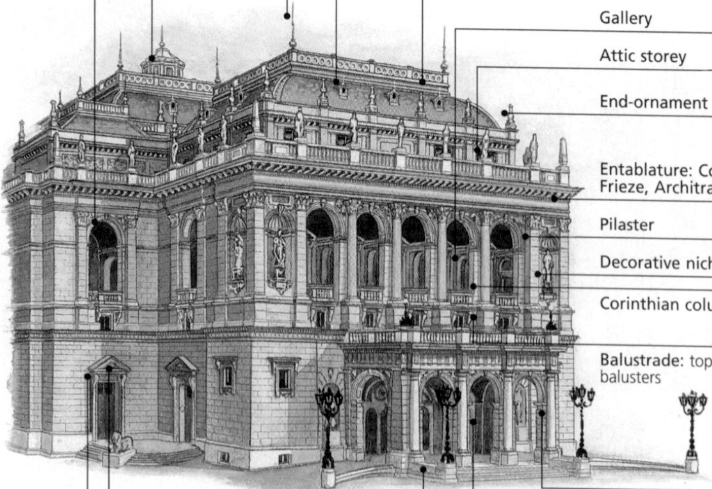

BUDAPEST – Former Post Office Savings Bank (end 19C-early 20C)

Majolica roof: Szolnay pottery decorated with motifs, garlands and coloured flowers.

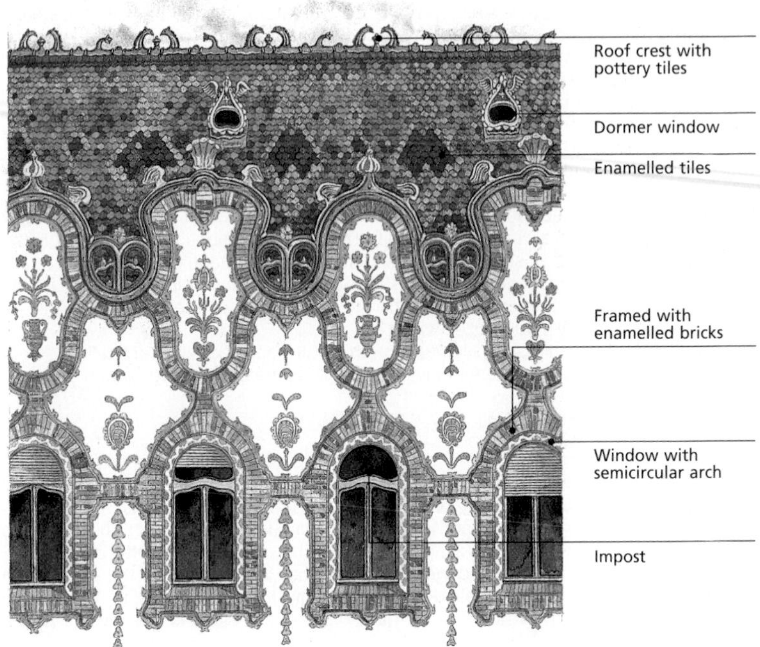

Religious architecture

PÁKS – Church (20C)

Hungarian Organic style: This style of architecture takes its inspiration from the symmetry of living creatures, human beings in particular.

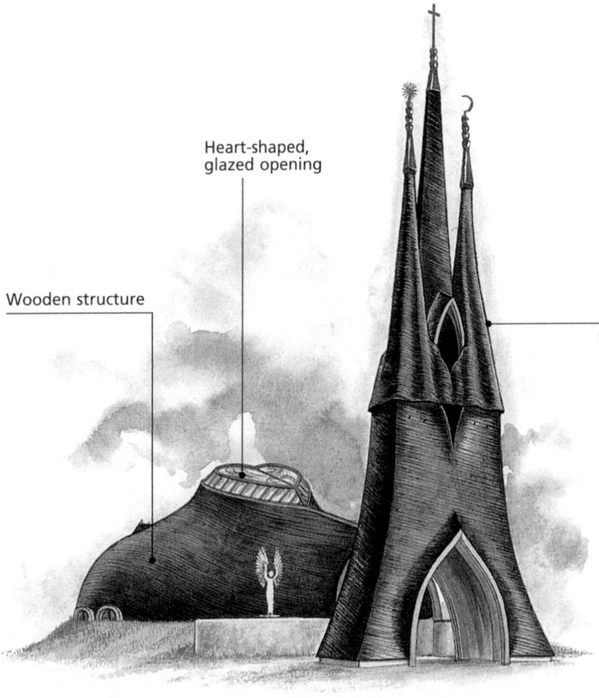

Heart-shaped, glazed opening

Wooden structure

Shingle roof

M. Guillou/MICHELIN

Hungary and the arts

Hungary has been a crossroads, a region through which tribes from all points of the compass have passed. It has been a place of confrontation, where one power has been substituted for another, where people passing through have stopped to settle and then been driven out, leaving traces of their culture, lifestyle and customs, abandoning their everyday objects and burying their dead. Those who settled here have left to conquer the world, and returned victorious or vanquished. They have travelled and traded. Hungary is a country with a wealth of inspirations drawn from other parts of the world, or invented. Those who call themselves Hungarian today have, through all the vicissitudes of history, formed a people that has been able to bring its intelligence, originality and personality to the fore – in a word, its genius.
Keeping alive a language spoken by 12 million people in a world of several billion inhabitants is something of a challenge in itself. To have this language produce so many works of literature and poetry that have enriched world heritage is proof of the imaginative strength of the Hungarian people. That it was a means of invention, placing its citizens' scientific discoveries – among the most important of the 20C – on an international scale, is confirmation of its vitality.
Hungary's literature, painting, sculpture, architecture and the great art called, sometimes disdainfully, folk art, have always powerfully expressed the Hungarian soul.

BEFORE THE ROMAN OCCUPATION

Only 25km/15mi from the present capital, at Vértesszőlős, the remains of *Homo sapiens paleohungaricus* were discovered. One of the first men to walk upright, he already had imaginative intelligence as he used fire and made the first artefacts.
Later, about 35 to 40 000 years BC, Neanderthal people settled in the Érd area (Budapest suburb) and in the Bükk Mountains, hunting, fishing and sheltering in caves; they also made tools and hunting weapons. However, it was more to the east, in the Great Plain, that civilisation expanded. Archaeological digs in the Tisza Valley have brought to light Neolithic relics and veritable objets d'art, such as the *Divinity with a Sickle* that dates from 3500 to 4000 BC.
The Celts arrived in the 3C and 4C, bringing with them the potter's wheel, which also indicates forceful imagination. They had themselves buried with their weapons and horses; archaeological sites have brought to light a great quantity of artefacts attesting to their art. All these riches can be seen at the Budapest National Museum.

THE ROMAN OCCUPATION

The Romans occupied a part of the territory that forms the Hungary we know today, and settled in the western part that they called Pannonia. They were to remain for nearly five centuries. They withdrew at the beginning of the 5C, not without leaving their mark on the country and its population. Among the towns of the Roman period that have preserved vestiges of varying degrees of significance are Intercisa (Dunaújváros) and Savaria (Szombathely). There are also roads, and Aquincum, the former capital of Lower Pannonia, is located in Budapest's Óbuda district.
Fortifications were built along the Roman walls that marked the borders they had defined. There are numerous statuary remains of this period, figures representing the gods they worshipped as well as a great many tombstones. Several Christian centres began to emerge during this Roman period, in the 2C and 3C. The Huns arrived in 492, driving the Roman population out of Pannonia. They were succeeded by the Ostrogoths, the Lombards and the Avars. Then came Charlemagne, who extended the Frankish Empire to the River Tisza.

ROMANESQUE STYLE

The late 10C and early 11C was the time of the Árpád dynasty. The conversion of Géza, followed by the baptism of his son Vajk, who became István (Stephen) and received the king's crown from the hands of the Pope's envoy, led to Hungary's being integrated into the Christian world. The king organised the country into *vármegyes* around the castles, which correspond to the present-day provinces. The regulations of these administrative units obliged the inhabitants to be baptised and to build a church for every 10 villages. At this time the king granted the monasteries and churches large sums of money. Ecclesiastics, monks or priests, were invited from France or Italy, and up until the Mongol invasion, Romanesque art flourished in Hungary (Pécsvárad Abbey, crypt at Tihany Abbey).
It was under Béla III that art and architecture received the most royal support. The widower of Anne of Châtillon, he took Margaret Capet for his second wife. French monks, workers and master craftsmen came to build and decorate palaces and churches. The styles could even be termed the Burgundy School and the Norman School. This period gave rise to the enlargement of Kalocsa, Eger, Győr, Ják Church (1212), the royal chapel at Esztergom, the start of the construction of Pannonhalma,

K. Szelényi/MAGYAR KÉPEK Kft.

Bélapátfalva Abbey

the Cistercian Abbey of **Bélapátfalva**, built by French Cistercians in 1232 and one of the most beautiful examples of Romanesque architecture, and Zsámbék, built by the French Aynard family who formed part of Margaret Capet's suite.
The style of the former Premonstratensian Abbey at Ócsa is between two periods and two styles; it is a rare example of a construction marking the end of the Romanesque and the beginning of the Gothic style. The chancel has fragments of 13C frescoes.

GOTHIC STYLE

Hungarian Gothic style came a century later than its French inspiration. It is simpler yet less severe than the Germanic version, most likely for technical reasons. Few traces remain, as the originals were incorporated into Baroque restorations.
Notable examples include Siklós Castle's chapel, which is a clear and luminous example in the closed environment of the castle. The Püspöki palota inside Eger Castle's fortifications has kept its Gothic gallery, as has the royal palace of Királyi palota in Visegrád. In Buda, on the castle site, Matthias Church has preserved only a few original elements and the same applies to Szent Miklós (St Nicholas) Church's cloisters, integrated into the Hilton Hotel. The town's parish church built at the Pest end of Elizabeth Bridge and built on Romanesque church ruins has kept a Gothic side chapel and several pointed-style openings. Note the non-Gothic feature, the *mihrab*, a souvenir of the time when the church was a mosque.
In Sopron, Szent Mihály Church suffered not from time, nor from the Turks, but rather from the ruthless Storno family who even added a bell-tower. In Nyírbátor, the Református templom in all its sobriety has a magnificent lacework of Gothic ribs covering the vault.

THE RENAISSANCE STYLE

Matthias Corvinus was made king at the age of 15. He did not take long to manifest the qualities of wisdom and strength attributed to the crow on his family coat of arms. He added to this a taste for books and things new, and transformed the court into a centre of culture. He brought artists from Italy, including Camicia, Chimenti and Giovanni Dalmate, and so transformed Buda Castle, and Visegrád Castle that their fame spread beyond the borders. Numerous examples of Renaissance art, fireplaces, floors and sculptures can be seen in the palace museum in Budapest. In Esztergom, Bakócz Chapel is a fine example of Renaissance art.

THE TURKISH PERIOD

This was disastrous for a large number of buildings and today there sometimes remains no more than a memory or a few stones. The Turks converted churches into mosques, which were later returned to Christianity. This was the case with Szigetvár Church. On the other hand, at Pécs, what is called the church-mosque was in fact originally a mosque. Again at Pécs, the Jakováli Hasszán Mosque is another small, well-preserved Turkish building. In Eger, the minaret is all that is left of the mosque. In Budapest, the Rudas and Király baths are extremely fine examples of the Ottoman period.

BAROQUE

Baroque blossomed in Europe between 1600 and 1800. In Hungary, what could be termed Early Baroque appeared in the part of the country that was not occupied by the Turks, between 1630 and 1710. The other two important periods of this style were 'mature' Baroque, from 1710 to 1760 and Late Baroque from 1760 to 1800. Baroque, in its various expressions, in terms of music, dance, painting and clothing, was considered the "art of appearance". The Baroque man had to "seem what he was, but above all be what he seemed". Of this spirit, architecture retained only the importance of appearance. It was representation to such an extent that artifice became the rule. *Trompe l'œil* replaced reality. It was the art of pretence. Marble was not marble, wood was an imitation, and the building's real structures often looked like false columns and false pilasters. On the other hand, apparently real columns supported nothing at all. While Baroque architecture paid no attention to function and needs, nevertheless space or spaces were dealt with in such a way that architectural volumes were created, making places where people felt at one with their surroundings. It is practically impossible to feel out of touch in a Baroque space.
A few examples of each of these periods will make it easier for visitors to get to know Hungarian towns. It should also be understood that the structures that look Baroque are the result of the Habsburgs' wish to annex Hungary and cover up all the elements of the Hungarian heritage that had escaped destruction under stucco, ornamentation and decoration.

Early Baroque – This is particularly noticeable in Sopron: the Fire Tower, Storno House and the Esterházy family mansion; in Győr, St Ignatius' Church.

Mature Baroque – Noticeable in all Hungarian towns, this is expressed in rounded, dynamic forms. The emphasis is on curves, which are found on twisted columns, for instance, and are used to accentuate the impression of space. Decoration uses light and shade effects and seeks to surprise with false perspectives, *trompe-l'œil*, excessive dimensions, interpenetration of volumes, all the component parts of appearance. A few examples of this period are as follows:
In Budapest: the University Church (Egyetemi templom), St Anne's Church, the town hall built by Martinelli (this looks more like an early Baroque structure, the volumes are simple, with large vaulted corridors off which run the rooms). In Eger: the Friar Minors' church, one of Hungary's most representative Baroque edifices; the County Hall and wrought-iron gates, created by Heinrik Fazola. In Ráckeve: the castle of Prince Eugene of Savoy (now a restaurant). In Gödölló: the royal castle. In Győr: the Carmelite Church. In Fertőd: the former Esterházy Palace.

Late Baroque – The **Copf style** is associated with Late Baroque. This style is a purified form of Baroque, a Central European variation. The name comes from the fact that the style used *copf* or garlands as a decorative element. Moreover, the style simplifies architecture by reducing the surface of the façade and the parts in relief to the extent that columns are replaced by pilasters or even painted onto walls. The architect who used this style to its best advantage was **Franz Anton Hildebrandt** (1719-97): he was architect to the royal court and administrator of all large projects.
Examples can be found in the royal palace in Buda, the cathedrals in Szombathely and Vác, and the bishop's palace in Székesfehérvár by the architect Jakab Rieder.

19C AND 20C

Classical architecture – This period expresses all the elements of the Classical School by integrating them into the architecture: columns, pediments and codified orders. It covers the first half of the 19C, and was a way of breaking with the Baroque and the Habsburg hegemony that followed the Ottoman domination. Hungary recovered from the hegemony, and its nobility became enterprising, growing rich and exhibiting the fact. The saying goes that "in Europe the Classical style is rigorous, while in Hungary it sparkles". This architecture reflected the end of feudalism in its various forms and started a period of activity and growth.
The period was characterised by great architects: **Mihály Pollack**, the creator of the County Hall in Szekszárd, and Budapest's National Musuem; **József Hild**, who built a great many residential and public buildings, and after building Eger Cathedral, participated in the final work on Esztergom Cathedral.

The Romantic style – This covered the end of the 19C. It opposed the strictness of Classical architecture and strove to satisfy imagination and emotion as opposed to reason. It introduced a certain exoticism and flashbacks to the past.
Miklós Ybl was trained in Vienna and in Munich, and worked in Mihály Pollack's workshop. He then began working on his own, and is now considered the greatest architect of the time. He was awarded the contract for the Pest Opera House. On the left bank of the Danube facing the Gellért Hotel he built the Customs House which later became the University of Economic Science. While Ybl's great achievements are known, two works, modest in terms of their dimensions, express his great qualities as an architect: Szent István Church in Nagycenk and the Evangelical Church in Kecskemét. In their simplicity and austerity they each create a very compact interior space.
Imre Steindl was the architect of the Budapest Parliament building, a great neo-Gothic structure with a richly decorated and painted interior.

Samu Petz followed in the footsteps of Gustave Eiffel by designing structures of cast-iron metal filled with brick or glass. This is the case with Budapest's large covered market near the University of Economic Science.
Albert Schickedanz and **Fülöp Herzog** are the architects of Heroes' Square, the Millennium Monument as well as the Fine Arts Museum and the Gallery of Arts opposite.

Eclectic architecture – This is sometimes called "Historicist" because it uses, and takes inspiration, from various historical styles. The style is perfectly illustrated in Budapest's Városliget area, with **Ignác Alpár**'s Vajdahunyad Castle.
During this period, the aim was to build quickly and as cheaply as possible, while, at the same time, buildings had to have an individual stamp. They built in brick and then put on a coat of plaster to imitate stone. Inspiration came from the taste of the customer or the architect's preference for a particular moment of history. Neo-Gothic, neo-Romanesque (Fishermen's Bastion in Budapest), neo-Renaissance (Hungarian Academy of Sciences or the Ethnography Museum), all flourished.

The Secessionist style and Art Nouveau – It was certainly a desire for liberty that incited creative people to free themselves from the yoke of classicist or historicist styles. They sought originality, a way of finding that there was a relationship in architecture between the exterior and the interior. Architects broke with all the neo-styles to invent their own. This was the Secessionist style, the appearance of fantasy, imagination, colour, and a search for harmony between the interior and the exterior, where the creators of a building interlinked all its constituent parts.
To express this in simple terms, this architecture was uniform. For example, there was full collaboration between the various trades, who used all their talents to produce the final work. The materials were used with so much care that their combination always seemed quite natural. To see some conspicuous examples, go into any bank lobby: from the door handle to the staircase balustrades, the floors, stained-glass windows, exit signs, everything is harmonious in terms of shape, colour and material. The functional part is integrated into the decor and the theme of nature is continued in the form of leaves and birds, a celebration of liberation.
The leader of this movement is without question **Ödön Lechner** (1845-1914). His most important works can be found in Budapest, Kőbánya Church (Kőbányai templom), the Museum of Applied Arts (Iparművészeti Múzeum), the Geology Institute (Földtani Intézet) and the former Post Office Savings Bank (Posta Takarékpénztár). An amazing example of Lechner's receptiveness and openness is in the 14th district, at n° 47 Hermina út. This is the National Association for the Blind (Vakok és Gyengénlátók Országos Szövetsége), originally a villa, with a greenhouse, the liberated and easy design of which says everything about its architect's creative freedom. Other architects built structures with the same degree of aesthetic success, such as the town hall (Városháza) in Kiskunfélegyháza, the town hall and Cifra Palace (Cifrapalota) by Sándor Baumgartner in Kecskemét, and Reök Palace , designed by Ede Magyar in Szeged.

F. Tulok/MAGYAR KÉPEK Kft
Kiskunfélegyháza – town hall

In this respect Budapest has nothing to envy in Brussels, Vienna or Paris. Art Nouveau, full of vitality, developed and fostered new forms of expression. There are numerous illustrations in Budapest of this new type of architecture, which would precede the Bauhaus movement and combine art with respect for the urban context. The building at n° 11/b in Váci utca dates from 1912; its architects, **Sámuel Révész** and **József Kollár**, are said to have been influenced by German Jugendstil and a certain Orientalism. The result is a building that blends in with its environment.
The influence of Gustave Eiffel, who designed the West Station, should be mentioned. The engineers and architects who worked for him followed in the same vein and constructed a number of covered markets according to the same principles. Budapest's main market is a fine example of this.

In the 1930s, influenced by Bauhaus ideas, about 20 Hungarian architects intelligently designed villas and small buildings which corresponded to people's needs at the time. Several examples of these structures can be seen on Napraforgó u. in the 2nd district (n°s 1 to 19 and 2 to 22), on Pasaréti út at n°s 96 and 97, the Franciscan Church (Szent Antal-templom) at n° 137 and the building at n° 32 on the corner of Trombitás u.

Organic architecture – During the Communist period, some architects made a statement through what is known in Hungary as Organic architecture. The leader was **Imre Makovecz**, who created the Hungarian pavilion for the 1992 World Exhibition in Seville. The name of **György Csete** can be associated with this as well. Hungarian Organic architecture does not refer to the American Organic architecture of Frank Lloyd Wright; here it is flavoured with a sort of regional or even nationalist spirit. Among numerous examples of this architecture are Sárospatak Cultural Centre, the Evangelical Church in Siófok, the church in Paks and some of the Ópusztaszer Memorial pavilions.

MAGYAR KÉPEK Kft

Ópusztaszer Memorial – House of the Crown

Painting – Hungary has always been rich in artists. During the Communist period many of them left their country to live abroad. Sculptors, painters, filmmakers, photographers and architects gained recognition for their work on the international scene. It is important to remember that Székely, Schöffer, Vasarely, Brassai, Capa, Vágó Szenes, Kertész and many others are of Hungarian origin.

This country, permanently unsettled by war and successive occupations, has not always been able to preserve the works of its artists. There are few old works, other than those preserved on floors or walls.

In this area, paint is too fragile to have left many traces. Here and there, a few pieces of frescoes, painting and sculpture remain. It can be said that, of the works prior to the 19C, the most beautiful pieces can be seen at Budapest's National Gallery and Esztergom's Christian Museum. The National Gallery also has works by all the great Hungarian painters. The portraitists **Miklós Barabás** and **Bertalan Székely** worked during the second half of the 19C. *The Portrait of Madame Bittó* shows the skill and delicacy of touch of a classic Barabás. Next to it, Bertalan Székely, who among other works painted scenes of war illustrating the history of Hungary, stands out for paintings such as *Zrínyi Breaking Out of the Castle* and *The Women of Eger*.

Gyula Benczúr, also interested in history, was an excellent portrait painter. He painted the portrait of Queen Elizabeth of Hungary, Sissy, as well as those of Count Andrássy and István Tisza. **Pál Szinyei Merse** (1845-1920) painted marvellous studies and sketches that unfortunately lost their richness on the final canvas. The *Poppy Field* (1902) is one of his best-known works. **Mihály Munkácsy** (1844-1900) was a joiner's apprentice; he learned the rudiments from a second-rate painter before he was helped by two well-known artists, Antal Ligeti and Mór Than; he was later part of the Barbizon School and came to paint the triptych exhibited in Debrecen's Déri Museum. He also painted much freer works, such as *The Dusty Road*, which is reminiscent of Turner. **Károly Ferenczy**, whose painting *October* is well known, and Mednyánszky were skilled painters who searched to find their own style. **Adolf Fényes** was part of the artists' colony at Szolnok, and probably its most prominent personality. His lively paintings attest to his mastery of Hungarian light, such as the canvas entitled *Morning in a Small Town*. Lastly,

K. Szelényi/MAGYAR KÉPEK Kft

Lazarine and Anella in the Park by Rippl-Rónai

the master of paintings from this period, **Rippl-Rónai** *(see KAPOSVÁR)*, grew artistically through his own reflections and analyses, and created highly personal paintings. From *The Woman in the Spotted Dress*, to *Lazarine and Anella in the Park*, as well as his *Stained-Glass Window for a Telephone Booth at the Café Japan*, he always shows himself to be a master of his art.

A Woman in a Black Hat by János Vaszary can be seen at the National Gallery. It is a work from his youth that was certainly influenced by his Parisian environment. In the long list of painters, the name of **Tivadar Csontváry Kosztka** (1853-1919) stands out as the creator of original, personal work. For those interested in his paintings, it would be worth visiting the Pécs Museum, which houses most of his important works. Budapest's National Gallery exhibits one of his most beautiful works, *The Seaside Cavalcade*.

Among Hungarian expatriate painters, there is obviously **Victor Vasarely** *(see BUDAPEST and PÉCS)*, as well as **Árpád Szenes** and **László Hajdú** who, among other works, painted an iconostasis of eight paintings inspired by Saint-John Perse's poetry.

Sculpture – This has always been a means of artistic expression particularly dear to Hungarians. Objects, statuettes and jewels allow us to identify the succession of peoples who passed through present-day Hungary. From the Romans to the Middle Ages and up to the modern era, we have carved traces left by Hungarian artists. The Christian Museum in Esztergom exhibits very beautiful wood sculptures. During the entire 18C and 19C, the Baroque gave sculptors scope for expression.

Works by 20C sculptors can be seen in every town and city. **Miklós Ligeti** is famous for a work in Budapest's Városliget area: the statue of Anonymous, the scribe monk with his face concealed under his hood. Born at the beginning of the 20C, **Imre Varga** is a prolific sculptor whose work can be seen in many Hungarian towns and cities: St Elizabeth in Sárospatak, Prometheus in Szekszárd and The Weeping Willow Monument near Budapest's Great Synagogue. **Ádám Farkas**, born after the Second World War, has an international reputation. He has produced sculptures in Japan and France; he also created the monument to the

MAGYAR KÉPEK Kft

Infinite Return by Ádám Farkas

Budapest – Police Headquarters

MAGYAR KÉPEK Kft

memory of the political prisoners of Recsk who died under the Communist regime.

Budapest urbanism – The late 19C and early 20C was a tremendous period for Budapest. In the 1890s, during the economic frenzy and the increase in building plans, Budapest's leaders grew worried. Taking inspiration from Vienna, they launched an international town planning competition to control the development of the capital in a country which then had a population of 15 million. Two major projects were decided upon: the laying out of Andrássy út and the laying out of Nagykörút (the Great Boulevard). Major transformations to the city began in 1894. Many aspects were modified and, it is true to say, a few beautiful elements sacrificed, but the present-day face of Budapest was built by enterprising men, among them "the greatest Hungarian", **István Széchenyi**.
Budapest has not undergone a town planning project worthy of a capital city since that time. A case in point is the national theatre, an old project that was open to national competition between Hungarian architects. Building began on Deák tér square but was interrupted after the 1998 elections, leaving a vast excavation area that is now intended for a park (the neighbouring bus station will be relocated). The theatre, relocated on another site on the banks of the Danube, opens in 2002, forming part of a new district built on the land formerly earmarked for the major universal exposition project, Expo 96. The Communist period saw the development of great housing projects without any apparent organisation. Since the change in regimes, a few major projects have seen the light of day, such as the one covering part of the West Station site. Budapest's new building sites chiefly favour hotels, shops and services.
Among contemporary architects, the name of **József Finta** comes up frequently. He was already well known before the change in regimes for the large hotels he built on the banks of the Danube. On Erzsébet tér, József Finta and Antal Puhl Associates designed the Kempinski Corvinus Hotel. This is contemporary architecture that does not yield to fashion, and approaches the layout of interior spaces in a variety of ways. The building on Teve utca should also be mentioned; it is home to the Police services and was also designed by Finta. On the banks of the Danube, the French Institute (Fő utca 17), opened in 1992, was designed by French architect Georges Maurios. The Hungarians regret that it "turns its back on the Danube". Its colour blends in with the urban context and its facing protects it from pollution. On the square in front of the institute a sculpture by Pierre Székely, a French artist of Hungarian origin, symbolises the friendship between the two nations.

Hungarian music

"...each of our folk melodies is a veritable model of artistic perfection. I consider them miniature masterpieces, in the same way as Bach fugues or Mozart sonatas are, in a larger form."

Béla Bartók

FROM THE ORIGINS TO THE 15C

The first manifestation of Hungarian music with a pentatonic scale (ie a five-tone system) appears in ancient sources. In the 7C a Greek historian, Theophylactus Simoccata informed his contemporaries of the existence of a Hungarian ancestral custom of Earth worship, taking the form of chants.

The scribe Anonymous, at the court of King Béla II (1131-41), enthusiastically relates the celebrations organised in honour of the chiefs of the seven Magyar tribes from Óbuda. During the festivities, the chants were accompanied by ancient instruments such as zithers and shawms (a wind instrument, ancestor of the clarinet).

With Christianity, the pagan period's literary and musical traditions definitively came to an end. The spirit of this originally nomadic people – warlike, with an impetuous, roving temperament, imbued with the melancholy of the steppes – has been perpetuated in characteristic Hungarian music: a slow lament, followed by an allegro *gioioso*. The early Christian songs were composed of Latin liturgies, later replaced by Hungarian hymns.

After the end of the Árpád dynasty, the Angevin kings offered a new dimension to secular music. The art of *chansons de geste*, called *regős* in Hungarian, developed during and after the reign of Sigismund of Luxembourg (1387-1437).

King Matthias Corvinus, son of János Hunyadi, who defeated the Turks, as well as his wife Beatrice of Aragon, the King of Naples' daughter, invited internationally renowned musicians to their court, Buda Regia.

THE 16C AND 17C

In the 16C, the ancient Hungarian legends of the Árpád period were revived in the form of epic songs. After the Turkish occupation of Buda (1541), in the heroic songs of the outstanding lutenist, **Sebestyén Tinódi Lantos** (*lantos* means lutenist), all the heroes of the past who fought against the old Ottoman enemy were revived. In his main work, *Cronica* (which appeared in 1554), he brought together some 23 historical, biblical, moral and satirical songs. It is true that Tinódi combined poetry with instrumental music in an original way, but the man still considered the most brilliant lutenist and composer of the century is **Valentine Bakfark** (1507-76).

A true "man of the world", Bálint (Valentine) Bakfark made several trips to a great many countries including Poland, Italy, Germany and France where, in 1552, his first tablature (notation for lute works) was published by Jacques Moderne in Lyon. Even Nostradamus praised him in his works.

The secret of this artist's popularity stems partly from his individual style: intense rhythm, exceptionally sensual sonority, and brilliant technique.

Prince **Pál Esterházy** (1635-1713) was also a great musician who drew his inspiration from religious music while adding Hungarian melodic twists. His work consists of nine choruses, 50 concertos and cantatas, the majority with instrumental or orchestral accompaniment.

MAGYAR KÉPEK Kft

THE 18C

The spirit of the Hungarian people expressed itself through *kuruc* songs during the War of Independence led by Ferenc Rákóczi II (1705-11). The *kuruc* were Rákóczi's soldiers who sang patriotic and satirical songs about the *labanc*, a nickname for the Hungarians who remained faithful to the Habsburg court.

The *kuruc* songs were the source of the famous *Rákóczi March*, which amazed its 19C public with the fascinating technique of Tzigane first violin **János Bihari**. Some say that before a battle against Napoleon's army in 1809, the Hungarian soldiers used this melody to fire up their courage.

The Hungarian translation of the French *Marseillaise* was by **Ferenc Verseghy** (1755-1822), a musician and propagator of Jacobin ideas in Hungary.
After 1750, Hungarian musical life was dominated by a new heroic style, the best example of this being without question the *verbunkos*, or "recruitment dance"(from *Werbung*, a German word meaning recruitment), accompanied by Tzigane music. The *palotás* dance – an imitation of the polonaise – mixes the slow Hungarian movement and the triple-time dance. The great connoisseur of these two types of dance was **János Lavotta**. The *verbunkos* and *palotás* traditions were then perpetuated by the *csárdás* (*csárda* means "inn", *csárdás* means "of the inn"). The *csárdás* has continued until the present day.

Opera – Very much appreciated by the public from the outset, opera soon found a specifically Hungarian character. The first Hungarian opera, *Prince Pikkó and Jutka Perzsi* was written by **József Chudy** (1793). Only its lyrics are known, as the music has entirely disappeared. The subject of the opera *Béla futása*, considered the first specifically Hungarian melodic work, goes back to the 13C, to the time of the Tartar invasion. Its composer, **József Ruzitska**, adapted *verbunkos* and *palotás* elements to the Viennese opera style, once very much in fashion.

THE 19C

This century was marked by national music, led by **Ferenc Erkel** (1810-93). A composer and orchestra conductor, he founded the National Opera where he produced his first historic work, *Mária Báthory* (1840). In 1844, in *László Hunyadi*, Erkel evokes the tragic story of King Matthias' brother. One of the principal roles was performed by the French singer, Anne Lagrange. The height of Erkel's artistic activity was in 1860, with the premiere of his opera ***Bánk Bán***, based on a tragedy by a contemporary playwright, József Katona. Erkel wrote the music for the national anthem with which his name is still linked.
The 19C musical world split into two groups. Ferenc Erkel created a conservative group whose members remained faithful to the traditions of Italian music, while at the head of the modernists stood Ferenc (Franz) Liszt.
Franz Liszt (1811-86) is a great name in Romantic music. A prodigious composer and pianist, he wrote, among other pieces, symphonic poems such as *Préludes* (1854), his famous *Hungarian Rhapsodies* (1846-85) and *Historical Portraits* (1884-86). It is in these works that this musical genius paid homage to his country, to which he did not return after years of study and travel in Europe until 1844. Budapest's Academy of Music, founded in 1875 by Liszt himself (it bears his name) quickly became the symbol of European musical education.

AKG Paris

Franz Liszt

THE 20C

The Academy of Music was the school and model for a large number of famous musicians throughout the world. These include the orchestra conductors **Ferenc Fricsay**, **Antal Doráti** (1906-88), **Jenő (Eugène) Ormándy**, **Georg Széll**, **Frigyes (Fritz) Reiner**, **János Ferencsik** and **Sir Georg Solti** (1912-99); pianists **Ernő Dohnányi** (1877-1960) and **Annie Fischer** (1916); violinists **József Szigeti** and **Ede Zathureczky**; and two giants who drastically changed 20C musical theory, Béla Bartók and Zoltán Kodály *(see KECSKEMÉT)*.
Like **Zoltán Kodály** (1882-1963), **Béla Bartók** (1881-1945) combined folk song with peasant music, which he considered the only reliable source of Hungarian music.
To discover and recover these sources, they travelled together through a great many villages in Hungary and Transylvania, and recorded about 15 000 folk songs. Their paths then divided, as Bartók chose musicology to analyse the samples from this collection, while Kodály put emphasis on his talent as a composer, inspired by the folk tradition. In 1923 he composed the famous *Psalmus Hungaricus*, his masterpiece for choir and orchestra. It was followed in 1926 by his comic opera, *Háry János*. Between 1930 and 1933 his two orchestral works, dominated by folk music motifs, were created: *Dances of Marosszék* and *Dances of Galánta*.
A strong attraction for French Symbolism as well as the desire to put Hungarian folk music in the spotlight led Bartók to write his first opera, *Duke Bluebeard's Castle* (1911). Kodály, who himself had begun his career on the heels of Claude Debussy with *Sonata for Cello and Piano* in 1912 and *Sonata for Cello* in 1915, compared the immense success of this opera with that of *Pelléas et Melisande* in France. For him, Bartók had created "a work of suggestive power, irresistible from the first to the last

measure, the most expressive he has ever written". The castle's seven doors symbolise man's inner world. By going beyond these barriers out of curiosity, even the deepest love ceases to exist. In 1916, at the request of Count Bánffy, the Intendant of the Budapest Opera, Bartók composed the music for the ballet *The Wooden Prince*. His Expressionist ballet *The Miraculous Mandarin* was created in 1919. His only choral work, the *Cantata Profana: The Nine Enchanted Stags*, appeared in 1930. He constructed the music around an ancient ballad of Magyar origin.

Bartók created a modern, original music by weaving together European and Hungarian traditions. Until his death in exile in New York, he devoted himself to researching personal concerns as well as problems common to people the world over. His humanism is present in every one of his works.

ROGER VIOLLET

Béla Bartók

A great many contemporary composers consider Bartók and Kodály as their spiritual masters. They include **Ferenc Farkas** (1905) and **Endre Szervánszky** (1911-77) who created a school of this new musical style, **György Ligeti** (1923), **György Kurtágh** (1926), **Rudolf Maros** (1917-82) and **András Szöllősy** (1921), composers with their own individual voices, and talented pianists such as **György Cziffra** (1921-94), **Zoltán Kocsis** (1952), **Dezső Ránki** (1951) and **András Schiff** (1953). The most imaginative composers of Hungarian opera include **Emil Petrovics** (1930), **Sándor Szokolay** (1931), **Sándor Balassa** (1935), **Attila Bozay** (1939) and **Zsolt Durkó** (1934).

Operetta – This musical category conquered the public very quickly. The first great name in Hungarian operetta was **Jenő Huszka** (1879-1960). He composed *Prince Bob*, *Gül Baba* and *Baroness Lili*. Another interesting name is that of **Pongrác Kacsóh** (1873-1924), composer of *János vitéz* and *Sleeping Beauty*.

Hungarian operetta has been known worldwide since **Imre Kálmán** (1882-1953), who had his first success with *The Gay Hussars*, followed later by *Gräfin Mariza* and *The Gypsy Princess*. *The Merry Widow* by the unforgettable **Franz (Ferenc) Lehár** (1870-1948) will be immortal in operetta history. His other masterpieces include *Gypsy Loves* and *Land of Smiles*. The best-known contemporary operetta composer is **Szabolcs Fényes** (1912); his greatest success is *Lulu*.

Folk art and traditions

Hungarian folk traditions are a valuable part of the nation's culture today. The variety of dance forms found in Hungary is unequalled in Europe. From the 11C folk arts gradually distanced themselves from professional crafts, and were influenced by the great movements of the following centuries, in particular the Renaissance in the 16C and the Baroque period in the 17C. The Renaissance brought considerable changes, notably in poetry, ornamentation, costume traditions and traditional architecture. In the 18C geographical, social and religious circumstances contributed to the blossoming of very different regional styles in embroidery, costumes etc. The 19C, however, brought a distinctive, **consistent peasant style**, which was reflected in all facets of peasant life: costumes, dwellings, textiles – fabrics, embroideries, bedclothes – and ceramics. It was in the 19C that the peasantry became guardian of the oldest elements of Hungarian culture and "peasant culture" became synonymous with "folk culture".

Attila-WOSTOK Press

NORTHERN HUNGARY

The traditional territory of the **Palóc** population lies between the River Ipoly and River Sajó in the Mátra, Bükk and Karancs mountains. Their folk art is carefully kept alive, and is characterised by their famous architecture, carved furniture, clothing, and embroideries which are all part of the traditional festivals held in numerous little villages. Among these traditions is the **festival of Palóc fabrics** which takes place in the summer in the towns of **Hollókő** and **Szécsény**. The **Sunday festival in Buják** and the fairs in **Kazár** and **Felsőtárkány** are also well known. During the annual **Palóc Festival** in **Parád**, the villagers present their traditional music, picturesque folk dances, traditional costumes and everyday objects from peasant and shepherd life in days gone by.

Hollókő, a village with a population of 450, lies on the slopes of Mt Cserhát. It was the first village to be registered on the Unesco World Heritage List, and has therefore been protected since 1987. The inhabitants make a living

M. Guillou/MICHELIN

from crafts and tourism. The village museum has a permanent **ethnographic exhibition** open to visitors, while the craftsmen's building shows the various techniques involved in woodcarving, beading and weaving.
The **Easter** festivities in **Hollókő** are faithful to tradition: an open-air Mass is celebrated followed by a village dance. Old customs, of course, take pride of place: egg-painting and splashing young girls with pails of water drawn from the well – symbolising fertility and ritual purification at one and the same time.
On the edge of the Hungarian plain live the **Matyós**, famous for their colourful costumes. *Mezőkövesd* embroideries from **Szentistván** or **Tard**, with intricate flower and leaf designs, little birds, twinned hearts or stars, are very much admired. The most beautiful examples of these techniques may be found in the **Matyó Folk Art Museum**. **Mezőcsát** is one of the best-known places for pottery. One of the specialities is the elongated Miska wine jug, with a neck resembling the head of a man wearing a *shako* (plumed military headgear). Music and dance traditions are alive owing to the impassioned work of several groups, such as the internationally known **Nógrád**, **Muzsla** from **Pásztó**, the **children's group Kenderike** from **Palotás**, and the **Vidróczki group** from **Gyöngyös**.

R. Mattes
Painted eggs

THE HUNGARIAN GREAT PLAIN

The folk traditions of horsebreeding, weaving, saddlery, lacemaking, embroidery, pottery, gingerbreadmaking, woodcarving and basketmaking are still respected and carried on to high standards.
Aside from its embroidered tablecloths and clothing, **Kalocsa** is renowned throughout the world for its paprika production. The women harvest the ripe paprika fruits, and dry them on village walls until they are ready to be ground in the windmills. These traditional preparation techniques are demonstrated at the Paprika Museum. As for the **onion**, the region's other speciality, **Makó's** Onion Museum contains an informative exhibition on the cultivation of this flourishing crop. **Szeged's** hand-sewn and embroidered slippers, or **papucs**, recall the time of the Turkish occupation. As the town that has organised the **open-air festival** since 1931, along with theatre plays, operas and ballets which take place every summer, **Szeged** has hosted the **International Folk Dancing Festival** for 30 years. **Kiskunhalas'** famous embroidery technique can be seen at its small institution devoted to lace. In September, villagers dressed in traditional folk costumes sing and dance as in the past at **Kalocsa**, **Kecskemét** and **Szeged folk festivals**, recalling the cheerful atmosphere of country weddings. In **Debrecen** and **Hajdúböszörmény** the results of meticulous labour can be admired – gingerbread preparation and decoration – while the trade of straw braiding is still practised in **Hajdúnánás**. Woodcarving is the traditional craft associated with the shepherds of the Puszta, as well as the making of objects out of leather or horn. **Hortobágy's International Horse Show** in July or the festivities in **Bugac** during August are excellent occasions to buy a few of these souvenirs.

TRANSDANUBIA

Southern Transdanubia is certainly one of the richest regions in Hungary for folk traditions; there are also a great number of old handicrafts kept alive here, such as painting on linen, pottery and the making of rugs, chests and even masks for the **Busó**

procession. This spectacular occasion, brought to life by southern Slavs from **Mohács**, is held in February to chase away the rigours of winter.

The **International Folk Festival** in **Pécs** and the **Whitsuntide Meeting** in **Buzsák** in May offer a wide range of regional folk traditions to spectators, such as the **preparation of the maypole** decorated with its multicoloured ribbons.

Among the customs linked to agriculture are the harvest and shepherd festivals, as well as the grape harvest festivities marking the end of work in the fields. The historical wine-growing regions of **Villány-Siklós**, **Szekszárd** and **Balatonboglár** produce the great vintages of southern Transdanubia – Kékfrankos, Kadarka and Bikavér – and organise **grape harvest festivals** in September.

In October Pécsvárad organises the Young Girls Fair on or around St Luke's Day; this is not an occasion for trading young girls, of course, but a folk-song festival. An equally famous event is the **Danube Countries Folk Festival**, held every three years, which revives the **Sárköz wedding ceremony**, and provides a show ground for handicrafts and folk culture.

Herend's hand-painted porcelain, sought after throughout the world, is made in several hundreds of forms and tens of thousands of patterns, many of which may be seen in the Herend Porcelain Museum with its workshops *(see under VESZPRÉM)*.

I. Benko/WOSTOCK PRESS

Mohács Carnival – The Parade of Masks

Literature, cinema and photography

LITERATURE

The sources of Hungarian literature are still as mysterious as the beginnings of its history. Thanks to **Hungarian chroniclers** – called **regős** – historical works in Latin have given us the songs and epics of the Magyar people, such as the *Legend of the Miraculous Stag* or the *Legend of the Turul* (*turul* is a bird of ancient Hungarian myth). With the adoption of Christianity came the written language of Latin, which quickly triumphed over the predominantly oral culture and became the official language. Chronicles, legends and hymns were the three preferred literary genres between the 11C and the 16C.

The first Hungarian prose appeared in the form of a funerary oration (c 1200); the oldest Hungarian poem is probably *Mary's Complaint* (c 1270).

The first Hungarian version of the Old and New Testaments, translated by two preachers – **Tamás** and **Bálint** – in around 1430 was the result of the spread of the Hussite movement throughout Hungary from the 1410s. The complete translation of the Bible, however, came in 1590, written by Calvinist **Gáspár Károlyi** (1529-91) who managed to create a biblical language of the time. **János Hunyadi**, the legendary vanquisher of the Turks who mobilised the European diplomatic community against the Ottoman invader, and his son, King **Matthias** (1458-90), were the creative spirits behind the **Renaissance** and humanism in Hungary. King Matthias invited Italy's greatest scholars and artists to his court, and created the Bibliotheca Corviniana, a library unequalled in Europe. Lyric poetry marked the Hungarian literature of this period, thanks to the first great poet, known as far away as Italy by the name of **Janus Pannonius** (1434-72). This genre remained important in Hungarian literature until the 1970s. It was in this cultural context that **Bálint Balassi** (1554-94) wrote his unique lyric poetry, resonant of both Hungary and the Renaissance. The work of this great soldier battling against the Turks consists for the most part of love poems, full of the Petrarchan poetical clichés then in fashion, while reflecting his true impassioned nature.

The 16C Reformation brought the Renaissance and Protestantism face to face, while the opposing Catholicism found its voice in the **Baroque** spirit of the early 17C. A statesman and great epic poet, **Miklós Zrínyi** (1620-64) wrote the famous *Siege of Sziget*, inspired by the Italian poet Tasso's works. This poem consists of 15 songs relating the heroic battle of Zrínyi's great-grandfather and his soldiers against Suleiman II's army in 1566.

Towards the end of the 18C, the philosophical ideas behind the **Age of Enlightenment** and the French Revolution aroused national awareness, giving new meaning to the idea of revolution. The pioneers of this school of thought were grouped around **Ignác Martinovics**: the great **Ferenc Kazinczy** (1759-1831) who revived the Hungarian language, and the poet **Mihály Csokonai Vitéz** (1773-1805). Owing to Csokonai's lively and colourful poetic language in his comic epic *Dorottya*, the great 20C poet, **Endre Ady**, considered him to be one of the precursors of **modern Hungarian lyrical poetry**. **Dániel Berzsenyi** (1776-1836) took up the torch of Classical poetry, providing a new setting for philosophical odes and poems conveying the notions of the Age of Enlightenment. Literature had a special place in the Hungarian battle for independence. **József Katona** (1791-1830) – who died before his work *Bánk Bán* came to be considered Hungary's greatest tragic piece – turned a 12C historical event into an analysis of the problem of foreigners holding power. The great political reform period beginning in 1825 paved the way for 1848's **revolutionary literature**. Four great Romantic poets dominated this time: Kölcsey, Vörösmarty, Arany and Petőfi. **Ferenc Kölcsey** (1790-1838) wrote the national anthem, and **Mihály Vörösmarty** (1800-1855) best portrayed Hungarian feeling by the reason, strength and personal will exemplified in his epic *Zalán's Flight*, the poetic drama *Csongor and Tünde* and *Exhortation*. **János Arany** (1817-82), a writer of epic poetry and the author of the *Toldi* trilogy, set his work in the 14C, at the time of Hungary's King Louis the Great. In *The Death of Buda*, however, he goes back as far as the mysterious period of Attila, which preceded the conquest of the country.

F. Szelényi/MAGYAR KÉPEK Kft

Sándor Petőfi

Even though Arany supported the revolutionary ideas of 1848 and attempted to justify them by recalling the past, it was his contemporary **Sándor Petőfi** (1823-49) who played a major role on 15 March 1848 by stirring up Pest's citizens with his poem *National Song*, a veritable clarion call to the battle for national liberty. As his body was never found after the battle of Segesvár on 31 July 1849, his name has become legendary. Hungarian literature went through a critical period during the years of disillusionment. The best writers and poets searched for a new way to ensure the survival of national existence. Among them was **Imre Madách** (1823-64), who incarnated this spirit in his dramatic poem *The Tragedy of Man*, tracing humanity's history while looking to a dark future. Pessimistic Madách demonstrates the disappointment of his hero Adam – an idealist constantly confronted with reality, who finds himself caught between unbelief and the desire to believe. **Mór Jókai** (1823-1904), novelist and Petőfi's friend during their youth, chose the path of reconciliation with Austria in the 1860s. His novels *A Man of Gold*, *A Hungarian Nabob* and *Zoltán Kárpáthy* are marked by this decision, and considerably influenced public opinion. **Kálmán Mikszáth** (1847-1910), considered Jókai's successor, evoked the strange world of landed nobility in small provincial towns. In representing this society in *A Strange Marriage*, *The Story of the Noszty Boy and Mari Tóth* and *The Beszterce Siege*, he breaks through the sad despair with typically Hungarian realism.

The early 19C was a major turning point, with the founding in 1908 of the review ***Nyugat*** (West), which rallied great literary minds such as **Endre Ady** (1877-1918), **Zsigmond Móricz** (1879-1942), **Mihály Babits** (1883-1941), **Dezső Kosztolányi** (1885-1936) and **Árpád Tóth** (1886-1928). Impressionism, Symbolism, Naturalism and Art Nouveau (called Secessionism in Hungary) as well as Realism were all united in the pages of *Nyugat*. Avant-garde literary movements were excluded. However, **Lajos Kassák** (1887-1967) created another review in 1916 called ***Tett*** (Act) which was to encourage modernity in literature, the fine arts and music. Among the novelists marking this period mention should be made of **Gyula Illyés** (1902-83) with his autobiography *People of the Puszta*, and **Gyula Krúdy**(1878-1933) with his world composed of the mysteries of *Sinbad* or *The Red Coach*. The greatest representative of poetry in the first half of the 20C was **József Attila** (1905-37), famous for his amazingly simple yet expressive language.

Lőrinc Szabó (1900-58), **István Vas** (1910-91), **Sándor Weöres** (1912-89) and **János Pilinszky** (1921-81) as well as **László Nagy** (1925-78), **László Lator** (b 1927) and **Ferenc Juhász** (b 1928) were also fundamental in the creation of **new lyrical poetry**.

The continued success of the novel from the 1970s would have been unimaginable without **Géza Ottlik** (1912-1990), **Miklós Mészöly** (1921), **Péter Nádas** (1942), or **Péter Esterházy** (1951), with his magnificent 1979 novel *Three Angels Watch Over Me*.

CINEMA

Pre-1945 – The Parisian and Viennese cinematographic traditions found fertile ground in Hungary. Films quickly became influential factors in cultural and political life. After 1912 **Sándor Korda** (1893-1956), the legendary cinematographic pioneer, ran several magazines with articles about the great contemporary writers, including Zsigmond Móricz. **Mihály Kertész** (1888-1962) directed the first Hungarian feature film, *Today and Tomorrow*.

From 1945 to 1954 – After the war, neo-Realist film-makers sought to reveal the truth about the war and Fascism's national origins. **Géza Radványi** (1907-86) produced most of the period's great works, a series of angry charges made against the world's inhumanity. At the end of the Rákosi period, from 1953, the effects of the intellectual revolution could be felt: **Károly Makk's** *Liliomfi* (1925), and **Félix Máriássy's** (1919-75) *Springtime in Budapest*.

Post-1956 – The Kádár regime sought reconciliation with the intellectuals, manifesting a realistic attitude to artistic "reality". From 1960 to 1963 four studios produced feature films, wholly funded and distributed by the State. The **Béla Balázs Studio**, founded in 1958, is one of the rare places where young film-makers are free to seek a new, unfettered and subjective form; **István Szabó**, **Sándor Sára**, **Pál Gábor** and **István Gaál** are among these film-makers. The two most important films from this period are **Zoltán Fábri's** *20 Hours* (1964) and **András Kovács'** *Frozen Days* (1966).

Miklós Jancsó completed his studies at the Film Academy in 1950. Since then he has significantly contributed to the wealth of Hungarian cinematography through his analyses of the essence of the Magyar character. This director from the generation of Bergman, Fellini and Resnais tirelessly creates new forms of expression. He has been particularly interested in the great moments of Hungary's history: *The Losers* (1965) recalls the 1848 post-Revolutionary period, *Light Waves* (1968) uses allegorical montages to reveal the true nature of power. Jancsó made a screen adaptation of Bartók's folk ballad *Cantata Profana* in his 1962 film *Cantata*. He interprets the events of 1956 through the story of a father who no longer recognises his sons because they have been turned into stags. In his 1972 drama *Red Psalm* he uses great lyricism in depicting the farm workers' revolt at the end of the 19C.

A scene from *Red Psalm* by Miklós Jancsó

After the great cinema movement of the 1960s and 1970s, a serious economic crisis drastically reduced film production: there were only eight films produced in all from 1987 to 1990.
The **Budapest School**, a movement started in 1980, includes documentary film-makers such as **Lívia Gyarmathy** and **Géza Böszörményi**, who worked at the **Társulás Studio** from 1981 to 1985.
A few examples of the best productions from the 1980s include: **Márta Mészáros'** *Private Journal* and *Journal for My Loves*; **István Szabó's** *Mephisto*, *Colonel Redl* and *Hanussen*; **Péter Bacsó's** *Dog's Life!*; **Károly Makk's** 1982 Cannes award-winner, *Another View*; **Péter Gothár's** *Time in Suspense*; and **Pál Sándor's** *Daniel Takes the Train*.

PHOTOGRAPHY YESTERDAY AND TODAY

Hungary's first *daguerrotypes* were presented in 1840, shortly after Jacques Daguerre's 1838 invention. During the Austro-Hungarian period the first images of war appeared; the events surrounding the great 1839 Millenary celebrations of the Hungarian nation followed, covered by the first photo-journalist, **János Müllner**.
The photo "message" genre is linked to **Károly Escher's** (1890-1966) work, in which he discovered the artistic value of everyday events and transmitted this to the public. Between the two World Wars, artists such as **Rudolf Balogh**, **Frigyes Haller** and **Tibor Csörgő** created a new *Magyar* style, characteristic of its authentic milieu – the Hungarian village. **Károly Divald** and **György Klösz** represent "pure" photography best, thanks to their magnificent images of Nature, in particular compositions of rustic landscapes. The Realist trend, called sociophotography in Hungary, made a brilliant impact with **Károly Escher**, **Kata Kálmán**, **Lajos Lengyel**, **Lajos Tabák** and **Judit Kárász**.
In the second half of the 20C, **Károly Gink**, **Péter Korniss** and **Tamás Fèner** worked freely with a variety of styles in most photographic fields, in sociography or applied photography, for example.
Today, the **Federation of Hungarian Artist-Photographers** guides the artistic photography movement; it has excellent support in the form of magazines – ***Fotó*** and ***Fotóművészet***. **László Cseri**, **Tibor Hajas**, **Péter Tímár**, **György Tóth**, **László Török** and **Attila Vécsy** may be counted among the artists who are Federation members. Other well-known artists of Hungarian origin have excelled in the art of photography. The names of **Gyula Brassai**, **Robert Capa** and **André Kertész**, with his unforgettable 1934 album, *Paris*, are world-famous.

Food and drink

Generous and spicy, but easy on the palate, Hungarian gastronomy today is the result of a long development that started with the movement of the Magyars from Asia. Culinary traditions reminiscent of their nomad days, such as the thick soups or the dumplings that they took on horseback with them, have been combined with a wide variety of culinary influences. Among them are Turkish, Bavarian and Bulgarian cuisine, not forgetting the Austro-Hungarian influence, which culminated in the art of making fine pastries and cakes.

MAIN DISHES

Ingredients – Home cooking is characterised by the use of a *roux*, called *rántás* in Hungarian, which consists of wheat flour browned lightly in lard, and seasoned very generously with red onion. This is then the base for a highly-spiced sauce flavoured with red paprika, the key element in Hungarian gastronomy, to the extent that the term *paprikás* is applied to all the dishes flavoured with this sauce, in particular fish, poultry and veal.

Hors d'oeuvres – The Turks introduced savoury *pogácsa*, little crusty rolls made from wheat or potato flour, mixed with lard and cheese or spices.

Starters – Soups have a predominant place; the thick *Jókai bableves*, for example, a bean soup garnished with slices of pork and smoked sausage. *Hortobágyi palacsinta* is a Great Plain speciality, a thick pancake with meat and onions. You can also start your meal with a slice of goose liver *(libamáj)*, generally served grilled or pan-fried.

Soups and meats – The most famous Hungarian dish is *gulyás*, named after the Great Plain shepherds who first prepared it. It is not a stew, as often believed, but a true beef soup flavoured with onions and paprika and accompanied by potatoes and carrots. The "goulash" people usually have in mind is actually called *pörkölt*; this stew of braised meat, tomatoes and green peppers, with a strong onion flavour, is the Hungarians' favourite Sunday dish. It can consist of beef or veal, or even pork or chicken. In *tokány*, another stew variant, the paprika is replaced with pepper. Roast pork hock *(csülök)* is just as popular, and has pride of place in small restaurants.

Poultry and game – Roasted or prepared in a sauce, game is much in evidence, especially in northern Hungary. The Great Plain has its poultry: chicken paprika *(csirkepaprikás)* is a speciality not to be missed, nor the chicken soup *(újházi tyúkhúsleves)* prepared with peas, mushrooms, carrots and noodles. As for goose liver, it can be served in a thick slice or cut into large cubes and fried in goose fat, and flavoured to perfection with garlic and onion.

Sausages – *Hurka* is a blood sausage stuffed with pieces of pork, spices and boiled rice, served as a hot dish. As for cold sausages, the variety is endless: one of the most renowned specialities is salami, especially the paprika-spiced smoked version from Szeged. In southern Hungary two neighbouring towns, Gyula and Békéscsaba, compete for the honour of making the best cold sausage. Békéscsaba holds an annual sausage fair.

Paprika

Obtained from red peppers, this fine powder is considered "typically Hungarian". In reality, it was in the 18C that paprika, originally from India or America, was introduced into Hungary. It is said that when Napoleon put an embargo on British goods, particularly spices, pepper became scarce and the Hungarians invented a "poor man's version". Paprika slowly took hold in Hungarian cooking, before the medical profession began to take an interest in it. It was found to be rich in vitamin C, as demonstrated by the Nobel prizewinner Szentgyörgyi in the 1930s. The spice is cultivated in the Kecskemét and Szeged regions, and exists in seven varieties ranging from extra sweet to strong.

Vegetables – Very often main dishes are served with rice, home-made noodles or dumplings *(galuska)*, or small round roasted dumplings *(tarhonya)* made from a mixture of flour and eggs. They are in fact inherited from the Magyar nomads who used to make them up in advance to cook for impromptu meals as needed. On the other hand, green vegetables are not normally served, except in luxury restaurants. When salad is on the menu, it consists of cucumbers, marinated cabbage, or pickled peppers.

Fish – The most famous is pikeperch, or *fogas*. This freshwater fish, weighing 8-10kg/17.5-22lb lurks in the waters of Lake Balaton. Transporting it is a delicate procedure, but its flesh is highly appreciated. It is best eaten, of course, freshly caught and cooked at the lakeside; all the good restaurants have it on the menu. Another choice fish, sturgeon *(tok)*, is caught in the River Tisza. Carp *(ponty)* is more common and eaten as a fillet fried in breadcrumbs ("Serb style"), dusted with the indispensible paprika. The angler's favourite dish is *halászlé*, an exclusively freshwater fish soup, consisting of carp, catfish and pike. It is an onion-flavoured fish soup with character; Hungarians cheerfully cut up an entire hot pepper and add it to the pot. In some restaurants and especially in the summer the dish is prepared in huge cauldrons in the open air, and often served very spicy.

DESSERTS AND OTHER SWEET THINGS

Pancakes – *Palacsinta* are thin crêpe-like pancakes served in a thousand different ways. They can be filled with curd cheese, hazelnuts or even apricot jam, or prepared "Gundel style": stuffed with walnut cream, folded in quarters, drizzled with hot chocolate and served *flambé*.

Cakes – Pastries made with poppy seeds, apples or walnuts are a tradition in Central Europe. The curd cheese and raisin strudel *(túró)* seems modest next to the *Dobos torta*, invented by the famous pastry-maker József Dobos; seemingly dozens of thin layers of cake are alternated with mocha butter-cream icing, decorated with chopped hazelnuts and finished with a hard and glassy caramelised top. The *Rigó Jancsi* is a flaky chocolate cream delight, and no one can resist the sponge cake *(somlói galuska)* flavoured with rum, filled with raisins and walnuts and crowned with whipped cream. Strudels, or *rétes*, are made with a kind of paper-thin flaky pastry with the particular flavour of gluten-rich Hungarian flour; they can be stuffed with apples, curd cheese and raisins, poppy seeds, walnuts or even cherries. *Túró Rudi*, curd cheese enveloped in chocolate, is very much appreciated by both the young and the young at heart.

WINES

Hungary, where the first vines were introduced in the Roman period, is the largest wine-producing region in Central Europe. Renowned for its high-quality vintages, the country produces 4 million hectolitres annually, 30% of which is red wine or rosé, and 70% white wine, which is better known. Hungary holds sixth place in the world for wine exports, sending two-thirds of its production abroad.
The wines generally bear the name of the town or region they come from, to which the suffix "i" is added: Badacsonyi, Egri etc. The grape variety's name is sometimes added as well. The country's vineyards extend over 135 000ha/333 585 acres, taking advantage of Hungary's plentiful sunshine and an often warm Indian summer. There are four wine-growing regions.

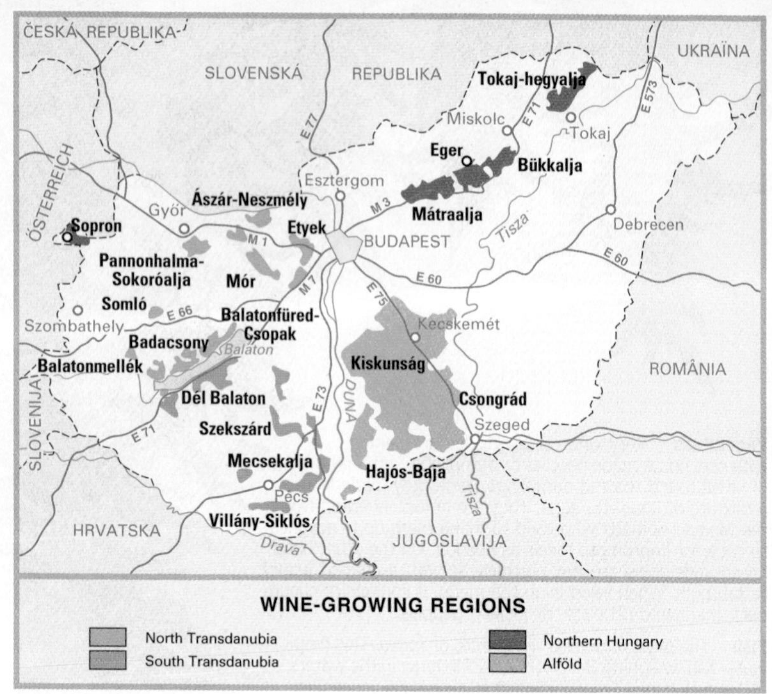

South Transdanubia

Mecsekalja – The Cirfandli grape produces a large selection of white wines here, ranging from very sweet to full-bodied. These wines are particularly fragrant.

Szekszárd and Villány-Siklós – The vines, which grow in a soil rich in loess and clay, produce full-bodied Kékfrankos and Kadarka reds. **Szekszárdi Bikavér**, a favourite of Franz Liszt, is today in competition with other vintages created with French vines, such as the velvety **Merlot** or **Villányi Cabernet** with its hints of blackberry and prune. These heady wines are delicious with stews or grilled meats.

Alföld

The Great Plain, between the Danube and the Tisza, represents half of the country's wine-producing territory. Grapevines were first introduced here to stabilise the *puszta*'s quicksand. This region produces excellent table wines, mainly whites.

Hajós-Baja – The German minority introduced Kadarka to the area south-east of Kalocsa: Rhenish **Rizling** and **Kékfrankos** have therefore become local wines.

Kiskunság – This area produces typical Great Plain wines from vines planted in sand; they are light, refreshing and sweet, such as **Olaszrizling**, which has a beautiful yellow colour. The town of Kecskemét produces a good white wine, **Kecskeméti Leányka**.

Csongrád – Further to the east, this sector enjoys the greatest amount of sunshine in the country (2 100hr annually). The rosé and red wines are characterised by the delicacy of their bouquet. The whites, such as **Tramini**, are slightly tangy; this wine goes well with game dishes.

North Transdanubia

Balatonfüred-Csopak – This area to the north of Lake Balaton is favoured with excellent climatic conditions for producing full-bodied wines with a subtle tang. The vines are grown in rich shale and sandstone soils. The most famous vintage is **Olaszrizling**, with its bouquet bearing hints of mignonette blossoms and bitter almonds. The Cabernet from the Tihany Peninsula is one of the country's best reds. It goes well with stuffed veal or chicken *paprikás*.

Badacsony – The whites are full-bodied and mellow when they come from the slopes of this originally volcanic massif. There are many varieties of vines here. **Kéknyelű**, with its rich bouquet, is a marvellous accompaniment for grilled lake pikeperch. **Olaszrizling** goes well with carp, but can also be appreciated on its own. **Muscat Ottonel** is enjoyable with desserts.

Balatonmellék – This area is known for its heady wines produced with Szürkebarát *(Pinot Gris* or *Moine Gris)*. Their fruity and spicy aromas blend well with poultry dishes. **Zöldvelteni** and **Zenit** are good with roast pork.

Sopron – This sector, located where the Alps meet the plain, produces red wines with a strong bouquet, made from **Kékfrankos grapes**. The soil, composed of gravel and sand, produces spicy whites made from **Veltliner vines**.

Somló – This little wine-growing area west of Lake Balaton is Hungary's smallest (500ha/1 235 acres of vines). Its wines are powerful and forceful, with a high level of acidity and alcohol. **Furmint** goes well with game and goose liver.

Mór – The basalt soil in this area between the Bakony and Vértes mountains favours dry wines with a high level of acidity. **Ezerjó** comes from here; of German origin, this wine has a complex and refined bouquet.

Ászár-Neszmély – The soil, a mixture of silt, sand and gravel, produces lively wines with rich bouquets. **Olaszrizling** goes very well with roast fillet of pikeperch, while **Rajnai Rizling** sets off grilled duck.

Etyek-Buda – South-west of Budapest, the soil is made up of sand and clay, producing **Chardonnay** and **Sauvignon Blanc**.

Pannonhalma-Sokoróalja – In a vineyard of 1 000ha/2 470 acres, the Olaszrizling, Rajnai Rizling and Tramini vines produce mellow and aromatic white wines.

Northern Hungary

Tokaj-Hegyalja – This region, with its volcanic soil covered with a layer of loess, is on the southern slopes of the Zemplén massif in north-eastern Hungary. It produces the most famous of Hungarian wines: **Tokay**, a golden nectar which is both sweet and soft. Tokay is made principally from **Furmint**, a smaller vine variety whose name comes from the French word *froment* ("wheat"), because of its yellow tint. Its subtle perfumes of bread, walnut and mushroom go perfectly with fish dishes. Tokay can also come from the **Hárslevelű grape**, producing a sweet and fruity wine, or from Muscat de Lunel. **Szamorodni** is the most common and least expensive Tokay, made with the entire bunch of grapes rather than from carefully sorted individual fruits. This rather strong drink may be served as an aperitif or with dessert.
The best Tokay is the **Aszú**, a mellow and exceptionally sweet nectar which figures among the world's most famous wines. Produced since the 16C, this was the first dessert wine obtained from dehydrated grapes. Louis XIV of France is said to have called it "the king of wines and the wine of kings". Its unforgettable bouquet blends well with goose liver or blue cheeses and it can also be served with dessert.

Eger – Hidden in the Mátra and Bükk massifs, Eger produces the famous *Egri Bikavér* ("Egri Bull's Blood"). Heavy and dark, it is made with several varieties of grapes. Its bouquet is reminiscent of vanilla and cloves. Another famous wine, **Egri Leányka** ("Eger Damsel"), is a semi-sweet white with a subtle aroma of honey. These strong wines, together with Egri Medoc (dark red) are very good with game.

Bükkalja – Gentle slopes, with a soil made up of clay and silt, produce whites with character such as **Olaszrizling**, excellent with trout, or mellow reds such as **Kékfrankos** which is pleasant with venison stew.

Mátraalja – Protected by the southern foothills of the Mátra Mountains, these vineyards produce heady white wines such as **Hárslevelű**.

OTHER ALCOHOLS

Spirits – The Hungarians rarely drink wine at lunch, particularly as the alcohol content runs to about 13 or 14 degrees. On the other hand, a great deal of **eau-de-vie** is consumed. The most famous is **barackpálinka**, a Kecskemét apricot brandy, which is the quintessential national drink. You may be offered a glass as an aperitif, or even in the middle of the day; this is one of the characteristics of Hungarian hospitality. A **Puszta cocktail** is an aromatic mix of Tokay wine (sweet or dry), apricot spirits and a flavoured liqueur. **Unicum** comes in unusual bottles and is a thick black liqueur, an acquired taste.

Beer – Among the national brands of beer *(sör)* are *Dréher* and *Kaiser*.

The recipe for Aszú wine

Sold in half litre bottles, *Aszú* wine is only produced in years when the first frosts coincide with the precise time of advanced ripening of the grape.
The grapes are then picked one by one, placed in graded baskets (28-30 litres/49-53 pints of grapes) where their own weight causes a first juice to be extracted, known as *aszú* essence. Between 1 litre/1.75 pints and 1.5 litres/2.6 pints are obtained, with a sugar content of 40 to 60%.
The grapes that have produced this essence are then kneaded into a paste which is added to wine in a Gönc barrel (from the name of the place where these 136 litre/30gal barrels are made). The *puttony* rating given to an *aszú* wine, corresponds to the number of baskets of paste that have been put into a barrel to macerate, from 2 to 6 *puttony*. *Aszú* takes at least four years and a maximum of eight years to mature, as follows: two years for the barrel, two years for the first two baskets and one additional year per basket of paste added. At the time of the Rákóczi princes, this wine became a sort of currency, sometimes used to obtain alliances and facilitate negotiations.

Sopron – Fő tér

G. Simeone / PHOTONONSTOP

Sights

AGGTELEKI NEMZETI PARK★★

AGGTELEK NATIONAL PARK – Borsod-Abaúj-Zemplén province

Michelin map 925 A 11 – Local map see BÜKK

Aggtelek National Park has been on the Unesco World Heritage List since 1995. It can be reached by taking roads 26 and 27, and is located about 63km/38mi north of Miskolc. The centre of the park is the hilltop village of **Aggtelek**. Its Reformed church, originally medieval, has undergone several transformations and now has a neo-Baroque bell-tower.

An exceptional underground world – The karst caves of Aggtelek-Jósvafő are in Hungary, while the Domica caves are in Slovakia. The entire network, known as Baradla, is spread over 25km/15mi; the Hungarian part covers 17km/10mi.
All told there are about 700 caves that have been hollowed out of the karst massif of the Bodva Valley through the ages (surface area of 560km^2/224sq mi). The caves are home to a biological reserve that has been protected since 1985. Numerous rivulets flow in and out of the swallow-holes (*barlang* in Hungarian) that are characteristic of karst regions. Slightly acid surface water filters through millions of small cracks, dissolving the soluble part of the limestone on its way. This water then slowly drips from the cave walls, leaving a deposit behind, and forming a decorative underground world of stalactites, stalagmites or other shapes, depending on where the drops of water fall.
The vegetation is typical of karst regions, with some rare species. As for the fauna to be found in the caves, over 500 species have been identified by Aggtelek speleologist-biologists.
This natural wonder was formed more than 200 million years ago. Man's presence in the caves has been verified and dates back about 35 000 years, while the oldest known documents and local map are from 1704. Modern man started to visit the caves at the beginning of the 18C.

AN UNDERGROUND TRIP INTO WONDERLAND

Visitors may choose between several tours: short (1.3km/0.8mi, 1hr); medium (2.3km/1.3mi, 2hr 30min); long (7km/4mi, 5hr); special (9km/5.4mi, 8hr).
There are two entrances on the Hungarian side, one at **Aggtelek** where the largest cave is, and the other at **Jósvafő**. The Aggtelek entrance is the most popular one and leads to the easiest tour. The Jósvafő entrance is less frequented but leads to an equally interesting tour. Not at all dangerous (no special footwear necessary).

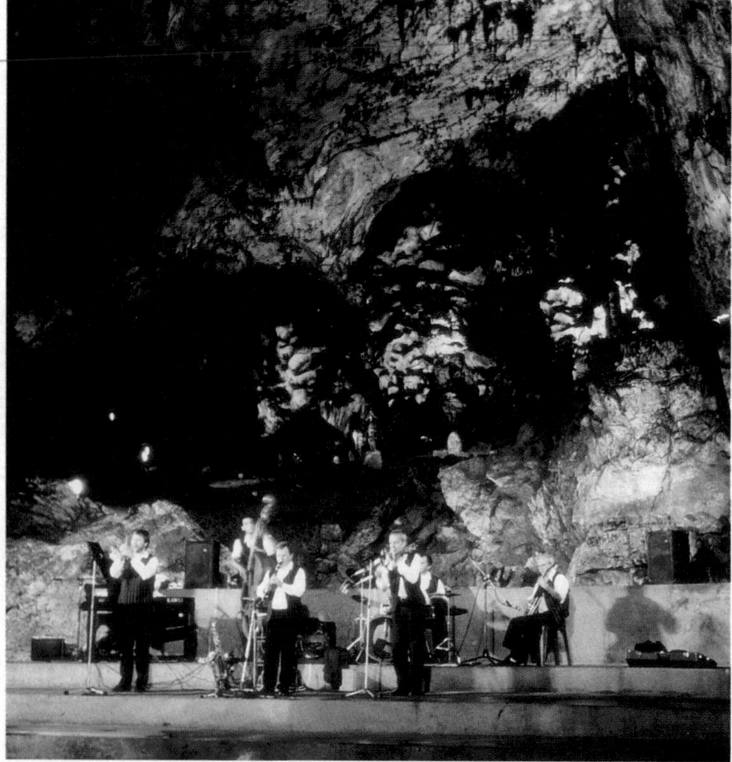

P. Borzsak/MAGYAR KÉPEK Kft

the tour takes place under pleasant conditions: there is no change in levels, the temperature is constant (9-10°C/48.2-50°F), the lighting is well planned and the music well adapted.
One tour is normally sufficient. The medium tour will give you time to admire and appreciate the acoustics in the natural concert hall on the Aggtelek side or in the immense cavern on the Jósvafő side.
If attending one of the summer **concerts**, don't forget to bring a light sweater.
The 5hr or 8hr visits are really intended for well-equipped sports enthusiasts and amateur potholers (helmets, boots etc). Register in advance by contacting park management: 3758 Aggtelek, Baradla Oldal 1. ☎/Fax 48/343 073.
Souvenirs are available next to the cave entrance, at the Cave and Speleology Museum. The exhibits were taken from the collections at Hungary's National Museum and Natural Sciences Museum.

Caves in Hungary

Hungary has created nine national parks. In five of them (Aggtelek, Bükk, Budapest, Upper Balaton and South Transdanubia), the caves are a major tourist attraction.
Of the 3 000 protected natural caves, 125 receive special protection. There are 26 caves that measure more than 1km/0.6mi in length, the two longest being Aggtelek's Baradla (17km/10.2mi) and Budapest's Pál-völgyi (11km/6.6mi), found in a district known as Rózsadomb (Roses Hill). Budapest has more than 30km/18mi of caves beneath the city.
Nine caves have facilities for tours and five are open to specialists; one of these functions as a public bath. The caves' watercourses often supply town drinking water (Pécs, for example) or are sometimes set aside for special use (Budapest's Chapel of the Order of St Paul in the Mt Gellért caves). Some caves have even been listed as having curative value. Climatic conditions in the caves are unusual and are beneficial for the treatment of bronchial ailments.
Special equipment is necessary for potholing tours, which are conducted under the aegis of the National Parks Directorate and the Association of Speleology and Karst Research. Certain travel agencies are specialists in Eco-tourism (EcoVISTA in Budapest's VISTA Travel Centre).

BAJA★

Bács-Kiskun province – Population 39 000

Michelin map 925 H 8

The River Danube and River Sugovica branch and cut across several islands, including Petőfi-sziget and Nagy-Pandúr-sziget, giving Baja the air of a resort town.
Several different ethnic groups live peacefully together here, Serbs, Croats, Germans, Tziganes and of course Hungarians.

Bridge over the Danube – *155km/93mi from Budapest, about 50km/30mi south of Kalocsa.* This is the last bridge over the Danube before the southern border. Baja, on the river's east bank, is a port with heavy river traffic, making it a busy trading centre. It was once used by merchants coming to buy wine and grain, which is why there are so many wine cellars and a cask-making industry. Grain, wine and flour were towed back up the Danube on little barges, while the wood for cask-making was floated downstream from the north. At Baja there were once as many as 70 watermills on the Danube and its small tributaries. The moneyed millers' guild used to celebrate its patron saint, St John Nepomuk during a festival, which still takes place in mid-May every year. The event, now known as the Johnny Floating festival, is an important folk occasion.
Both cars and the railway use the bridge that crosses the Danube. Baja serves as a point of call. To the west, rich Transdanubia is wooded and heavily populated. To the east, a plain between the Danube and the Tisza heralds the **Alföld** (the Great Eastern Plain), already faithful to the image of the *puszta*, with its vast expanses, horses, dunes and cantilevered wells. This region is more sparsely populated.

The festivals – The **Fish Soup Festival** and the **Minorities Festival** run concurrently. Antal Grassalkovich, who commissioned the construction of a palace that is now the town hall, signed a contract with the town which stipulated that the Council would always consist of three ethnic groups, each with one-third of the seats. He also established an alternating judicial power system. The judge was chosen each year from a different ethnic group.

Fish Soup Festival

Every year on the second Saturday of July, Szentháromság tér, or Holy Trinity Square, is overrun by a mass of cooks, gourmets and ordinary food-lovers who come to taste the **halászlé** (fish soup). The soup is made with fish from the Danube and nearby rivers or lakes. It is cooked in more than 1 000 large copper kettles set over open wood fires. The event is worth seeing and the soup is good too. Here as elsewhere, it is the cook's secret touch that adds zest to the normal recipe.

SIGHTS

Városháza (Town Hall) – *Szentháromság tér.* Holy Trinity Square, bordering the River Sugovica on its western side, is surrounded on the other three sides by Baroque buildings that include the town hall. This was built in the mid-18C by Antal Grassalkovich, intendant to Maria Theresa, who also built Gödöllő Castle. It is not open to the public but visitors can cross the courtyard and leave via the opposite façade, facing **Ferences templom** *(Bartók Béla u. 1).* This Franciscan church contains a perfectly tuned Baroque organ.

★ **Türr István Múzeum** ⏲ – *Deák Ferenc u.1.* The museum bears the name of István Türr (1825-1908) who was born in Baja. He was a hero in the War of Independence (1848-9) and later forced into exile. During the Crimean War he served the English who showed their gratitude by saving his life after his capture by the Austrians in 1856. He then saw action alongside Garibaldi, returned to Hungary in 1867, and worked on regulating river flow and canal systems. This led to his participating in preparatory work on the Panama and Corinth canals.

The museum's largest and most interesting exhibition shows life on the Danube. Visitors can discover aquatic flora and fauna, and how fishermen lived, fished and built their boats. There are also models of watermills, which are actually boats permanently moored along the river bank, with a large wheel attached that is turned by the water current. An ethnographic collection represents the various peoples who live in Baja and the surrounding area. An exhibition on Hungarian contemporary painters completes the tour.

On leaving the museum, return to Szentháromság tér, go past the town hall and along **Eötvös János utca**, Baja's entirely pedestrianised main shopping street.

★ **Nagy István Képtár** ⏲ – *Arany János u. 1.* Go past Tóth Kálmán tér, and take Vörösmarty u. to the square of the same name. You will find a town house, now a museum, exhibiting works by painters who for the most part lived here after 1946 and are known as the **Alföld School**. It makes for a pleasant visit, and gives a good presentation of the provincial art of the time. There are also works by painter Gyula Rudnay and sculptor Ferenc Medgyessy. A few metres further on, András Jelky Square is interesting in name only. This globe-trotter was born in Baja in the 18C. He was a tailor's apprentice who left for Paris and later returned to his mother country to write his memoirs after travelling through China, Japan, Ceylon and many other countries.

A place to stay, a place to eat

Hotel Duna – *Szentháromság tér. Rooms at €23.* Standing on the quietest corner of the square, the hotel affords an interesting view of the Sugovica branch of the Danube.

The quays at the foot of the bridge leading to Petőfi-sziget have been developed all along the Sugovica. Here you will find **cafés** and **restaurants**, as well as **Infotourist**, which provides information on regional sights.

Vizafogó Panzió – *Petőfi-sziget, Március u. 15. ☎ 79/326 585. Rooms at €18.* On the banks of an arm of the Danube, a charming *panzió* with five rooms and a fish restaurant.

Sugovica Hotel – *Petőfi-sziget. ☎ 79/321 755. Rooms between €18 and €46.* Modern hotel with clean and comfortable rooms.

Véndió Vendéglő – *Petőfi-sziget, ☎ 79/325 195.* On the quiet little island of Petőfi-sziget, a restaurant with a large terrace. Special fish dishes.

Fadd-Dombori – *22km/13.6mi north of Szekszárd.* A leisure and holiday complex has been developed around a Danube backwater consisting of small family homes and campsites. Bungalows are available. This stretch of water is over 7km/4.2mi long and approximately 0.5km/0.3mi wide. Hungary's rowing team practises here.

Campsite: Hullám *(The Wave)*, **Kemping Tolna Tourist Kft.** – *71333 Fadd-Dombori, Nyirfa u. 5. From 15 April to 15 October.*

Szerb ortodox templom – *Táncsics Mihály u. 21.* The most interesting of Baja's two Serbian Orthodox churches has a beautiful 19C iconostasis.

Petőfi-sziget – A bridge links the city centre to Petőfi-sziget. This small island has beaches, a yachting harbour, the Sugovica Hotel, campsites, and playing fields shaded by huge trees that grow in the moist ground providing pleasant, shady places to stroll. Everything about the setting is restful. In summer, however, it is difficult to find a spot on the beaches or at the campsites.

EXCURSIONS

★★ **Train or boat tour in the Gemenc Nature Reserve** – This is a trip for nature lovers. You can go on weekends from 1 May to 30 October, although the boat trips stop on 15 October. The trip by narrow-gauge rail (run by the MÁV, the Hungarian State train system) is 30km/18mi long; the local agent is **Gemenci Erdő és Vadgazdaság Rt.** *(6500 Baja, Szt Imre tér 2. ☎ 79/324 144)*. It is also possible to combine the train tour with a boat trip on the Sió Canal, which links Lake Balaton to the Danube.
The **Gemenc Forest**, which extends over 20 000ha/48 000 acres, is an illustration of what the areas along the Danube and Tisza that were liable to flooding were like before the flow of these rivers was controlled. The flora and fauna are extremely rich and varied. There are deer, boar and waterfowl, as well as vegetation peculiar to areas subject to flooding. Companies such as **Trófea Vadászatszervező** and **Vadászatelszámoló Kft.** *(7100 Szekszárd. Arany János u. 3. ☎ 74/316 718)* organise hunting parties. Fishing is restricted but many spots are completely open to visitors.

Őcsény – *38 km/23mi north-west along roads 55 and 56; then take a small road on the right before Várdomb.*
A small airport between Baja and Szekszárd hosts the **Gemenci Vitorlázó Repülő Bajnokság** (Glider Championship) every year at the end of July. The **Nemzetközi Hőlégballon Találkozó** (International Hot-air Balloon Meeting) takes place in early August. All kinds of air sports are possible at this airport, where you can also find accommodation and camping facilities. For further information, contact **Gábor Talabos**, *7143 Öcsény Pf. 6, ☎ 74/496 265.*

Szekszárd – *37km/22mi north-west along roads 55 and 56.* Like Kalocsa, Szekszárd lay on the banks of the Danube until the end of the 19C. Today, however, river flow regulation has left this old Roman town surrounded by land. Szekszárd spreads out along an avenue that is successively called Béri Balogh Ádám, Széchenyi and Rákóczi. At the point where the avenue changes its name from Béri Balogh Ádám to Széchenyi, turn left and go up to Béla tér. Here, in the **Megyeház (County Hall)** ⓥ courtyard, visitors can see the foundations of a Benedictine monastery that Béla I had built in 1061. Returning to cross the avenue, go past Liszt Ferenc tér and go into Mártírok tere (Martyrs' Square). The **Wosinsky Mór Múzeum** ⓥ★★ is at n° 26, named after a priest and archaeologist who excavated widely in the region. The museum was built at the end of the 19C to exhibit the collections that can be seen today; they include numerous pieces of Celtic and Avar jewellery. There is an excellent exhibition on the first floor covering life in Hungary at the turn of the century.
Szekszárd is also the birthplace of several famous people, including **Mihály Babits**, one of Hungary's great poets. The **house where he was born** ⓥ *(Babits u. 5)* is open to the public. **János Garay**, a writer born in Szekszárd, is well known as the creator of the eloquently boastful Háry János. Kodály used this character for a musical work that is extremely popular in Hungary.

BALATON★★★

Veszprém and Somogy provinces

Michelin map 925 F 4 and 5, G 3

The largest lake in Europe – Approximately 100km/60mi from Budapest, in the heart of Transdanubia, Lake Balaton stretches for a distance of 77km/45mi. Its width varies from 1.5km/0.9mi at the Tihany Peninsula, to 14km/9mi at its broadest part. It has an area of 598km²/231sq mi and an average depth of 2.5m/8.2ft. Near the Tihany Peninsula it is only about 12m/39ft deep, which explains the relatively high water temperature (close to 25°C/77°F), much appreciated by swimmers.

THE HUNGARIAN SEA

The name of the lake is thought to have come from the Avar word *blatno*, which means stagnant water. The presence of marshland, and therefore water, probably has something to do with this.

Balaton has always been a source of life throughout history. Fish, game and reeds have drawn from its waters the vital element for their evolution. It has been a place of contemplation and meditation because of the beauty and luminosity of its natural sites. It has also been a sort of natural frontier, which, in the 16C separated the Habsburgs from the Turks. However, the Turks managed to reach the north shore which they laid waste. In the 18C, Germans, Croats and Slovaks came and settled in the region. At the end of the 18C, Balatonfüred and Hévíz started to resemble summer resorts where the rich families from Buda, Pest and Austria came to spend long holidays.

The **railway line** joining Nagykanizsa to Buda was built on the south shore in 1861. The one on the north shore was built in 1909. It was then that the lake, part of which was filled in, took on its current shape, and tourism really started to develop.

After the First World War, 50 000 to 60 000 people would come here on holiday. Twenty years later, on before the Second World War, the figure had risen to nearly 250 000.

The Riviera of the Communist countries – The socialist regime, instituted in Hungary after the Second World War, made efforts to develop social tourism for the workers. This was subsequently followed by the **nationalisation** of existing facilities, the expropriation of villas and the establishment of holiday camps.

During the Communist regime, Lake Balaton enabled German families from the West and the East to meet with greater ease. People from the West did not have much difficulty in entering Hungary and, for the East Germans, it was easier to come to a brother country than to cross the Iron Curtain. In addition to the holiday camps opened by companies or workers' organisations, certain sectors, such as the Balatonaliga holiday camp were reserved for "party members". In this protected complex, the hierarchy was strictly respected. The areas made available and the quality of service and facilities depended on the social status of the holidaymaker. The large accommodation complexes, converted in the 1990s into hotels, date from this era.

And today... – The Balaton region has played a major role in the development of tourism in Hungary and is still one of its driving forces. After Budapest, it is the most visited area in the country. Every year over 950 000 tourists come and stay in accommodation on the shores of the lake or further inland. The vast majority of tourists are German. The roadsides are decorated with *Zimmer frei* signs put up by local inhabitants, as bed and breakfast accommodation is common. German is certainly the most widely spoken foreign language in the Balaton area, whether in shops, hotels, restaurants, cafés or nightclubs. Of the number of nights spent by tourists in Hungary, 32% are spent in this region. In the summer season, with its long weekends, the people of Budapest come to swell the ranks of tourists. This region, often known as the "Hungarian Sea", owes its success not only to the quality of the environment and the micro-climate, but also to the facilities available, all of which make the area an immense holiday resort.

Holidaymakers who wish to enjoy a sporting activity or simply relax, can do so on one of the 130 beaches around the lake. This is not the only centre of interest in the region, however, for the hinterland is also pleasant and picturesque.

Between Budapest and Lake Balaton, **Lake Velencei** *(see SZÉKESFÉHÉRVÁR: Excursions)* and the western tip of the inland sea, **Kis-Balaton** (Little Balaton), are twin paradises for ecologists and nature lovers.

A TOUR OF THE LAKE

North-south, the two shores – The north and south shores are very different. The landscapes, which bear witness to an eventful past, the natural reserves of fauna and flora, the thermal springs, beaches and vineyards all provide a wealth of interest for visitors, who can also enjoy the abundance of handicrafts, wines and folklore.

/MAGYAR KÉPEK Kft

On the shores of the "Hungarian Sea"

★★The north shore

Coming from Budapest, leave the M 7 by taking road n° 71, which runs along the eastern tip of the lake.

This is the most interesting side. There are several holiday resorts and also vines growing on the volcanic slopes, which produce pleasant white wines.

Balatonalmádi – The first major resort of interest to visitors is Balatonalmádi which has a permanent population of about 8 500. It has been a holiday resort since the late 19C and boasts the Hotel Aurora, Budatava beach and water-sports establishments.

2.5km/1.5mi further on, take a small road on the right in the direction of Veszprém.

Felsőörs – A charming little 13C Romanesque church made of red sandstone standing in the middle of the village is not really worth a trip in itself but the climb up towards Felsőörs takes you through an area that has retained all its character. In this vineyard country the stone from nearby quarries colours the old houses. Basalt and volcanic rock are black, whereas the limestone is white and the sandstone decidedly red.

Return to the main road.

Balatonfüred – This is the oldest of the lake's north shore resorts and thermal spas. Visitors have been coming here for the beaches and thermal spa treatment for over 200 years.

The old centre of Balatonfüred lies to the north of the railway line, which cuts the town in two. The road that runs parallel to the railway line in the south marks the boundary of the resort part of Balatonfüred built on the shores of the lake. With over 6km/3.7mi of beaches, this area offers all the facilities of a holiday resort. On the continuation of Jókai Mór utca, there is a landing-stage where you can take a boat to Tihany, Siófok or Keszthely.

Balatonfüred has kept its aristocratic appearance which goes back to the time when it was a meeting place for people from the world of politics, culture and entertainment. The resort originally became popular as the actress and singer **Lujza Blaha** (nicknamed the nation's nightingale) had her holiday villa here; it has since been turned into a hotel *(Blaha Lujza utca 4)*.

It was in Balatonfüred that István Széchenyi inaugurated the lake's first steamer in 1846. Several Hungarian writers and poets have stayed in the town. **Sándor Kisfaludi** established the first Hungarian-language theatre here. **Mór Jókai**, a friend of Sándor Petőfi, and prolific novelist, much appreciated in the Anglo-Saxon world, wrote over 100 novels here. He is sometimes compared to Charles Dickens. The famous winner of the Nobel prize for literature, the Indian writer **Rabindranath Tagore**, came to Balatonfüred for treatment in 1926 and planted a lime tree before he left (a tree-lined avenue bears his name). Since then, numerous famous people have followed his example.

Vineyards on the north shore of the lake

Jókai Múzeum ⓥ – *On the corner of Honvéd utca and Jókai Mór utca.* In this villa, now a museum, Jókai, who was also a member of Parliament, wrote almost his entire work in purple ink, on official headed notepaper.
On the opposite corner of the crossroads, you can see the **round church** (Kerek templom), built at the end of the 19C.

★ **Gyógy tér** – In the middle of Treatment Square is the Kossuth Lajos drinks stall (built in 1800). Between 1 May and 30 September, you can taste Balatonfüred's sulphurous water, without having to be a patient.
In the 18C, the **bitter water** from the carbonic-gaseous springs was served with ewe's milk to treat stomach-ache. It was also used as a remedy for tuberculosis. Towards the end of the 19C, the curative and therapeutic properties of these waters were discovered and have since been used to treat heart conditions and problems of the circulatory system.

Szanatórium – This large building was constructed in 1810 (in Hungarian the word *szanatórium* means a place for convalescence). Every year, **Anna's Ball** takes place in the great hall. This tradition has been perpetuated since 1825 when the rich Szentgyörgyi-Horváth family used to spend their holidays at Balatonfüred. On 26 July, St Anne's Day, they used to give a large ball in honour of their daughter, Anna. If you are here on 26 July, you will be able to admire the guests, dressed in period costumes. The first ball was given in the Horváth villa *(on the corner of György tér and Blaha Lujza utca)*. After being used as a convalescent home for miners, it was left derelict and is now awaiting restoration. Under the sanatorium's arcades, the Balaton Pantheon will tell you the names of the famous people who have been to Balatonfüred. Commemorative plaques bear the names of learned people, artists, writers, musicians and politicians, both Hungarian and foreign.
Leaving these rather crowded shores in summer, you will find a completely different atmosphere in the hinterland dominating the lake, with its hills and valleys where forests and vineyards alternate, depending on the orientation. If it is not sunbathing weather, or if you wish to escape, take a walk or ride on horseback along the paths reserved for nature lovers.
A few hundred metres from the road between Aszófő and Pécsely *(7km/4mi beyond Balatonfüred)* stands an inn-cum-riding centre (forest rides available).
From Pécsely continue towards Barnag;, turn right towards an old "Pony Express" stopping place. Modelled on the American West, the Hungarians created a sort of Pony Express to carry the post on horseback.

Nagyvázsony – Nagyvázsony is a historic stopping place on the post route. This is where the **Postakocsi** (post coaches) changed their teams, composed of six horses.

Kinizsi-vár – Called after its owner, Kiniszi Castle is astonishing. **Pál Kinizsi** was a miller reputed to be as strong as Hercules. The town where he was born is not known with any certainty because several places have what they claim to be

Kinizsi's millstone on show – the millstone that he could lift with only one hand when he was just a youth. Strong, courageous and intelligent, Pál Kinizsi made himself so useful to King Matthias that the king appointed him one of the leaders of his army and, as a reward for services rendered, gave him Nagyvázsony Castle.

A hero for Hollywood – Many tales are told to illustrate the strength of the hero who made mincemeat of his adversaries. It is said that, in a victorious battle against the Turks, he took three prisoners, one under each arm, the third held between his teeth, and swung them round and round before casting them into the distance. He also quelled the rebellion of the King's black guards who were demanding to be paid after returning victorious. Kinizsi had more than 1 000 massacred. He was given the castle in 1492 and died two years later.

Tour – The castle is now a museum. Hungarian castle life is illustrated by an exhibition of furniture and objects. During the 18C the place served as a prison, evidence of which is displayed. Kinizsi's tombstone is exhibited in the restored chapel where a few documents illustrate his life.

★★ **Posta Múzeum** – The Post Museum recalls the means, through time and space, that man has used to communicate. In the summer, visitors can post letters that will be stamped with the museum's postmark.

Return to the lake and take road n° 71 again.

At the foot of the Tihany Peninsula, the road makes a sudden turn.

★★★ **Tihany** – *See this name.*

If you do not have the time to go right around the lake and wish to return to the south shore, take the ferry from the far end of the peninsula *(the crossing takes 15min)*. It can get quite busy in the summer. Souvenir shops and cafés are a pleasant way of passing the time.

★ **Örvényes** – This village has preserved a watermill in working order. Inside, there is a small ethnographic museum with everyday objects and handicrafts.

Balatonudvarí – In the cemetery, see the heart-shaped tombstones (late 18C-early 19C).

Révfülöp – The origins of Révfülöp go back to the 11C when it was a fishing village. Destroyed by the Turks in the 16C, it only came back to life in the 18C when it was transformed into a holiday resort. Here, far from the larger complexes, the lakeside is quiet and restful, in a good position at the foot of Mt Fülöp.

Badacsony – The name refers to a small town, a massif, a holiday resort, a wine-growing area and, above all, a protected site. Like Tihany, Badacsony has a fine location on a 438m/1 437ft hill dominating the lake. Of volcanic origin, it would appear to have been set down there for the beauty of the gesture and to offer ramblers magnificent walks with splendid **views**★★ over Lake Balaton. The road through the town takes the name of Balatoni út. Heading north of this, you leave the lakeside and cross the railway line to get to the hiking pathways. If hiking and steep slopes do not inspire you, there are four-wheel drive vehicles to take you to the top of the massif. They leave from the post office on Sétány Park. Experienced hikers will find detailed maps on sale in shops or at the tourist office. The path with blue markings leads to the **Kisfaludy belvedere**, offering a fine **view**★★ over Lake Balaton and the volcanic cones. On the way up, take a breather at the **Kisfaludy ház** terrace to admire the landscape.

A wine-growing region – According to legend, an earthenware flask over 2 000 years old, which had contained wine, was supposedly found at Balatonfelvidék. This would disprove the story that says that it was the Romans who introduced the vines and the wine-making techniques. Be that as it may, Badacsony are excellent white wines, to be consumed in moderation, of course.

Szigliget – Once an island and now a small picturesque village, Szigliget is dominated by the ruins of a 13C castle, flying the Hungarian flag. There is a view over the vineyards and the lake from the top of the tower.

★★ **Keszthely** – *See this name.*

Hévíz – *See this name.*

The south shore

Return to Keszthely and continue along road n° 71.

This side of the lake is less attractive as it is lined with almost indistinguishable holiday resorts such as **Fonyód**, **Balatonboglár**, **Balatonlelle**, **Balatonszemes** and **Balatonföldvár**, which are jam packed in the summer.

Szántód – Landing-stage for Tihany and Balatonfüred. Large campsite.

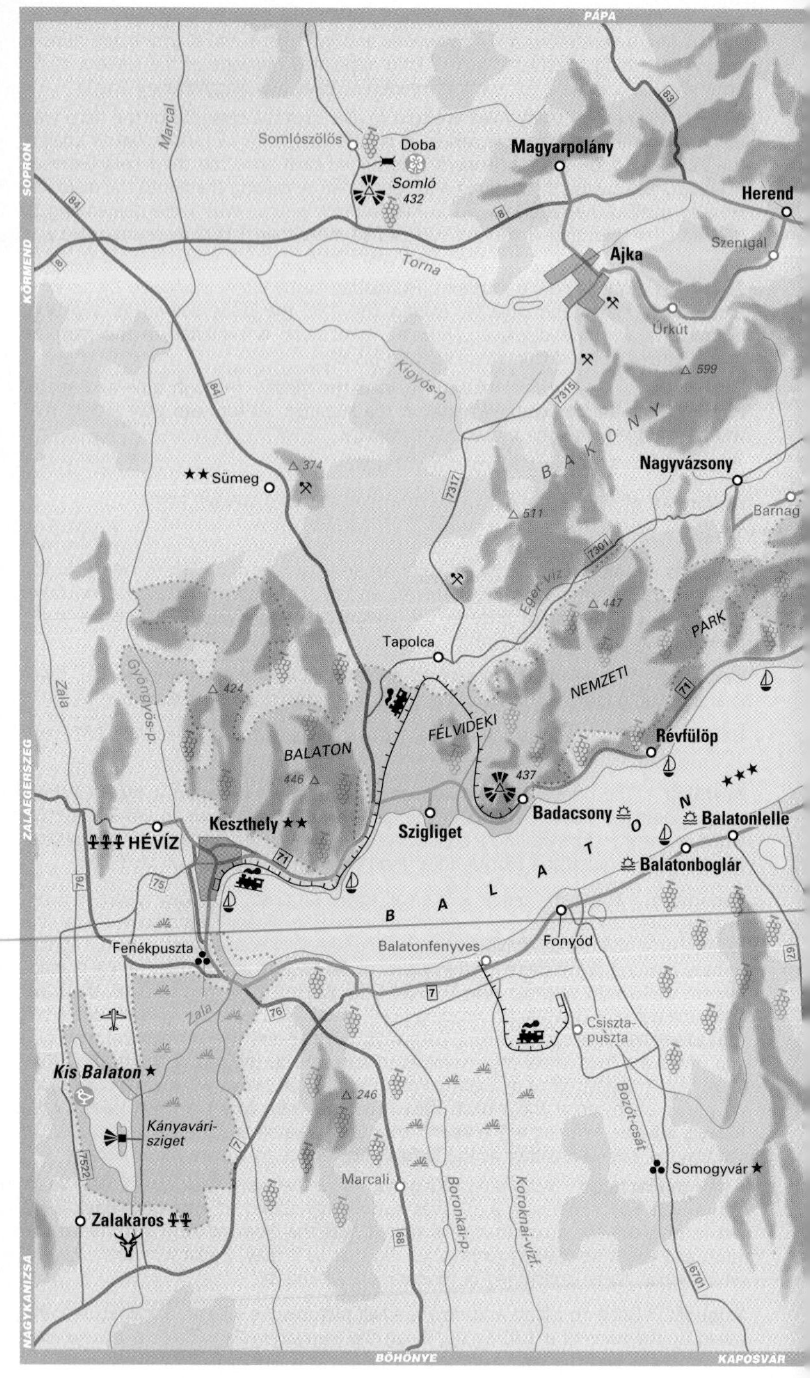

The area between Szántód and Siófok forms a stretch of urban development where the majority of summer visitors are to be found.

★ **Szántód-puszta Majormúzeum** Ⓥ – This tourist and cultural centre is comprised of a group of 18C and 19C buildings that have been perfectly restored, giving visitors an idea of the rural environment of the time. Farms, storerooms and stables etc can be visited. There is an aquarium with several species of Balaton fish. Folk

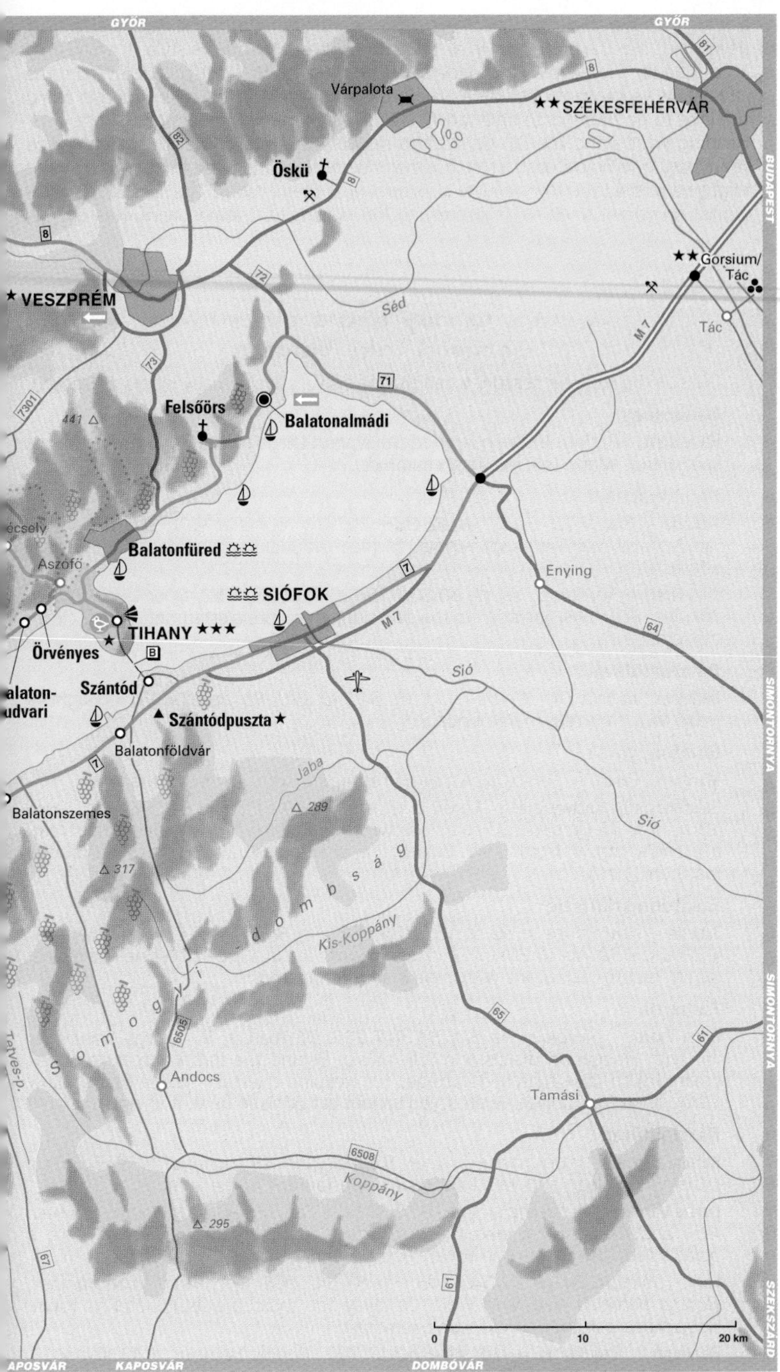

art also has a prominent place. Horse-riding and rides in open carriages are available. Accommodation should be booked well in advance. A comfortable *csárda* with a terrace serves classical Hungarian food.

Siófok – The holiday resort *par excellence* for those who like crowds. The lakeside beaches are overlooked by villas, hotels, campsites, restaurants, discotheques and shops (clothes, bags and souvenirs).

It was after the construction of a railway line at the end of the 19C that Siófok developed, like Balatonfüred, in a rather elegant and bourgeois style. It was easily accessible for the people of Budapest and the lakeside brought cool relief from the city air. As years went by, Siófok was forced to extend for several kilometres along the lake to accommodate and satisfy steadily increasing numbers of visitors.
Heading west along the Sió Canal, two resorts, Ezüst-part (the Silver Coast) and Aranypart (the Gold Coast) stretch either side of the canal near the harbour. What might be termed the town centre is located near the harbour. The station (Vasútállomás) on Váradi Adolf tér is interesting for its early 20C atmosphere. Nearby, the

A place to stay and a place to eat around Lake Balaton

Outside the summer season, when the area is very lively, many places are closed.

Badacsony

Halászkert – *Park u. 5. Open April to November.* Large restaurant with numerous specialities. Many folk events in summer.

Balatonalmádi

Viktória – *Bajcsy Zs. u. 42. ☎ 88/338 940. 10 rooms at €31.* Charming little family hotel with well-kept rooms. Terrace overlooking a garden. An excellent address!

Club Hotel – *Neptun u. 15. ☎ 88/339 150, Fax 88/339 152. Open June to September.* Very well located at the lakeside, this hotel-restaurant offers clean, modern rooms.

Balatonföldvár

Budalakk Üdülőház Kft – *Petőfi u. 11. ☎ 84/340 270. Rooms at €13.* A delightful place at a very reasonable price.

Balatongyörök

Margaréta Panzió – *Eötvös u.* A *panzió*-restaurant with a view of the lake.

Balatongyöröki Kastélyszálló – *Petőfi u. 2. ☎ 83/349 510, Fax 83/346 001. Open 15 April to 15 October. 36 rooms between €13 and €26.* In a quiet little street, a stone's throw from Lake Balaton, a prestigious hotel in a neo-Baroque mansion (1945).

Balatonmáriafürdő

Janette – *Ady Endre u. 93. ☎ 85/376 522, Fax 85/376 027. Rooms between €22 and €32.* About 20km/12mi from Keszthely, in a little street near the lake, family *panzió*-restaurant with rooms and bungalows.

Zamárdi

Kocsi Csárdi – *Siófoki u. ☎/Fax 84/349 010.* On road n° 7, a large traditional inn with Hungarian dishes and folk music. Behind the inn, a street has been created with little thatched cottages for sleeping quarters (house for 5: allow €90). Ideal for families. Even if you cannot eat or sleep here, it is worth a look!

Balatonfüred

Korona Panzió – *Vörösmarty u. 4. ☎ 87/343 278. 18 rooms at €39.* Beautiful *panzió* with clean and well-kept rooms. Restaurant in the summer.

Balázs Villa – *Deák Ferenc u. 1. ☎ 87/580 060, Fax 87/580 061. Rooms between €31 and €46.* A charming villa with every possible comfort tucked down a quiet street away from the town centre. Pool, sauna and solarium.

Park – *Jókai u. 24. ☎ 87/343 203, Fax 87/342 005. Open April to September. Rooms between €46 and €62.* Certainly the most beautiful hotel in town. Rooms decorated in an old-fashioned style.

Flamingó – *Széchenyi u. 16. ☎ 87/343 707. Rooms between €49 and €62.* Modern hotel with no particular charm but has the major advantage of being open all year round. The rooms are spacious. Pool open in summer with a view of the lake.

Koloska Csárda – *Koloska Tál. Open April to October.* At the top of the village in the forest, an immense traditional inn, specialising in grilled meats.

Borcsa – *Tagore Sétány. Open February to December.* On the shore of Lake Balaton, one of the town's best-known restaurants. Terrace with a view over the water. Specialities: grilled meat and fish.

Arany Korona – *Kossuth L. u. 11.* Very popular no-frills restaurant. Hungarian specialities: fish and poultry.

Stefánia Vitorlás Étterem – *Tagore Sétány. Open all year round.* A tourist restaurant in a beautiful house. Large terrace overlooking the lake.

concrete **water tower** (Víztorony) is a classified monument. It houses the Tourinform Tourist Office. At n° 2 Sió utca, the **József Beszédes Museum**, called after the hydraulics engineer, tells the story of how the flow of the Danube and waters of Lake Balaton were regulated. The **Imre Kálmán Múzeum** ⓥ *(Szabadság tér)* is dedicated to the operetta composer (he composed the famous *Princess Csárdás*) and relates the life of this musician who emigrated to the United States. Lastly, the **Evangelist Church★** (Evangélikus templom) situated in Oulu-park is an example of contemporary architecture, of the Organic style, designed by Imre Makovecz.

★KIS-BALATON (LITTLE BALATON)

Kis-Balaton, which is part of the Upper Balaton National Park (Balaton Felvidéki Nemzeti Park), used to be part of Lake Balaton. This area was gradually filled in by the alluvial deposits from the River Zala. Around 3 500ha/8 600 acres remain, covered with reeds and interspersed with shallow pools of water. Around 100 species of birds have made their home in the area. It is also a resting place for migrating birds. The park is protected and visitors require a permit. Some 1 400ha/3 400 acres are currently protected; however, there is an observation point for visitors which does not require a permit on **Kányavári sziget** (Kányavár Island), which is located 2km/1.25mi to the north of the centre of Balatonmagyaród. A **bridge** with wooden arches leads you to an observation tower.

-MAGYAR KÉPEK Kft

Zalakaros – This extremely popular spa to the south of Kis-Balaton has every facility for tourism and spa (and dental) treatment. It provides a variety of accommodation, hotels, a holiday village, villas and campsites. There are 13 swimming pools, one of which is an indoor pool built by Makovecz. Only the indoor pool is open all year round; the others are open from May to September. Visitors are principally German and Austrian. All the usual facilities of a holiday resort are available to visitors and, if you are lucky, peace and relaxation too.

View of Buda

G. Simeone/PHOTONONSTOP

Budapest

Travellers' addresses

ACCOMMODATION IN BUDAPEST

You can also consult the **Michelin Red Guide Europe**, which offers a selection of hotels in the Hungarian capital. The addresses that we suggest here have been chosen for their setting, location or character. We also mention some guest-houses, called *panziók* (*panzió* in the singular) in Hungarian. These small family-style hotels are often located in a quiet district away from the centre, and are good value overall.

The establishments chosen have been classified into three categories to cover all budgets. Given the fluctuations of the Hungarian currency (the forint), many places give their prices in euro. These prices generally include breakfast. The **Budget** category suggests hotels that offer a double room in season for up to €61. Every room has a bath or shower and a TV. The furnishings may be a little outmoded. The **Moderate** category proposes hotels that are more central, with prices for a double room in high season substantially higher than €61. On the **Expensive** list you will find charming, well-appointed hotels, with prices that naturally match the setting and facilities.

Hotels and panziók

BUDGET

Papillon Hotel – *Buda II., Rózsahegy utca 3/b.* ☎ *212 4750. Fax 212 4003. 20 rooms between €30 and €61.* On Roses Hill, a quiet little hotel, very easy to get to. Breakfast on the terrace.

Noé Hotel – *Buda III., Királyok útja 301.* ☎ *454 0742. Fax 243 9400. 18 rooms between €30 and €40.* 15min drive from the centre. Extremely peaceful location in a park. All the rooms have a view of the Danube. Restaurant. Fully equipped bungalows for rent.

Kék Duna Panzió – *Buda III., Nánási út 1/c.* ☎*/Fax 240 5040. 16 rooms between €47 and €61.* Quiet, pool in summer. Garden and barbecue. Small restaurant downstairs.

Vénusz Hotel – *Buda III., Dózsa György utca 2-4.* ☎ *368 7252. Fax 368 6407. 77 rooms between €45 and €50 (breakfast €3).* Not far from the Aquincum Roman ruins, this motel-like establishment has simple rooms on the ground floor. Pool and sauna.

MODERATE

Délibáb Hotel – *Pest VI., Délibáb utca 35.* ☎ *479 8600. Fax 342 8153. 34 rooms between €56 and €76.* In a former Eszterházy mansion and very close to Heroes Square and the M 1 underground station, 15min from the centre of Pest. Rooms a little old-fashioned but clean. Noisy on the street side despite double glazing. Good price in view of the location.

Korona Panzió – *Buda XI., Sasadi utca 127.* ☎ *319 1255. Fax 319 5734. 8 rooms between €56 and €62.* A pleasant place far from the noise of the city. Garden, meals available.

Kapu Panzió – *Buda XI., Ugron Gábor 9.* ☎ *319 2985. Fax 319 2986. 10 rooms between €52 and €62 and a suite with Roman bath.* An elegant house with a large wooden gate, in a restful setting. Sauna. Terrace. Private garage. Small dining room.

Beatrix Panzió – *Buda II., Széher út 3.* ☎ *275 0550. Fax 394 3750. 18 rooms between €55 and €65.* The spot is quiet, surrounded by greenery. Garden.

Queen Mary – *Buda XII. Béla Király utca 47.* ☎ *274 4000. Fax 395 8377. 22 rooms between €38 and €55.* In the peace and quiet of the Buda Hills. Rooms with a little terrace and a view. Sauna. Car park.

Centrál Hotel – *Pest VI., Munkácsy utca 5-7.* ☎ *321 2000. Fax 322 9445. 42 rooms between €24 and €72.* A small building in the quiet embassy district. Spacious rooms. Restaurant.

Radio Inn – *Pest VI., Benczúr utca 19.* ☎ *322 0237. Fax 322 8284. Rooms between €55 and €72.* In the quiet embassy district. Every room (nice old furnishings) has a kitchenette. Pleasant flower garden in summer.

Panzió Gold Hotel – *Pest XIV., Ungvár utca 45.* ☎*/Fax 252 0470. 24 rooms between €56 and €70.* Far from the hectic pace of central Budapest. Family atmosphere. Private car park.

City Panzió Mátyás – *Pest V., Március 15 tér 8.* ☎ *338 4711. Fax 317 9086. 56 rooms between €64 and €84.* Excellent location, just next to Elizabeth Bridge. Comfortable rooms with standard furnishings, noisy on the street side. An added extra is that breakfast is served downstairs in the cellar, which is decorated with historical frescoes from the Mátyás Pince restaurant.

City Panzió Pilvax – *Pest V., Pilvax köz 1-3. ☎ 266 7660. Fax 317 6396. 32 rooms between €64 and €84.* Also very well located near the pedestrian district.

City Panzió Ring – *Pest XIII., Szent István krt. 22. ☎ 340 5450. Fax 340 4884. 39 rooms between €64 and €84.* Located on the Main Boulevard. Same level of comfort as the two entries above (same owners, same furnishings). Choose a room looking out onto the little street.

EXPENSIVE

Nemzeti Hotel – *Pest VIII., József körút 4. ☎ 477 9310. Fax 314 0019. 76 rooms between €105 and €135.* Very well located on the Main Boulevard, a stone's throw from the Blaha Lujza tér underground station. A building with a beautiful blue façade. The inside has been very carefully renovated. Art Nouveau decor. Light and airy rooms entirely revamped, refurnished and redecorated. Very beautiful dining room.

Gellért Hotel – *Buda XI., Szent Gellért tér 1. ☎ 385 2200. Fax 466 6631. 233 rooms between €125 and €204.* A monument, an old luxury hotel with early-20C decor and, best of all, free access to the thermal baths and pool (robes provided). A dream come true?

Art'Otel – *Buda I., Bem rakpart 16-19. ☎ 487 9487. Fax 487 9488. 165 rooms between €125 and €143.* A cross between a hotel and an art gallery. The ensemble includes four attractively restored Baroque houses. The rooms are spacious and, like the rest of the establishment, have been decorated with works by Donald Sultan, a contemporary American artist. View over the Danube, Parliament or Castle Hill.

Youth hostels and Campsites

The Travellers' Youth Hostel chain has a certain number of youth hostels in Budapest. To reserve: *XII., Dózsa György út 152. ☎ 329 8644. Fax 320 8425. Internet: www.travellers-hotels.com and E-mail: travellers@mail.matav.hu*

Citadella Hotel – *Buda XI., Citadella sétány. ☎ 466 5794. Fax 386 05 05. 17 rooms between €41 and €47.* Inside the Citadel fortifications at the top of Mt Gellért.

Museum Youth Guest House – *Pest VIII., Mikszáth Kálmán tér 4. ☎ 318 9508. Fax 266 8876. Rooms with 2, 4 or 6 beds from €20 per bed.* 10min on foot from the Danube and not far from the National Museum.

Best Hostel – *Pest VI., Podmaniczky utca 27 (ring doorbell at n° 33). ☎ 332 4934. Fax 269 2926. Rooms with 2, 4, 7 or 8 beds. Between €15 and €20 per bed.* Very good location on the corner of the Main Boulevard. Well equipped. Bicycle hire.

Zugligeti Niche Campsite – *Buda XII., Zugligeti út 101. ☎ 200 8346. Open all year.* In a good, shady spot in the Buda Hills.

Római Campsite – *Buda III., Szentendrei út 189. ☎ 368 6260. Fax 250 0426. Open all year.* A "small town" with pool. Bungalow rental.

Mikro Campsite – *Buda III., Rozgonyi Piroska utca 19. ☎ 240 1072. Open May to October.* Small, shady campsite.

Guesthouses

Ibusz – *Pest V., Ferenciek tere 10. ☎ 317 3500. Fax 338 4987.*

Budapest Tourist – *Pest V., Roosevelt tér 5. ☎ 317 3535.*

RESTAURANTS IN BUDAPEST

The restaurants described below have been chosen for their setting, atmosphere, typically Hungarian food, or their unusual character. We have established three categories: **Budget** (allow 2 500Ft for a meal, drinks included), **Moderate** (between 2 500Ft and 5 000Ft), and **Expensive** (prices substantially over 5 000Ft). For a selection based particularly on culinary criteria, consult the **Michelin Red Guide Europe**.

Don't be surprised in restaurants if they ask you what you would like to drink almost as soon as you sit down. It is customary to order a drink before choosing your dishes.

BUDGET

Fakanál – *Pest IX., Vásárcsarnok. Closed in the evening and on Sundays.* A pleasant corner in the upper gallery of the main market, where you can have something decent to eat, quickly. Self service: cold dishes on a trolley; hot dishes on a rustic, cast iron stove.

Kádár Étkezde – *Pest VII., Klauzál tér 9. Open from 11.30am to 3.30pm.* The prices here defy all competition. Situated in the heart of the Jewish district, this restaurant has a regular clientele. It is very simple, almost like a canteen, but there is a wide choice of good food, and the place is friendly. You help yourself from the bottle of soda water on the table and pay for it by the glass. You pay at the cashdesk as you leave and then return to tip the waitress. There are photos of famous customers on the wall, including Italian actor Marcello Mastroianni as a young man.

Kispipa Vendéglő – *Pest VII., Akácfa utca 38. ☎ 342 2587.* The menu is in several languages with an almost unbelievable choice of dishes. Bistro decor, old posters on the wall and a piano playing in the evening. You can try the game, foie gras, fish from Lake Balaton and good desserts, all at very reasonable prices with Hungarian wine included.

Fészek – *Pest VII. Kertész utca 36. ☎ 322 6043.* The proprietor, menu and prices are the same as at the previous restaurant, but with an entirely different decor. There is a club atmosphere, since this used to be a club for artistes only. A large and rather dim dining room and an inner courtyard that is very pleasant in summer.

Mérleg Vendéglő – *Pest V., Mérleg utca 6. ☎ 317 6911.* Rather crowded, especially at noon when nearby office-workers come here for lunch. Simple Hungarian cooking, a good choice and reasonable prices.

MODERATE

Rondella – *Pest V., Régi posta utca 4.* This is in a stone-walled cellar, very cool in summer. It has a rustic feel and a varied menu at reasonable prices. The wine is served in an unusual sort of fountain.

Fatál – *Pest V., Váci utca 67 (entrance Pintér utca). ☎ 266 2607.* People queue to get in, probably because of the restaurant's atmosphere and originality. The decor consists of a long vaulted cellar and solid wood tables, while the food (copious and filling) is served on wooden boards (*fatál* in Hungarian) or directly from the stoves. For large appetites...

Sir Lancelot – *Pest VI., Podmaniczky utca 11. ☎ 302 4456.* Return to the Middle Ages in this stone cellar, with heavy tables and rustic benches. Musicians playing Renaissance music in the evening add to the atmosphere. Abundant food (grilled meat or chicken, for example) served on wooden boards by damsels and squires in period costumes. The tableware is in keeping with the style.

Múzeum – *Pest VIII., Múzeum körút 12. ☎ 338 4221.* A famous restaurant next to the National Museum. Stylish. Very good for a dinner by candlelight in a pre-1940s style setting; effective ceramics and mirrors.

Bagolyvár – *Pest XIV., Állatkerti út 2. ☎ 343 0217.* An annexe of the neighbouring Gundel, but at prices that are substantially more affordable. Beautiful dining room with wooden ceiling. Traditional cooking with carefully prepared dishes. In the evenings a cimbalom-player will add a certain charm to your meal.

Cyrano – *Pest V., Kristóf tér 7-8. ☎ 266 3096.* If you saw the film *Cyrano de Bergerac*, you will perhaps recognise the chandelier in the middle of the metal-and-ceramic Gaudiesque decor. The food is delicious, the prices reasonable.

Horváth Gösser Restaurant – *Buda I., Krisztina tér 3. ☎ 375 7573.* This restaurant is favoured by former football player Ferenc Puskás (star of Réal Madrid and the 1958 Hungarian football team). His table is reserved and there are several photos on the walls. Food is reasonable and prices not exorbitant.

Régi Sipos Halászkert – *Buda III., Lajos utca 46. ☎ 368 6480.* Traditional cooking. A good place for fish-lovers. Gypsy music to accompany your meal.

Csalogány Étterem – *Buda I., Csalogány utca 26. ☎ 212 3795.* Menu in several languages and the food is good. Very good value for money.

Remíz – *Buda II., Budakeszi út 5. ☎ 275 1396.* Near the tramway depot, this restaurant offers quality Hungarian cuisine, such as filet of fogas (pikeperch), roast goose, sautéed foie gras with apples, and succulent pastries. Good wine list. In summer, choose a table out in the garden.

Náncsi Néni – *Buda II., Ördögárok utca 80. ☎ 397 2742.* In the Buda Hills, far from the centre but in a quiet and cool setting. Good traditional home cooking, accompanied by a little accordion music. Very pleasant garden in summer. Reservations advisable.

EXPENSIVE

Gundel – *Pest XIV., Állatkerti út 2. ☎ 321 3550.* The setting, the atmosphere, the summer garden and the music, all contribute to the restaurant's renown. The prices match the high standard of cuisine.

Alabárdos – *Buda I., Országház utca 2. ☎ 356 0851.* Vaulted Gothic dining room decorated with weapons, armour and shields (the restaurant's name means Beefeater). Grilled medallion of foie gras, poultry, game and various meats. The menu is mouth-watering, the food delicious.

Living in Budapest

By air – International and domestic flights arrive at Ferihegy International Airport (24km/15mi south-east of the capital), terminal A or B. The best way to get to the centre of Budapest is to use the **Airport Minibus Service** shuttles (white Ford vehicles seating eight to nine people, with Airport Minibus written on them). Go to the LRI Airport Passenger Service counter and indicate where you would like to go, be it a hotel or a private address. You will pay about 1 800Ft (Return trip 3 300Ft) and then you must wait for the driver to call out the name of the hotel or address. There is a 15% discount if you buy a **Budapest Kártya** (Budapest Card) at the same time.

For the return journey, you can ask your hotel reception to arrange for the Airport Minibus. You can also reserve it yourself from a private home or a public phone box. It is recommended to reserve the day before the return trip. The shuttle will arrive at the exact time and place requested. It will cost you the same price for the return. However, if you buy a return ticket when you arrive, you will receive a discount on the total (ticket valid for three months).

Reservations: ☎ 296 8555, Fax 296 8993.

Car hire – International firms at the airport and in the city:

– Europcar: District IX, Üllői út 60-62, ☎ 313 14 92,
– Avis: District V, Szervita tér 8, ☎ 318 4240,
– Hertz: District V, Apáczai Csere János u. 4, ☎ 296 0997 or 266 4344,
– Budget: District 12, Krisztina körút 41-43, ☎ 214 0420.

TOURIST INFORMATION

Tourinform: Tourist office– Pest main office: Sütő utca 2. ☎ 438 8080; open 8am-8pm. Vörösmarty tér: open 24hr a day. There is also a Tourinform counter at Ferihegy International Airport 2. Other tourist offices in Pest include Nyugati pályaudvar (West Station) and Liszt Ferenc tér. In Buda, there is one in Szentháromság tér.

Internet: www.budapestinfo.hu

Vista Travel Agency – Andrássy út 1, H-1061 Budapest. All kinds of tourist-oriented goods and services: trips, excursions, maps, guides, luggage etc.

Street names – To find your way around Budapest, you should be aware that the capital is divided into 23 districts, indicated in Roman numerals on maps, in addresses or on street signs. Districts I and XI (right bank) comprise the Buda Castle District and Mt Gellért; districts V, VI, VII and VIII (left bank) comprise the most popular parts of Pest. An address is written in the following way:

V. Sütő utca 2. The Roman numeral indicates the district, followed by the name of the street and the number. When it involves the name of a person, the first name comes after the surname, such as Clark Ádám tér, Liszt Ferenc utca.

A few useful terms to help you find your way around:
utca (abbreviation, 'u.') means street
út = road
körút (abbreviation, *'krt.'*) means boulevard
tér or *tere* means square
rakpart means quay
híd means bridge
sétány means lane
sugárút means avenue
köz means passage
pályaudvar means station

Post code – The two middle figures in the address indicate the district. For instance, 1062 Budapest means that the address is in District VI. 1113 Budapest is in District XI etc.

Dates – In several European countries the date is written as follows: 10/12/03 for 10 December 2003. The Hungarians write 2003/12/10, the year coming before the month and the day.

Budapest Kártya/Budapest Card – This tourist card is recommended for those wishing to visit the museums and use the public transport systems without restriction, inside city limits (further afield, you will have to present your card and buy a ticket supplement at your point of departure). Among the services that come with the card:

– discount for the Airport Minibus,

– free unlimited use of the public transport system (underground, bus, trolleybus, tramways, HÉV suburban trains),

/DR

– free admittance to most of the museums and cultural spots,

– discounts for certain performances, reductions in some shops, restaurants, cafés, pubs and swimming pools

– discounts on some car hire and bicycle hire on Margaret Island (Margit-sziget).

The *Budapest Kártya* (card) is on sale at the airport, at Tourinform, in the major underground stations, travel agencies and wherever you see the card's sticker. Price: 3 400Ft, valid for two days; 4 000Ft, valid for three days. Do not forget to sign it. A small guide is given to each purchaser, describing all the advantages that come with the card.

Publications – The ***Budapest Panorama*** brochure (available free from the Tourinform offices and in most hotels), published every month in five languages (English, German, Italian, Russian and French), gives the programme of cultural events, shows, the addresses of stores, restaurants, museums, religious services etc. The free, monthly brochures, ***Programme in Hungary*** (in German and English), ***Where Budapest*** and ***Budapest Pocket Guide*** (in English only) also give a great deal of practical information.

Brochures such as ***Budapest Guide, Budapest Baths, Budapest Museums***, as well as a map of the city are available free of charge in several languages at the tourist office (Tourinform Sütő utca 2). Night owls may ask for the ***Budapest Night Life Guide***.

The magazine ***Budapest Week*** can be bought at kiosks. If you understand Hungarian, buy *Pesti Műsor*, a very complete entertainment guide.

Banks, currency exchange, credit cards – The banks are generally open Monday to Friday from 8am to 4pm. Several foreign exchange bureaux can be found in the Váci utca district; rates can vary, so shop around and ask for a receipt. Cash dispensers or ATMs where you can withdraw money with a credit card are marked *Bankomat*. Avoid changing money in the hotels, as the rate of exchange is not good. You are strongly advised against changing money in the street with people who illegally offer you attractive rates.

Credit card payment is quite customary.

Coins: 1, 2, 5, 10, 20, 50, 100 and 200Ft. **Banknotes**: 200, 500, 1 000, 2 000, 5 000, 10 000 and 20 000Ft.

Museums and sights – Most museums are closed on Mondays. In season, opening hours are from 10am to 6pm.

Shopping – Stores are open from 10am to 6pm (8pm on Thursday and 1pm on Saturday). Food shops are often open from 7am to 7pm (3pm on Saturday). There are also small non-stop food shops open 24hr a day (good in an emergency to buy a bottle of mineral water, a beer or a snack).

M. Guillot/MICHELIN

Media – The BBC World Service can be picked up on short-wave radio and both BBC and CNN are available on television. The major British and American newspapers are sold in kiosks and hotels in the town centre. British newspapers and other literature can be consulted at The British Council, Benczúr utca 26, H-1068 Budapest. ☎ 00 36 1 478 4700, Fax 00 36 1 342 5728/352 8779. E-mail: information@britishcouncil.hu

Post (Posta) – Post offices are open from 8am to 6pm.

The **Main Post Office**, Petőfi Sándor utca 13-15, is generally open daily from 8am to 8pm (3pm Saturday), except Sundays.

There are also offices at the West Station (Nyugati pályaudvar) and East Station (Keleti pályaudvar).

Postboxes are easy to recognise. They are often red and decorated with a hunting horn.

Useful telephone numbers and addresses

Emergencies – 104, 112
Police – 107, 112
International information – 199
British Council – VI., Benczúr utca, ☎ 478 4700
Lost and found/Tafált tárgyak – VII., Akácfa utca 18, ☎ 322 6613
Day and night services:
Doctors – ☎ 200 0100. II., Kapy utca 49/B.
Chemists/Gyógyszertár – II., Frankel Leó út 22; III., Szentendrei ut 2/A; IV., Pozsonyi út 19; VII., Szigony utca 2; IX., Boráros tér ; X., Liget tér; XII., Alkotás utca 1/B; XIV., Örs vezér tere.

Telephone – Public telephone booths work with coins (10, 20, 50 and 100Ft) and cards. The cards are sold in post offices, kiosks or State-licensed tobacconists' *(Trafik)*, underground stations, and most hotels. Price: 900Ft for 50 units, 1 800Ft for 120 units.

To telephone abroad, dial 00 + the relevant country code (44 for the United Kingdom, 1 for the USA and Canada, 61 for Australia, 64 for New Zealand etc).

To telephone from inside Budapest, dial the seven-digit number (without the prefix for the city).

To telephone from Budapest to the provinces, dial 06 + the city code + your correspondent's number.

GETTING AROUND BUDAPEST

As in most big cities, traffic and parking problems are such that it is better to leave your vehicle in a car park or garage, and go on foot, by public transport or taxi.

Parking – Fee-paying car parks often look like a piece of waste ground between two buildings. The attendant who sells the tickets is usually in an old booth or a caravan.

The multi-storey car parks are quite different. The main ones are the following:
– District V: Szervita tér; Türr István utca 5 (pay booth and exit at Aranykéz utca 4-6)
– District VII: Nyár utca 20
– District VIII: corner of Üllői út and Baross utca; Futó utca 52.

For parking meters, have 5, 10, 20, 50 or 100Ft to hand (3hr of parking). If you run over time or park in an unauthorised space, you may well have your car towed away or immobilised with a wheel clamp... Complications to be avoided.

Taxis – There are lots of taxis, either company owned or independent. Negotiate the price for the trip before you start and keep an eye on the meter. The possibility of being cheated should definitely not be excluded. The following taxi firms have good reputations, and their names appear on the car or on the indicator lamp on the roof:
– Főtaxi ☎ 222 2222
– Rádiótaxi ☎ 377 7777
– City Taxi ☎ 211 1111
– BudaTaxi ☎ 233 3333
– 6x6 ☎ 266 6666
– Teletaxi ☎ 355 5555

Public transport – *Map on the inside back cover of this guide.* This is run by one company, BKV, and generally functions from 4.30am to 11pm. The main transfer stations are:
– Buda: Batthyány tér and Moszkva tér
– Pest: Deák tér and Blaha Lujza tér.

Tickets – *Also see Budapest Kártya above.* It is important to emphasise that tickets cannot be bought on buses, tramways or trolleybuses. They can only be bought in underground stations (indicated by the letter **M**), at kiosks, and at the BKV counters at large crossroads and terminals. They are bought singly (about 100Ft) or in books of 10 or 20. They need to be punched (red or orange machines) before starting your trip on each underground line, HÉV train or on the buses, trolleybuses or tramways. There are also several worthwhile formulas for unlimited travel inside Budapest's city limits; if you wish to go beyond, you must buy a ticket supplement at your departure point and display your card:
– 3 or 7-day cards: between 1 600Ft and 1 950Ft.
– 14-day card: for those under 25, around 2 500Ft.
Do not forget to sign your name, otherwise you may be fined on the spot.
There are also cards for 7, 14 or 30 days' travel (between 1 700Ft and 3 500Ft). You will need a photograph.

Underground – There are three underground lines in Budapest: the M 1, M 2 and M 3. The lines are represented by different colours: the M 1 is yellow, the M 2 is red and the M 3 is blue. The M 1 is called the little underground (three little carriages) and was the first line to open on the Continent. It practically follows the same route as Andrássy út, linking Budapest city centre to City Park.

The doors open and close automatically. Each station is announced beforehand in each carriage. All the lines pass through Deák tér. **To change lines or direction you must punch a new ticket**. Tickets are checked often, and the inspectors do not wear uniforms but can be recognised by their red armbands. If you are fined, make sure you are given a receipt.

In the world of the underground, two signs are important: *bejárat*/entrance and especially *kijárat*/exit. The lines are indicated by their colour, and their destination is on each corresponding platform.

Some stations are well below ground level; the escalators are steep and go rather fast, so be careful not to lose your balance as you get on or off.

Buses and trolleybuses – Buses are blue and trolleybuses red. The buses with black numbers pull up at every stop, those with red numbers are express buses. The names of the stations are indicated at each stop. The times between pick-ups are marked on the blue panels at every stop (the wait is generally from 5 to 15min depending on the time of day). There are 15 night lines.
Sometimes the stops are announced; press the button over the door to request one.

Tramways *(Villamos)* – The yellow cars (with one or two rare exceptions) travel all over the capital, in every direction. The network is very good and very practical. The stops are sometimes announced, and there are two night lines.

The lines most used by tourists, serving several tourist destinations or districts are:

– lines n°s 4 and 6, which follow the Main Boulevard to Moszkva tér,
– line n° 2 , which runs along the Danube on the Pest side from Közvágóhíd to Jászai Mari tér (near the bridge and Margaret Island),
– line n° 19, which runs along the Danube on the Buda side up to Batthyány tér.

M. Guillot/MICHELIN

HÉV – These three letters designate the suburban trains serving districts beyond the capital's city limits. The lines are the following (the first name indicates the name of the departure station in Buda or Pest):
– Batthyány tér-Szentendre,
– Batthyány-tér-Békásmegyer,
– Örs vezér tere (M 2 underground line terminus)-Gödöllő,
– Örs vezér tere-Cinkota,
– Vágóhíd-Tököl,
– Boráros tér-Csepel.

Budapest by sightseeing bus – Several companies offer this service in various languages:
– holders of a Budapest Kártya receive a 50% discount with Ibusz Travel/Budapest Sightseeing, V. Erzsébet tér, ☎ 318 1139/1043,
– Budatours, V. Roosevelt tér, ☎ 353 0550 or 331 1585 or 312 4037,
– Queenybus, V. Erzsébet tér, ☎ 246 4755,
– Cityrama, ☎ 302 4382.
– N-Bus, ☎ 369 9089.

Budapest by boat – Another way to discover the banks of Buda and Pest is to go on a trip on the Danube.
– Holders of a Budapest Kártya receive a 24% discount on Mahart trips: the Danube Bella and Danube Legenda boats leave from Quay n° 6 Vigadó tér, ☎ 317 2203.

You may also feel like a cruise with dinner on board and gypsy folk entertainment. Boat trips on the river operate from May to August, Thursday to Sunday, from 9am to 5pm. They link Boráros tér to Római Fürdő and stop at several places.

Budapest by bicycle – Good luck. Ask for the Kerékpárral Budapesten map at Tourinform. This indicates recommended itineraries, bicycle routes, hire and repair shops.
Margaret Island (Margit-sziget) is closed to cars and ideal for getting your legs into shape.

Chair-lift (Libegő) – No, you are not seeing things; the chair-lift is real although surprising in a city like Budapest. Take the n° 158 bus from Csaba utca near Moszkva tér, get off at the Zugliget terminus, and take off to Mt János. A 15min trip in absolute quiet to a difference in height of 262m/859ft. The view is impressive.

Flight over Budapest in a hot-air balloon – Depending on weather conditions, a 1hr flight (maximum two people) to discover the city from above. A minibus service takes passengers to the take-off site and brings them back.

Reservation: **Sup-Air Ballon Club** ☎ 322 0015.

THE BATHS

Gellért – *Buda XI., Szent Gellért tér 1. ☎ 466 6166. Outside pool; in summer, open daily from 6am to 7pm, indoor pool from 6am to 5pm; in winter, indoor pool (swimming cap provided) open Monday to Friday from 6am to 7pm, Saturday and Sunday from 6am to 5pm; steam baths: open Monday to Friday from 6.30am to 6pm, Saturday and Sunday from 6am to 5pm. Bus nos 7 and 86, tramways nos 18, 19, 47 and 49.* The most sumptuous baths of all, these have marvellous Art Deco decoration. Classified a historical monument, Gellért is part of the Gellért Hotel. Its hot waters (37°C/98.6°F), slightly acid and radioactive, are excellent for treating rheumatism. The indoor pool alone, with its marble columns and lion heads spouting water, is worth the trip. The large outdoor pool, built in 1918, was Central Europe's first artificial wave pool.

Király – *Buda II., Fő utca 84. ☎ 315 3000. Open from 6.30am to 7pm, Tuesday, Thursday and Saturday for women only, and Monday, Wednesday and Friday for men. M 2 Batthyány tér, bus nos 60, 86.* The most Turkish of Budapest's baths, picturesque with its green cupola decorated with a Turkish crescent.

Széchenyi – *Pest XIV., Állatkerti körút 11. ☎ 321 0310. Thermal baths open Monday to Friday from 6am to 7pm, Saturday and Sunday from 6am to 12pm; pool open 1 June to 30 September, daily from 6am to 7pm and 1 October to 30 April, Monday to Friday from 6am to 7pm and Saturday and Sunday from 6am to 2pm . M 1 Széchenyi fürdő, bus nos 4 (red), 20, 30 and 105, trolleybus nos 70, 72, 75 and 79.* In the middle of winter, when the pools are surrounded with ice and snow, you can bathe while having a friendly game of chess (water at 38°C/100.4°F) in a cloud of steam.

Rudas – *Buda I., Döbrentei tér 9. ☎ 356 1322. Open Monday to Saturday from 6am to 6pm, Sunday from 6am to 1pm. Bus nos 7, 7A and 86, tramways nos 18 and 19.* These baths date from the time of the Turkish domination and have separate sections for men and women. The water temperature in the pools varies from 28°C/82.4°F to 40°C/104°F. The swimming pool is mixed.

Palatinus Strand – *XII., Margitsziget. Bus n° 26, tramways nos 4 or 6.* An immense complex including thermal baths and pools. Overcrowded in summer.

SHOPPING

Value-added tax reimbursement – This does not apply to objets d'art or antiques. The value of articles purchased in Hungary must be over 50 000Ft. Be sure to keep your receipts or bills. For payments by credit card, reimbursements will be made by bank transfer. Cash reimbursements are made by various offices of the Ibusz agency (in the city: at Pest Ferenciek tere), at the airport, Keleti station and border posts. For information contact the **Hungary Global Refund**, II., Bég utca 3-5, ☎ 212 4906.

Shopping centres

Mammut – *Buda II., Lövőház utca 2-6. ☎ 345 8020. Close to Moszkva tér (bus, trams, underground). Open seven days a week.* Statue of a mammoth in front. Over 180 shops on several levels around a large central patio. On the top floor you have a choice between several types of restaurant: fast food, cafeteria, Greek food, fish, pizzeria, Asian food etc. There is also a games room and a gym.

West End City Center – *Pest VI., Váci út 1-3. ☎ 238 7777. Open seven days a week.* An immense glass complex set off by cascades and fountains near the West Station. There are some 400 shops, restaurants serving Hungarian or foreign fare, and also a Hilton Hotel. Major brand names in clothes, audiovisual goods, decoration etc. Rooftop garden.

Duna Plaza – *Pest XIII., Váci út 178. ☎ 465 4220. Open Monday to Saturday 10am to 9pm. M 3 underground, Gyöngyösi utca station and bus n° 4.* A shopping centre with avant-garde architecture, consisting of 150 shops (including Central Europe's largest Virgin Megastore), numerous restaurants and bars (open seven days a week). The centre also has leisure facilities (skating rink, electronic games room, cinemas, billiards and bowling alley).

Pólus Center – *Pest XV., Szentmihály út 131. Open Monday to Friday from 9am to 7pm (5pm Saturday, 3pm Sunday). Bus nos 7 or 130 from Nyugati pályaudvar and Keleti pályaudvar.* A shopping complex with restaurants, cinemas, games, skating rink, bowling alley etc.

Embroidery

Beautiful examples of folk art such as Kalocsa embroideries, Matyó patterned blouses, Sárköz fabrics (blue cloth) and carved wooden objects can be purchased from the numerous stands set up on Vigadó tér, in the famous main market (Vásárcsarnok), in the shops in Budapest town centre and especially on Váci utca or in Castle District.

Folkart Centrum – *Pest V., Váci utca 14.* A great many traditional art objects and embroideries (men's and women's clothing, table linen etc).

Népművészeti Kft – *Pest V., Régiposta utca 12, Budapest V. ☎ 185 143.* Kalocsa embroideries, typical traditional objects and produce.

Herend and Zsolnay porcelain, Ajka crystal

Herendi Porcelán – *Pest V., József Nádór tér 11. M 1 underground, Vörösmarty tér terminus.* Sumptuous pieces with prices to match. A visual delight.

Ajka Kristály – *Pest XIII., Szent István krt. 18. ☎ 340 5083. Open Monday to Friday from 10am to 6pm and Saturday from 10am to 1pm.* Black ceramics, 'Miska' ceramic jugs.

Zsolnay Márkabolt – *Pest V., Kigyó utca 4. ☎ 318 3712. Open Monday to Friday from 10am to 6pm, Saturday from 9am to 1pm.* Magnificent shop with splendid Zsolnay porcelain exhibited in the windows.

Herendi Márkabolt – *Pest V., Kigyó utca 5. ☎ 118 3439. Open Monday to Friday from 10am to 6pm and Saturday from 9am to 1pm.* Very beautiful choice of Herend porcelain table services and figurines.

Kínál kft. – *Pest XIII., Nyugati tér 4. ☎ 131 51 37. Open from Monday to Saturday from 8am to 7pm and Saturday from 8am to 2pm.* A wide choice of shapes and colours.

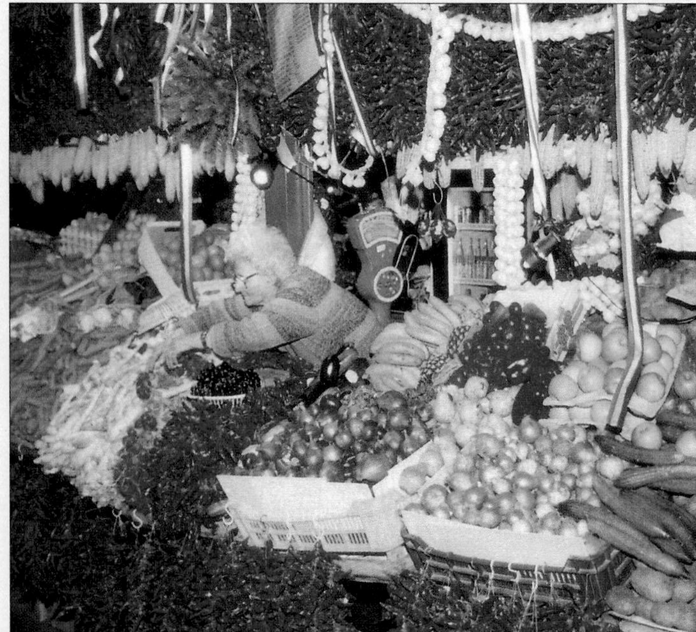

/MAGYAR KÉPEK Kft

Wines, food products

We suggest you take some Tokay (Tokaji) Aszú home with you *(see Introduction: Food and drink)*. Other typical products: Pick salami, foie gras, apricot or cherry brandy and of course the famous Kalocsa or Szeged paprika to be found in all its various forms.

Magyar Borok Háza – *Buda I., Szentháromság tér 6. ☎ 212 1031. Open Monday to Saturday from noon to 8pm.* Here you can taste and purchase 470 types of wine from the 22 Hungarian wine-growing regions. Explanations are provided to help visitors understand the Tokaji Aszú wine-making process and discover some of the Egri Bikavér (Bull's Blood) cellars.

J.-C. Saturnin/MICHELIN

Flea markets galore!

Wine City – *Pest V., Párizsi utca 1. ☎ 118 26 83.* Wide choice of good quality wines (about 400), from all the country's wine-producing regions. Small wine museum and wine tasting in the cellar.

Menedzser Shop – *Pest V., Váci utca 74 (corner of Szerb utca).* A wide choice of Hungarian and foreign wines. Wine tasting.

Marcipán – *Pest V., Párizsi utca 3. ☎ 117 3643. Open Monday to Saturday from 10am to 7pm.* For lovers of sweets and ice cream, but marzipan in all its forms and colours has pride of place.

Markets

Vásárcsarnok (Main Market) – *Pest IX., Vámház krt. Open Monday to Friday from 6am to 7pm and Saturday from 6am to 1pm.* Famous covered market that was inaugurated in 1897 and has been magnificently renovated. The ground floor is filled with food shops (butcher-delicatessens, fruit and vegetables, garlands of paprika, garlic and onions, as well as foie gras, salamis, wines and spirits). Upstairs on the first floor the gallery has numerous stands with local crafts and embroidery (wide choice of tablecloths and napkins), a few of which deserve a special mention: Játék (K 10), wooden toys; Fajka Erzsébet (K 15), glass objects and wooden chess games; Forrayné Ancsa (K 16/A), magnificent dried flower compositions; (K 23) wine by the glass.

Ecseri piac – *Pest XIX., Nagykőrösi út 156. Take the ordinary 54 bus from Boráros tér, or the red 54 bus from the Határ út underground station. Open Monday to Friday until 4pm, Saturday until 1pm.* A **flea market** where you can find just about everything, as flea markets should be. If you are looking for a spare part you stand a chance of finding it, unless your attention is caught by an old phonograph, an icon, a medal of the Order of Lenin, or a Red Army cap. Go on Saturday, when the place draws people from all over.

Bookshops

Litea – *Buda I., Hess András tér 4.* A pleasant place in the Castle District. You can look at the books and magazines here, and have some tea. CDs also for sale.

Király – *Buda II., Fő utca 79. ☎ 214 09 72. Open Monday to Friday from 9am to 6pm and Saturday from 10am to 5pm.* A French and English bookshop selling all sorts of books, as well as newpapers and magazines. A friendly, welcoming place.

Párizsi udvar – *Pest V., Petőfi Sándor utca 2. ☎ 118 3136. Open Monday to Friday from 9am to 7pm and Saturday from 10am to 1pm.* Wide choice of travel guides, photography books about Budapest and Hungary, foreign language books (English, German, Italian and French).

Írók boltja – *Pest VI., Andrássy út 45. ☎ 322 1645.* In this bookshop most of the works are in Hungarian (small international magazine department). You can leaf through chosen books while you have a cup of tea or coffee in the small lounge area.

Libri – *Pest V., Váci utca 32.* This bookshop in the pedestrian area has numerous foreign books for sale.

Könyvesház – *Pest XIII., Váci utca 19.* Immense general bookstore. Newspapers and magazines (Hungarian and international) and music department (CDs, cassettes).

Pont – *Pest V., Mérleg utca 6.* Well supplied with books and guides on Hungary and Budapest. Small lounge area to flick through books in peace.

Corvina – *Pest V., Kossuth Lajos utca 4.* The Corvina publishers' bookshop, on the third floor of a building. Numerous foreign titles.

M. Guillot/MICHELIN

Music

Zeneszalon – *Pest V., Vörösmarty tér.* Wide choice of CDs and cassettes of all types.

Amadeus CD Szalon – *Pest V., Duna korzó.* Wide choice of classical music CDs.

Rózsavölgyi – *Pest V., Szervita tér 5.* CDs, sheet music and cassettes.

CAFÉS, TEA SHOPS

Budapest and its art of living is also the art of drinking tea or coffee and savouring succulent pastries. There is nothing like a *cukrászda* (Hungarian for a pastry shop-cum-tea shop); this will be a memorable experience.

Gerbeaud – *Pest V., Vörösmarty tér 7.* The most famous tea shop, bought in 1884 by Émile Gerbeaud, the famous Swiss confectioner. His portrait hangs in one of the rooms. Very popular with tourists from the world over. A real institution. Terrace open in summer.

Ruszwurm – *Buda I., Szentháromság utca 3l.* With its Biedermayer decor and its *Krémes* specialities, this is one of the oldest and most popular tea shops in Hungary. Tourists often queue here for a table in the charming little tea room.

Kid-Kervella/HOA QUI

Gerbeaud tea-room

Angelika – *Buda I., Batthyány tér 7. Open Monday to Saturday from 10am to 11pm.* On the banks of the Danube in the Buda district, whether on the terrace on a fine summer's day or inside in one of the tastefully decorated rooms, you can enjoy one of the numerous pastries offered, including a house speciality: *Angelika torta* (a sort of chocolate and vanilla layer cake).

Gellért Hotel – *Buda XI., Szent Gellért tér 1. ☎ 385 2200.* The Viennese café decor is magnificent, and the cakes are excellent.

Művész – *Pest VI., Andrássy út 29. ☎ 352 1337. Open from 9am to midnight.* A classic, very near the Opera House. Large mirrors and imposing chandeliers decorate the interior. Tempting pastries.

Lukács – *Pest VI., Andrássy út 70.* It is above all for the pastries that you enter this establishment. You will taste the best *Somlói galuska* (soft sponge cake, covered in chocolate and whipped cream) in the city here. Upstairs, there is a fine carved marble fireplace and beautiful crystal chandeliers.

Centrál kávéház – *Pest V., Károlyi Mihály u. 9. ☎ 266 4572. Open seven days a week.* This dates back to 1887. After being closed for many years, it is now reviving the tradition of the Hungarian cafés of yesteryear, although it has adopted modern furnishings on its two floors. One of the ciy's most recent venues, a fashionable place where it is not easy to find a table.

Mozart Café – *Pest VII., Erzsébet krt. 36. ☎ 352 1392. Open Monday to Friday and Sunday from 9am to 11pm and Saturday from 9am to midnight.* Frescoes and a musical ambience will take you into the world of the famous composer. Service by staff in traditional costumes. A haven of peace, quiet and cool on this busy boulevard.

PUBS AND BARS

Beer in Hungarian is *sör*, a normal beer (0.3 litres) *pohár*, a large beer (0.5 litres) *korsó*. Wine is called *bor*.

More and more pubs are flourishing in Budapest and often food is available at any time of the day.

Crazy Café – *Pest VI., Jókai utca 30. ☎ 302 4003. Open daily from 10am to 1am.* This establishment in a long, vaulted cellar has particularly original decoration on the walls, comprising the portraits of 145 famous Hungarians from various fields, including sport, show business and politics. Extensive drinks menu (100 beers and nearly 120 spirits). Theme evenings offered practically every day (concerts, karaoke and variety shows).

Old Man's Music Pub – *Akácfa utca 13. ☎ 322 7645. Open daily from 3pm.* Known for its vaired concerts (among others, blues, country and rock) every evening from 9pm. A lively cosmopolitan clientele.

Miró Café – *Buda I., Úri utca 30. ☎ 375 5458. Open daily from 9am to midnight.* A stone's throw from the Matthias Church, in a tourist area, this unusual-looking bar will take you into the world of the Catalan artist Miró, with its decoration (paintings) and furnishings. Theme evenings are regularly organised.

For Sale Pub – *Pest IX., Vámház krt.* Straw on the floor, a shotgun and two revolvers on the walls, beer on the counter. You could imagine you were in a saloon in the American Wild West. Upstairs, farm tools on the walls, rather like a country barn. Music in the evening draws large crowds.

Beckett's – *Pest V., Bajcsy-Zsilinszky út 72. ☎ 311 1035. Open Monday to Saturday from 11am to 2am and Sunday from noon to 10pm.* Irish pub frequented by a good number of expatriates. Irish beer, of course. For football fans, several television screens broadcast important matches. Live music every evening. Very crowded.

Ball'n Bull – *Pest VIII., Rákóczi út 29. ☎ 338 2429.* This is a place where keen supporters of American sports meet. Matches are broadcast on a giant screen and on TVs. A great many autographs of famous athletes (Pelé, Ali, Joe Montana) decorate the walls. Choice of over 100 cocktails, light food.

Kisrabló Pub – *Pest XI., Zenta utca 3. ☎ 209 1588. Open daily from noon to 2am.* A pub with unusual decor. A short flight of steps takes you into an old ship. There is a room downstairs for those who like dancing (pop music).

Art Café – *Pest V., Vörösmarty tér 1. ☎ 267 0297.* Its immense terrace, with tables and chairs covering part of the square and its location between Váci utca, the most frequented shopping street in the city and Vigadó tér make this one of the liveliest cafés in Budapest. Live music and variety shows on the terrace in fine weather give it a festive air.

Paris Texas Café – *Pest VIII., Ráday utca 22. ☎ 218 0570. Open daily from 10am to 1am.* Far from the noise in the city centre, this bar is also very different from the majority of the other establishments. It is a meeting place for students from the nearby university and the ambience is friendly. The decor (old photos on the walls, old phones, lamps) and the unusual furnishings create a pre-1940s atmosphere.

Le Bistrot Pierrot – *Pest V., Aranykéz utca.* A pleasant little bar in a modern style, with restrained decor. The light food has names like Pierrot Salad or French Bacon.

The Stage – *Pest V., Aranykéz utca 5. ☎ 267 0309. Open Monday to Saturday from 11am to 2am and Sunday from 7pm to 2am.* Large beer bar that operates as a cybercafé. On the first floor, several computers are available for Internet fans.

Fat Mo's – *Pest V., Nyári Pál utca 11. ☎ 267 3199. Open daily from noon to 2am.* Near the Váci utca pedestrian area. The name harks back to the days of Prohibition. A painted wall, some steps and a vaulted cellar with a decor entirely devoted to America in the 1920s. On concert evenings (from 9pm) it is practically impossible to find a table and difficult to even make a path through the crowd. The three bars, including a cocktail bar, get very busy.

Incognito – *Pest VI., Liszt Ferenc tér 3. ☎ 351 9428. Open Monday to Friday from 10am to midnight.* Opposite the Academy of Music, this is the favoured place for the music lovers who frequent the district. In summer it is very pleasant to have a drink on the shady terrace.

Fregatt Pub – *Pest V., Molnár utca 26. ☎ 118 9997. Open daily from 5pm to midnight.* Pub with a decor like the inside of a boat. Wide choice of beers (Irish, Czech and German). Darts games. Musical entertainment at weekends.

Irish Cat Pub – *Pest V., Múzeum körút 41. ☎ 266 4085. Open daily from 11am to 5pm.* Popular and typical Irish pub, in a cellar where beer and whiskey flow. Mostly regulars.

Morrison's – *Pest VI., Révay utca 25. ☎ 269 4060.* Near the Opera House. A British atmosphere in the cellar, perhaps because of the London telephone box.

NIGHTLIFE

Fortuna Revü Bár – *Buda I., Hess András tér 4. ☎ 155 8713. Open daily from 10pm to 5am.* Nightclub and dance spot with a dinner-show cabaret, put on by singers, dancers and variety artists, followed by a band to round off the evening. Adjoining discotheque open Wednesday, Friday and Saturday from 10pm to 4am.

Made Inn – *Pest VI., Andrássy út 112. ☎ 311 3437.* The restaurant serves Italian, Greek and also Hungarian food. From Wednesday to Sunday, the discotheque offers entertainment on various themes (karaoke and several types of music).

High Life Disco Club – *Buda III., Kalap utca 14. Open Friday and Saturday from 10pm to dawn.* The capital's fashionable discotheque, where Budapest's young people come to dance in a frenzy of lights and decibels. Disco music, rock, funk, house and techno depending on the floor. A cocktail bar, café and restaurant complete this establishment.

CASINOS

In addition to slot machines, these have the entire panoply of traditional games (roulette, black jack, poker).

Casino Las Vegas – *Pest V., Roosevelt tér 2. ☎ 317 6022.*

Várkert Casino – *Buda I., Ybl Miklós tér 9. ☎ 202 4244. Open daily from 7pm to 2am.*

Casino Tropicana – *Pest V., Vigadó utca 2. ☎ 327 7250.*

SHOWS

The programmes are indicated in the various brochures mentioned above. For reservations, contact the box office of the establishment, your hotel, or:

– **Vigardó Ticket Office:** *Pest V., Vörösmarty tér 1. ☎ 327 4322. Open Monday to Friday from 10am to 6pm (closed 1.30pm to 2pm)*

– **Central Ticket Office:** *Pest VI. Andrássy út 18. ☎ 312 0000. Open Monday to Thursday from 9am to 4pm (3pm Friday)*

– **Music Mix 33:** *Pest V., Váci utca 33. ☎ 317 7736. Open Monday to Friday from 10am to 6pm (1pm Saturday)*

– **Publika Ticket Office:** *Pest VII., Károly krt. 9. ☎ 322 2010. Open Monday to Friday from 10am to 5pm*

– For credit card holders *☎ 266 0000 between 8am and 8pm.*

Classical music, opera, operetta

Zeneakadémia – *Pest VI., Ferenc tér 8.* The leading concert venue in the capital, where the most famous musicians have appeared, including Liszt, Wagner, Brahms and Richard Strauss. In season, music-lovers can listen to the country's best symphonic orchestras.

Pesti Vigadó – *Pest IV., Vigadó tér 2.* Variety shows and operettas.

Magyar Állami Operaház (Hungarian National Opera) – *Pest VII., Andrássy út 22.* One of Europe's most prestigious opera houses. As in the past, the works of the greatest names in music are played here.

Erkel Színház – *Pest VIII., Köztársaság tér 30.* Art Nouveau decor in a hall that seats 2 400.

Folk music

Bábszínház – *Pest VI., Andrássy út 69. Performance at 8pm, alternating with Budai Vigadó and Duna Palota.* Rajkó Folk Music Ensemble founded in 1952.

Budai Vigadó – *Buda I., Corvin tér 8. Performance at 8pm, alternating with Bábszínház and Duna Palota.* Hungarian National Folk Music Ensemble founded in 1951.

Duna Palota – *Pest V., Zrínyi utca 5. Performance at 8pm, alternating with Budai Vigadó and Bábszínház.* Duna Folk Music Ensemble founded in 1957.

Petőfi Csarnok – *Pest XIV., Zichy M. út 14.* In summer, there are several events each month: theatre and ballet performances presented by world-famous companies. It is advisable to book.

Jazz

Jazz Café – *Pest V., Balassi Bálint utca 25.* One of the city's oldest jazz clubs. Very existentialist, smoky atmosphere during the numerous concerts organised here.

The Long Jazz Club – *Pest VIII., Dohány utca 22-24. Open daily from 6pm to 2am.* Groups perform every evening from 9.30pm in the L-shaped room, on a stage in the corner. Often the evening ends with a group singalong.

Fél 10 jazz Klub – *Pest VIII., Baross utca 30.* Establishment on three floors, with bare metal decor. The somewhat chilly atmosphere warms up considerably on concert evenings. Student crowd.

Pop and rock

Petőfi Csarnok – *Pest XIV., Zichy M. út 14.* This is the venue for the city's rock music concerts. Each year the Hungarian Jazz Festival also takes place here. In the adjoining beer garden there is musical entertainment every Tuesday and Wednesday in summer.

Laser Theatre – *Pest X., Népliget, Planetarium.* It is here that world-famous groups have performed, including the Beatles, Pink Floyd and JM Jarre. This temple of music uses all today's special effects: laser, light play and pyrotechnics.

BUDAPEST AND CHILDREN

Állatkert (Zoo) – *Pest XIV., Állatkerti krt. 6-12. Open 1 May to 31 August, daily from 9am to 7pm and 1 September to 30 April from 9am to 5pm. M 1 Széchenyi fürdo bus n° 4.* Thought to be one of the oldest zoos in the world (opened in 1866), it has over 500 mammals, 700 birds and 1 500 reptiles and fish.

Nagy Cirkusz (Circus) – *Pest XIV., Állatkerti krt. 12. Shows Monday, Thursday and Friday at 3pm, Saturday at 10am, 3pm and 7pm, Sunday at 10am and 3pm. M 1 Széchenyi fürdő underground, bus n° 4.* World-famous Hungarian artistes perform here. Clowns, wild animal tamers and their charges, acrobats and others are acclaimed by the numerous children (and adults) at each performance.

Vidám Park (Amusement park) – *Pest XIV., Állatkerti krt. 12. Open April to September, daily from 10am to 8pm and October to March from 10am to 6pm. M 1 Széchenyi fürdő underground, bus n° 4.* The funfair is near City Park and offers a multitude of attractions for old and young alike: Ferris wheel, big dipper, merry-go-rounds, bumper cars and quad circuit. Be sure to take a look at the 19C carousel. There is also a play area for small children.

Planetárium – *Pest X., Népliget. Open Tuesday to Sunday at 7pm. M 3 Népliget underground.* This institute serves to popularise astronomy and related sciences for as wide a public as possible. Exhibitions and projections.

Budavári Labirintus (Buda Castle maze) – *Buda I., Úri utca 9. Open daily from 9.30am to 7.30pm.* Unusual and mysterious.

Gyermekvasút (Children's Train) – *Buda, Mt Széchenyi-Hűvösvölgy. See also Around Buda.* Small train with open-sided carriages. All the staff, except those running the engine itself are children aged 10 to 14, dressed in the uniforms of the Pioneers (a youth movement from the Communist era).

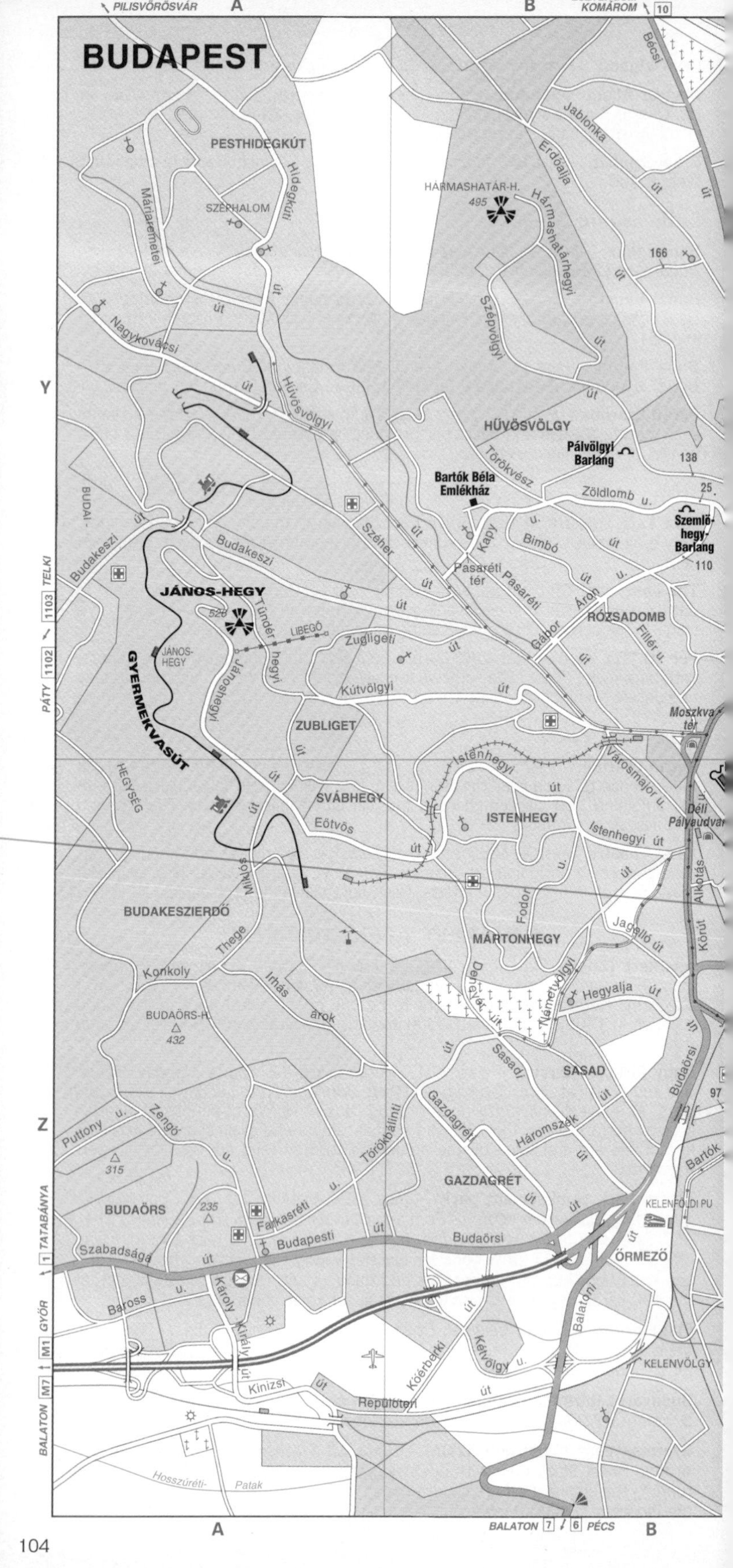
BUDAPEST
PILISVÖRÖSVÁR
ESZTERGOM
KOMÁROM
10
A
B
Y
Z
PESTHIDEGKÚT
SZÉPHALOM
HÁRMASHATÁR-H.
495
HŰVÖSVÖLGY
Pálvölgyi Barlang
Bartók Béla Emlékház
Szemlő-hegy-Barlang
JÁNOS-HEGY
526
JÁNOS-HEGY
LIBEGŐ
GYERMEKVASÚT
RÓZSADOMB
ZUBLIGET
SVÁBHEGY
ISTENHEGY
Moszkva tér
Déli Pályaudvar
BUDAKESZIERDŐ
MÁRTONHEGY
BUDAÖRS-H.
432
SASAD
GAZDAGRÉT
BUDAÖRS
315
235
KELENFÖLDI PU
ÖRMEZŐ
KELENVÖLGY
Hosszúréti- Patak
PÁTY 1102
1103 TELKI
BUDAI-HEGYSÉG
1 TATABÁNYA
M1 GYŐR
M7 BALATON
BALATON 7 6 PÉCS
166
138
25
110
97

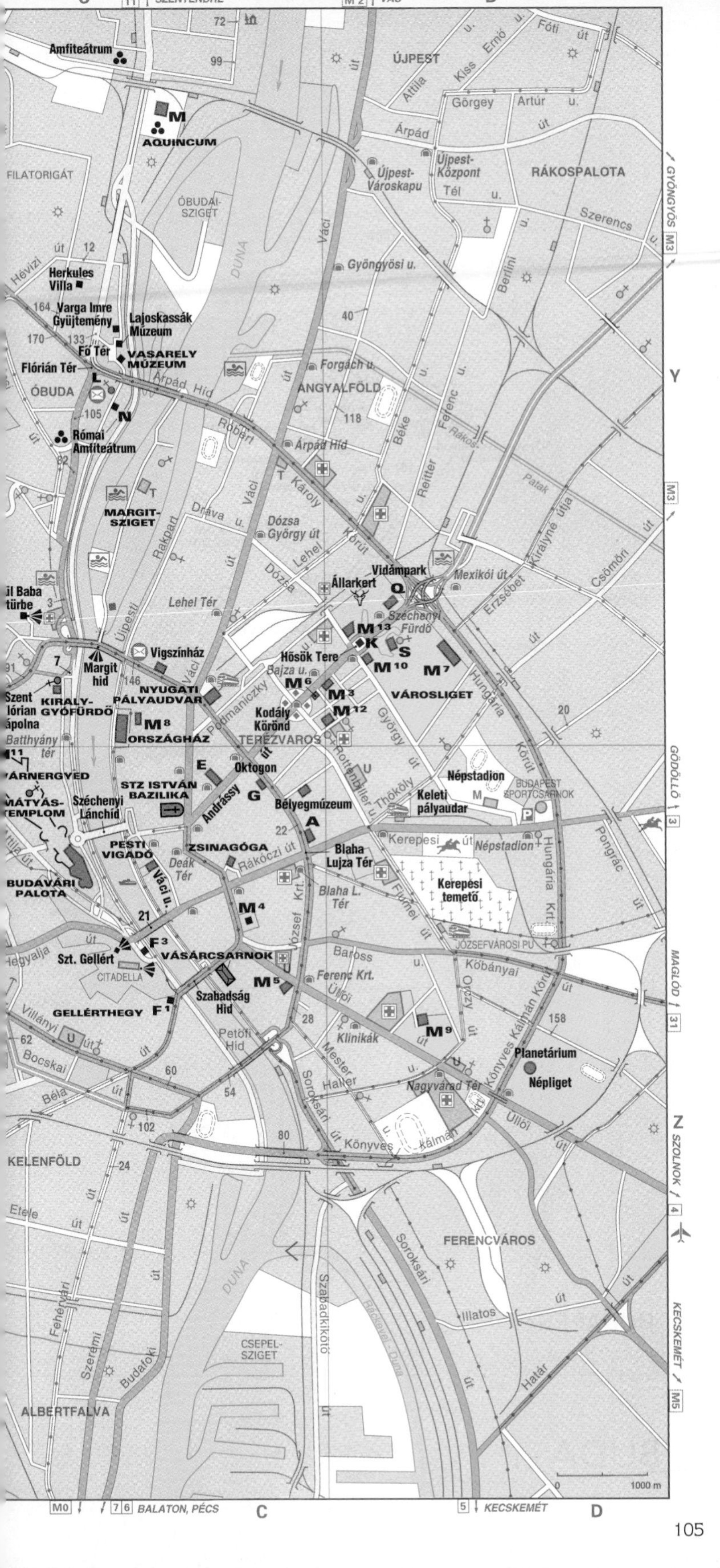
SZENTENDRE
VÁC
ÚJPEST
RÁKOSPALOTA
Amfiteátrum
AQUINCUM
FILATORIGÁT
ÓBUDAI-SZIGET
DUNA
Herkules Villa
Varga Imre Gyüjtemény
Lajoskassák Múzeum
Fő Tér
VASARELY MÚZEUM
Flórián Tér
ÓBUDA
Római Amfiteátrum
MARGIT-SZIGET
Újpest-Városkapu
Újpest-Központ
Gyöngyösi u.
Forgách u.
ANGYALFÖLD
Árpád Híd
Dózsa György út
Vidámpark
Állarkert
Széchenyi Fürdő
Hősök Tere
VÁROSLIGET
Lehel Tér
Vigszínház
Margit híd
NYUGATI PÁLYAUDVAR
KIRALY-GYÓFÜRDŐ
ORSZÁGHÁZ
TERÉZVÁROS
Kodály Körönd
Oktogon
STZ ISTVÁN BAZILIKA
Széchenyi Lánchíd
Bélyegmúzeum
Népstadion
BUDAPEST SPORTCSARNOK
Keleti pályaudvar
PESTI VIGADÓ
ZSINAGÓGA
Deák Tér
Blaha Lujza Tér
Kerepesi temető
BUDAVÁRI PALOTA
Szt. Gellért
CITADELLA
VÁSÁRCSARNOK
Szabadság Híd
GELLÉRTHEGY
Petőfi Híd
Klinikák
Nagyvárad Tér
Planetárium
Népliget
KELENFÖLD
FERENCVÁROS
CSEPEL-SZIGET
ALBERTFALVA
GYÖNGYÖS
GÖDÖLLŐ
MAGLÓD
SZOLNOK
KECSKEMÉT
BALATON, PÉCS
1000 m

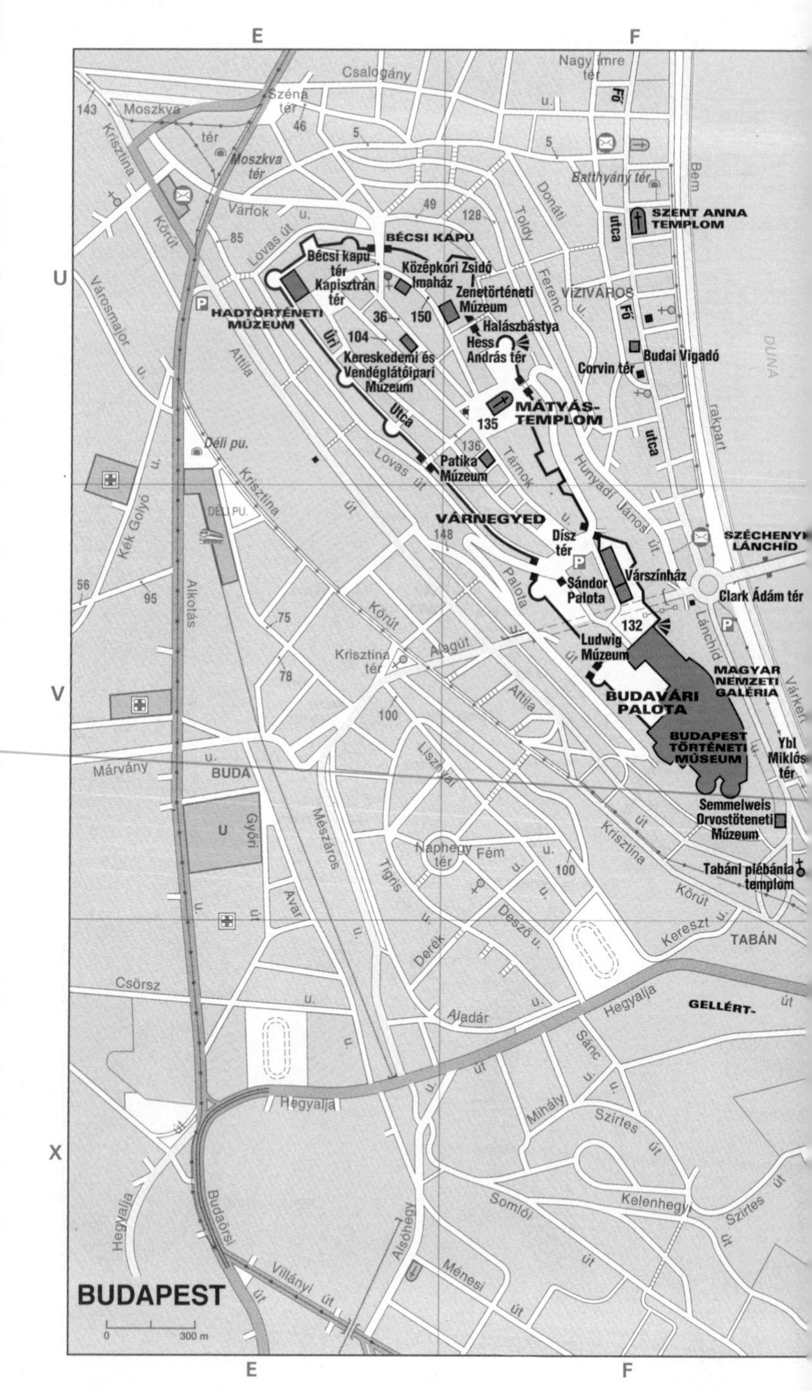
BUDAPEST
0 300 m
BÉCSI KAPU
Bécsi kapu tér
Kapisztrán tér
Középkori Zsidó Imaház
Zenetörténeti Múzeum
HADTÖRTÉNETI MÚZEUM
Halászbástya
Hess András tér
Kereskedelmi és Vendéglátóipari Múzeum
MÁTYÁS-TEMPLOM
Patika Múzeum
VÁRNEGYED
Dísz tér
Sándor Palota
Várszínház
Ludwig Múzeum
BUDAVÁRI PALOTA
MAGYAR NEMZETI GALÉRIA
BUDAPEST TÖRTÉNETI MÚZEUM
Semmelweis Orvostörténeti Múzeum
Tabáni plébánia templom
SZENT ANNA TEMPLOM
Budai Vigadó
Corvin tér
Batthyány tér
VÍZIVÁROS
SZÉCHENYI LÁNCHÍD
Clark Ádám tér
Ybl Miklós tér
DUNA
TABÁN
GELLÉRT-
Széna tér
Moszkva tér
Déli pu.
Krisztina tér
Naphegy tér
Nagy Imre tér
BUDA
E
F
U
V
X

BUDA...

… PEST

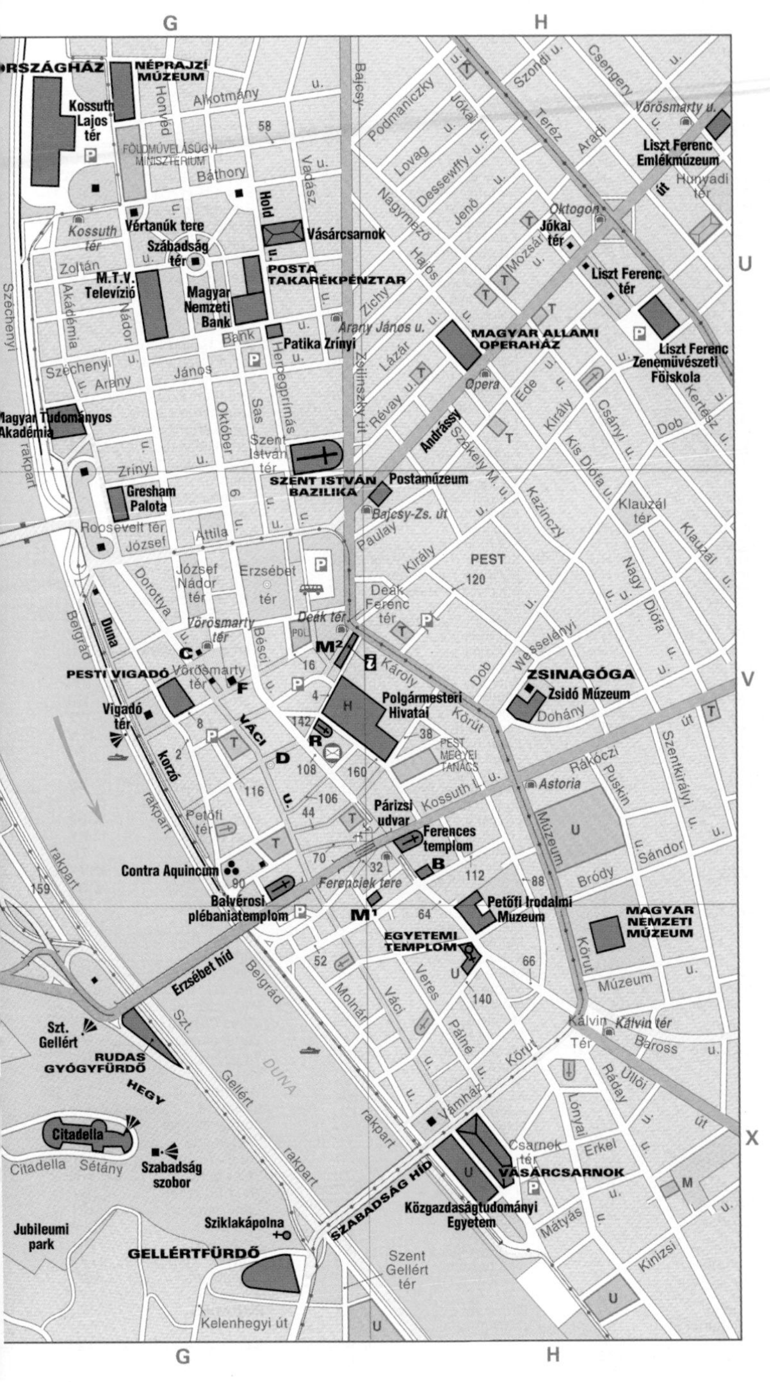
G
H
U
V
X
NÉPRAJZI MÚZEUM
Kossuth Lajos tér
FÖLDMŰVELÉSÜGYI MINISZTÉRIUM
Alkotmány
Báthory
Honvéd
Vadász
Hold
Vértanúk tere
Szabadság tér
Vásárcsarnok
POSTA TAKARÉKPÉNZTÁR
M.T.V. Televízió
Magyar Nemzeti Bank
Patika Zrínyi
Nádor
Akadémia
Zoltán
Széchenyi
Arany János u.
Hercegprímás
Október 6 u.
Sas
Szent István tér
SZENT ISTVÁN BAZILIKA
Postamúzeum
Gresham Palota
Roosevelt tér
József Attila
József Nádor tér
Erzsébet tér
Deák tér
Deák Ferenc tér
Vörösmarty tér
PESTI VIGADÓ
Vigadó tér
Duna korzó
Váci
Polgármesteri Hivatal
PEST MEGYEI TANÁCS
Párizsi udvar
Ferences templom
Ferenciek tere
Petőfi tér
Contra Aquincum
Belvárosi plébániatemplom
EGYETEMI TEMPLOM
Petőfi Irodalmi Múzeum
MAGYAR NEMZETI MÚZEUM
Astoria
Rákóczi
Kossuth L. u.
Múzeum
Kálvin tér
Baross
Üllői út
Ráday
Lónyay
Erkel
VÁSÁRCSARNOK
Közgazdaságtudományi Egyetem
SZABADSÁG HÍD
Erzsébet híd
Szt. Gellért
RUDAS GYÓGYFÜRDŐ
HEGY
Citadella
Citadella Sétány
Szabadság szobor
Sziklakápolna
Jubileumi park
GELLÉRTFÜRDŐ
Szent Gellért tér
Kelenhegyi út
DUNA
Belgrád rakpart
Szt. Gellért rakpart
Vámház
Kinizsi
Mátyás
Molnár
Veres Pálné
ZSINAGÓGA
Zsidó Múzeum
Dohány
Wesselényi
Dob
Király
Kazinczy
Klauzál tér
Nagy Diófa u.
Kis Diófa u.
Csányi u.
Kertész u.
Andrássy
MAGYAR ÁLLAMI OPERAHÁZ
Opera
Liszt Ferenc Zeneművészeti Főiskola
Liszt Ferenc tér
Jókai tér
Oktogon
Liszt Ferenc Emlékmúzeum
Vörösmarty u.
Hunyadi tér
Teréz
Aradi
Csengery
Szondi u.
Podmaniczky
Jókai
Lovag
Dessewffy
Nagymező
Jenő
Mozsár
Hajós
Zichy
Lázár
Révay u.
Székely M. u.
Bajcsy-Zs. út
Paulay
Károly
Kossuth
Múzeum
Sándor
Bródy
Szentkirályi
Puskin
PEST

STREET INDEX FOR MAP OF BUDAPEST

BUDAÖRS

SIGHTS ON MAP OF BUDAPEST

(M) = **see Museums**

Sight	Map	
Ady Endre Emlékmúzeum (M)		
Állatkert (Zoo)	DY	
Amfiteátrum (M)		
Andrássy út	HU	
Aquincum (M)		
Bartók Béla Emlékház	BY	
Batthyány tér	FU	
Bécsi kapu tér	EU	
Bécsi kapu	EU	
Belvárosi plébánia templom	GHV	
Bélyegmúzeum (M)		
Budai Vigadó	FU	
Budapesti Történeti Múzeum (M)		
Budavári palota	FV	
Café New York	CZ	**A**
Citadella	GX	
Clark Ádám tér	FV	
Corvin tér	FU	
Deák Ferenc tér	GV	
Dísz tér	FV	
Dohány utcai zsinagóga	HV	
Egyetemi Könyvtár	HV	**B**
Egyetemi templom	HX	
Erzsébet híd	GX	
Ferences templom	HV	
Ferenciek tere	GHV	
Flórián tér	CY	
Fö tér	CY	
Földalatti Vasúti Múzeum (M)		
Gellértfürdő	GX CZ	**F**[1]
Gellérthegy	FGX	
Gerbeaud Cukrászáda	GV	**C**
Gresham palota	GUV	
Gül Baba türbe	CY	
Gyermekvasút	AYZ	
Hadtörténeti Múzeum (M)		
Halászbástya	FU	
Herkules villa	CY	
Hermész-diszkút	GV	**D**
Hopp Ferenc Kelet-Ázsiai Múzeum (M)		
Hősök tere	DY	
Iparművészeti Múzeum (M)		
János-hegy	AY	
Jubileumi park	GX	
Keleti pályaudvar	DZ	
Kerepesi temető	DZ	
Király Gyógyürdő	CY	
Kodály körönd	CY	
Kodály Zoltán Emlékmúzeum (M)		
Középkori Zsidó Imaház (M)		
Közgazdaságtudományi Egyetem	HX	
Közlekedési Múzeum (M)		
Lajos Kassák (M)		
Liszt Ferenc Emlékmúzeum (M)		
Liszt Ferenc Zeneművészeti Fõiskola	HU	
Ludwig Múzeum (M)		
Luxus (Áruház)	GV	**F**
Magyar Állami Operaház (M)		
Magyar Kereskedelmi és Vendéglátóipari Múzeum (M)		
Magyar Nemzeti Bank	GU	
Magyar Nemzeti Galéria (M)		
Magyar Nemzeti Múzeum (M)		
Magyar Televízió (M.T.V.)	GU	
Magyar Természettudományi Múzeum (M)		
Magyar Tudományos Akadémia	GU	
Március 15 tér	GV	
Margit híd	CY	
Margitsziget	CY	
Mátyás templom	FU	
Milléniumi emlékmű	DY	**K**

Museums

Museum	Map	
Ady Endre Emlékmúzeum	GHV	**M**[1]
Amfiteátrum	CY	
Aquincum	CY	
Bélyegmúzeum	CZ	
Budapesti Történeti Múzeum	FV	
Földalatti Vasúti Múzeum	GHV	**M**[2]
Hadtörténeti Múzeum	EU BZ	**M**[11]
Hopp Ferenc Kelet-Ázsiai Múzeum	CDY	**M**[3]
Iparmûvészeti Múzeum	CZ	**M**[5]
Kodály Zoltán Emlékmúzeum	CDY	**M**[6]
Középkori Zsidó Imaház	EFU	
Közlekedési Múzeum	DY	**M**[7]
Lajos Kassák	CY	
Liszt Ferenc Emlékmúzeum	HU CZ	**G**
Ludwig Múzeum	FV	
Magyar Állami Operaház	HU CZ	**E**
Magyar Kereskedelmi és Vendéglátóipari Múzeum	EU	
Magyar Nemzeti Galéria	FV	
Magyar Nemzeti Múzeum	HVX CZ	**M**[4]
Magyar Természettudományi Múzeum	DZ	**M**[9]
Műcsarnok	DY	**M**[10]
Néprajzi Múzeum	GU CY	**M**[8]
Patika Múzeum	FU	
Petõfi Irodalmi Múzeum	HV	
Postamúzeum	HUV	
Ráth György Múzeum	CDY	**M**[12]
Semmelweis Orvostörténeti Múzeum	FV	
Szépmüvészeti Múzeum	DY	**M**[13]
Varga Imre Gyüjtemény	CY	
Vasarely Múzeum	CY	
Zenetörténeti Múzeum	EFU	
Zsidó Múzeum	HV	

Sight	Map	
Mücsarnok (M)		
Néprajzi Múzeum (M)		
Népstadion	DZ	
Nyugati pályaudvar	CY	
Óbudai plébánia templom	CY	**L**
Óbudai Zsinagóga	CY	**N**
Országház	GU	
Pálvölgyi Barlang	BY	
Párizsi udvar	GHV	
Patika Múzeum (M)		
Patika Zrinyi	GU	
Pesti Vigadó	GV	
Petõfi Irodalmi Múzeum (M)		
Planetárium	DZ	
Postamúzeum (M)		
Postatakarékpénztár	GU	
Ráth György Múzeum (M)		
Római Amfiteátrum	CY	
Roosevelt tér	GUV	
Római Amfiteátrum	CY	
Rudas Gyógyfűrdő	GX CZ	**F**[3]
Semmelweis Orvostörténeti Múzeum (M)		
Szabadság Szobor	GX	
Szabadság tér	GU	
Széchenyi Gyógyfürdõ	DY	**Q**
Szemlõ-hegyi Barlang	BY	
Szent Anna templom	FU	
Szent Flórián kápolna	CY	
Szent Gellért	GX	
Szent István bazilika	GUV	
Szentháromság tér	FU	**135**
Szépmûvészeti Múzeum (M)		
Szervita tér	GV	
Szervita templom	GV	**R**
Sziklakápolna	GX	
Tabáni plébánia templom	FV	
Tárnok utca	FUV	
Vajdahunyad vára	DY	**S**
Varga Imre Gyüjtemény (M)		
Várszínház	FV	
Vásárcsarnok	GU	
Vásárcsarnok	HX	
Vasarely Múzeum (M)		
Vértanúk tere	GU	
Vidám Park	DY	
Vígszínház	CY	
Víziváros	FU	
Vörösmarty tér	GV	
Zenetörténeti Múzeum (M)		
Zsidó Múzeum (M)		

Visiting Budapest

The tourists flocking into Central Europe are delighted to include the Pearl of the Danube in their tour.
Budapest stretches on either side of the legendary Danube, which rises in Germany's Black Forest; its majestic waters flow over a distance of 2 850km/1 770mi before reaching the Black Sea.
There is a surprising geographical contrast between the two banks of the river. On the right bank Buda is situated on a number of wooded hills, which give it a countrified, residential or even aristocratic feel, with its expensive-looking little houses and villas and well-tended gardens. In contrast, Pest on the left bank is flat – a plain extending as far as the eye can see, punctuated for the most part by old buildings and residential flats on the outskirts.

E. Baret
Your carriage awaits!

Budapest has 2.1 million inhabitants. Administratively it is divided into 22 districts covering a total area of 525km²/203sq mi (the island of **Csepel** in the south, an industrial and port area, makes up the 21st district).
Budapest is a veritable melting-pot with a variety of cultures, each of which has left permanent traces and forms part of the national heritage. Budapest is a unique city that combines the essence of East and West. It is also, of course, a city of public baths, a reminder of the Roman period and the Turkish occupation. And Budapest is one of the showcases for the Art Nouveau style, which was at its height at the turn of the 19C. Budapest is a city where dance and music reign, be it with the classical music of Liszt, Kodály, Bartók, the operettas of Lehár, or gypsy music, not forgetting jazz and rock. Budapest is a city where the atmosphere of legendary tea rooms is to be savoured (at Gerbeaud and Művész in Pest, or Angelika and Ruszwurm in Buda) along with that of old literary cafés. Finally, Budapest is a city where famous wines – Tokay, Egri Bikavér and Barakpálinka – should be tasted and enjoyed.
Enjoy your stay in the Magyar capital, you will certainly find it impossible to remain indifferent to its charms.

One day in Budapest

Morning in Buda – **Budávari palota★★★**: exterior – **Várnegyed★★**: **Mátyás-templom★★** – **Halászbástya**: **view★★**

Afternoon in Pest – **Széchenyi Lánchíd (Chain Bridge)★★** – **Váci utca★** – **Vásárcsarnok★★** – **Hősök tere: Milleneumi emlékmű**

Two days in Budapest

First day in Buda – **Budávari palota★★★** and **Magyar Nemzeti Galéria★★** – **Várnegyed★★**: **Mátyás-templom★★** and **streets** (**Táncsics Mihály utca★★**, **Fortuna utca★★**, **Úri utca★★**) – **Halászbástya**: **view★★**

Pest – **Gellérthegy★★**: **view★★★** of the Citadel – **Országház★★★** – **Széchenyi Lánchíd (Chain Bridge)★★** – **Vörösmarty tér★** – **Váci utca★** – **Vásárcsarnok★★**

Second day in Pest – **Magyar Nemzeti Múzeum★★** – **Andrássy út★★** – **Hősök tere: Milleneumi emlékmű★** – **Szépművészeti Múzeum★★★** – **Király gyófürdő★★** – **Városliget★**

Three days in Budapest

The two-day programme and the third day – **Margit-sziget★★** and **Gyermekvasút★** (the children's train in the Buda Hills).

In any event, do not miss the chance to sample a pastry in a tea room, such as at **Ruszwurm** or **Angelika** in Buda, or at **Gerbeaud★**, **Művész** or **Centrál** in Pest, if only to enjoy the setting of these establishments.

Historical table and notes

1-4C AD	The **Romans** found the province of Pannonia (western part of today's Hungary), then establish the military camp of Aquincum on the site of Óbuda. Aquincum quickly becomes a flourishing city, the capital of Lower Pannonia in the reign of Emperor Trajan.
5C	The **Huns**, led by Attila, take Aquincum. Several successive barbarian invasions bring the Roman presence to an end.
896	The **Magyars**, led by Prince Árpád, cross the Carpathian Mountains. Árpád establishes his summer encampment on the island of Csepel.
1241	Buda and Pest are devastated by Tartar invasions.
1243	King **Béla IV** builds Buda Castle.
1458-1490	Buda becomes an important cultural centre in Europe during the reign of **Matthias I Corvinus**.
1541	The **Turks** take Buda.
1686	Christian armies led by the Habsburg, **Charles of Lorraine**, liberate the city. Buda becomes an Austrian army garrison town.
1825	Count István Széchenyi founds the Academy of Sciences and donates a full year's income.
1838	Terrible floods devastate half of Pest.
1848-1849	Uprising and **Hungarian War of Independence** against the Habsburgs. Death of poet Sándor Petőfi, fierce advocate of national independence.
1849	The Chain Bridge (Széchenyi Lánchíd) is inaugurated.
1867	Hungarian Compromise with Austria and Dual Monarchy set up. Emperor Franz Josef and his wife Elizabeth (Sissy) are crowned sovereigns of Hungary in Matthias Church in Buda.
1873	Three independent towns – Buda, Pest and Óbuda – are joined to form Budapest.
1896	Inauguration of the first underground train line (today's M 1) on the Continent. The 1 000th anniversary celebrations. Major festivities, particularly in Városliget.
1902	Inauguration of the Parliament.
1925	First international Fair.
1944	Arrow Cross, allied with the Nazis, conducts a reign of terror.
1945	The Red Army liberates the city.
1949	**László Rajk's** trial and execution.
1950	Creation of Greater Budapest and inauguration of Ferihegy Airport.
23 October 1956- November 1956	Hungarian Uprising. In November **Imre Nagy** returns and announces several measures including the country's neutrality and its withdrawal from the Warsaw Pact. Soviet tanks close in on the capital and crush the insurrection. Some 3 000 people are killed and many buildings damaged by bullets and shells. 200 000 Hungarians leave the country. Arrests and executions are to follow.
1973	Mayors from Europe's capitals plant trees in Buda's Europe Park (Européaliget) to celebrate the city's centenary.
1985	The Buda Castle District and the panoramic view over the Danube are put on Unesco's World Heritage list.
1989	Imre Nagy (executed in 1958) is officially rehabilitated. Budapest honours him with a national funeral and reburial. On **23 October** the People's Socialist Republic of Hungary becomes the **Republic of Hungary**. The red star is to disappear from public buildings.
1991	The last Russian troops leave Budapest.
August 1998	European athletic championships take place in the Népstadion, the People's Stadium.

TURN-OF-THE-CENTURY ART OR ART NOUVEAU

The second half of the 19C was marked by several major events which were to boost Budapest's remarkable modernist movement. In 1867, after two centuries of Austrian domination, Hungary was finally recognised as an independent nation; in 1873 the city of Budapest came into being; and 1896 was the 1 000th anniversary of the Magyar invasion of the Carpathian Basin. The city was prosperous, its industry dynamic, the population growing, the standard of living high and intellectual exchange was abundant, particularly through the creation of many schools, theatres and an opera. The eyes of the world were on Budapest; great construction projects were being undertaken, in particular the Continent's first underground train line, the world's largest stock exchange, the world's largest Parliament and the world's largest bridge (Erzsébet). A strong nationalistic spirit developed with the recovery, manifesting itself in the glorification of national heroes and events and finding its expression in a mix of academic Romanticism and an idealising Classicism. Mihály Munkácsy's work, *The Conquest*, exhibited in Budapest's Parliament is a typical example of this official art.

At the turn of the century the Hungarian artistic community largely rejected this academic style of Historicism. The will to create a national art based on the Hungarian people's Magyar origins inspired a great many artists. Art became a means of expressing their social, ethical and utopian ideas and paved the way for the society to come. Several new artistic movements, linked to artistic developments elsewhere in Europe, swept across Hungary: Naturalism and open-air painting, Art Nouveau and Symbolism – Hungary was giddy with excitement. Individual artists searched for the right means of expression and in so doing brought about artistic renewal and while their styles were sometimes in complete opposition to each other, they were all agreed in their rejection of academism.

Art Nouveau burst onto the scene and became the best means of expressing the new modernity; while it was part of the international fashion, in Hungary it took on an authentically national character. In architecture, the Hungarian Art Nouveau style was inspired by Transylvania's picturesque medieval architecture, recently rediscovered, as well as Scandinavian architecture. Without any doubt the pioneer in the field was the famous Hungarian architect **Ödön Lechner** (1845-1914). From the 1890s he established a new style of architecture going back to the Hungarian people's origins in the East. Eastern Moorish and Byzantine motifs and architectural forms as well as elements from Hungarian folk art, especially tapestries, inspired him. He used majolica ceramic from the famous Zsolnay works to ornament roofs and adorn façades with what has been termed a richly embroidered national costume. He strengthened his style, on the fringes of the Classical ideas of his time, with the construction of the **Museum of Applied Arts**, between 1891 and 1896. The East is very much present in his first modern steel constructions, as can be seen in the patterns decorating the museum's main entrance, the spectacular exhibition hall encircled with Islamic double arcades, and the dome and roofs with their coloured tiles also suggestive of the East. On the other hand, the organic forms and gracefully flowing lines also found in the museum's main entrance are typically Art Nouveau. Ödön Lechner's most successful work is probably the former **Post Office Savings Bank**, built between 1899 and 1902. The façade, decorated with mosaics and plant designs, is of a very high technical and artistic standard. The roof in majolica tiles is overrun with floral and animal patterns. The ever-present mythological references reflect the nationalistic spirit then in vogue; thus the recently discovered bull's head refers to the Hungarian legend of Attila's treasure. From 1905, architecture took on a social character. While drawing on exploratory work by Ödön Lechner, the new generation of architects, represented in particular by Béla Lajta and Károly Kós, addressed problems of technology and hygiene. Their goal was to create a better environment in perfect harmony with nature, as expressed in Hungarian folk art. **Béla Lajta** (1873-1920) combined Hungarian Art Nouveau and typically Scandinavian brick architecture in his Institute for the Jewish Blind, 1905-08. **Károly Kós** (1883-1977) re-established continuity with the past through references to the Magyar people and the Huns. The Budapest **Zoo**, designed by Dezső Zreumeczky (1908-09), consists of medieval-style wood constructions using architectural forms typical of Transylvania (turrets, spires and balconies), reworked by his imagination.

The notion of harmony with nature preoccupied the artistic community. The works of Hungarian painter **Károly Ferenczy** (1862-1917) developed a lyrical approach where man developed in harmony with nature. He gave a mystical and religious meaning to art, which linked him with the Symbolist movement in Europe. In *The Three Magi*, executed in 1899 and exhibited at the National Gallery, man is at one with nature, in a mystical atmosphere lending itself to the miraculous. **Simon Hollósy** (1857-1918) found fulfilment in the open-air painting of the French Impressionists, while drawing his inspiration from the landscapes of Transylvania.

WATERSTONE'S BOOKSELLERS
Please refer to the Waterstone's
Customer Satisfaction Guarantee,
displayed in store, for our refund
and exchange terms and conditions
220-226 Chiswick High Rd
London W4 1PD Tel: 020 8995 3559
Thank you for shopping at Waterstone's

111 CASH-1   2065 0112 002

HUNGARY, BUDAPEST	QTY 1	9.99
9782061542019		
	TOTAL GBP	**9.99**
CASH		10.00
	CHANGE	.01

VAT No GB 710 6311 84

28.10.03 14:47

Hungarian Art Nouveau

STF/SUNSET

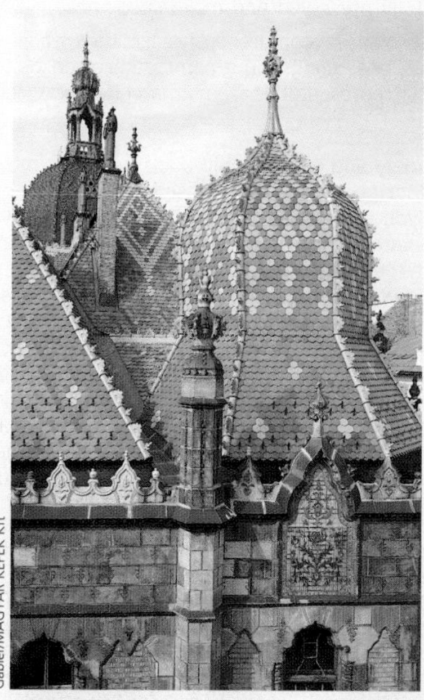
Gabler/MAGYAR KÉPEK Kft

Et. Revault/PIX

Et. Revault/PIX

J.-C. Saturnin/MICHELIN

THE BATHS: A RITUAL AND AN INSTITUTION

You may be surprised to see a number of people carrying small plastic bags in the early morning or evening. In fact, they are going to or coming from the baths *(open from 6am)* and are carrying shampoo, soap and personal effects! The baths, a distant echo of the Roman period and the Ottoman occupation, are part of the everyday life and health routine of the people of Budapest. They go to the baths to treat aches and pains, to chat, play chess or simply relax.

It is true that you feel a deep sense of well-being, and that you feel good – very good – after a session at the baths, rounded off with a steam bath, a massage session and then of course a good shower. You feel much more relaxed and probably a bit peckish. It is an experience not to be missed before leaving Budapest, if only to admire the magnificence of certain establishments.

The area around Budapest has a number of hot springs. About 100 may be found here, some of which supply the capital's public baths or spa complexes. The Romans did not overlook the water's healing qualities and made great use of them; the ruins of the baths at Aquincum are proof enough. In the 16C the Turks, who occupied Hungary for over a century, developed public baths and built establishments that were small architectural jewels; these are carefully preserved and maintained today.

It goes without saying that we cannot provide a comprehensive list here of all of Budapest's spas, pools and public baths. Consequently, the names are given of the better-known establishments or those most representative from an architectural viewpoint.

★★★ **Gellért gyógyfürdő** – There are men-only and women-only pools, and two mixed pools (indoors and outdoors). The indoor pool or carbonic-gaseous bath is famous for its decor in the early 1900s style; you see it in all the tourist brochures. It was built in 1934 where the hotel's conservatory once stood. To bathe here, you have to don a blue plastic cap provided at the entrance. The rectangular pool is surrounded by twisted columns decorated with floral motifs, a great metal and glass dome arching overhead. The columns support a mezzanine walkway, itself decorated with green plants and pillars sheathed in Zsolnay ceramic. The outdoor pool is appreciated for its artificial waves and sunbathing area. The hot-spring baths tiled with magnificent blue mosaics are worth a visit. You do not need a bathing costume – each visitor is given a wrap before enjoying a dry bath (sauna), a steam bath or a dip in the pools where the temperature varies from one pool to another. The visit is rounded off by lying down for a few moments' rest to become accustomed to normal temperatures again.

★★★ **Széchenyi gyógyfürdő** – One of the most popular establishments. This enormous spa has a sunbathing area and an outdoor pool where chess is played in water at 27°C/80.6°F (even in winter), in addition to an indoor pool. The Széchenyl baths resemble an enormous neo-Baroque palace, with their domes prominent in the middle of Városliget (City Park). The main entrance hall leading to the baths is really worth a look; the mosaics on the dome and vaults are superb. The entrance to the sunbathing area is on the other side, on Állatkerti körút. The main pool is 50m/55yd long (water at 27°C/80.6°F); there are two semicircular pools on either side. On the right the water is at 38°C/100.4°F, and on the left, 34°C/93°F.

★★ **Rudas gyógyfürdő** – From the outside these Turkish baths do not seem particularly attractive. And yet, after leaving your clothes in a cubicle (an employee dressed in white locks it for you), it is time to make your way to the inner sanctum – clad in the white loincloth provided at the entrance. A real surprise and novelty await the uninitiated! You come to an area in half-darkness, built in 1566 by the pasha Mustapha Sokoli. A moist heat, rising vapours, and in the middle a great octagonal pool in red marble, surrounded by eight columns bearing a dome set with pieces of glass, all create a strange decor and atmosphere. There is a pool in each corner with water temperatures varying from very cold to very hot. You may also have a steam bath (two rooms, 45°C/113°F and 55°C/131°F) and an energetic massage by giants who first coat you with oil. After a refreshing shower, swathe yourself in a bath towel, take a few minutes' rest if you like, and then leave, feeling really fit.

★★ **Király gyógyfürdő** – The Király baths, set back from Fő utca, can be recognised by their cupolas topped with the Turkish crescent. They were completed in 1566 by the pasha Mustapha Sokoli. The name Király is the Magyar version of the German König, the name of the family who owned the baths at the end of the 19C. Like the Rudas baths, these are a beautiful example of Ottoman architecture. The octagonal pool, surrounded by blind arcades, has a great dome overhead.

Famous baths

G. Giulio/WOSTOK PRESS

Széchenyi

MAGYAR KÉPEK Kft

Gellért

F. Szelényi/MAGYAR KÉPEK Kft

Király

R. Mattès

Széchenyi

MAGYAR KÉPEK Kft

Rudas

BUDA

VÁRHEGY (CASTLE HILL)

Surrounded by ramparts, the hill rises about 45m/150ft above the Danube. When it is lit up at night, it takes on an entirely different dimension. The castle or royal palace, with its immense dome, the Matthias Church with its glazed roofs, the Fishermen's Bastion seen from the left bank of the Danube on the Pest side, are all resplendent with a thousand lights.

To get to the hill from Pest on foot, cross Chain Bridge and take the **funicular railway** ⓥ *(Sikló)*. Just before the lower station on Clark Ádám tér is a stone sculpture on the left; this is the **zero kilometre point**, from which all distances from Budapest are calculated. A little further on, against the wall can be seen mosaics of the Hungarian coat of arms, surrounded by those of the former provinces.

From the upper station, there is already an interesting **view★** of the Danube and Pest (telescope).

★★★Budavári palota (Royal Palace)

Béla IV, king from 1235 to 1270, decided to raise a fortress on this spot in order to warn Buda of Mongol invasion. The castle was extended during the reign of Sigismund of Luxembourg (1387-1437). It was with Matthias Corvinus (1458-90), however, that the glory of the palace reached its peak. This brilliant sovereign, a man of letters and a Humanist made this a temple of art and science, developing it in the Renaissance style. In 1686 it was at the centre of the siege to drive out the Turks, and sustained considerable damage. In the 18C and 19C the Habsburgs wanted to make it into a royal residence, on a scale appropriate to their rank. Firstly Maria Theresa had an imposing Baroque construction raised; then, in 1890, Franz Josef entrusted Miklós Ybl and Alajos Hauszmann with remodelling the edifice to give it a neo-Baroque look. In fact, the Emperor only made rare, brief visits to the palace that he had wanted to be so imposing and sumptuous.

The festival of arts and trades – Every year for four days in the month of August, the former palace of Buda becomes a hive of activity. Among others, stone and wood carvers, blacksmiths, weavers, potters, toy-makers and bakers set up their stands and workshops all around the palace to bring their old trades back to life, and to sell their products. Folk dancing, music and games accompany the festival. Worth seeing.

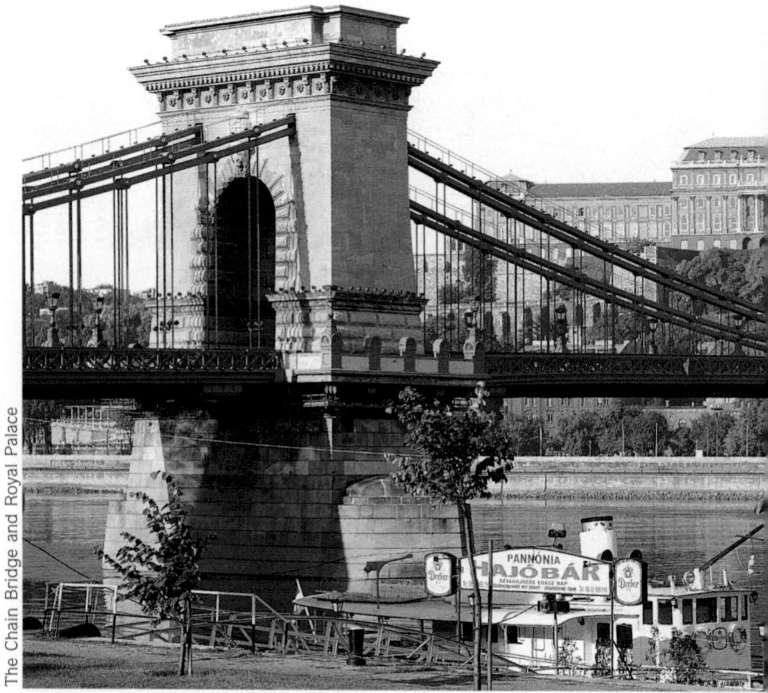

The Chain Bridge and Royal Palace

Exterior

A gigantic bird of prey with outspread wings, clutching a sword in its claws, seems about to take off from a pillar of the neo-Baroque wrought-iron gate to the castle's fortifications. This mythical bird is a **turul** (pronounced too rool), the emblem of the Magyar tribes often to be seen in Hungary.
The royal palace's Baroque façade stretches over 300m/984ft and overlooks the Danube. A dome in the centre rests on a group of twinned columns. The **equestrian statue of Eugene of Savoy**, one of the liberators from the Turkish occupation, dominates the vast terrace with its panoramic view. There are two scenes of the Battle of Zenta (1697) on its pedestal. Continue along this promenade until you reach an overhang, overlooking the river. A good place for taking photos; the **view★★** here is magnificent. From left to right you can readily distinguish Margaret Island, the Parliament, Chain Bridge, St Stephen's Basilica, Elizabeth Bridge, Liberty Bridge and then, a little further on, Gellért Hill, the citadel and Liberation Monument.

Take the passage to the right of the National Gallery entrance.

The principal attraction on the square (statue of a groom in the centre) is without question the **Matthias Fountain★**. You cannot miss it, people stop to study it in detail, photograph it, or be photographed in front of it. This bronze sculptural group, the work of Alajos Stróbl (1904), represents Mattias Corvinus in a hunting scene. The subject was inspired by a ballad by the 19C Romantic poet, Mihály Vörösmarty, in which Matthias meets a beautiful young girl, Ilonka, when he is out hunting.
To the left beyond the fountain, is the **inner courtyard** by the **Lion Gate**, so called because of the stone lions standing guard at the entrance. Stand in the middle of this beautiful paved courtyard to enjoy the majesty of the surrounding buildings. **Széchényi National Library** (Nemzeti Széchényi Könyvtár) stands in the centre to the right. Founded by Count Ferenc Széchényi in 1802, this is the country's largest library; its reading room is open to all.
At the far end of the courtyard, cross the entrance hall of the Budapest History Museum (Budapesti Történeti Múzeum) and go down the stairs to the southern ramparts and **Mace Tower** (Buzogány-torony) with its conical roof, a vestige of the medieval fortifications. Visitors can leave the castle fortifications through a nearby gate, Ferdinand Gate, set into the ramparts, and see the barbican, a semicircular work built in the 14C and 15C. Beyond the gardens stretches the Tabán district.

G. Siméone/PHOTONONSTOP

Prince Eugene of Savoy

Eugene of Savoy-Carignan was born in Paris in 1663. His parents had decided he was destined for a career in the church, but he committed himself to Louis XIV's army. When the Sun King refused to give him the command of a regiment, the prince, his pride hurt, left the French army – at the age of 20 – and joined the Habsburg army of Leopold I, Germanic Emperor, Archduke of Austria, King of Bohemia and Hungary. At this time the Turks dominated the greater part of Central Europe, and Buda was in their hands. In 1683, Vienna was besieged by the Grand Vizir Kara Mustapha. Pope Innocent XI sent several Christian armies to help the Austrians and deliver the city. Eugene of Savoy was sent to join the Allied army of the King of Poland, John III Sobieski. On 12 September the Christian victory of Kahlenberg heralded the reconquest. Charles of Lorraine liberated Buda in 1686. Eugene of Savoy took part. He became a generalissimo of the Austrian Imperial troops and won fame in the War of Liberation against the Ottoman Empire: the Battle of Zenta (1697), the Karlowitz Peace (1699) and the Treaty of Passarowitz (1718), which fixed the Habsburg Empire's territorial limits. He also played a role of prime importance in the conflict over the Spanish Succession. A skilled and influential politician, he imposed the 1714 Rastatt Peace on Louis XIV, thereby ending the war. Austria showered him with glory and money. In Vienna he had the Belvedere built as his summer palace, and the Prinzen Eugen Stadtpalais as his winter palace (today's Ministry of Finance.) It was here that he died in 1736. His remains are in the Austrian capital (the Tirna Chapel in St Stephen's Cathedral).

Interior

The main building of the royal palace and the wings house three musuems.

★★ **Magyar Nemzeti Galéria (Hungarian National Gallery)** ⏱ – This museum is entirely dedicated to Hungarian pictorial and sculptural art from the Middle Ages to the 20C. The collections are divided among the four floors (names of works in English and Hungarian). In the former Throne Room on the first floor, there is a beautiful collection of late-Gothic **altarpieces★**. Altarpiece art flourished from the 15C to the early 16C, and is represented by triptychs and polyptychs. Some huge altarpieces come from the former administrative provinces of Szepes *(Szepes Altar)*, Sáros *(Mary Magdalene Altar)*, Liptó *(St Andrew's Altar)*, Zólyom *(St Martin's Altar)* and Csík *(Main Altar of the Descent of the Holy Spirit)*. Among the 19C painters, **Mihály Munkácsy** and **László Paál** should be mentioned, linked by their friendship. The first studied in Berlin, Munich and Paris. In *Condemned Cell*, he wanted his painting to be realistic and dramatic. On the other hand, his *Firewood Carrier*, painted during his stay at Barbizon, has a more lyrical style, with a landscape background. Paál was greatly influenced by the Barbizon School and gained fame for his landscape painting *(Noon, Path in Fontainebleau Forest, Landscape with Cows)*. Note Pál Szinyei Merse's *Picnic in May*, a subject often painted by the Impressionists. The museum also has a collection of monumental works on historical subjects, such as the *Baptism of Vajk* (the future King Stephen I) by Gyula Benczúr or, on the first floor landing, a portrayal of *Miklós Zrínyi at the Battle of Szigetvár* by Peter Krafft, a compelling work.

★ **Budapesti Történeti Múzeum (Budapest History Museum)** ⏱ – Explanations are in English and Hungarian. The contents of this museum can be summarised as Budapest through the ages. Archaeology, the Middle Ages, the modern period (the great moments in the life of the city) and the construction of the castle are retraced in a series of rooms exhibiting various collections: objects from archaeological digs, jewels, ceramics, everyday objects etc. On the ground floor, the **Gothic Sculpture Room** has very beautiful limestone statues and statuettes that are often very expressive and enhanced by the special lighting (take a map at the entrance to the room to follow the numbering more easily). The lower parts and basements of the museum, the medieval part of the castle, have beautiful rooms with quadripartite vaulting (imposing hall with a faience stove) mostly dating from the time of Sigismund of Luxembourg, king from 1387 to 1437. The **royal chapel** also merits a visit, built in the 14C during the reign of the Angevin kings. Lit by three glass bays, it is decorated with a triptych in the middle of the room.

Ludwig Múzeum ⏱ – A museum for lovers of contemporary art. Permanent works and temporary exhibitions (ground floor and second floor). In the entrance hall hangs a portrait of the donors Irene and Peter Ludwig (a German industrialist and great collector). Among the best-known names illustrating the major movements in contemporary art throughout the world are Roy Lichstenstein, Jean Tinguely, Frank Stella, Joseph Beuys, Robert Rauschenberg and Claus Oldenburg. See also a work by Yoko Ono (the widow of John Lennon, who was murdered in New York in 1980): a white chess set on a white table. The Hungarian avant-garde movement (1956-58) has not been forgotten, nor the new generation of artists represented, among others, by László Bartha, Béla Kondor and István Mazzag.

★★ VÁRNEGYED (CASTLE DISTRICT)

After a walk inside the fortifications for the view, or a visit to the museum, stroll around the old district just for pleasure, stopping here and there to look at a shopfront, a façade, a monument, or to film and take photos. If you start to feel peckish or thirsty, this is not a problem, you can choose between the many street vendors and cafés.

Szent György tér – This square in front of the main entrance to the castle is flanked on the right by two buildings: the neo-Gothic **Sándor Palace** (Sándor palota), the former residence of the Prime Minister, and the **Castle Theatre** (Várszínház) with its Rococo façade, a former Carmelite convent dissolved in 1782 on the order of Joseph II and turned into a theatre in 1787 by Farkas Kempelem, an architect and the inventor of a chess-playing automaton. The first Hungarian-language performance was given here on 5 October 1790.

Dísz tér – This square has consecutively been named Pasha Square, St George's Square, and then, since the 19C, Parade Square (an allusion to the military parades of the past). It used to be the heart of the district in the Middle Ages. Several Baroque and neo-Classical buildings surround it, such as the ochre-coloured post office (Posta). A statue of a Hussar, dressed in the uniform of the time of Maria Theresa, stands where the square joins Szent György utca. Further on, the *Honvéd statue* commemorates the Hungarian uprising against the Habsburgs in 1848-49. The Honvéd, a soldier in the national army, is represented here, holding a sword in his right hand and brandishing a flag in his left. Behind him an angel symbolically holds the laurels of victory.

Tárnok utca – Treasurer's Street (an allusion to the king's finance minister), overrun with German merchants in the Middle Ages, is bordered with beautiful houses with painted corbelled façades, or decorated with Baroque elements. The buildings are mostly shops selling souvenirs, traditional clothes and embroideries, or café-restaurants. This is undeniably a tourist street. Some façades deserve a closer look, such as the Tárnok café at **n° 14**. This house, restored in the 1950s, dates from the 14C and 15C.

Patikamúzeum (Pharmacy Museum) ⌚ – *At n° 18.* This was a 15C merchant's home before becoming the Arany Sas pharmacy (the Golden Eagle, as the wrought-iron sign over the door reminds us) in the 18C. Today this little museum displays pharmaceutical objects, pots and instruments from the 16C to the 19C. Two rooms are particularly interesting: the re-creation of an 18C apothecary's shop and a laboratory reminiscent of an alchemist's den.
A little further on, take a look at **Balta köz** (Axe Passage) to the left, a dangerously cut-throat alley during the Middle Ages.

Szentháromság tér – The main square in the Castle District, Trinity Square, is called after the **Trinity Column★** adorning its centre. This Baroque monument by Fülöp Ungleich was raised in the 18C to commemorate the plague epidemics in the 17C and 18C. It was the custom at the time for survivors to raise a monument to the glory of God, to thank Him for sparing them. A great many towns have a similar votive column. Carriages wait by the monument, ready to take visitors for a ride around the district. To the right of the square is the Matthias Church with its bell-tower, a veritable lacework of stone, and its gleaming tiled roofs. A Baroque palace built at the end of the 17C by an Italian architect, on the corner of Szentháromság utca, used to be Buda's town hall. A pinnacle turret with a clock rises over the former chapel. In the corner, in a niche over an oriel window, is a statue of Athena, protectress of the city. The goddess has a shield carved with Buda's coat of arms held in her right hand. On the other side of the square is a neo-Gothic building that used to be the Ministry of Finance.

Magyar Borok Háza (Hungarian Wine Centre) ⌚ – *At n° 6.* Hungary is a wine-producing country. While Tokay is the best-known wine abroad, there are other names to be discovered. The 20 wine-producing regions with their various grape varieties and vintages are clearly presented by a map and explanatory signs (in English and Hungarian). There are hundreds of labelled bottles. Tasting and sale of wine.

★★ Mátyás-templom ⌚ **(Matthias Church)** – Originally this church was called Our Lady of the Assumption, taking on its current name in the 19C in homage to King Matthias Corvinus. He had extended the building and celebrated his first wedding here to Catherine of Podebrady, Princess of Bohemia, in 1461, and his second one to Beatrice, daughter of the King of Naples, Ferdinand of Aragon, in 1476.
In the 13C King Béla IV had a basilica built on the site of the church dedicated to the Virgin, with a nave and two side aisles. In 1309 Charles Robert of Anjou was crowned king here (after being crowned in Székesfehérvár by the bishop of Esztergom, according to the custom of the time). The building took on its current dimensions during the reigns of Sigismund of Luxembourg (14C) and Matthias (15C) who added the south tower. When the Turks were masters of Buda in 1541, they completely destroyed the Christian furnishings, transformed the church into a mosque, and covered the walls with carpets.

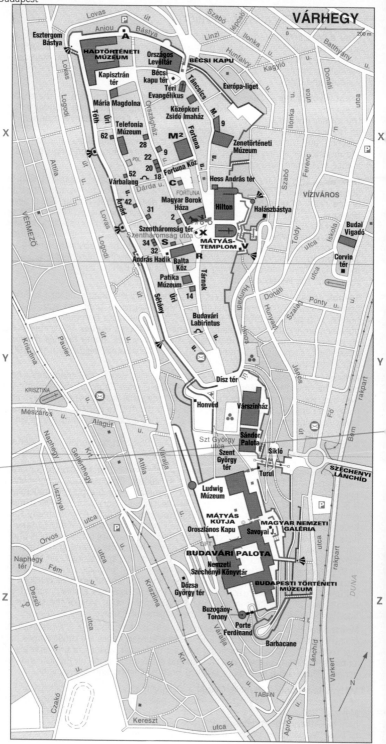

When the Christian armies liberated Our Lady in 1686, King Leopold I gave it to the Jesuits, who endowed it with Baroque elements. In 1867 the Emperor of Austria, Franz Josef I and his wife Elizabeth (Sissy) were crowned as sovereigns of Hungary. Franz Liszt composed a *Coronation Mass* for the occasion and conducted it himself. The king then decided to give the church a Gothic appearance.

SIGHTS IN THE VARHEGY QUARTER

(M) = see Museums

Sight	Map	
Abdurrahman Abdi Pacha	X	A
András Hadik	XY	
Balta Köz	Y	
Budai Vigadó	X	
Bécsi kapu	X	
Bécsi Kapu tér	X	
Budapesti Történeti Múzeum (M)		
Budavári Labirintus	Y	
Budavári palota	Z	
Buzogány torony	Z	
Dísz tér	Y	
Esztergom Bástya	X	
Európaliget	X	
Fortuna utca	X	
Hadtörténeti Múzeum (M)		
Halászbástya	X	
Hess András tér	X	
Hilton	X	
Kapisztrán tér	X	
Könyvkereskedés Litea	X	C
Középkori Zsidó Imaház (M)		
Ludwig Múzeum (M)		
Magyar Borok Háza	X	
Magyar Kereskedelmi és Vendéglátóipari Múzeum (M)		
Magyar Nemzeti Galéria (M)		
Mária Magdolna templom	X	
Mátyás Kútja	Z	
Mátyás templom	X	

Museums

Sight	Map	
Budapesti Történeti Múzeum	Z	
Hadtörténeti Múzeum	X	
Középkori Zsidó Imaház	X	
Ludwig Múzeum	Z	
Magyar Kereskedelmi és Vendéglátóipari Múzeum	X	M[2]
Magyar Nemzeti Galéria	Z	
Patika Múzeum	Y	
Telefónia Múzeum	X	
Zenetörténeti Múzeum	X	

Sight	Map	
Nemzeti Széchenyi könyvtár	Z	
Országház utca	X	
Országos Levéltár	X	
Patika Múzeum (M)		
Régi Budai Városháza	X	R
Ruszwurm Cukrászda	X	S
Sándor palota	Y	
Savoyai j.	Z	
Sikló	YZ	
Szent György tér	YZ	
Szent István szobor	X	V
Szentháromság tér	X	
Szentháromság Szobor	X	X
Táncsics Mihály utca	X	
Tárnok utca	Y	
Telefónia Múzeum (M)		
Téri Evangélikus Templom	X	
Tóth Árpád Sétány	XY	
Turul	Z	
Úri utca	XY	
Várbarlang	X	
Várszínház	Y	
Zenetörténeti Múzeum (M)		

An architect, Frigyes Schulek, was given responsibility for the project, which lasted for 20 years. After the Second World War, the reconstruction work took another 20 years. Today the edifice has once more regained its past splendour, and is one of the most visited places in the capital.

Exterior – The **Matthias Tower** on the main façade sweeps 80m/262ft up into the sky. Four-sided at the base, it becomes octagonal in its upper levels to finish with a stone spire. The **Béla Tower** to the left of the portal is smaller and in the Romanesque style. The main portal is surmounted with a tympanum representing a Virgin with Child and two angels. The church's roofs are covered with beautiful enamelled tiles, a much-used material in the 15C. The south portal *(to the right)*, or the **Mary Portal**, goes back to the time of King Louis the Great (or Louis I). A bas-relief on the pediment shows the Virgin kneeling between the Apostles. At the top of the vault, God reigns over the world, with a royal crown and the terrestrial globe. Statues of St Stephen and St Ladislas stand on either side.

Interior – *Enter through the Mary Portal.* When you step inside, the profusion of paintings comes as a great surprise. The church appears Byzantine at first sight because the vaulting, walls and pillars are abundantly decorated with paintings – geometrical or plant motifs of either medieval or Art Nouveau inspiration. The flags in the nave are souvenirs of the 1867 coronation; they were brought from Hungary's various provinces. The neo-Gothic main altar in the chancel, a work by Frigyes Schulek, has a statue of the Virgin in a mandorla, lit by golden rays. The four Evangelists and the Fathers of the Church figure on the pulpit.

Go around the church, starting to the left of the chancel.

St Ladislas' Chapel – Frescoes illustrating the life of the 11C saint, king and knight, painted by Károly Lotz.

Trinity Chapel – King Béla III of the Árpád dynasty and his wife Anne of Châtillon are buried here.

St Imre Chapel – Beautiful triptych. In the central panel Prince St Imre is shown with his father, St Stephen, and his tutor, Bishop St Gerard.

Baptismal font – This is a beautifully carved stone ensemble. The basin is supported by four small columns, decorated with a lion base. The cover of the basin is made of bronze.

Lorette Chapel – Closed by a beautiful wrought-iron door, this is entirely devoted to worship of the Virgin. Note the red-marble Virgin with Child; she is wearing the Imperial Crown of Austria.

C. Morgan/HOA QUI

The roof of St Matthias' Church

Egyháztörténeti Gyűjtemény ⓥ **(Museum of Ecclesiastical Art)** – *Stairs in the chapel to the right of the chancel.* First cross the crypt (a red-marble tomb containing the remains of the Árpád dynasty kings that were found in Székesfehérvár, coat of arms of the Knights of the Order of Malta) and then climb to St Stephen's Chapel (bust of Elizabeth – Sissy – in Carrara marble at the entrance), which exhibits the bust-reliquary of the saint. The stained-glass windows depict Hungary's saints and blessed. A spiral staircase leads up to the Royal Oratory, where St Stephen's Crown of Hungary is displayed along with photographs and explanatory panels (in English, German and Hungarian). Next, there is a gallery exhibiting vestments and religious objects (chalices, patens, monstrances and pyxes).

Halászbástya (Fishermen's Bastion) – The **statue of St Stephen**, a bronze work by Alajos Stróbl, stands regally before the Fishermen's Bastion. Stephen I, the first king of Hungary, is represented on his caparisoned horse, wearing his coronation mantle and the Holy Crown and holding the double apostolic cross that symbolises the country's conversion to Christianity. The halo around his head alludes to his canonisation in 1083. The imposing neo-Romanesque pedestal (by Frigyes Schulek) is a beautiful example of carved limestone. The bas-reliefs depict important scenes from Stephen's reign. You will also notice that on each side are the symbols for each of the four Evangelists: a man or angel for Matthew, a bull for Luke, an eagle for John, a lion for Mark.
Raised in the late 19C or early 20C and designed by Frigyes Schulek, the **Fishermen's Bastion** is a neo-Romanesque group of ramparts and turrets reminiscent of a fairy-tale castle. The origin of its name is uncertain. Two explanations are possible: in the Middle Ages a fish market may have been held nearby, or perhaps the name is linked to the fishermen's guild that actively participated in the town's defence from the original ramparts. This grouping was built for the city's Millenary celebrations in 1896. The seven towers symbolise the seven Magyar tribes, each chief being represented by a statue. The watch-path should not be missed. Tourists crowd here for the extensive **views**★★ over the Danube and Pest on the other side. From the bastion, there is an equally interesting view over the coloured roofs of the Matthias Church. Continue to the far end of the rampart that reflects in the tinted-glass of the Hilton Hotel. A double staircase leads down to the Víziváros district. There is a statue of Janós Hunyadi at the bottom; this military leader defended Belgrade against the Turks in the 15C.

Hess András tér – This square bears the name of the first printer established here in 1483. He was the publisher of the *Buda Chronicle*, the first work to be printed in Hungarian. The statue in the centre is of Pope Innocent XI, whose role was of primary importance during the war against the Turks. The statue was raised during the celebrations of the 250th anniversary of Buda's liberation. Behind the statue at n° 3 can be seen an old house called the Red Hedgehog House, because of the charming little animal decorating the upper part of the door. On the left, the Fortuna restaurant building has a beautiful yellow façade.

★★ **Táncsics Mihály utca** – A journalist, Mihály Táncsics (1799-1884) gave his name to this street, which is lined with beautiful houses bearing a series of colourful façades in Baroque or neo-Classical style. Táncsics was a hero in the battle for national independence, and was a fierce partisan of emancipation for the serfs.

Hilton Hotel – The hotel belonging to the well-known chain is a modern building that is out of keeping in a district that has been classified as historical. It was built on the site of a former Dominican convent. On the wall of the church's old St Nicholas' Tower is a bas-relief to the glory of Matthias Corvinus (it is a copy, the original being in Bautzen in Germany, in Ortenburg Castle). The king is represented enthroned, with a sceptre in his hand. Two angels hold the royal crown over his head. Go into the hotel lobby to see the remains of the nave (view of the Parliament) and the old cloisters.

Zenetörténeti Múzeum (Music History Museum) ⓥ – *At n° 7.* This beautiful Baroque mansion with its wrought-iron balcony was once the Erdődy Palace. Beethoven was a visitor here in 1800 for a concert he gave at the Buda castle theatre. The museum exhibits a large number of musical instruments (wind, string and folk instruments) and some re-created lute workshops. A section is devoted to Béla Bartók: several original music manuscripts, as well as medals, statuettes, drawings and photos pay homage to the great composer.
In the nearby house at **n° 9**, two plaques on the yellow façade indicate that Kossuth Lajos and Mihály Táncsics were imprisoned here. Before it became a Habsburg prison, this was a royal residence.

Középkori Zsidó Imaház ⓥ **(Museum of the Former Medieval Synagogue)** – *At n° 26.* In the Middle Ages Táncsics Mihály utca was the main street in Buda's Jewish district (at n° 23, archaeological digs in the garden have revealed the remains of a synagogue, indicating the presence of a Jewish community). Expelled from Hungary in 1360 on the decision of King Louis I (the Great), the Jews were able to return to Buda in 1386 and resettle in this district. In 1686, the Jews suffered from renewed persecution by the city's liberating Christian armies.

The synagogue, or rather the prayer room, is divided by two Gothic pillars. On the upper part of the walls there are 17C inscriptions. Visitors can also see tombstones from an old Jewish cemetery.

Bécsi kapu tér – The Saturday market used to be held on this peaceful square. It is surrounded by little Rococo houses with multi-coloured façades, decorated with plaster ornamentation (see nos 3 and 5). On the corner of Táncsics Mihály u. stands the **Lutheran Church** (Evangélikus templom), built in the late 19C. Near the entrance there is a plaque in memory of Pastor Gábor Sztehlo, who saved 2 000 children during the Second World War. The neo-Romanesque building of the **National Archives** (Országos Levéltár), recognisable by its beautiful enamelled roof, is on the north side of the square. The monument to Ferenc Kazinczy (1759-1831), writer, poet and great defender of the Hungarian language, represents a woman holding a lamp in her right hand.

★ **Bécsi kapu (Vienna Gate)** – The Vienna Gate, once the second main gate to the city, was rebuilt in 1936 for the ceremonies celebrating the 250th anniversary of Buda's liberation. A plaque on the inside of the gate honours the soldiers of different nationalities who died in the fight to free Buda from Ottoman occupation. The **monument to the reconquest of Buda** (1936) shows an angel with a woman's face, brandishing a double apostolic cross symbolising the victory of Pope Innocent XI's Christian armies.

Go through the gate and turn right.

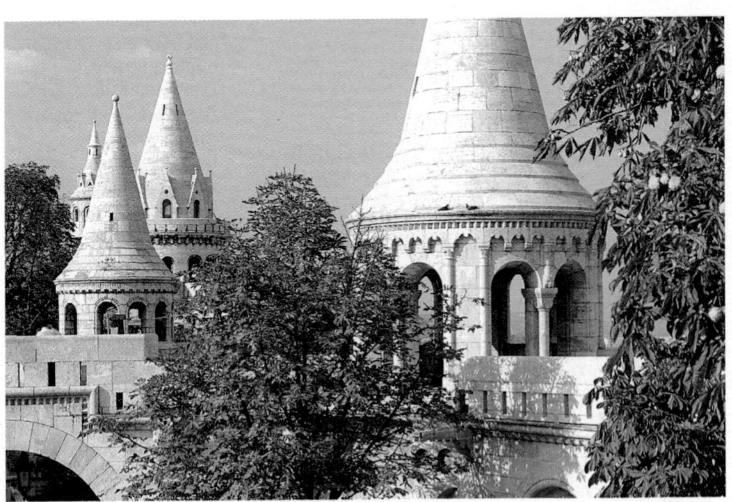

E. Baret

The Fishermen's Bastion

You come to a little open area called **Europe Park** (Európaliget). It was created in 1973 to commemorate the centennial of the foundation of Budapest. The mayors of several capitals and large European cities each planted a tree marking the event (each tree has a plaque indicating which city donated it). A sculpture by Imre Varga represents the musician Zoltán Kodály sitting on a bench. A little further on, a balcony offers a beautiful view of Margaret Island and Pest.

★★ **Fortuna utca** – This is another street, characteristic of the Castle District, where visitors can admire the façades of historical old houses.

Magyar Kereskedelmi és Vendéglátóipari Múzeum ⓥ (Museum of Hungarian Commerce and Catering) – *At n° 4.* This is a pleasant little museum that will take you a few years back in time to relive the great years of the development of Hungarian trade and tourism in Budapest. The city accomplished incredible feats for the 1896 Millenary exhibition, in terms of restaurants and hotels for the visitors and guests. Old posters, photographs, a set table, waiter and waitress uniforms, menus, are all souvenirs of this era. It is impossible to refer to gastronomy and the restaurant business without mentioning Émile Gerbeaud, the celebrated confectioner, or Károly Gundel, the great Hungarian chef who gave his name to a chic Budapest restaurant and a succulent dessert (*Gundel palacsinta* – a pancake drizzled with hot chocolate sauce and served flambé). The golden age of cafés – similar to the Viennese coffee-house age – when they were places to meet and exchange ideas, is featured in one of the rooms. There is also a re-creation of a 1918 Gellért Hotel room.

Just before Hess András tér, take Fortuna köz to the right.

This passage leads to a courtyard with souvenir shops and the **Litea bookshop** (a wide choice of books in foreign languages, records, as well as a tearoom).

Országház utca – A main thoroughfare in the Middle Ages, Parliament Street has borne its current name since 1790, when the assembly met in a former convent of St Clare nuns at n° 28. This is now one of the buildings of the National Academy of Sciences. Several houses still have Gothic features (n°s 2, 9, 18, 20 and 22).

Várbarlang (Castle Caves) ⓥ – *Entrance Dárda utca.* This walk is similar to the one through Úri utca labyrinth, where visitors can discover a network of natural caves, equipped and used by the city's various occupants over the years. During the Second World War, this veritable underground city sheltered over 4 000 people, with air shafts to the surface providing the necessary ventilation. The German, Hungarian and Russian armies used these underground hiding places to store arms and munitions and even serve as a military hospital.

From Szentháromság tér, take Szentháromság utca.

At n° 7, the **Ruszwurm Cukrászda** pastry shop founded in 1827 is unlikely to leave you indifferent. In season, tourists queue up to buy one of their superb cakes or to sit in the small adjoining room. The turn-of-the-century decor is also worth seeing. The **equestrian statue of András Hadik** in Hussar uniform stands on the corner of Úri utca. Hadik gained honour during Maria Theresa's reign, when he earned promotion to general. He took part in Austria's War of Succession and in the Seven Year War between Austria and Prussia.

★★ **Úri utca** – A walk along the longest street in the Castle District is a must to admire the splendid façades of most of the Baroque houses. The succession of fine houses lends the street a residential air and an atmosphere of peace and comfort.

Budavári Labirintus ⓥ – *At n° 9.* The **labyrinth** under the Castle District is a fascinating and intruiging attraction, particularly for children. The galleries and caves were used as shelters during different wars and also as military warehouses. Low-ceilinged passages, sometimes vaulted with

Gothic alcoves

In several of the streets in the Castle District, it is interesting to go under the vaulted porches to see the alcove seats, with trefoil lancet arches (often in groups of three). At first sight they look rather like the stone choir stalls used by canons in medieval churches – so their presence in middle class homes seems a bit odd. In Úri utca look at n°s 31, 32, 34 and 42. Several interpretations have been given. They may have served to display wares, shelter servants waiting for their masters, or perhaps, more simply, they may have been part of a fashion, an extra ornament for the house, with each owner trying to outdo his neighbour.

City streets...

E. Baret

MAGYAR KÉPEK Kft

Gabler/MAGYAR KÉPEK Kft

R. Mattès

E. Baret

water trickling down the walls *(take a light sweater)*, various rooms, a pale light, a strange musical background, statues (including a crowned head coming out of the ground), a fountain flowing with wine are mysterious to say the least. The prehistoric and historic part ends, inevitably, with a café-bar in a vaulted cellar. You can leave the Castle District through the labyrinth by taking the Lovas út exit.

Telefónia Múzeum ⓥ **(Telephone Museum)** – *At n° 49.* In the era of the mobile phone, this is a small trip back in time for those interested in a means of communication that has completely changed our way of life. Among the rather exceptional pieces in the museum are telephones which belonged to Emperor Franz Josef, King Charles IV and other sovereigns, and closer to our time, an impressive collection of telephone cards, from Europe, Asia, America, Africa, Arab countries and Australia.

Continuing along the same street, the façades at nos 52, 54, 56, 58, 60 and 62 are worth particular attention.

Úri utca opens onto Kapisztrán tér.

Kapisztrán tér – János Kapisztrán (1386-1456), a Franciscan monk of Italian origin who fought the Turks with Janós Hunyadi, has given his name to this square. The monument to his memory (by sculptor József Damkó), shows him dressed as a monk, exhorting his soldiers to battle with a banner in his hand. A Turkish soldier lies at his feet, next to a Hungarian who is sounding the trumpet to mount the attack. This quiet square is lined with majestic buildings.

Mária Magdolna templom – A Gothic bell-tower is the main element of the **remains of St Mary Magdalene Church**, which may be seen on the square. During the Ottoman occupation this was the only Christian edifice authorised by the Turks. Catholics and Protestants met here on a rota system. Temporary exhibitions are organised inside the tower. Visitors can even climb up (not for those with leg or respiratory problems) to the top and, on their way, have a look at the bells (outside) that chime regularly.

★ **Hadtörténeti Múzeum** ⓥ **(Military History Museum)** – Recognisable by the two rows of cannon, this is in a former barracks dating from 1830. Like most military museums, this one houses weapons, uniforms and decorations. However, on the ground floor, visitors may be particularly interested in some of Hungary's roles in aid missions, such as during the Vietnam War. On the first floor the Hungarian Revolution and the War of Independence rightly have their place, together with the Second World War and the October 1956 Uprising.

Take a few steps to the right on leaving the museum and go to the Esztergom Bastion where the national flag flies, symbolising the end of the Turkish occupation. There is a view from the bastion over part of Buda, the Buda Hills and Mt János behind. A little further on, along the Anjou Bastion, beyond another row of cannon, there is a tomb surmounted with a turban. Abdurrahman Abdi Pasha, Buda's last Turkish governor, is buried here. He died at the age of 70 while defending the city against the Habsburg soldiers. This monument was raised to him as a form of reconciliation, on the initiative of the family of a Hungarian soldier, György Szabó, who fell on this same spot. The inscription in Hungarian and Turkish could be translated as: "He was a heroic enemy, may he rest in peace."

Ph. Roy/HOA QUI

The *turul*, the emblem of the Magyar tribes

★ **Tóth Árpád sétány** – The **Rampart Promenade** stretches from the Esztergom Bastion to Dísz tér, and follows the ramparts built in the Middle Ages. The interest of this walk is the view it offers of Buda's western quarters, from the hills of the same name to Mt Gellért.

★★ GELLÉRTHEGY (MT GELLÉRT)

Set between Elizabeth Bridge and Liberty Bridge, Mt Gellért is one of the most characteristic features of the right bank. The wooded hill rises to an altitude of 235m/770ft.
To reach the hill from Pest on foot, cross Elizabeth Bridge, turn left and walk along until you get to some steps, then climb up. In the 19C the slopes were covered with vineyards which were wiped out by phylloxera. According to legend, Mt Gellért was much appreciated by witches and sorcerers who met here for the witches' sabbath. At the foot of the hill there are several thermal springs feeding the Gellért, Rudas and Rác spas.

Fireworks on 20 August

This is a national holiday. Hungarians pay homage to their first king, Stephen I, or St Stephen.
In Budapest, fireworks are traditionally set off from Mt Gellért, generally at about 9pm. It is a great day for the people of Budapest who start to invade the Danube's banks at 6pm – especially the left bank on the Pest side, and the bridges. It is a sight in itself to watch the buses emptying their crowds of passengers from outlying districts, both parents and children eagerly awaiting the day. Exactly on time, the lights go out and Mt Gellért is lit up, as is Liberation Monument. The show lasts about 30min, a beautiful performance, a marvellous succession of multi-coloured tableaux met with cries and cheers. Then it is darkness for a brief moment, before everything lights up again, and the human tide gradually withdraws to return the following year.

St Gellért Monument – Gellért (Gerald) was made first bishop of Csanád County in 1030. He lived during Stephen I's reign and was called by the king himself from his Benedictine monastery of San Giorgio in Venice to serve as a tutor to the royal successor, Prince Imre. His actions also culminated in the baptising of numerous pagans. The pagan revolt that followed Stephen's death in 1038 led to Gellért's martyrdom in 1046. It is said that he was thrown from the top of the hill, in a barrel. Canonised in 1083, St Gellért is today highly honoured in Hungary. The monumental bronze statue by Gyula Jankovits (1904) stands on the site of his martyrdom, half way up the hill, in front of a peristyle of classical inspiration. Gellért seems to be blessing the city, holding a cross in his raised right hand. A converted pagan is shown at his feet. The **view★★** is excellent.

Citadella – The **citadel** crowns the hill. It was built in 1851 on the order of Emperor Franz Josef. As the Hungarian revolt (1848-49) had shaken the Austrians, the latter saw this defence structure as a good way to keep the city under control. A hotel and a restaurant occupy part of the buildings.
Visitors can go inside the fortifications and walk around the watch-path. From here the **view★★★** is magnificent and particularly extensive. You can contemplate the town below and Pest on the opposite bank. In the distance, to the left, can be seen one of the city's green spots, Margaret Island.

Liberation Monument – This is a colossal monument such as those seen in many other Central European countries. On a limestone base, a woman (14m/46ft high) in a very dignified pose bears a palm leaf aloft that she seems to be offering to the sky. This monument was built in 1947 in memory of the city's liberation by Red Army soldiers.
There is a **view★★** of the river, Buda and Pest from the terrace. On the right the bird's-eye view of the Gellért Hotel and baths enables you to appreciate the architecture of the site as a whole.

Take the path that runs alongside the citadel on the left.

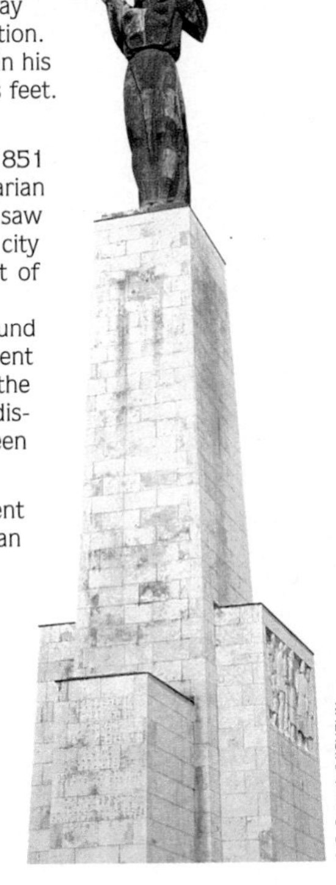
J.-C. Saturnin/MICHELIN

Jubileumi Park – Jubilee Park was inaugurated for the 40th anniversary of the October Revolution. It makes for an interesting walk, with shady paths, flowerbeds and lawns. Take the path down to the Gellért baths.

★★★**Gellértfürdő and Gellért Hotel** – *See The Baths.* The Gellért baths and hotel are probably the most prestigious thermal bath and hotel complex in the Hungarian capital. The name conjures up the grand age of luxury hotels. The Art Nouveau exterior is a monument in itself. The thermal spa complex (entrance on Kelenhegyi út) even includes a Thai massage centre and a dental surgery (Hungarian dental care is famous, and attractively priced). The Hotel entrance is on Szent Gellért tér, and the lobby is worth a quick visit.

Stand on the other side of the square next to the Danube for an interesting view of the hotel's façade. Turn to the right to get a good view of Liberty Bridge and the majestic buildings of the University of Economic Sciences on the opposite bank.

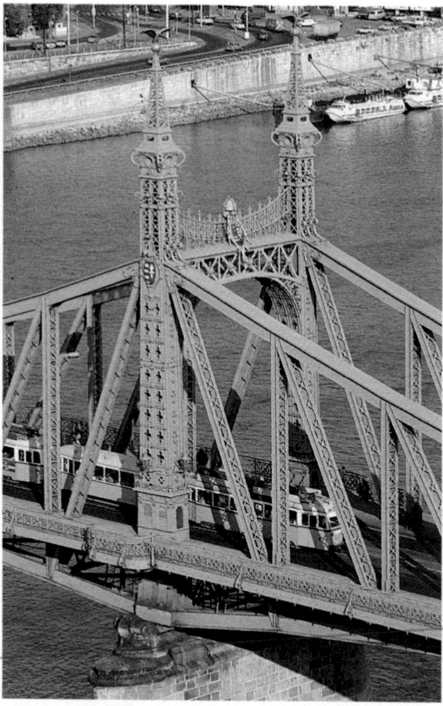

G. Durand/PHOTONONSTOP

Liberty Bridge

Sziklakápolna (Chapel in the Rock) – *Opposite the Gellért spa entrance.* A gate opens onto a cave divided into several chapels cut into the rock itself. One of them contains the Polish eagle and a replica of the famous Black Virgin from Jasna Góra Monastery (Czêstochowa, Poland).

★★**Szabadság híd (Liberty Bridge)** – With Chain Bridge, this is one of the most original bridges in the city. It has a span of 331m/1 086ft, and is a beautiful example of metal architecture. Budapest owes much to the three engineers: János Feketeházy, Aurel Czekélius and Virgil Nagy. Named the Franz Josef Bridge, it was inaugurated in 1896 by the emperor himself. It took on its current symbolic name in 1946, the year of its reconstruction.

The *turul*, Hungary's mythical bird, decorates the four turrets surmounting the bridge's piers. At each end, the Hungarian coat of arms with St Stephen's Crown at the top is visible on the arches.

TABÁN

This district stretches from Elizabeth Bridge at the foot of Mt Gellért, to the foot of Castle Hill.

The name *tabán* is a Turkish word meaning tannery. During the Ottoman occupation, Serbian tanners occupied this district, living in miserable conditions.

Erzsébet híd (Elizabeth Bridge) – This modern suspension bridge bears the name of Elizabeth of Wittelsbach, the wife of Franz Josef, Empress of Austria and Queen of Hungary, known as Sissy.

On the right, beyond the bridge, coming from Pest, you can cross a little park with György Zala's sculpture representing the queen so dearly loved by the Hungarians. A little further on, on the corner of Attila út and Apród utca, stand two graffiti-covered sections of the **Berlin wall**, which have been placed here symbolically. Further up, on the grassy slope, is a naïve-style monument commemorating the October 1956 Uprising.

Tabáni plébániatemplom – **Tabán Parish Church** is dedicated to St Catherine of Alexandria. It is a Baroque edifice built on the site of a former medieval church that the Turks turned into a mosque.

Semmelweis Orvostörténeti Múzeum ⓥ – This **Museum of the History of Medicine** is housed in the birthplace of Ignác Fülöp Semmelweis (1818-65), a famous gynaecologist and obstetrician who also specialised in infectious diseases. He is buried in the garden. In Room 3, which is partly dedicated to the doctor (furniture and personal objects), are furnishings from the former Holy Spirit pharmacy (18C-19C).

Ybl Miklós tér – There is a monument to architect Miklós Ybl (1814-91) on this square, as well as an eye-catching pavilion, even more impressive at night when it is illuminated. The pavilion is an old pumping station that has been turned into a casino-restaurant (Várkert Casino and Valentine Restaurant).
Beyond the square you come to steps leading up the slopes of Castle Hill. You will then be able to see a neo-Classical group of terraces, arcades and statues, the work of Miklós Ybl.

★ VÍZIVÁROS (WATER TOWN)

As early as the Middle Ages this district, the lower town, was called water town because of the many thermal springs.

★★ **Széchenyi Lánchíd** – Chain Bridge, the city's oldest bridge, is also called Széchenyi Bridge, after the person who commissioned its construction. It is to Count István Széchenyi that Budapest owes what is one of the symbols, or perhaps *the* symbol of the city. In December 1820 the young aristocratic Hussar captain learned that his father had died in Buda. He came to Pest to take the ferry, but found it impossible to cross the Danube as the ice had interrupted all traffic on the river. Forced to stay put for several days, the idea of building a bridge took root in his mind. Several projects were presented and two British engineers, William Tierney Clark and Adam Clark, were given responsibility for the project. The work lasted from 1842 to 1849.
The bridge has a span of 380m/1 246ft and is 15.7m/51ft wide. The use of stone and iron has created a beautiful Classical ensemble, that should be seen when lit up at night; the suspension cables linking the two piers, in the form of a triumphal arch, look like garlands of light. Two stone lions proudly guard each end, crouching on pedestals.

Clark Ádám tér – This square is very busy with the thousands of vehicles going into and coming out of the tunnel cut into Castle Hill that leads to the Kristinaváros district. The tunnel was designed by the British engineer Adam Clark, who supervised the construction of Chain Bridge. To the left, beside some bushes, you will notice a sculpture marking the **zero kilometre point** from which all distances from the capital are measured.

Fő utca – The district's main street runs parallel to the Danube and is lined with an assortment of buildings.
N^{os} **30 and 32** are a former Capuchin convent and its adjacent church. They stand just before **Corvin tér**, a square bordered with Baroque houses (n°s 2 to 5). On the north side, the **Budai Vigadó** Theatre with its neo-Classical layout (Buda's concert hall, not to be confused with the Pest Theatre on Vigadó tér) is where the Hungarian Folk Music Ensemble appears (Magyar Állami Népi Együttes). Further up on the right, note the red-brick, neo-Gothic **Calvinist Church**.

Tongueless lions?

Have you noticed that the Chain Bridge lions do not have tongues? According to legend, a shoemaker's apprentice noticed this on the day of the inauguration and commented on it aloud. The audience at the ceremony broke up in hilarious laughter, and the sculptor, János Marschalkó, threw himself into the Danube. A sad end. In fact, this is not true. The lions do have tongues, but they are so small you would have to climb up on the pedestal and get close to their mouths to see them, if you felt so inclined. As for the sculptor, he died much later, of old age.

Batthyány tér – This is a central point for urban transport, and very useful for tourists (underground line n° 2, tramways, HÉV suburban train terminus). Count **Lajos Batthyány** (1806-49), a liberal politician supporting the Austrian Compromise, was Prime Minister of the first Hungarian government in 1848. He resigned from his post following a disagreement with Lajos Kossuth, head of the liberal movement during the 1848 Revolution, and was executed by the Austrians in 1849 after the Hungarian revolution failed.

★ **Szent Anna-templom (St Anne's Church)** – This graceful Baroque church, with two identical bell-towers, overlooks the square. You can make out allegorical statues of Faith, Hope and Charity over the portal. In the centre of the façade is a statue of St Anne

J.-C. Saturnin/MICHELIN

The Chain Bridge

with Mary. The interior, like all Baroque churches, is profusely decorated. This is the case with the main altar framed with marble columns, the cupola's frescoes representing the Trinity, the gilded pulpit ornamented with cherubs, and the organ case. The **Café Angelika** is near the church; go towards the Danube, and you will find it slightly lower down. The café, a former literary coffee shop, is a pleasant place to come for cakes and to admire the decor set off by beautiful hangings and panelling. The Café Miró is also on the square, and is decorated with works by the Catalan artist. Cross the avenue for an impressive overall view of the Parliament on the opposite bank.

G. Siméone/PHOTONONSTOP

Castle Hill Funicular

At **n° 3** on the square, near the 19C market (Vásárcsarnok, in reality a supermarket), is what was once the *White Cross Inn* where plays were also performed. This house stands out for its reliefs of the four seasons as well as its two wrought-iron balconies on either side of the central building, Rococo on the right and Baroque on the left. The entrance is through the porch below. A bar sign with the name of Casanova reminds patrons that the famous adventurer and seducer supposedly came here when he toured Europe at the end of the 18C.

Just beyond Nagy Imre tér, an imposing building bounded by four streets could raise a few questions. What was concealed behind the austere wall of this brick edifice? The answer (depending on the period of history you are talking about): the military tribunal, the political police, the Gestapo.

★★ **Király gyógyfürdő (Király Baths)** – This is one of the oldest establishments dating from the Turkish occupation (16C). The characteristic features of this period can be clearly seen by stepping back on Fő utca. Note the green cupolas, the largest of which was raised in 1556 on the order of Pasha Mustapha and is surmounted by a Turkish crescent.

Szent Flórián kápolna – **St Florian's Chapel** is a charming little Baroque edifice built between 1759 and 1760 by architect Mátyás Nepauer. Statues of St Nicholas and St Blaise decorate the façade. The main altar has paintings showing the saint's apotheosis.

Bem József tér – Numerous gatherings took place here during the October 1956 Uprising. **József Bem** (1794-1850) is a symbol for Hungarians. An ardent defender of liberty, this general, of Polish origin, took an active part in the 1848 revolution. The great Hungarian poet Sándor Petőfi paid homage to him with verses engraved on the pedestal of his statue, which represents him wounded and exhorting his men to battle.

PEST

BELVÁROS (THE INNER CITY)

Pest's historical centre, referred to as Belváros, is basically delimited by Margaret Bridge (Margit híd), the Little Boulevard and Liberty Bridge (Szabadság híd). The district is very busy in the daytime, with numerous banks, government offices, shops, cafés and restaurants.

Lipótváros

The Lipótváros district – **Leopold Town** – gets its name from Leopold II, King of Hungary from 1790 to 1792.

Kossuth Lajos tér – An immense crowd gathered on this square on 23 October 1989 to celebrate the proclamation of the Hungarian Republic. The red star decorating the tip of the Parliament dome's spire was taken down. The square bears the name of **Lajos Kossuth**, one of the leaders of the War of Independence from 1848 to 1849. His statue (to the right facing the Parliament) shows him surrounded by other figures. Opposite, on the other side of the square, is an equestrian statue of Ferenc Rákóczi II, the hero of the 1703-11 war against the Habsburgs.

★★★ **Országház** ⏲ **(Parliament)** – Budapest's Parliament has an arcaded façade on the Danube and another on Kossuth Lajos tér. It is a gigantic neo-Gothic monument with a cathedral-like appearance. With its dome, small bell-towers, pinnacles, spires, arcades and galleries, it is reminiscent of the British Parliament in London or even Milan Cathedral. It was built between 1885 and 1902 to plans by Imre Steindl. In 1896 the Assembly sat here to mark the 1 000th anniversary of the foundation of the country.
Eighty-eight statues representing Hungarian sovereigns, princes and military leaders line the façades. On each side of the central building, two symmetrical wings join each other under the dome. They were built when the Assembly was divided into two chambers: the Chamber of Deputies and the Upper Chamber.
Today the Parliament is the seat of the Republic's Presidency (south wing), the Government (north wing) and the National Assembly.
On the square, the principal entrance decorated with stone lions leads to the main staircase.

Interior ⏲ – *The guided tour of the inside only covers a part of the building.* Majestic, sumptuous and brilliant is how the main staircase and the lobby can be described, given the glitter of the profuse gilded decoration. The ceiling is decorated with quadripartite vaulting and frescoes by Károly Lotz, *The Apotheosis of the Legislation* and *The Glorification of Hungary.* At the foot of the stairs, in a niche in the left wall, there is a bronze bust of architect Imre Steindl, by Alajos Stróbl.

M. Guillou/MICHELIN

The immense, **circular room with a cupola** contains many years of history represented by statues of successive sovereigns as well as the coats of arms of the former administrative districts. The room also contains the **Crown jewels★★**. These were moved here from the National Museum on the occasion of the 1 000th anniversary of the coronation of Stephen I (1 Jan 2001). The Crown of St Stephen, as it is known, was returned to Hungary by the Americans in 1978. It had been securely guarded up to this date in the United States, where it had found refuge after the Second World War. It figures on the country's coat of arms and is a magnificent example of goldsmith's work, probably created in the 11C. Its lower part is of Byzantine inspiration, and is composed of small plaques of cloisonné enamel of the saints and archangels, inset with precious stones. In the centre figures the Byzantine emperor, Michael Ducas. The upper part, of Latin inspiration, is made up of two wide enamelled crossover gold strips, with a Christ in Majesty and portraits of two Apostles whose names are inscribed in Latin. The whole is topped by an oblique cross (the fact that it is oblique has aroused much questioning. However, it has simply been damaged over the years).
The **sceptre** made of silver and rock crystal is said to be of both Egyptian and Hungarian origin. The orb, a **globe** surmounted with the patriarchal cross and adorned with the coat of arms of the House of Anjou, is believed to date back to the 14C (reign of King Charles Robert of Anjou). The **sword** comes from a 16C Venetian workshop.
The statues in the **Commons** are allegories of the main trades of commerce and industry. The **Debating Chamber**, entirely in wood, is also lavishly gilded. The President directs the debates facing the deputies who are in a semicircle in front of him, or more accurately, given its shape, in a horseshoe. You will notice a few spaces in the corridors with benches reserved for the deputies and numbered cigar holders (each number corresponding to a Member of Parliament).
From both the inside and outside you will notice two sorts of half-buried pavilions on the square. These are iceboxes, an early form of air-conditioning! They contained ice and, linked to the building by conduits, served to bring a little cool air to the inside.

★★ **Néprajzi Múzeum (Ethnography Museum)** ⓥ – This neo-Renaissance palace, the former Magistrates' Court and former Appeals Court, was built at the end of the 19C. Above the pediment resting on six columns is a sculpture reminding us of the building's first function. It represents the goddess of Justice with a chariot harnessed to three horses. The extremely large collections give a good idea of the rural world from the 18C to the early 20C, before the Treaty of Trianon. Agriculture, fishing, craftsmanship, fairs and markets, the family (from birth to death) and traditional festivals (Carnival, Easter, Christmas, New Year) are clearly illustrated with photos, costumes, everyday objects, tools, furniture etc.

As you leave the museum, turn left, cross Altotmány utca and walk alongside the Ministry of Agriculture (Földművelésügyi Minisztérium).

You come to a little square, **Vértanúk tere**, with a **statue of Imre Nagy** standing on a bridge (symbolising totalitarianism giving way to democracy), his eyes turned to the Parliament. Recalled to head the Hungarian government

during the insurrection in October 1956, Imre Nagy recommended radical reforms to liberalise the regime and break free of the Soviet yoke. The intervention of Soviet troops did not take long to follow. Nagy made a moving broadcast appealing for the protection of Western powers. Condemned to death, he was executed in 1958 and his memory rehabilitated in 1989.

★ **Szabadság tér** – Liberty Square has a certain style despite its slightly ostentatious air. It was created on the site of an old Austrian barracks. Large and open, it is lined with buildings with majestic façades, such as the former Stock Exchange (today **MTV Televízió**, the national television), and opposite, Hungary's national bank **(Magyar Nemzeti Bank)**. These two edifices, although very different, are by the same architect, Ignác Alpár. If you are interested in the history of currencies, go into the bank to see the **coin and banknote collection (Bankjegy és Érmegyűjtemény)** ⓥ. As you leave, on the corner of Arany János utca and Hercegprímás utca, the small **Zrínyi pharmacy** deserves to be visited for its original wood furniture and its old jars (1803). North of the square, in the middle of the lawns laid out in a half-circle, is the only remaining monument dedicated to the Soviets. It is an **obelisk** to the memory of Red Army soldiers who liberated the city in 1945. On the other side of the street is the American Embassy, by pure coincidence, of course! The United States is honoured here in the person of **General Harry Hill Bandholtz**, whose **statue** stands on the square. After the Council Republic fell in 1919, he saved the treasures of the National Museum from looting by Romanian troops.

Hold utca – At n° 4 on this street is one of Ödön Lechner's works; he had a hand in virtually every building in the Art Nouveau style in Budapest. Here the structure is the **former Post Office Savings Bank**★★ (Posta-Takarékpénztar, *see illustration in the Introduction*). It is true that the design of this ensemble was somewhat fanciful, to the extent of being overly ornate. But the decoration, colours, and shapes, all in a mixture of brick, mosaic and ceramics, make an extremely original composition.
Almost opposite, at n° 13, a **covered market** (Vásárcsarnok) deserves a look for its metal architecture and stalls.
Further north you come to a triangular crossroads. In the centre, in a bronze lamp on a pedestal, burns the **Eternal Flame** in homage to Lajos Batthyány, the Prime Minister of the first Hungarian government, shot here by an Austrian squad on 6 October 1849.

★ **Szent István Bazilika (St Stephen's Basilica)** – This building was begun in 1851 and completed in 1906. József Hild, the architect of Esztergom and Eger, began the project, which was taken over after his death in 1867 by Miklós Ybl. It was Ybl who gave it its colossal look, almost crushingly so, that was inspired by the neo-Renaissance style. The façade, still austere, has a porch at its main entrance, surmounted by a carved pediment showing the Virgin surrounded by the Hungarian saints. A number of statues by Leó Fessler can be seen outside: the four Evangelists (at the base of the dome), the Fathers of the Church (towers), the Twelve Apostles (east end, which you will find if you walk around the building to the right).
The interior, which is laid out in the shape of a Greek cross, surprises with its grandeur and ornamentation, especially the mosaic cupola (96m/315ft high) and the chapels one after the other in the side aisles. On the main altar, the statue of St Stephen is in Carrara marble, and there are low reliefs showing scenes from his life. **St Dexter's Chapel** (to the left of the chancel) contains one of the church's most valuable pieces; this is a reliquary, thought to be St Stephen's right hand, which is carried in a procession on 20 August, the day devoted to the first Hungarian king, Stephen, canonised in 1083.

MAGYAR KÉPEK Kft

Couronne de saint Étienne

North Tower ⓥ – From the top of the tower there is a fine **panorama**★★ of the whole town.

Take Zrínyi utca.

Roosevelt tér – The square used to be a market place in the early 19C. Today, it bears the name of Franklin Delano Roosevelt, the President of the United States from 1933 to 1945 (commemorative plaque on the corner of József Attila utca on the wall of the Ministry of the Interior – Belügyminisztérium). At each end of the square stand two statues that make a pair. To the right, looking in the direction of Chain Bridge, is a statue of István Széchenyi and to the left, a statue of Ferenc Deák. Roosevelt tér is a very busy square; all the vehicles coming from or going to Buda via the bridge have to go through it.

Gresham palota – This is another example of the Art Nouveau style in Budapest. Gresham Palace (1907) has clearly aged badly, but it is still one of the most important buildings in the city. It is named after a London insurance firm that itself borrowed the name of the founder of the first London stock exchange, the Royal Exchange. Thomas Gresham lived from 1519 to 1579 and was financial councillor to the Crown when he undertook the construction of the Royal Exchange. His bust can be seen in a niche at the top of the edifice. The façade looking onto Roosevelt tér is decorated with carved stone reliefs. There was a Gresham Café, between the two World Wars, a meeting place for a great many artists. Today the palace contains offices and a casino.

Magyar Tudományos Akadémia – On the other side of the square, facing the Inter-Continental Hotel, is the **Hungarian Academy of Sciences** (19C) housed in a neo-Renaissance building by Berlin architect Friedrich August Stüler. During the first Diet from 1825 to 1827, Count István Széchenyi gave a year of his income to build this Academy. On the top floor, the six statues represent the first six departments of the Academy: law, science, mathematics, philosophy, linguistics and history. On the Danube side are other allegorical statues: Archaeology, Poetry, Astronomy and Political Science. On the corners of the building are statues of Newton (English mathematician, physicist and astronomer), Lomonossov (Russian physicist), Galileo (Italian mathematician, physicist and astronomer), Révay (Hungarian linguist), Descartes (French mathematician, physicist and philosopher) and Leibniz (German mathematician and philosopher).

Kiskörút **(Little Boulevard)**

The Little Boulevard, as it is called locally, forms a curve following Deák tér, Károly körút, Kálvin tér and Vámház körút. The historical centre lies between this limit and the Danube. The great Bajcsy-Zsilinszky út, the avenue linking Deák tér to Nyugati tér, can be considered an extension of the Little Boulevard; one runs into the other.

Deák Ferenc tér – A strategic place for all those visiting the capital, since all the underground lines stop here as well as several bus and tramway lines. The square is named after **Ferenc Deák** (1803-76), lawyer, moderate politician and Minister of Justice in 1848, who participated in the celebrated Compromise of 1867, making Austria and Hungary two associated States. The **Lutheran Church** stands on the square and can be recognised by its neo-Classical façade. Erzébet tér, with its small park and coach station, is near the square.

Földalatti Vasúti Múzeum (Underground Museum) ⓥ – This little museum, in the Deák tér subway station, deserves a short visit. Along the platform, explanatory panels (in English and Hungarian) and old photographs retrace the construction of Line n° 1, which was the first subway line on the Continent, inaugurated on 2 May 1896. Moreover, the line is rather amazing, with its three little yellow carriages, it seems to come from a model city. You can also see three carriages from different periods (1896 and 1973) including one made in Hungary.

Take Sütő utca (Tourinform – tourist office – at n° 2), leading to a busy little square decorated with the Fountain of the Nereids (Szomory Dezső tér), then continue along Bárczy István utca until Szervita tér. Go a short way along Városház utca, which branches off to the left to admire n°s 9 to 11, the façade of the **City Hall** (Polgármesteri Hivatal). Once a military hospital, then a barracks under Joseph II in 1784, the biggest Baroque building in the city was constructed by Martinelli in the early 18C. There are statues of Atlas and allegories of War and Peace over the porch.

Szervita tér – From the middle of this square you have a good view of the Art Nouveau (or Secessionist) **mosaic** decorating the upper part of a building with a clothes shop on the ground floor (n° 3). The theme of the mosaic (by Miksa Róth) is the Glorification of Hungary. There is the Virgin, the patron saint, surrounded by angels bearing the coats of arms of the country and of Magyar heroes.

Szervita templom (Servite Church) – The Servite Order was given permission to establish itself in Hungary in 1686 during the reign of Leopold I. The Baroque church is dedicated to St Anne. There are statues of St Augustine and St Philip on the façade's balustrade. Above the portal, a bas-relief features the Order's patron saints. There is a single nave, and a statue of St Anne at the main altar.

M. Guillot/MICHELIN

Vigadó tér

Vigadó tér – This square on the banks of the Danube is extremely busy in the summer season. The restaurant terraces are packed. Groups of musicians, and stalls selling souvenirs, handicrafts and clothes draw visitors who stroll along the promenade known locally as the **korzó** or **Duna korzó**. This is a pleasant walk that goes along the river from Roosevelt tér to Petőfi tér (statue of poet Sándor Petőfi in front of the Marriott Hotel) and which provides a good **general view** of Castle Hill and Mt Gellért.

★**Pesti Vigadó** – This concert hall is considered a remarkable example of Hungarian Romanticism. It was built between 1859 and 1864 to plans by Frigyes Feszl and was designed to hold ceremonies, concerts, balls and performances of all kinds. It still is an important venue, one of the city's famous concert halls. The façade facing the square is marked out by columns topped with crowns. Abundantly decorated with sculptures, it forms an unusual ensemble.

★**Vörösmarty tér** – Every tourist visits this square at least once, simply on account of its location in the heart of the pedestrian district. In the centre there is a **monument to Mihály Vörösmarty** in Carrara marble. This Romantic poet from the first half of the 19C was a fervent patriot. On the statue's base are lines from his famous poem *Szózat* (*Appeal*, 1840), which has become something of a second national anthem, to be heard at the end of solemn gatherings. It begins like this:

Be faithful to your country,
Oh Hungarian! It is your cradle.
With its flesh it has nourished you
And it will be your tomb.

All around the monument in summer, day and night, are musicians, painters, portraitists and caricaturists. The café terraces can barely cope. The famous pastry shop **Gerbeaud**★ is here, a meeting place for the sophisticated crowd in the early 20C. Émile Gerbeaud, a Swiss confectioner, created this establishment in 1884. Step inside to admire its turn-of-the-century charm, and, while there, treat yourself to one of the marvellous cakes. On the corner of Deák Ferenc utca, the **Luxus** clothes and fashion accessory shop dating from 1911 deserves a look.

★**Váci utca** – Not to be missed along with Vörösmarty tér and Szabadsajtó út. This is the ultimate shopping street. With its foreign exchange offices and all types of shops with very tempting windows, it is also popular with tourists. People come here to window-shop or buy clothes, tableware, embroideries, music, books, jewellery, leatherwork etc. In high season, amateur musicians, mime artists and other entertainers perform for passers-by while hoping for a few forints in return. There are also stallholders selling postcards, guides and illustrated books about the city. Váci utca is also a street where it is interesting to look up and admire a few façades: n° 5, n° 11a (Art Nouveau), n° 13 (the oldest neo-Classical building in the street), n° 15 (carved wood façade), n° 18 (ceramics).

On a little square on the corner of Régiposta utca stands the **Hermes Fountain** (Hermészdíszkút), celebrating the messenger of the gods who was, among other things, protector of trade.

In the district next to Váci utca there are other shopping streets worth a short walk: **Petőfi Sándor utca, Párizsi utca, Haris köz, Kígyó utca**.

★ **Párizsi udvar** – **Paris passage** is one of Pest's sights, not for its shops, but for its architecture! Byzantine, Moorish or both at the same time, or perhaps Venetian, or Art Nouveau. A strange mixture in any case. The name goes back to the 19C and alludes to the covered passages then fashionable in Paris at that time. Note the glass cupola.

Március 15 tér – This square stretches out near Elizabeth Bridge. Its name recalls the first day of the 1848 revolution. Below, there are some Roman ruins called **Contra Aquincum**. These are the remains of a fortified camp built at the end of the 3C during the reign of Emperor Diocletian. On the square itself there is a modern sculpture of Roman legionaries.

★ **Belvárosi plébániatemplom** – The **Inner City Parish Church**, the oldest church in the Hungarian capital, was built on the site of a Roman fortress. It is among the city's most famous images, with its two symmetrical bell-towers rising on either side of a porch surmounted by a pediment. Various styles have been used on the building, illustrating several periods of construction. This is noticeable from the outside where Gothic buttresses contrast with the Baroque façade.
As soon as you go through the door, you see the triumphal arch and the Gothic chancel with its ribbed vaulting beyond. The Baroque nave has barrel vaulting. There are red-marble tabernacles on the walls, separating the chancel from the nave. During the Turkish occupation, the church, like so many others, was turned into a mosque. The mihrab, visible in the fourth niche in the apse to the right of the chancel, is a reminder of this. The pulpit is a beautiful work of Baroque-style carved wood.

Ferenciek tere – From this square, always very busy in the day, there is an underground passage (M 3 underground line station) to the Váci utca pedestrian district. From the entrance to the underground railway, you can see Elizabeth Bridge with Mt Gellért behind it. In the foreground are the **Clotilda Palaces** (Klotild paloták), two perfectly identical buildings, on each side of Szabadsatjó utca. They are named after the wife of Joseph, the Palatine Prince, and illustrate the early 20C style; both are topped with small lanterns. On the other side of the avenue take a look at the building on the corner of Petőfi Sándor utca. Its upper part is a beautiful example of the Art Nouveau style.
The **Nereids Fountain** in the middle of the square dates from 1835.

★ **Ferences templom** – The **Franciscan Church's** main entrance is through a porch framed with columns and surmounted by the Order's coat of arms. There are three niches on the façade that contain statues of St Peter of Alcantara, St Anthony of Padua and St Francis of Assisi. The interior is decorated in the Baroque style, and does not have side aisles. For a time Franz Liszt withdrew to the Franciscan monastery nearby (which no longer exists as such). The place where he sat during Mass is indicated on a pew. The ceiling frescoes have the Life of the Virgin as their theme. There is a beautiful carved wooden pulpit decorated with the Twelve Apostles.

M. Guillot/MICHELIN

Gerbeaud cake and tea shop

A little further on to the left, beyond the *Kárpátia* restaurant, stands the **University Library** (Egyetemi Kônyvtár), founded in 1635 and built here in the 19C. Stand on the other side of the street to have a better view of the neo-Classical façade.

A great name in Hungarian literature

Endre Ady was born in Érmindszent in Transylvania on 22 November 1877. After studying law in Debrecen and Nagyvárad (now Oradea in Romania), he worked for several newspapers and was soon noticed for his frank style. During a stay in Paris (1904-05), he discovered Symbolism, the literary movement created in reaction to Parnassian poetry. With his literary review *Nyugat (West)* he established himself as one of the leaders of the revival in Hungarian literature. His *New Poems* published in 1906 only confirmed this change, in both form and spirit. In his political poems the image he presented of his country was disconcerting, Hungary was no longer the illustrious land of the Magyars but a more modest and isolated country. On the theme of religion, Ady showed himself to be an iconoclast, a blasphemer. Tormented, ill and worn down by alcohol and drugs, he died in Budapest in 1919. The country gave him a national funeral.
His major works include *New Poems* (1906), *Blood and Gold* (1907), *On Élie's Chariot* (1908), *I Would Like to Be Loved* (1910) and *Leading the Dead* (1918).

Ady Endre Emlékmúzeum (Endre Ady Apartment Museum) ⏲ – *Veres Pálné utca 4, first floor*. The furniture in the study (bookcases, desk with personal objects), the dining room and the bedroom recall the last two years that the poet spent with his wife before his death.

Petőfi Irodalmi Múzeum (Petőfi Literary Museum) ⏲ – *Károlyi Mihály utca 16*. This museum called after Sándor Petőfi, the illustrious poet (of whom there is a statue on the staircase), is housed in the former palace of the Károlyi counts. The street bears the name of Mihály Károlyi, politician and first President of the Hungarian Republic (1919). This well-renovated building, in the Classical style, is by András Mayerhoffer. The museum is more for literary buffs than passing tourists, presenting the life and work of Hungarian authors less well-known than Sándor Petőfi, to whom an entire room is devoted.

★ **Egyetemi templom (University Church)** – This is probably the most popular Baroque church in the city. Originally it was part of a monastery of monks of the Order of St Paul, the only religious order founded in Hungary in the 13C, which was abolished in 1782 during the reign of Joseph II. The exterior is very imposing. The façade, surmounted by a pediment decorated with the Order's emblem, is framed by two onion-domed bell-towers each topped with a cross. The statues of St Paul

"Stand, Magyar, your country needs you."

These words, dear to the Hungarian heart, were the signal for revolution. They were pronounced by **Sándor Petőfi** on 15 March 1848 and are extracts from the poem *National Song* that he wrote to exhort the national spirit to battle against the Habsburgs. Considered one of the heroes of the revolution of 1848-49 as well as the greatest Hungarian poet, Petőfi was born in Kiskőrös in 1823, to a family of modest means. Very early on he left school to join a theatrical troupe, then to work for a newspaper. He later served as a volunteer – a *honvéd* – in the national army and played an active part in the War of Independence. He was General Bem's aide when he fell under enemy fire on 31 July 1849 during the Battle of Segesvár (today Sighišoara, Romania).
He published his first poem in 1842 in a literary review, followed two years later by his first collection, *Poems (Versek)*, in which he unveiled his personal experiences, feelings, and outlook on life, nature and the world. The same year he brought out *János vitéz (John the Valiant)*, a masterpiece of populist literature. Collections such as *Cypress Branches from Etelke's Tomb (Cipruslombok Etelke sirjáról)* and *Clouds (Felhők)* express a period of extreme pessimism. His political poems manifest the revolutionary spirit and fierce love of liberty that would make him a symbol of national independence. In 1955 a group of young intellectuals and anti-authority communists founded the **Petőfi Circle** to fight against the political purges exercised by the Moscow-controlled government.
Sándor Petőfi will always be a symbol of national independence.

the Hermit and St Anthony are visible at the top of the pediment. A beautiful carved wood door opens onto an interior with a sumptuous decoration of frescoes (see those in the vaulting representing scenes from the Life of the Virgin), false marble, gold and carved wood. In the chancel over the altar there is a copy of the Black Virgin in the Jasna Góra Monastery (Czêstochova, Poland). The **pulpit★★**, like other decorative features in the church (confessionals, the balustrade of the organ loft, pews) was carved out of wood by the monks.
Near the church on Egyetem tér, the **Lórand Eötvös University** (Law Faculty) is in a neo-Baroque building.

Continue along Kecskeméti utca and at Kálvin tér (Calvinist church with a four-columned portico) take Vámház körút on the right to the tramway station in front of Liberty Bridge.

★★ **Vásárcsarnok (Main Market)** – In all towns, main markets are obviously among the places that tourists like to stroll and get a feel for local life. Already from the outside, the brick façade with its neo-Gothic towers, the roofs covered with Zsolnay majolicas, the arches and the clock on the middle section all have something attractive about them. The place, it has to be said, also looks a little like a railway station.
It was built at the end of the 19C as part of a project for five covered markets. The plans were drawn up by Samu Petz. The municipal authorities had decided on this type of market to replace the open-air markets, considered a health problem because of the bad smells emanating from them.
The interior, a vast hall with metal vaulting, has multi-coloured fruit and vegetable stalls on the ground floor, with garlands of garlic and the famous paprika; as for the cold meats, the no less famous salamis are hanging to their best advantage. The foie gras is here as well as the local spirits such as the celebrated apricot brandy *(barackpálinka)* or *Unicum* liqueur.

Et. Revault/PIX

The gallery upstairs goes right round the building. There is a succession of bars, fast food outlets, handicrafts, Hungarian wine, and, to conclude, stands with a wide choice of embroidered table linen that visitors will find hard to resist.

Near the main market on Fővám tér an imposing neo-Renaissance building stands on the corner of Közraktár utca. This is the old Customs House, today the **University of Economic Sciences**. This historic classified structure was built between 1870 and 1874 by Miklós Ybl. The façade looking out over the Danube is ornamented with a group of 10 allegorical statues by Viennese sculptor Auguste Sommer. Together with the main market, it is illuminated at night, and well worth a look.

★★ **Magyar Nemzeti Múzeum (Hungarian National Museum)** Ⓥ – Founded in 1802 by Count Ferenc Széchenyi, the museum today occupies a neo-Classical palace with a great Corinthian-columned portico. The carved tympanum represents allegories of Pannonia, surrounded by the Sciences and the Arts. The statue in front of the museum is of the great 19C Hungarian poet, **János Arany**. There are other statues of scholars, poets and statesmen embellishing the garden around the museum.
On the ground floor, the coronation **mantle** in purple Byzantine silk was a gift from King Stephen I and his wife to the Church of the Virgin in Székesfehérvár. It forms part of the Crown jewels that are currently being exhibited in the Parliament.
On the first floor, the rooms present the great moments in the country's history in chronological order, from the arrival of the Magyar tribes to the period after Communism.

Each period is well illustrated with maps, plans, paintings, art objects, everyday objects, weapons, furniture, clothing, videos etc.
In Room 5, devoted to the period of Mathias/Mátyás Hunyadi – Matthias Corvinus – there are very beautiful Gothic stalls from Bártfa Church. In the next room (which shows the Ottoman occupation, second half of the 16C to the early 17C), other stalls from Nyírbátor's Franciscan church are a marvel of Hungarian woodwork.
Note the extremely delicate details and the degree to which the artists have created a veritable lacework in wood. See also in Room 8, devoted to the expulsion of the Turks, a beautiful ceramic coffered ceiling. The contemporary period (rooms 19 and 20) clearly shows the role Hungary played and how the country suffered under dictators like Miklós Horthy. Horthy became an ally of Hitler's Germany and let the sinister Hungarian Nazis, the Arrow Cross, act as they thought fit. Mátyás Rákosi orchestrated the Red Terror in the 1950s. Then there was the 1956 Uprising, the end of Communism and the proclamation of the Hungarian Republic on 23 October 1990.

THE FORMER JEWISH DISTRICT

Delimited for the most part by Károly körút, Erzsébet körút, Dohány utca and Király utca, the old Jewish district is ideal for a walk, to breathe in the special atmosphere of its streets and imagine what it was like in the past.

The Jewish community – The Jews came principally from Central Europe in the 17C and 18C, and settled first in Buda in the Castle District. The first years proved difficult for this community, who were considered foreigners until Empress Maria Theresa signed a Tolerance Decree granting them the same rights as the Christians.
It was mainly in the second half of the 19C that the Jewish community moved to Pest, after the introduction of a law permitting them to own land. Workshops, shops, restaurants and clubs appeared, making the district a hive of activity. By the end of the century, the Jewish community was one of the best integrated in Europe, making a cultural and economic contribution to the country. In 1900 it consisted of about 170 000 people. After the First World War the White Terror struck part of the Jewish population.
In 1920 Parliament limited the access of Jewish students to higher education to 5%. In 1938, allied to Hitler's Germany, Hungary promulgated a first anti-Semitic law, followed a year later by a second law. It was at this time that a ghetto was formed in which Jewish people were confined and their possessions confiscated. In 1944 the mass extermination and deportation of thousands of Jews was organised with the help of Hungarian Nazis, the formidable Arrow Cross.
It was during this tragic period that **Raoul Wallenberg**, the First Secretary of the Swedish Embassy, risked his life to provide safe-conduct for numerous people, saving them from death. A monument in Buda on Szilágyi Erzsébet fasor recalls

Theodor Herzl (1860-1904)

It was in this house, now the site of the Jewish Museum that the founder of Zionism was born. A plaque in the stairwell commemorates this event. He received a primary and secondary education at the Jewish school, and at the age of 18, the victim of anti-Semitism, left Budapest for Vienna, with his family. He then studied law and became a lawyer before turning to journalism and literature. In 1891 he settled in Paris as a correspondent for the *Neue Freie Presse*, an Austrian newspaper with a liberal tendency. Already marked by anti-Semitism, he was deeply shocked by the Dreyfus Affair, which exploded in France in 1894. The same year he wrote *The New Ghetto*, a play in which he clearly showed his ideas in favour of the emancipation of the Jews and recognition of their rights. In 1896, in his book entitled *The Jewish Condition* he set out his idea of Zionism, aimed at bringing Jews together in an independent state in Palestine. In 1897 he organised the first world Zionist congress in Basle in Switzerland, and even created the Jewish National Bank and the National Jewish Fund for the purchase of land in Palestine. He died in Edlach in Austria in 1904, without achieving his dream. On 14 May 1948 the State of Israel was born. The following year the mortal remains of Theodor Herzl were transferred to Jerusalem.

the courage and devotion of this man. After the capital's liberation, the Red Army took him to the USSR, where he disappeared in mysterious circumstances. In the year 2000, the Russians officially recognised that he was executed on a decision taken by the Soviet powers.

Zsidó Múzeum (Jewish Museum) The history of Hungary's Jewish community, Jewish traditions, and the Holocaust are well illustrated in this museum, by means of explanatory panels (in English, Hungarian and Hebrew), ritual items, manuscripts, textiles and paintings.

★★ **Dohány utcai zsinagóga (Great Synagogue of Dohány Street)** – Europe's largest synagogue was built between 1854 and 1859 to plans by the Viennese architect Ludwig Förster. Of Byzantine-Moorish inspiration, it is a beautiful edifice in coloured brick, decorated with ceramics and two onion-domed towers resembling minarets. Two levels of wooden galleries run around the inside, which is lit by two large chandeliers, each weighing 1.5t. The total effect is majestic. Note the richness of the decoration, especially on the ceiling and the Ark that naturally draws the eye when you first come in. This is where the Scroll of the Torah, the roll of parchment upon which the Mosaic Law is written is carefully preserved.

If you go a short way along Wesselényi utca, you come to the **Weeping Willow Monument**. This silver sculpture by Imre Varga was raised in 1987 to the memory of Hungarian Jews who died during the Second World War. In Dob utca is a curious **monument to Carl Lutz**. It represents a man on his back, trying to get up to ask for help from the angel who seems to be coming out of a nearby recess. Carl Lutz was a Swiss emissary who, like Raoul Wallenberg, helped a great many Jews while risking his own life.

G. Durand/PHOTONONSTOP

Part of the Great Synagogue tower and dome

NAGYKÖRÚT

(GREAT BOULEVARD)

The Great Boulevard, as it is commonly known, is a sort of ring road extending for 4.5km/2.7mi between the Petőfi and Margaret bridges. It in fact consists of five boulevards: Ferenc krt., József krt., Erzsébet krt., Teréz krt. and Szt. István krt. While the first two have only limited interest, it is worth spending a few hours visiting the others. They are extremely busy in the daytime. Continuous waves of passers-by invade the pavements, while streams of vehicles, buses and trams cram the roads. All along this great thoroughfare are thousands of shops, cafés, restaurants and cinemas.

If you would like to get an idea of the constant dizzying activity on Nagykörút without tiring yourself, take a trip on tramway line 4 or 6 at Petőfi híd or Margit híd.

★★ **Iparművészeti Múzeum (Museum of Applied Arts)** – *Üllői út 33-37. Underground line M 3, Ferenc krt. station.*

Inaugurated in 1896 on the occasion of the Millenary celebrations, the building itself is one of the events not to be missed. Architect Ödön Lechner (façade statue), nicknamed the Hungarian Gaudí, wanted to illustrate the Secessionist style, the Hungarian branch of Art Nouveau in which Eastern influences are obvious. You will have to step back and look up to appreciate this form of art on the roofs and façades evidenced by a profusion of coloured ceramic ornaments with floral and animal motifs. See also the ceiling of the entrance lobby, a veritable floral constellation. The more restrained interior is just as surprising. Under a huge metal-framed glass roof, a large room is surrounded with brilliant white multifoil arches and balustrades. A permanent exhibition presents hundreds of objects on the theme of European arts and trades. Within this theme, there are five principal sections: porcelain, ceramics, glasswork; the art of the book, leather, bookbinding, paper; textiles; wood, joinery, cabinetmaking; and metal and ironwork. The temporary exhibition, which may last for several years, is devoted to the 1900 style in several European countries and in the United States. There is furniture (very beautiful English pieces including a sideboard carved from solid oak by The Bath Cabinetmakers Co), ceramic and porcelain displays (Denmark polar bear), textiles and tapestries (from Hungary, tapestry representing a peasant couple), and leather.

Blaha Lujza tér – This important crossroads is at the junction of the Great Boulevard and **Rákóczi út**, a large shopping thoroughfare that extends from Kossuth Lajos utca and leads to the East Railway Station (Keleti pályaudvar). The name of the crossroads derives from Lujza Blaha (1850-1926), who was a very popular actress in the days when the National Theatre stood here.

★★ **Bélyegmúzeum (Stamp Museum)** ⏲ – *Hársfa utca 47.* A small museum but with an extraordinary collection of postage stamps displayed by continent, which will delight connoisseurs.

★ **Nyugati Pályaudvar (West Station)** – Did Gustave Eiffel have a hand in this? Yes, indeed! The station, a clever combination of glass and iron that fits in perfectly with the brick buildings and which bears the architect's mark, was constructed between 1874 and 1877 by the firm that built the famous Eiffel Tower in Paris. Take a quick look at the old station restaurant, today an American fast food outlet. The Art Nouveau decor is magnificent.

Take the underground passage that crosses Nyagati tér and continue along Szent István Körút until Margaret Bridge. At n° 14, set back from the boulevard, is the Variety or **Vígszínház** Theatre. There are two busts in front of this neo-Baroque edifice: to the left Miklós Zrínyi (1620-64), a poet of Croat origin and fervent partisan of the expulsion of the Turks, and to the right, the poet Sándor Petőfi.

M. Guillot/MICHELIN

The West Station

ANDRÁSSY ÚT TO HŐSÖK TERE

★★ **Andrássy út or Budapest's Champs-Élysées** – This straight avenue, 2.5km/1.5mi long, is the most elegant in the capital. At the time of the Austro-Hungarian Dual Monarchy, Budapest flourished and this period was particularly marked by great urban projects. After a trip to Paris in 1858, Count Gyula Andrássy, the Prime Minister of the Hungarian government, had the idea of

Literary cafés and coffee houses

The taste for cafés, which later became a veritable way of life, was brought by the Turks in the 16C. At the time of the Millenary (1896) Budapest had about 600. At the turn of the century, Budapest, like Vienna and Paris, experienced a great period of literary cafés. In 1914 Dezső Kosztolányi wrote in *Füst* "The Englishman with excessive pride declares, 'My home is my castle!' The man of Budapest can answer him with equal pride: 'My café is my castle!'"

A home to men of letters and journalists, the cafés played a vital role in the blossoming of Hungarian literature and even became places of work. As for the coffee houses that welcomed the middle classes, they stayed open day and night, especially those on Andrássy út and Rákóczi út. People came to talk, read (numerous newspapers or reviews in various languages were made available to regulars) or play billiards. After the First World War, the period of decline began. The number of cafés dropped radically, leaving behind a deep sense of loss.

After the Second World War, several cafés, such as the Belvárosi opened their doors again, but the golden age was a dim memory. Jenő Heltai expressed this very well in *Szemtanú* in 1949, "When I think about the deplorable tragedy of the cafés, and the manner in which they blossomed and then declined, I feel like the legendary Rip van Winkle, who looks at the world around him after waking from a sleep of 20 years... The old man looked in vain for the cafés of his youth, where he felt at home. Cafés have gone from being the star of the show to a walk-on part."

creating a main thoroughfare linking the Little Boulevard to the City Park. The route of the avenue was drawn up in 1872, and work lasted about 20 years. The year of the Millenary celebrations saw a magnificent avenue, lined with eclectic buildings and expensive mansions. The avenue changed names several times, depending on history. First Sugár út (Main Avenue), then Andrássy (on the count's death in 1890), Sztálin (in 1947), and then Népköztársaság (for the People's Republic) from 1957 to 1990 when it reverted to Andrássy.

Postamúzeum ⓥ **(Postal Museum)** – Two old letter boxes mark the location of this museum, which can be reached from an inner courtyard that itself deserves a look for its decorated galleries. On display are re-creations of service windows, telephone booths, vehicles, uniforms and a long list of other items.

★★ **Magyar Állami Operaház** ⓥ **(National Opera House)** – The neo-Renaissance style Opera House was built between 1875 and 1884 by Miklós Ybl. The façade has a projecting porch that supports a loggia. On either side of the entrance there is a niche with a statue of a great Hungarian composer. To the right is Franz Liszt (1811-86) and to the left **Ferenc Erkel** (1810-93). Erkel, who was born in Gyula and died in Budapest, was also a talented pianist and orchestra conductor. He wrote Hungary's national anthem as well as several operas. The concert given at the formal inauguration of the Opera House, held on 27 September 1884, was conducted by Ferenc Erkel who, among other works, directed the overture to his opera *László-Hunyadi*.

The first-floor part of the façade has a five-arched gallery, marked by Corinthian columns. The upper part of the building is also decorated with a balustrade surmounted by statues of famous composers (Mozart, Beethoven, Rossini, Wagner, Tchaikovsky, Smetana etc).

The **interior** is sumptuous. The main staircase, the lobby, the smokers' hallway, the auditorium (fresco by Károly Lotz on the ceiling, showing the Apotheosis of Music), the formal reception room, and the royal staircase are all resplendent with gilding, wood panelling, frescoes, paintings and marble.

The arcaded neo-Renaissance palace on the other side of the avenue is the seat of the National Institute of Classical Dance. A little further on, at n° 29, the **Művész pastry shop** and tea room has kept its turn-of-the-century charm. This is a good place to have some cake and coffee. The avenue cuts across Nagymezö utca which is nicknamed **Broadway** because of its numerous theatres and cafés. You then come to two squares that are very busy in summer, **Liszt Ferenc tér** (statue of poet Endre Ady) and on the other side of the avenue, **Jókai tér** (statue of Romantic writer Mór Jókai, 1825-1904).

Liszt Ferenc Zeneművészeti Főiskola (Franz Liszt Academy of Music) – The great composer's bronze statue, by Alajos Stróbl, decorates the façade. This famous music conservatory has an amazing library on Hungarian music. Take a look at the **lobby★** with its opulent decoration *(Király utca entrance)*.

Andrássy út then goes across the **Oktogon**, an octagonal square that crosses the Great Boulevard.

There is also evidence here that Budapest has not escaped the fast food invasion. Beyond the Oktogon, the avenue opens up with side pathways originally reserved for riders.

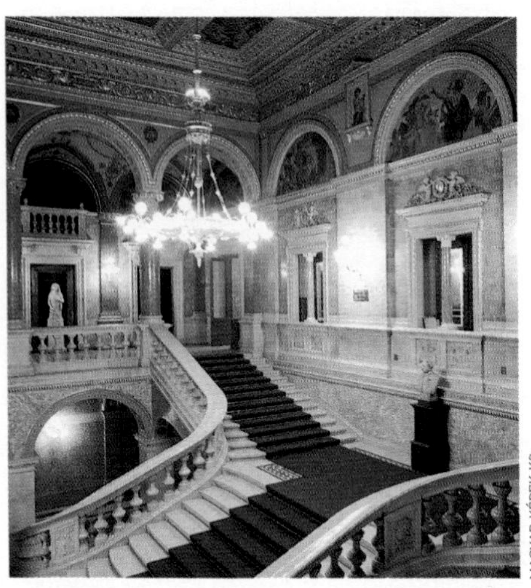
MAGYAR KÉPEK Kft

The main staircase of the Opera House

Liszt Ferenc Emlékmúzeum ⓥ – *Vörösmarty utca 35*. Three rooms comprise the **apartment** that Franz Liszt lived in during the last five years of his life, when he came regularly to spend the winter in Budapest. There is a plaque on the wall opposite the front door that indicates the times the musician would receive callers. The bedroom was also a study. On the desk several personal objects are exhibited, including tuning forks, a pince-nez and letters, and in the wardrobe, a hat, cane and gloves. On a small table, there is a bronze mould of Liszt's right hand, by Alajos Stróbl. In the sitting room, the Bösendorfer piano was his favourite instrument.

Kodály körönd – This is an elegant square with four symmetrical buildings forming an arc of a circle. Decorating the lawn, there are four imposing statues of individuals who won glory in the battle against the Turks.

Kodály Zoltán Emlékmúzeum ⓥ – Together with Béla Bartók, Zoltán Kodály made a deep impression on 20C Hungarian music. The **apartment** he lived in from March 1924 to his death in March 1967 contains souvenirs of the great composer: pianos, library and books, desk, sheet music. A little-known facet to his talent is also revealed – he made pottery (collection of pots and vases in the dining room).

Beyond Kodály körönd, Andrássy út looks completely different. A chic residential district unfolds. Old and sometimes run-down buildings with their façades often decorated with sculpture give way to beautiful villas and expensive mansions. A large number of embassies are to be found in this part of the avenue.

Hopp Ferenc Kelet-Ázsiai Múzészeti Múzeum (Far East Museum) ⓥ – Ferenc Hopp (1833-1919), an optician and great traveller, donated to the country the objects he brought back from his great many trips to Asia. This museum, his former villa, exhibits them in rotation.

★ **Ráth György Múzeum** ⓥ – *Városligeti fasor 12*.
An eclectic-style villa is home to this museum entirely devoted to Indian and Far Eastern art: sculptures, statuettes, jewels, and hangings. In the Japanese art section (Room 6 and first floor) the beautiful collections of ivory and gold-lacquered combs, pipes and pipe holders and a re-creation of the tea ceremony with all the appropriate utensils are particularly interesting.

Hősök tere (Heroes Square) – This gigantic square has the Fine Arts Museum on the left and the Art Gallery on the right. In the centre is a column and behind two colonnades in an arc with a group of statues and sculptures is the Millenary Monument. Heroes Square is the work of architect Albert Schickedanz. Through the years it has always been the venue for mass events, celebrations or general rejoicing.

★ **Milleneumi emlékmű (Millenary Monument)** – As its name indicates, the monument commemorates the 1 000th anniversary of the Magyar conquest. It was inaugurated in 1896. In the centre, a column 36m/118ft high holds a statue of the Archangel Gabriel, standing on a globe, bearing the Hungarian crown and the apostolic cross. On the pedestal an imposing group of sculptures shows the Magyar Prince Árpád on horseback, accompanied by the six other Magyar tribal chiefs. The colonnade is divided into two symmetrical parts. At the top there are allegorical

M. Guillot/MICHELIN

Árpád and the Magyar chiefs

statues representing Work and Abundance (left), Knowledge and Glory (right). The chariot of War and the chariot of Peace stand facing each other. Between each column you can see statues of the historical figures (sovereigns and princes) who left their mark on the country's history. A relief under each statue depicts a scene from the life of these figures. Some of the kings represented are Stephen I, Béla IV, Louis the Great, and Matthias Corvinus. There are also princes of Transylvania, Gábor Bethlen and Ferenc Rákóczi II, and a man of the people, Lajos Kossuth, the hero of the revolution of 1848-49.

★★★ **Szépművészeti Múzeum (Fine Arts Museum)** – The Fine Arts Museum is a colossal neo-Classical edifice. Its porch consists of eight Greek Corinthian columns (the pediment is a replica of the one in Olympia's Temple of Zeus). The **Egyptian Antiquities** department is downstairs, and includes remarkable pieces that illustrate the various periods of Ancient Egypt. Among the exhibits are a painted wood sarcophagus of an Amun priestess (Third Dynasty period, 1735-1580 BC), a bronze statuette of a seated cat (Ptolemaic Egypt, 320-30 BC) – in Ancient Egypt the cat was venerated as a sacred animal – and a **bronze statuette of Imhotep** (Third Dynasty doctor and architect). Note the fine detail and proportions. A contemporary art collection is exhibited downstairs.
Greek and Roman Antiquities are on the ground floor, together with drawings and engravings, then 19C art.
However, it is especially on the first floor, in the **Old Masters Gallery**★★ that most of the key pieces are located, demonstrating the great 13C-18C schools.

Italian painting – *Rooms to the right at the top of the stairs.* Among the great periods illustrated, the Quattrocento (15C), the early Italian Renaissance, is represented here by artists of the Urbino and Florence schools, such as Giovanni Santi and Domenico Ghirlandaio *(St Stephen)*. Gentile Bellini with his *Portrait of Cararina Cornaro, Queen of Cyprus* is also on display. Carlo Crivelli's graceful *Virgin and Child* with its refined colours exemplifies 15C Venetian painting. The next century, the Cinquecento, included some great names. Among them, Raphael, a prolific portraitist whose paintings of the Virgin Mary were extremely soft and gentle. Note his *Portrait of Pietro Bembo* and the *Esterházy Madonna*. There is also work by Titian, who before turning to mythological or religious subjects, was an excellent portraitist *(Portrait of the Doge, Marcantonio Trevisani)*. Paintings by Veronese *(Portrait of a Man)* and Tintoretto are also shown. The Baroque rooms contain works by Tiepolo, Bellotto and Guardi.

Dutch painting – The 16C is represented by Hans Memling and Gerard David *(Nativity)*.

Spanish painting – By El Greco, note the sensual and mystical *Mary Magdalene*, and a more sombre painting, *Agony in the Garden*. By Velasquez, note *Peasant's Repast*, a genre painting showing peasants at a table talking together while a woman carefully pours the wine. Goya's *Young Girl with Pitcher*, is another example of genre painting, in which the artist puts the accent on the main character, merely sketching the surroundings. His *Portrait of the Wife of Juan Augustin, Ceán Bermúdez* shows great care in depicting the detail of clothing. Paintings by Murillo, characterised by images full of tenderness and mysticism *(The Child Jesus Distributing Bread to the Pilgrims)*, and José de Ribera, known for his vigorous realism, complete the Spanish School.

German painting – In his great composition, the *Dormition of the Virgin*, Hans Holbein paid the greatest attention to representing the Apostles. The German Renaissance is represented by Dürer *(Portrait of a Young Man)* and Lucas Cranach the Elder.

Portrait of Pietro Bembo by Raphael

English painting – The 18C school is represented by several portraits, including Reynolds' *Portrait of Admiral Edward Hughes*. At the end of the century, landscape painting found an indisputable master in Constable.

French painting – Nicolas Régnier *(Card Players)*, Simon Vouet *(Apollo and the Muses)*, Jacques Blanchard *(St Jerome)*, Claude Lorrain *(Villa in the Roman Countryside)*.

Flemish painting – Works by Rubens, Van Dyck, Jordaens – prestigious names from the 17C, considered the golden age of Flemish painting, together with the 15C.

Műcsarnok (Exhibition Hall) – On the other side of Hősök tere, this building that looks like a Greek temple (note the mosaics on the façade) is reserved for temporary exhibitions principally of contemporary art.

★VÁROSLIGET (CITY PARK)

It is difficult to imagine that this place was a royal hunting ground and an enormous marsh in the 15C. In the middle of the 18C, Empress Maria Theresa decided to have the marshland drained and to plant new species of trees to make a public promenade. Towards 1810 Palatine Prince Joseph, a man of refinement who appreciated beauty and nature, suggested creating a commission to embellish Pest. Henrik Nebbie, a landscape gardener of French origin, was given the responsibility of drawing up the plans to turn this into a large recreation and leisure park. By the end of the 19C it had taken on its present form.
Városliget and Margit-sziget are very popular in summer when the city gets sticky. Families come here, seeking a shady spot to get some fresh air. They go for walks and enjoy boating (in winter the lake is drained and turned into an ice rink).
As you walk through the park beyond the castle, you can see the **statue of George Washington**, the first President of the United States, on the edge of the lake. It was put here in 1906 with donations from Hungarian émigrés.

★**Vajdahunyad vára** – Vajdahunyad Castle is an unusual ensemble (designed by Ignác Alpár), built on the occasion of the Millenary celebrations to illustrate the architectural styles existing in Hungary. Therefore, no one should be surprised to see a mixture of Romanesque, Gothic, Renaissance and Baroque all within this limited area. The main part draws on the style of Honedoara Castle (formerly Vajdahunyad) in Transylvania, now part of Romania. A three-arched bridge leads to the castle's courtyard, where one can see **Ják Chapel** to the left. The portal is decorated with sculptures representing the Twelve Apostles, similar to those in the old 13C Benedictine abbey of Ják. In front of the Baroque part of the castle, a strange character, his face hidden under a monk's hood, is seated on a marble bench. This is **Anonymous**, a scribe at the court of King Béla III (12C), a bronze sculpture by Miklós Ligeti (1903).

Magyar Mezógazdasági Múzeum (Museum of Agriculture) ⌚ – A large exhibition on working the land, animal breeding, fishing, hunting, forestry and wine-growing in the past and present. Explanatory panels in English and Hungarian.

★★★**Széchenyi gyógyfürdő (Széchenyi Baths)** – *See The Baths.*

The Municipal Circus, **Fővárosi Nagy Cirkusz**, faces the baths; it is known even outside of Hungary.

Vidám Park – *See Budapest and children.*

Állatkert (Zoo) – *See Budapest and children.*

★**Közlekedési Múzeum (Transport Museum)** ⓥ – *Városligeti körút 11.* Explanatory panels in English, German and Hungarian.

This museum creates an interesting panorama of the development of transport in Hungary, by rail, road, air and water routes. To the left, at the entrance to the hall reserved for rail transport, there are beautiful engines and old carriages (1860 locomotive, 1887 carriage from the Mohács-Pécs line). Model train lovers will enjoy the fascinating collection on a scale of 1:5. Still on the ground floor, but on the opposite side of it, are old motorcycles and cars. The oldest is an 1898 Peugeot. There is also an 1899 Oldsmobile (for those keen on speeds of 35kph/21mph) and a 1901 Peugeot convertible (30kph/17mph). From the Hungarian automobile

T. Hortobagyi/MAGYAR KÉPEK Kft

Vajdahunyad Castle

industry there is a Csonka from 1908-12, with a four-cylinder engine, capable of 50kph/32mph and several MÁG models: a 1928 Magosix (40hp), a 1928 Magotax taxi (25hp). Upstairs, river transport is well represented by models of boats, navigational instruments, not forgetting the Óbuda and Újpest naval projects and the Balaton and Danube cruise ships.

EAST OF THE GREAT BOULEVARD

The long Rákóczi út, which cuts across the Great Boulevard at Blaha Lujza tér, leads to **Baross tér** (statue of Gábor Baross, the Minister of Transport who developed the Hungarian railway system) and to the East Station.

Keleti pályaudvar (East Station) – The biggest station in the capital (international traffic) has an eclectic-style façade (statues of James Watt, the inventor of the steam engine and George Stephenson, the inventor of the steam locomotive). See the lobby decorated with mural paintings.

Kerepesi temető – *Fiumei út 16.* Budapest, like all capitals, has its own cemetery, its National Pantheon, where famous people are buried. We suggest you buy a map at the entrance. In this vast landscaped area, the Lajos Kossuth monument, or rather mausoleum, is undoubtedly the most impressive and dominates the entire cemetery. The mausoleums of Ferenc Deák and Lajos Batthyány are of interest, as well as the Pantheon of the Working Class Movement, reserved for faithful servants of the Communist regime (as the inscription says: "They lived for Communism and for the People"). There is a small museum (if you are interested in this kind of thing) devoted to funerals, with a room with illustrations of the national funerals of famous individuals such as Imre Nagy, Cardinal Mindszenty, Béla Bartók, Zoltán Kodály, Miklós Horthy and János Kádár (First Secretary of the Communist Party, 1956-88).

Népstadion – In 1998 the **People's Stadium**, which is part of an immense sports complex consisting of several halls, a skating rink and a hotel, was the venue for Europe's athletics championships. Take the **Ifjúság útja** walk, lined with monumental sculptural groups celebrating sport and the army.
North of the stadium is a district mainly consisting of individual houses. The Geology Institute – **Földtani Intézet** – at n° 14 **Stefánia út**, is a beautiful example of the Secessionist style, by Ödön Lechner.

SOUTH-EAST OF THE GREAT BOULEVARD

Magyar Természettudományi Múzeum (Hungarian Museum of Natural History) ⓥ – *Ludovika tér 2. Underground line M 3, Klinikák station.* Near **Orczy Kert**, a park planted with about 100 species of trees, the museum, through its Man and Nature in Hungary exhibition, shows how humans, since their appearance on earth, have used nature for their own ends. Rational use or abuse, with the pollution created, whether of nuclear origin (Chernobyl) or due to irresponsible dumping are all covered. Animal protection is symbolised by Noah's ark.

Planetárium – *Underground line M 3, Népliget station.* In the People's Park, **Népliget**, a dome measuring 23m/75ft in diameter indicates the location of the planetarium, where you can take off for the stars. Shows at very precise times.

Wekerletelep – *Underground line M 3, Határ út station, then bus n° 194 or 99 to Kós Károly tér.* A country town! That is the impression you have as you walk around this part of the Kispest district, with Kós Károly tér park at the centre. The architecture of the housing for government and municipal employees, from 1908 to 1925, is quite surprising – blocks of streets meeting at sharp right angles and green spaces.

★★ MARGIT-SZIGET (MARGARET ISLAND)

Access: Tramway lines 4 or 6 to Margit híd or lines 2 or 2A from Vigadó tér along the Danube to the Jászai Mari tér terminus, then on foot, via the bridge.

Margaret Island is a long almond-shaped stretch (2.5km/1.5mi long and 0.5km/0.3mi wide) between the Margaret and Árpád bridges to which it is linked. A haven of peace and greenery, it is justly considered as one of the capital's most beautiful parks. With the exception of a bus (n° 26) that crosses the island, and a small train on tyres that runs around it, traffic is forbidden. Only cyclists are allowed to use the various lanes. Hiring a bicycle is actually a good way to visit the island (hire near the roundabout at the entrance, to the left, a map of the area is provided to help you find your way around). Sports fields, pools, a rose garden, a Japanese garden, a small zoo, shady lanes, lawns, picnic areas, all contribute to making this an ideal place for leisure, amusement and relaxation. On Saturdays and Sundays in summer, Budapest families come here, to the great delight of their children (small electric cars can be hired for them) and of course, itinerant vendors. As a thermal spa, Margaret Island is well endowed in terms of balneotherapy and accommodation.

Margit híd – Margaret Bridge is the work of French engineer Ernest Gouin, who with the Batignolles Construction firm was chosen from among the other foreign candidates to carry out the project. The work began in 1872 and was finished in 1876. This unusual bridge is made of two arms that meet at the island at a 150° angle. The statues decorating the pillars are also of French origin, from the Parisian Thabart workshop.
Stand in the middle and enjoy the **view★** of the Danube, spanned by Chain Bridge. On the two banks can be seen, to the right, Buda's royal castle and Matthias Church, and, to the left, Pest and the Parliament. Far off on the right you can distinguish Mt Gellért and Liberty Monument.

From Hare Island to Margaret Island – The Romans who lived in the neighbouring town of Aquincum already frequented the island regularly because of its curative thermal waters. The place then became a royal game reserve for the Árpád dynasty kings, hence its first name, Hare Island. In the 12C, monks settled here and built monasteries. The 13C was the era of the Mongol invasion. After several defeats, King Béla IV vowed that his daughter Margit (Margaret) would devote her life to God as soon as the country was freed. Faithful to his word, he built a convent – the ruins of which are still visible – for Dominican nuns, and entered his daughter at the age of nine. Her life was rather brief, as she died at the age of 28. The Turkish occupation brought about the destruction of the island's religious buildings and it was deserted until it became the property of Joseph, Archduke of Austria and

MAGYAR KÉPEK Kft

Hire a pedal car and take off!

Palatine Prince of Hungary, at the end of the 18C. He turned it into an enormous landscaped park, planting grapevines and numerous species of trees.

Tour – The Centennial Monument sweeps upward near the fountain marking the far southern tip of the island. It is a daring bronze sculpture in the form of flames, inaugurated in 1972 on the occasion of the centennial of the unification of Buda, Pest and Óbuda. Take a look inside the monument at a curious group of objects (including a ship's rudder, a propeller and a cogwheel).
You then have a wide choice of directions to take through the verdant oasis. The middle part is the most romantic, thanks to the many species of trees and flowers that decorate the flower beds.
Opposite Buda along the Danube is the immense **Palatinus Baths** complex, which has several pools, an artificial wave pool and a beach, and has room for some 20 000 people. The Dominican convent ruins where Princess Margaret lived are visible in the greenery in the centre of the island. Not far off, Artists' Walk (busts of famous Hungarian artists including Franz Liszt, Ferenc Erkel and Mór Jókai) leads to a neo-Romanesque chapel. At the foot of the old water tower (1911) that rises to a height of 57m/187ft, is an **open-air theatre** where theatre and dance performances take place in summer. To the north of the island, as you approach Árpád Bridge, there is a small circular monument on columns that was once a **musical fountain**.

ÓBUDA

Access: HÉV suburban train from Batthyány tér in the direction of Szentendre, get off at Árpád híd or at Aquincum to go directly to the Roman town.

This district, or rather suburb of the 3rd district, was independent until 1873. It is the oldest part of Budapest – its name means old Budapest. You could well have doubts about this if you consider the numerous characterless buildings and blocks of flats that mushroomed here as a result of the gigantic city development plan in the 1960s, and which totally changed the verdant setting. At first sight, it is not particularly inviting, but with a minimum of effort you can find a few little corners among the concrete, places where it is pleasant to walk and pause for a while. This is the case with **Fő tér** and the little streets and tiny squares nearby. Óbuda was a part of the old Roman Pannonia that corresponded to Transdanubia.

At the time of the Romans

While remains going back to prehistory have been discovered, it is the Roman period that has deeply marked the history of this suburb. The Romans established a military camp (about 6 000 legionaries) and founded the town of Aquincum, capital of Lower Pannonia during the reign of Emperor Trajan. A number of ruins of the military camp and civilian town of this era can be found scattered over a few square kilometres.

Military camp amphitheatre – *Corner of Pacsirtamező utca and Nagyszombat utca.* This had seating for about 15 000 spectators who would have attended the competitions, races, combats and games (by comparison, the Roman Coliseum had 45 000 seats) that took place in the arena (131m/430ft long and 107m/351ft wide).

Flórián tér – In the area around Óbuda, which itself is a kind of crossroads where communications converge, archaeological digs during the construction of the elevated railway brought to light fragments from the thermal baths in the military camp (caldarium or hot bath, frigidarium or cold bath).

Hercules villa – *Meggyfa utca 19-21. Bus nos 6, 34 or 42 from Flórián tér to Bogdáni utca.*
Slightly hidden in the middle of blocks of flats, Hercules Villa, a fine patrician mansion is named after its floor mosaic illustrating the myth of Hercules (3C).

★ **Aquincum** ⓥ – *Szentendrei út. HÉV suburban train from Árpád híd or Batthyány tér, get off at Aquincum or take bus n° 42 from Flórián tér.*

The ruins of this town founded in the 1C are quite impressive and are shown off to advantage; they are enhanced by an archeological museum inside the site. The civilian town, 600m/1 968ft long and 400m/1 312ft wide, surrounded by protective walls, was at its peak in the 2C and 3C. It was largely peopled with merchants and craftsmen and was very busy. The two towns consisted of 60 000 inhabitants in all. In AD 124, under Emperor Hadrian, Aquincum became a municipality (directed by its own laws while remaining under Rome's authority), then in AD 194, under Emperor Septimius Severus, a Roman colony. At the end of the 4C, the Roman town was attacked by invaders from the East. The town fell into decline in the 5C, the Huns delivering the final blow. The Romans abandoned Aquincum, but not before they had concluded a pact with Attila, the new master.

The field of ruins clearly shows the layout of the town: streets at right angles to each other, the network of sewers and pipes, the location of various buildings. To the right (opposite the museum) were the public baths and the large open market *(macellum)*, and, further on, the craftsmen's workshops, merchants' shops and houses. At the far end of the site, in a small building (a former bathhouse that was part of a private home), is a fragment of a mosaic representing a wrestling scene. Over to the left is another small building (a sundial at the entrance) that has several beautiful examples of mosaics.

If you retrace your steps and go towards the museum, you will see the temple to Mithra, a Persian sun god who was worshipped by the Greeks and later by the Romans. The **archaeological museum** has a peristyle at the entrance, and contains relics from digs (statues, bas-reliefs, coins, pottery, tools, everyday objects). There is an unusual piece, a 3C hydraulic organ.

Civilian town Amphitheatre – *Near the underground passage of the HÉV suburban train station.*

Of more modest dimensions than the military town amphitheatre, this could hold 8 000 spectators.

Provincial charm

★ **Fő tér** – You do not expect to find this little paved square with its very provincial atmosphere at the foot of impersonal blocks of flats. It is worth taking a short walk around the surrounding streets with their colourful houses and echoes of days gone by.

The square is bordered with wealthy Baroque-style buildings. In summer the restaurant and café terraces in this peaceful district are an invitation to passers-by to sit down for a while.

Zichy kastély – This mansion was built for Count Miklós Zichy and his wife, members of the Óbuda nobility in the 18C. You have to go into the courtyard (concerts in summer) to admire the beautiful façade and staircase. The **Kassák Lajos Múzeum** ⓥ on the first floor is devoted to this writer and painter (1887-1967), considered one of the leaders of the Hungarian avant-garde. Three rooms contain an exhibition of his work, including paintings, drawings and photographs.

At the corner of Hajógyár utca and Laktanya utca, you will come upon a curious group of four women, sheltering under their umbrellas. These are bronze sculptures by Imre Varga.

J.-C. Saturnin-MICHELIN

Umbrellas and their charm
Waiting by Imre Varga

Varga Imre Gyűjtemény ⓥ – *Laktanya utca 7.*

The Imre **Varga Museum** has several rooms and a garden containing completed pieces and models by this prolific contemporary sculptor. He created numerous sculptures or monumental groups that can be seen all over the capital and Hungary itself. Sculptures on religious themes, famous people (Liszt, Bartók, Lenin, Mihály Károly), patriotic subjects, scenes of everyday life: the sources of inspiration are multiple. There is a glass case with a collection of medals he received in recognition of his accomplishments.

★**Vasarely Múzeum** ⓥ – Victor Vasarely (see also PÉCS) donated several hundred of his works to his country of origin. The pieces are exhibited in the part of the Zichy mansion overlooking Szentlélek tér. The compositions (paintings, drawings and tapestries) show the evolution of his art, which systematically used optical illusion in a combination of geometric shapes and colours.

Óbudai plébániatemplom- *Lajos utca, on the other side of the expressway.* Óbuda's Baroque-style parish church was built for the Zichy family in the 18C. There are two niches on the façade with statues of St Sebastian and St Roch.

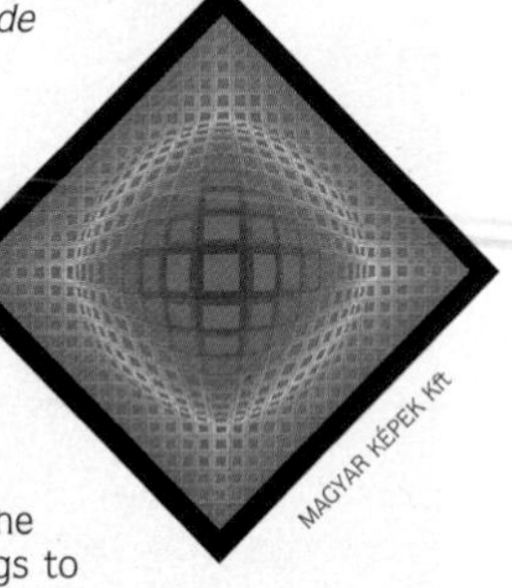

Óbudai zsinagóga (Former Synagogue) – *Lajos utca 16.*
This edifice is distinguished by a six-columned neo-Classical porch. The building itself is set back from the street, near the modern Aquincum Hotel and an array of council house acccommodation. On the tympanum are the stone tablets with the Mosaic Law. The old Óbuda synagogue today belongs to the Hungarian television network and is used as a studio.

AROUND BUDA

Rózsadomb

Hill of Roses is a small residential community with comfortable homes and little gardens.

Gül Baba türbe ⓥ – *Mecset utca 14. From Pest, tramway lines 4 or 6 in the Moszkva tér direction, get off after Margit híd (Margaret Bridge).*
Take Torok utca on the right, which forks into Margit körút, then Gül Baba utca on the left, a picturesque little street that climbs sharply (uneven paving stones) and forks off at the foot of the hill. Half way up, a set of stairs on the left leads to Gül Baba's Mausoleum, an octagonal edifice topped with a dome and a Turkish crescent. The mausoleum, maintained by the Turkish government, is a pilgrimage site for Muslims the world over. Gül Baba, Father of the Roses, was a dervish in the Bektachi Order (statue at the entrance, representing him with a rose in his turban). He lived in the 16C, participated in the Buda conquest and is said to have introduced the first roses. He died during a religious ceremony in Matthias Church, which had been turned into a mosque. Sultan Suleiman the Magnificent attended his funeral in person. The tomb is covered in a green cloth with verses from the Koran on it. Prayer rugs and objects of worship are also visible inside the mausoleum.
There is a view over the city from the little tower outside the sacred precinct.

Budai-hegység

For Budapest's citizens or tourists seeking a real breath of fresh air, the Buda Hills offer footpaths through woods, picnic areas and viewpoints, a surprisingly verdant setting only a few kilometres from the turbulent city, which can be stifling in summer.

★**Gyermekvasút** ⓥ –The **Children's Railway** or Pioneers' Train (a youth movement created under the old regime) is a unique attraction, to be recommended. The most pleasant way to reach it is by taking the little rack railway in front of the Budapest Hotel, easily recognised by its cylindrical shape (Szilágyi Erzsébet fasor 47). From the upper terminal, walk towards the television transmitter; the Children's Train station is near it. Except for the engine driven by an adult, all the services (ticket sale, ticket-checking, departure signal) are taken care of by children (boys and girls from 10 to 14 years old), who wear a regulation uniform and salute each departure and arrival in a military manner. The train trip, through woods for the most part, is very pleasant. Several stops punctuate the journey, over a total of about 12km/7.2mi. At each stop you can go for a walk in the countryside. From the terminus (Széchenyi-hegy) you can return by the n° 158 bus or n° 56 tramway to Moszkva tér.

János-hegy – Mt János (John) is the highest hill around Buda (526m-1 735ft) and can be reached by chair-lift. Take the n° 158 bus in Csaba utca near Moszkva tér (stop near the post office, which looks like a medieval castle)ⓥ. Get off at the Zugliget terminus, which is the departure point for the **chair-lift** *(Libegő)*. At the top, take the road on the right up to the neo-Romanesque observation tower, where there is a magnificent panoramic **view**★★. You can also get to this tower by the Children's Railway. In this case, get off at János-hegy station, then take the scenic path (about 30min walk).

Szelnyi/MAGYAR KÉPEK Kft

All on board...

Pál-völgyi Barlang (**Pál-völgyi Cave**) ⓥ – *Szépvölgyi út 162. Bus n° 65 from Kolosy tér, get off at Pál-Völgyi cseppköbarlang. Certain passages are difficult and you need strong legs and lots of breath. Temperature about 11°C/51.8°F in summer. Take a light sweater.*

This cave with its concretions (inhabited by hundreds of bats in winter) was discovered at the end of the 19C. The visit involves a little climbing but you can see weird formations with names suggesting evocative images, including the Organ, the Zoo, the Cabaret, Sword of Damocles, Snow White and the Seven Dwarfs.

Szemlő-hegyi Barlang (Szemlő-hegyi Cave) ⓥ – *Pusztaszeri út 35. Take bus n° 29 and get off at Szemlő-hegyi Barlang.*

The visit involves less climbing than Pál-völgyi Cave; the sights here include a number of cauliflowers and a witch!

Bartók Béla Emlékház (**Béla Bartók House Museum**) ⓥ – *Csalán út 29. Take bus n° 5 from Március tér or Moszkva tér, get off at Pasaréti tér, then continue on foot along Csévi utca, following the signs.*

The great composer (statue in the garden) lived in this villa from 1932 to 1940 before leaving to settle in the United States (he gave his last concert in Budapest on 8 October 1940). On the first floor is a concert room (18C coffered ceiling). On the second floor the artist's life is retraced: photos, recordings (with Kodály or alone, playing the piano), his own piano, peasant furniture carved for him, a pen-holder with five nibs for drawing sheet-music scales etc.

J.-C. Saturnin/MICHELIN

The Park of Statues

The south-west

★ **Nagytétényi Kastélymúzeum** ⓥ – *15km/9mi from the centre of Budapest. Take bus n° 3 from Móricz Zsigmond körtér, get off at Petőfi Sándor utca. By car, take Budafoki út, then follow Nagytétényi út all the way to Kastélypark.*

A richly endowed and very interesting collection of furniture is on show in Száraz-Rudnyánszky Castle. This was built in 1700 on the site of an old fortified town called Campona, dating from the time of the Roman Empire. The castle changed hands several times, coming into the possession of Julianna Száraz and her husband József Rudnyánszky, nephew of Antal Grassalkovich, the man who built Gödöllő Castle. Sets of furniture that will fascinate lovers of period pieces are clearly displayed in beautifully restored rooms. Visitors will thoroughly enjoy the tour not only because of the quality and diversity of the items presented but also because the displays have been organised to highlight the relationships between each object and period. Through the displays, which cover a period ranging from the Middle Ages to the 19C, you will be able to admire the skill and invention of the craftsmen who built the furniture.

Szoborpark (Statues Park) ⓥ – *15km/9mi. Take the yellow Volánbusz bus n° 6 from the terminus at Bukarest utca near Kosztolányi Dezső tér. The trip takes about 20min.*

A large number of statues and monumental groups raised during the Communist era were taken down and set up here in this park, created for this purpose. Lenin, Marx and Engels are here to welcome visitors and the Internationale and other partisan songs can be heard as soon as you cross the threshold. T-shirts are sold making fun of the old regime. Each statue is numbered. Visitors can buy a brochure published in several languages to locate where things are. Enshrining moments of glory for this or that celebrity (Béla Kun, Endre Ságvári, Ferenc Münnich), and monuments to the worker movement, the Soviet-Hungarian friendship, the Hungarian Brigade during the War in Spain, the group is rather impressive. Families often come here – perhaps for a lesson in history?

EXCURSIONS

By boat or hydrofoil *Departure from Belgrád rkpt. or Vigadó tér*

★★★ **Dunakanyar (Danube Bend)** – *See this name.* Given the different stops, the boat trip to Visegrád takes about 3hr 25min, that to Esztergom about 5hr 30min. By **hydrofoil** allow 1hr 20min.

★★ **Szentendre** – *See this name.* Trip 1hr 30min by boat.

The town – The boat goes around Margaret Island and after Liberty Bridge (Szabadság híd) turns around to return to the starting-point. A quiet trip (recorded commentary in English, German, Italian and Hungarian) to take in good weather to see the Buda and Pest monuments on the banks of the Danube from a different angle.

Excursion to Bratislava or Vienna – By **hydrofoil**, the Slovakian capital (valid passport) is 4hr 40min from Budapest, whereas the Austrian capital is 6hr 20min away. The trip begins by taking in the Danube Bend.

By car or train

★★★ **Dunakanyar (Danube Bend)** – *See this name.*

★★ **Szentendre** – *See this name.*

★★ **Gödöllői Király-kastély** – *See this name.*

Zsámbék – *30km/18mi west along the M 1 motorway and then road n° 1104 on the right.*

Hungary has few Romanesque churches, which is why this village deserves a short trip to see the ruins of its 13C church once belonging to a Premonstratensian convent. There is substantial restoration work being done, which detracts from its appearance at first glance, but you can gain an impression of the past importance of the site. A small underground museum explains the archaeological dig and the restoration. A Turkish well can be seen in the village.

Ráckeve – *45km/27mi south. Leave Budapest by taking the M 5 then take the M 0 on the right and then road n° 51 towards Solt. After the village of Kiskunlacháza leave this road to take a little road on the right. Access also by the HÉV suburban train at the tramway n° 2 terminus, Kvassai Jenő út.*

This is a pleasant town in summer with its beach laid out along an arm of the Danube. Anglers like it here and tourists come to see the **Serbian Orthodox church** (Szerb templom, *Viola utca*), famous for its frescoes and Baroque iconostasis. If you take Kossuth Lajos utca in a northerly direction, you come to **Prince Eugene of Savoy's Castle**. This Baroque edifice, now a restaurant (Savoyai Kastély Étterem) has a central building flanked with two wings turning back at right angles. As with the Belvedere Palace in Vienna, Austria, the Prince of Savoy commissioned the Viennese architect Johann Lukas von Hildebrandt to draw up plans for the castle.

BUGAC-PUSZTA★★

BUGAC PUSZTA – Bács-Kiskun province

Michelin map 925 G 9 – 40km/24mi south of Kecskemét

Access: by car from Kecskemét, take road n° 54, then after about 25km/15mi take a small road on the left to Bugac. If you are not travelling by car, you are strongly recommended to take the train from Kecskemét. The journey is like a pleasure trip, as the small train whisks you to Bugac and Bugacuszta, past fields, woods, vineyards and stock farms. The Pásztormúzeum station is signposted.

THE GREAT PLAIN OR PUSZTA

The very word **puszta** *(see Introduction: Faces of Hungary)* evokes a particular image: a little house with its well and bucket, the setting sun, a silhouette on horseback, and a tremendous sense of freedom as the endless plain beckons with opportunities for riding.

Puszta does not necessarily mean desert, but rather a place where there is nothing, even if Bugac's dry *puszta* with its sand dunes is reminiscent of arid climes. The *puszta* is the great plain, the **Alföld** that originally occupied all the eastern and south-eastern part of the country, from the Danube to the Romanian border and to Hungary's southernmost limits.

The *puszta* can take on very different appearances.

The great civil engineering works to regulate the flow of the two rivers, the Danube and the Tisza, have significantly changed the landscapes of the Great Plain. Economic necessity and agricultural development have gradually eroded the wild parts of these immense areas. Fortunately, the most typical parts have been protected with the creation of the Nemzeti Park (Kiskunsági National Park), which includes Bugac and Hortobágy.

It is not possible to see all of the places of interest in the Kiskunsági Nemzeti Park by car. It covers 76 000ha/182 400 acres of protected land, 48 000ha/115 200 acres of which are part of the park itself and have been divided into nine sectors. The rest of the territory is made up of protected landscapes and nature reserves. Two-thirds of the park have a Biosphere Reserve status. Lake Izsák Kolon-tó and Lake Alkáli-tó, which are rich in carbonates are also protected. Every effort is made to make visits pleasant for tourists, such as the numerous small horse-drawn carts ready to set out to discover the *puszta*. Springtime and autumn are the quietest seasons, when the sandy tableland of long grass and conifers leaves visitors feeling very small against the immense horizon.

TOUR

From the excursion train station of Pásztormúzeum, you walk for 15min along a packed-sand path and come to an inn *(csárda)* at the park entrance. There you may take one of the light carts to the Shepherds Museum and to a complex with a stud farm, inn and show ground for riding events.

Be warned about the carts. Their springs are not all in good condition, and as the tracks are rather bumpy those with sensitive backs should take care. The Pásztormúzeum looks like an enormous Chinese hat resting on a great prairie of wild grass.

M. Guillou/MICHELIN

★ **Pásztormúzeum (Shepherds Museum)** ⏱ – This resembles the huts built by shepherds on the *puszta*, consisting of tepee-like structures covered in bundles of rushes, and sometimes surrounded by an enclosure also made of reeds. The *pásztor*, responsible for keeping *racka* sheep (*racka* have long corkscrew horns, and the lambs are black and the adults white), lived in these temporary villages. Here the shepherds kept everything they needed during their stay: essentials for living, for raising and caring for the animals, making cheese etc. They were helped in their work by *puli*, a small round version of a black poodle, tiny creatures in comparison with the large sheep but extremely efficient nevertheless. In addition to the shepherds there were the *csikós*, who watched over horses, and *gulyás*, or cattlemen. In the museum you will see what these men made to pass the time: carved wooden pipes, decorated canes, and all the domestic articles they carried with them in their narrow little carts.

Cowboys of the puszta – Next to the museum stands a complex consisting of a stud farm, a restaurant and a horse-riding centre. The *csikós* put on riding shows several times a day. While it is true that these shows are all alike, they are generally quite good and should not be missed.

In addition to the equestrian exploits of the riders you will see a herd of grey cattle far off on the horizon. Driven by dogs and *csikós*, they will eventually come right up to you. You will hear whips cracking around your ears, and see the famous five-in-hand – a single rider stands with each foot on a galloping horse, while he holds the reins of another three *(see illustration under Hortobágy-Puszta).*

A place to stay

Táltos Lovas Panzió – *Nagybugac 135.* ☎ *76 /372 633. Rooms between €22 and €32.* Complex with rooms, bungalows and apartments. Organises horse riding competitions and rides. Meals available.

Gedeon-tanya Panzió – *Tanya 150, 6078 Jakabszállás.* ☎ *06/76/722 800. Rooms at €36.* A little paradise! Halfway between the main 54 road and the town of Bugac, away from everything, this family *panzió* consists of two thatched houses. Horse, Hungarian cattle and goat breeding. Guaranteed peace.

A place to eat

Bugaci Csárda – ☎ *76/372 522.* Between Bugacpusztaháza and Bugac, a famous traditional inn with Hungarian music and dancing.

BÜKK★★

Heves and Borsod-Abaúj-Zemplén provinces

Michelin map 925 B 10 and 11

The Bükk massif, classified as a National Park under the name of **Bükki Nemzeti Park**, forms part of the northern mountain chain extending beyond the Mátra massif from Gyöngyös to Miskolc along the Slovakian border. This mountainous area, whose summit, **Istállós-kő**, is only 959m/3 100ft high, is composed of limestone rock and a karst plateau surrounded by steep cliffs. In the north, it is bordered by the River Sajó, in the west by the River Eger, and in the south by the Great Plain. The region is unusual for its numerous caves (over 800 have been recorded); the most characteristic of these can be visited at Lillafüred.

The Bükk Mountains, slightly less than an hour by car from the capital, deserve their reputation. The air is healthy, the countryside beautiful and the walks and pathways well laid out. Here you will find the peace and solitude of walks in the forest – the forests are mainly composed of beech trees, *bükk* means beech – lively traditional festivals, as well as a wide variety of flora and fauna.

FROM EGER TO MISKOLC

55km/34mi – allow half a day

★★ **Eger** – *See this name.*

Leave Eger heading north along road n° 25 then, a few miles after Szarvaskő, turn right along road n° 2506.

The film of dust on the houses and vegetation will indicate that you are close to Bélapátfalva.

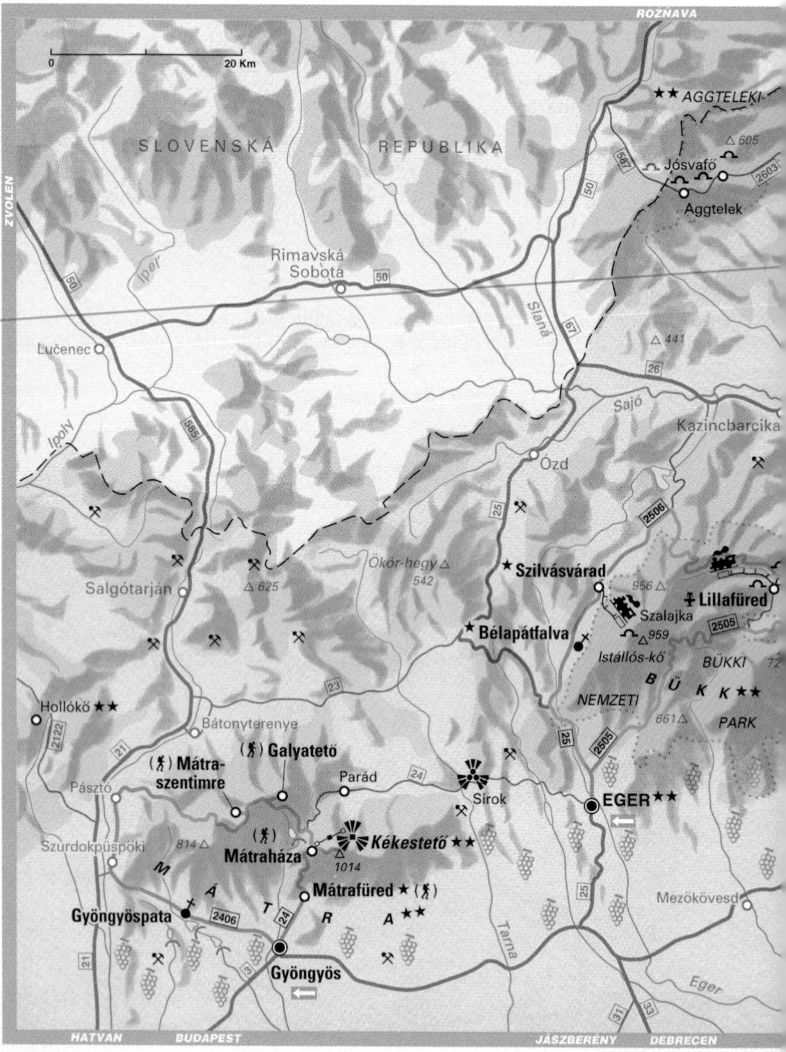

★ **Bélapátfalva** – A small town stretching along a dusty valley. In fact, nothing suggests that one of the best-preserved collections of Cistercian art in Hungary is to be found in this industrial area, dominated by a cement works.

On the right-hand side of the main street, lined with houses and industrial buildings, you will see a small sign for the **Apátság Múzeum**. The road leads to the site of Bélapátfalva Abbey whose church has been preserved and restored and appears almost intact. It is nestled in a small vale of greenery, resting on the limestone cliff that provided the stone to build the abbey and now supplies the cement works.

Next to the **church** ⓥ, you will find the remains of the abbey whose foundations were found and uncovered in 1964. The Bishop of Eger, Kilit, founded the abbey of Bélháromkút in 1232; several other abbeys were founded by the Cistercian monks including those on Mt Pilis and Mt Bélapátfalva. Construction of the abbey was interrupted by the Mongols and resumed on their departure. The monks stayed at Bélapátfalva until the Turks arrived. They cleared and cultivated the ground and dug a pool to provide fish for periods of abstinence from meat. First the Turks and then the Wars of Religion drove the monks out and it was only in the 18C, thanks to the fervour of a hermit, that the Bishop of Eger had the church restored. The organ case, pulpit, sacristy and main and side altars date from this Baroque era. Some 35 different stonemason's marks have been found in various places in the church, which, among its works, contains examples of Romanesque art.

The road continues northwards and the drive through the forest is extremely pleasant.

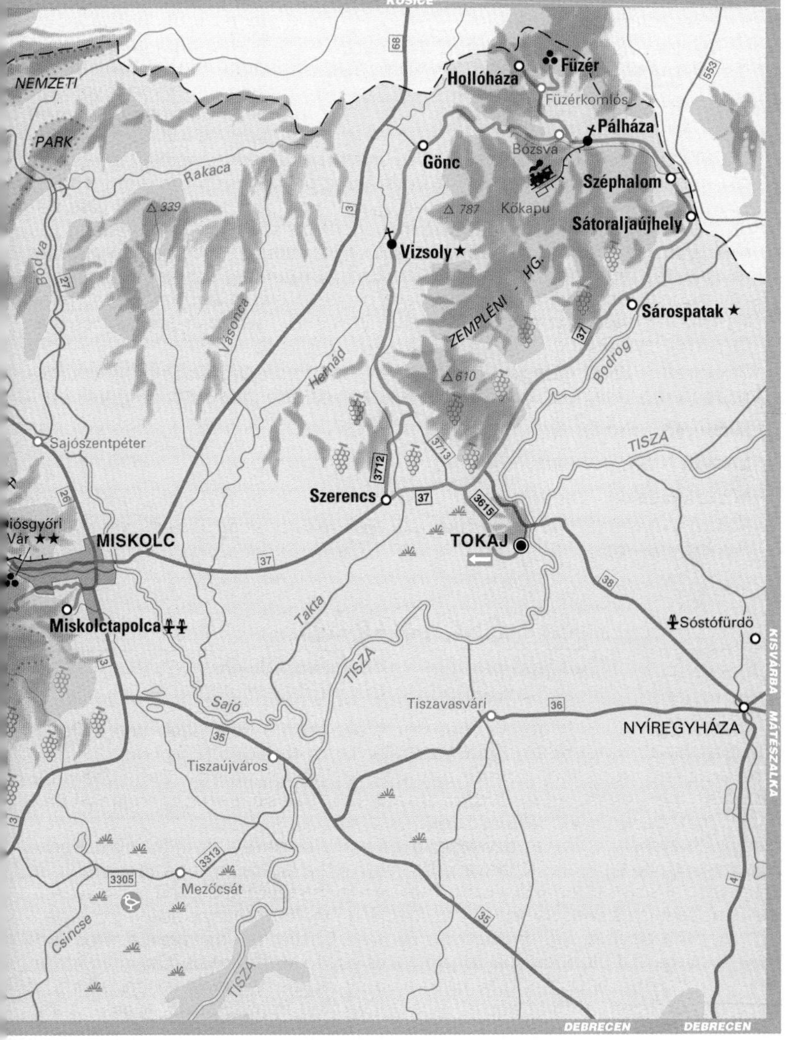

★ **Szilvásvárad** – The town of the famous Lipizzaners, magnificent white horses, is worth a visit. The horses were brought from Lipica in Slovenia where they had been bred since the 16C. Due to their intelligence, strength and endurance, Lipizzaners are used for horse riding at the highest level. In fact, the riders of the famous Spanish Riding School in Vienna use Lipizzaners. A **Horse Museum** ⓥ(Lipicai lótenyésztés-történeti kiállítás) contains an exhibition of pictures, drawings and photos of the most famous of these creatures. Visitors can also see, or rather admire them during dressage, in the meadows or in their boxes. It is possible to ride them or take a lesson in *kocsi* driving *(see Tata: Surrounding areas)*. Szilvásvárad is an important centre for team-driving, with teams of two, three or as many as seven horses. Everything relating to the horses is done with great skill; they are magnificently combed, brushed and bridled in finely worked leather harness. At the weekend in summer, you can watch demonstrations or races; it is worth spending an afternoon at these traditional events. The atmosphere is something like a fête. Doughnuts, *lángos* (a sort of fried pastry, seasoned with oil and garlic) and other kinds of sustenance are offered along the streets and alleyways. This village also opens onto the forest, which you can explore on a small train, a delight for children. To get to the station, turn right at the point where Egri utca takes a right-angled turn to the left. You can park your car here. Go along the stream and you will see the station 150-200m/165-220yd further on. The small train operates about 10 trips per day during the summer season. With its three or four open carriages, it takes you for a charming ride; leaves brush against your face and you will pass waterfalls, rivers and forest paths. The train stops off at **Szalajka-Fátyolvízesés**. If you wish, you can return by the same means of locomotion, but it is also pleasant to make the return journey on foot. It takes approximately 2hr to walk back and you can enjoy the peace and the sounds of the forest. In **Szalajka**, see the **Forest Museum** and **Istállóskő cave**, one of the sites in Hungary where ancient pottery has been discovered.

A place to eat

Vadász Bistro – *Kossuth u. 8, Répáshuta.* ☎ *46/390 159.* 14km/8.4mi from Lillafüred, in the Bükk National Park, a traditional, no-frills restaurant in a small country village. A good place for meeting Hungarian farmers. Restaurant interestingly decorated with deer antlers and goatskins. Guaranteed that you will feel far from home!

Szalajka – *Egri u. 2, Szilvásvárad.* Very good trout to be eaten here, sold by weight.

Take road n° 2506 again towards the north. Just before Dédestapolcsány, take the small road on the right, go through Mályinka and take the next turning left.

⚘ **Lillafüred** – *See Miskolc.*

Miskolc – *See this name.*

⚘⚘ **Miskolctapolca** – *See Miskolc.*

Return to road n° 2505 which takes you back to Eger along a small road through Bükkszentkereszt.

CSONGRÁD

Csongrád province – Population 20 000

Michelin map 925 F 10

A town, a river, a wide avenue, but where are the 20 000 inhabitants? This is puzzling on a first visit to Csongrád, especially during the summer months.

A royal capital, Csongrád never recovered from the Mongol invasion. Destroyed in the early 13C, the royal seat was moved to Szegad. Csongrád slumbered on from that time until it came back to life in the mid-20C.

The town's architects astutely developed a sense of effacement; along the main avenue lime trees, plane trees and other varieties conceal the façades and give the visitor an impression of strolling through a park. There is a stylish touch at the end of the avenue, the Gimnázium, a secondary school in a charming Art Nouveau style building complete with majolica ceramic tiles, in line with Fő utca. Further on, the avenue, lined with flowers, lawns and the occasional square, takes you to Múzeum-Ház. Csongrád has an intangible charm... a charm to be discovered by bicycle, the most common form of transport. Csongrád, with its annual wine festival held from 13 to 15 August, is also considered to be the town of wine-growing and wine.

A place to stay

Eat, sleep and live in a fisherman's house – The village houses are simply but comfortably equipped, very reasonable and even cheap. To rent one, contact Szeged Tourist (Fő utca 14). Eight types of houses are available.

Belsőváros – To rent a 45-82m²/482-883sq ft house in the old village (that is to say, including kitchen, bath and 1 to 4 bedrooms) write to Szeged Tourist well in advance. The houses are all furnished and equipped.

Erzsébet Hotel – *Fő utca 3. ☎ 63/483 960, Fax 63/483 631. 13 rooms. Prices around €25.* A classic Hungarian hotel, decently equipped but with a rather dark decor. The restaurant serves traditional dishes, *gulyás*, beef stews, pork stews etc. Accommodation located near the baths (tickets available at the hotel).

Tisza Hotel – *Fő utca 23. ☎/Fax 63/ 483 594. 15 rooms with TV at around €40.* More modern, it is also located on the main avenue and in the very centre of the town. Dental and medical care available. Restaurant. Car park.

Ifjúsági Szálló – *Körös-torok Halász u. 30. ☎/Fax 63/ 474 842. Around €6 per person.* A well-kept youth hostel in a pretty setting.

If you really like crowds – The **Körös-toroki Partfürdő** is a resort – campsite, bathing area, games, beach etc – at the junction of the two rivers 300m/330yd from the old village. Virtually from sunrise the crowds are here to enjoy the sand and water. Vendors sell sandwiches, *palacsinta* (pancakes), *lángos* (savoury fried pastries with various toppings, from grated cheese, with or without cream, to garlic crushed in oil) etc.

A place to eat

Kertvendéglő – *Dózsa Gy. tér.* A good restaurant with a garden in summer. The terrace is linked to the open-air pool of the baths. The cooking is simple and traditional, and as always the portions are more than generous.

Kemence – *Öregvár utca 54. ☎ 63/383 340. Open daily from noon to 10pm.* This is in a former fisherman's home. In fine weather you can eat outside; they make excellent fish dishes. You can drink Csongrádi Kadarka, a local red wine with your food.

Fahídi (wooden bridge) **pinceborozó** (wine cellar restaurant) – *Kereszt tér 22. ☎ 63/470 061 or 63/ 471 193.* The decor echoes the name; the restaurant is in a vaulted cellar, with wooden tables separated by pierced partitions also made of wood. The specialities are fish and *bográcsos* dishes (cooked in a pot over an open wood fire) prepared to order or as they come. Wine from the barrel or by the bottle.

SIGHTS

Gyógyfürdő és Uszoda – The **thermal baths** can be reached by taking Dob utca, and are located in a 7 000m²/8 372sq yd park. The hot spring that supplies the water (46°C/114°F) is 1 091m/3 578ft below the surface. The baths consist of an indoor pool for the winter, an open-air pool open June to August (weekdays 10am to 10pm), a children's pool and a sauna. The spa specialises in diseases of the joints, rheumatism and gynaecological problems. While the setting is a little antiquated, the quality of treatment here is renowned.

★**Tari László Múzeum** ⓥ– *Iskola utca 2.* István Széchenyi is often admired for his vision in understanding the need to control the flow of Hungarian rivers, particularly the Tisza, along with preparation work and relevant decision-making. Less is known, however, of the conditions of the men who worked on the project. The 19C *kubikosok*, the workers who dug up and removed thousands of tonnes of rubble to retain the waters of the rivers, lived like slaves, working 12 to 16 hours a day in mud and dust, badly paid, poorly fed and ill-housed, far from home.

The László Tari Museum was created by a Csongrád dentist in homage to the many people who left their home town and region for these far-off worksites.

MAGYAR KÉPEK Kft

The old village – At the junction of the Tisza and its tributary, the Körös, and the Holt-Tisza, an oxbow of the Tisza, Csongrád has always been associated with fishing. The present-day village is no different from the fishing village of 200 years ago.

Continue on Fő utca, take either Gróf Andrássy utca or Gróf Apponyi Albert utca, then Öregvár; go along the banks of the Tisza to the far end of the town and the museum-village.

★ **Múzeum-Ház** – *Gyökér utca 1.* Two old houses are linked by a thatched passage. In one house there is an open fireplace, a guest bedroom and everyday objects. The other house has fishing tackle on display.

DEBRECEN★

Hajdú-Bihar province – Population 210 000

Michelin map 925 D 13

Debrecen, surrounded by great stretches of tableland, lies at the heart of the expanse to the east of the River Tisza. Debrecen is the urban centre of the Hortobágy region, the well-watered *puszta* that constitutes the nature reserve of the great east-southeast plain.

Debrecen, both Protestant and Reformed, is known as Calvinist Rome. It is considered a *civis* town by Hungarians, that is, strict, civic and righteous – the citizen's city.

A SHORT HISTORY

The Slovaks called the region **Dobre Zliem** (fertile ground) when they settled here sometime before the 9C; this is perhaps the origin of the modern name of Debrecen.

Today's city was founded in the 14C by one of King Louis the Great's military chiefs. The king called it the village of song, owing to its many singers, a tradition, which has continued up to the present time. In 1405 King Sigismund granted the same rights to Debrecen as to Buda, including the right to hold three fairs a year; a century later this number was increased to eight.

Debrecen's upper middle class owned great properties on the western plain. There were worked by peasants, known as **Hajdúk**, who raised horses and cattle and did much of their work on horseback, driving their beasts several thousand kilometres to be sold at Debrecen. The Hajduk, who were also soldiers, fought against the Habsburgs.

From 1536 Debrecen's inhabitants opted for the Reformed religion. The town became a Calvinist centre. In 1538 the **Reformed College** was founded. In 1541 the first printing house devoted to serving the Reformation was created. In 1693 Leopold I gave Debrecen the status of a royal independent city.

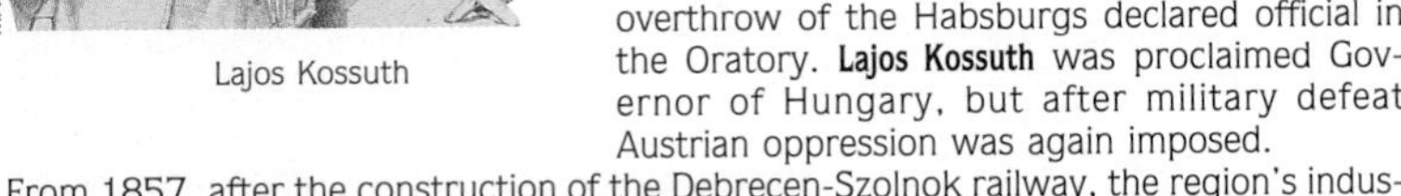

MAGYAR KÉPEK Kft

Lajos Kossuth

Under the Habsburgs the town was continually endangered and burned several times. During the 1848 Revolution and the fight for independence, Debrecen was the seat of the National Assembly. In 1849 imperial authority was cast off and the overthrow of the Habsburgs declared official in the Oratory. **Lajos Kossuth** was proclaimed Governor of Hungary, but after military defeat Austrian oppression was again imposed.

From 1857, after the construction of the Debrecen-Szolnok railway, the region's industrialisation began (sugar and tobacco production, furniture making).

After the Treaty of Trianon, Debrecen became a border city, where thousands of political exiles came from the divided territories.

In late December 1944, on Russian initiative, a provisional government was created at Debrecen, which prepared the municipal and general elections in September and November 1945.

THE CITY

Piac utca – This is Debrecen's main street, running from the railway station in the south to Kálvin tér, the city's main square in the north. Its very name (Market Street) recalls Debrecen's former calling as a city of fairs and markets. In the 16C over 75 000 head of livestock were sold annually. The Hadjúk drove cattle throughout Europe.

★ **Nagytemplom (Great Church)** – This dominates primarily because of its size, being able to seat close to 3 000 worshippers. This Reformed church is the largest Protestant sanctuary in Hungary. Visitors may be lucky enough to hear the great organ, often used for rehearsals. Lajos Kossuth's seat is kept here.

★ **Református Teológiai Akadémia (Reformed College)** ⓥ– This was built in the Classical style between 1803 and 1816, and then enlarged between 1870 and 1874. Dating from the Middle Ages, the very famous school became and long remained northern Hungary's greatest educational establishment, aided and supported by the nobility, as well as by financiers of the time and, of course, the Reformed Church. A school had previously existed on the site of the present College. Up until the late 18C discipline was severe, and students had to rise at three o'clock in the morning.

★ **Museum** – This is essentially devoted to the history of the College, whose fame was such that students came from virtually every European country. A beautiful **collection of religious objects★** is exhibited on the ground floor. The **kopjafa** are particularly interesting; a sort of totem, these carved wooden objects mark burial sites.

The walls of the staircase leading to the library and the oratory (1938) are decorated with frescoes telling the story of the College. There is a stained-glass window, on the second-floor landing, in memory of a former student who later become a famous mathematician. Orwald Thoroczkai once directed the philosophy and mathematics department.

MAGYAR KÉPEK Kft

Debrecen – Reformed College Library

★ **Library** – This is the largest collection of documents concerning the Reformed Church. There are over 500 000 volumes, including 200 versions and various translations of the Bible.

★ **Oratory** – Debrecen was the cradle of Hungarian Calvinism. It is a city that has always cared deeply about its independence, and has always affirmed its desire for liberty. It is therefore not surprising that the Hungarians chose Debrecen for the official declaration of the overthrow of the Habsburgs; it was in the oratory that Hungary's proclaimed Parliament voted this decision in May 1849. The names of the members present at the assembly, including that of Lajos Kossuth, are engraved on brass plates. In the same way the 1944 provisional Assembly was established in Debrecen until the liberation of Budapest and Hungary.

★★ **Déri Múzeum** ⓥ– Four Ferenc Medgyessy sculptures on the square in front of the museum represent Science, Art, Archaeology and Ethnography.

The museum is named after its principal donor, **Frigyes Déri**, who died in 1924 and who had no particular tie to Debrecen. Born in Hungary, Frigyes Déri studied in Vienna and manufactured silk fabrics there. He was a collector who wished to donate his collection to a museum located in a university town. The museum was built between 1926 and 1928. It is now home to various collections, a painting gallery, a Far East collection, antique, archaeological and ethnographic collections, and a nature and fauna museum. The part devoted to Debrecen daily life is very interesting.

A place to stay

Centrum Panzió – *Péterfia u. ☎ 52/416 193. 20 rooms between €35 and €61.* Small town-centre hotel, charming, clean and modern, with rooms overlooking the garden.

Péterfia Pension – *Péterfia u. 37. ☎ 52/423 582. 18 rooms at around €31.* Next to the above hotel. Modern rooms.

Grand Hôtel Aranybika – *Piac u. 11-15. ☎ 52/416 777. 237 rooms between €57 and €69.* Immense hotel with a 300-year-old façade extending along the town's main thoroughfare. This is one of the oldest hotels in town. The Art Nouveau lobby and restaurant are splendid. The best rooms look out on the street, which unfortunately means they are noisy.

A place to eat

Dante – *Piac u. 22. ☎ 52/451 806.* Fashionable restaurant with Italian decor. Hungarian and international cuisine. An extensive wine list. Rather expensive.

Halásztanya Étterem – *Piac u. 70-74. ☎ 52/410 106.* The façade is not particularly attractive, but behind it is hidden an excellent fish restaurant. Traditional and pretty decor.

Flaska Söröző – *Miklós u. 4. ☎ 52/414 582.* In a vaulted cellar, this is a little neighbourhood restaurant frequented mostly by local people. Very inexpensive. Perhaps the best address.

Városháza Étterem – *Piac u. 20. ☎ 52/444 767.* Hungarian and international cuisine. Menus between €8 and €23.

One of the museum's key works is Mihály Munkácsy's **triptych★★**. The first panel, *Christ Before Pilate*, was completed in 1881 and exhibited in several European cities. Munkácsy finished the second panel, *Golgotha*, in 1884. The two panels were then exhibited in the United States and presented by the artist himself. A Philadelphia entrepreneur later bought them and exhibited them every year at Eastertide. This tradition continued until 1988, when they were sold at auction at Sotheby's in New York. A Hungarian gallery owner bought *Golgotha*, while *Christ Before Pilate* was bought by the Museum of Toronto. Both works were on loan to the Déri Museum and were returned to the United States in 2001.

Nagyerdő – This wooded area stretches north of the city. A part has been urbanised, mainly to establish the medical school there. A residential area has also been created in this green part of the city.

DUNAKANYAR★★★

DANUBE BEND – Pest and Komárom-Esztergom provinces

Michelin map 925 D 8, C 8 and 7

Duna, the Danube... In the romantic setting of the Danube Bend, the River Danube is more beautiful than ever. From its source in the Black Forest – the actual spot is a much debated question – the Danube is the cosmopolitan river that links the West to Asia. Along a parallel, it flows from west to east, crosses southern Germany and Austria, visits Bratislava, runs through the Czech Republic for a few miles and, following the directives of the Treaty of Trianon, draws the border between present-day Slovakia (Czechoslovakia at the time) and Hungary. Here it passes north of the Gerecse Mountains, cutting between the Pilis and Börzsöny hills, and then flows around Szentendre Island. Beyond the island it heads towards the capital and then continues south across the Great Plain.

Dunakanyar is the Hungarian word to describe the river's magnificent curve, known as the Danube loop, elbow or bend. We will use the last expression since this corresponds to the Hungarian term. After leaving Esztergom, the coronation town, the Danube bends due south. Up to this point Europe's second longest river has not met many major obstacles along the route from its source but here it seems to have heard the call of the Great Plain and succumbed to the temptation of idleness.

THE DANUBE BEND BY CAR

Round trip from Budapest – 140km/87mi – allow a full day

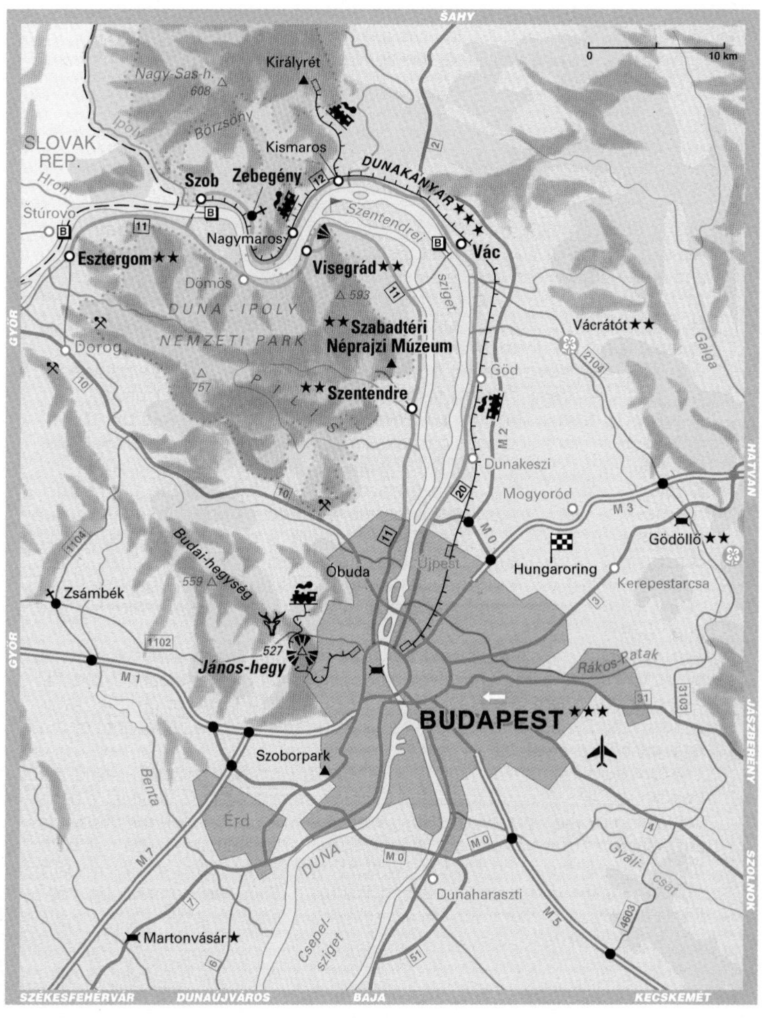

The right bank as far as Esztergom

★★★ **Budapest** – *See this name.*

Leave Budapest on the right bank, following the Danube and take road n° 11 to Szentendre.

The road goes through Óbuda and large residential blocks before it runs past the Roman ruins of Aquincum.

★★ **Szentendre** – *See this name.*

★★ **Visegrád** – *See this name.*

The most spectacular **view★★★** of the Danube Bend is from Visegrád.
There was definitely a reason why kings and queens built their castles and royal residences here. Obviously, there were strategic motives but, above all, there was the beauty of the setting itself. Numerous sovereigns, guests at the palace whose reputation had spread throughout Europe, were able to admire the setting and the river, which flows more slowly here before embracing Szentendre Island. At the foot of the fortress is the town of Visegrád, with Charles Robert of Anjou's palace and Solomon's Tower. Opposite, between the river and Mt Zebegény is Nagymaros. From this viewpoint, you can also see the remains, on the Hungarian side, of the Nagymaros Dam.

Beyond Dömös, you can see Slovakia from the road on the other side of the river.

★★ **Esztergom** – *See this name.*

The left bank

You can return to Budapest via the left bank of the Danube. From the sharply winding road above the river you can see the opposite bank and its relief. In the late afternoon, in fine weather, the light is splendid, giving the countryside a

The Bős-Nagymaros Dam

This is an old project that began in the fraternal context of the Communist regimes. The dam was not built as planned, the project is still not finished and a few differences of opinion still remain between the protagonists.
At the outset, there were two principal partners, Czechoslovakia and Hungary. A third, Austria, was providing the resources, which were to be reimbursed in the form of electricity.
Originally, the idea stemmed from a desire to conquer nature with science and with the power of tools forged by man. The idea dates from the first years of the establishment of the Communist regimes, just before the 1950s. Studies were made and decisions taken, but work only began in 1983. It was strongly opposed by Hungarian ecologists, and was in process when the Berlin Wall fell. Another consequence of the collapse of the Communist regimes was that Czechoslovakia became two States, the Czech Republic and the Slovak Republic. Only the Slovak Republic is currently involved in the construction of the dam. Ecological protests stem from the fact that, in the area where the waters of the dam were to be contained, the Danube flows over a bed of gravel, sand and permeable sedimentary layers, filtering out impurities.
The waters of the river, slowed down by the dam, would then deposit the elements carried along and, over time, might seal off the cracks in the filtering layers. There is said to be around 60km³ /14 cu mi of ground water beneath the Danube and it is this fabulous reserve that the opponents of the dam wish to protect.
The Slovaks have already built part of the dam on their territory, called the Gabcikovo Dam. They estimate that their investment, which should have been completed by the work on the Hungarian side, will not bring in the dividends anticipated and are asking for compensation. The Hungarians do not wish to continue with the construction, which they consider too costly, technically out-of-date and dangerous for the environment. They wish to break the contract. A difficult problem for the International Court of Justice in The Hague which has inherited the case...

special brilliance. On this bank numerous residences once belonged to the lords and ladies of the court who took advantage of the beauty of the setting, the game, the forests and the wealth of the land.

Return to road n° 11 in the opposite direction. At Basaharc, turn left along a small road and take the ferry to the left bank of the river.

Szob – Frontier post for Slovakia. See the **Börzsöny Museum (Börzsöny Múzeum)** ⓥwhich relates the country's history (objects found in archaeological digs), the life of the country and the fauna and flora.

Continue on road n° 12, which runs alongside the Danube.

Zebegény – This small town radiates peace. Visitors come here to rest and spend time with their families. It is worth stopping to visit the **parish church** *(Petőfi tér)* designed by the architect, Károly Kós. It dates from 1909 and is an example of Art Nouveau architecture. The exterior is simple and well proportioned. The highly decorated interior has been inspired by folk art. It was painted by students from the Higher School of Decorative Art, under the direction of Aladár Kriesch. Above the altar, the *Apotheosis of the Holy Cross* is surrounded by garlands of flowers. Zebegény happened to be the permanent residence of a 20C Hungarian painter, István Szőnyi, whose house has been turned into a museum where drawing and painting courses are held every year. The garden is used as a campsite for young artists.

Nagymaros – Famous for the name of the dam and also for its red fruit and raspberries now grown to make jam and cordials.

Kismaros – A small train takes you for an 8km/5mi trip to Királyrét (the King's Field) through the Morgó Valley. The King's Field is a hollow in the middle of the hills where the beautiful Beatrice of Aragon, wife of King Matthias Corvinus, used to bathe in a pool.

Vác – *See this name.*

Road n° 20 takes you back to Budapest through the industrial outskirts of Újpest.

THE DANUBE BEND BY BOAT FROM BUDAPEST

Landing-stage on the Pest side: Belgrád Rakpart near Vigadó tér.

A pleasant way to appreciate this magnificent waterway and have a completely different vision of the countryside is to take a boat trip.
Some excursions include a stop-off at Visegrád, others go as far as Esztergom. Some boats do the return journey from Budapest to Visegrád without stopping. We recommend the full trip to Esztergom *(allow at least 5hr)*. Take an early morning boat. The trip is cool and comfortable. Once you have crossed the northern part of the capital, you reach Szentendre Island quickly. Travelling on one of the branches of the river that encircles the island, the boat goes along its coast for a few kilometres before moving forward on the Danube in all its grandeur between Nagymaros and Visegrád. The boat then slips between the Börzsöny and Pilis hills, along the Slovak side and the town of Štúrovo until it reaches Esztergom, heralded by its monumental basilica which seems to be watching over the river.

EGER★★

Heves province – Population 65 000

Michelin map 925 C 11 – Local map see BÜKK

Eger is a beautiful, attractive city, nestled in the hollow between the impressive Bükk and Mátra mountains, which protect it from the north wind and give it an ideal climate for growing vines. **Egri Bikavér** or Bull's Blood, the reputedly strength-giving wine, needs virtually no introduction. The hero of the battle against the Turks, István Dobó, made his men drink it to give them strength; but the story does not tell us whether or not Eger's women also used some of this potion to take part in the fray!

The 18C was to see the revival of Eger, when the city took on its current Baroque appearance – a look which never fails to charm visitors.

A great captain – **István Dobó** was born in 1500 and died in 1572. He was a seasoned captain but also quite simply a man of great character. As a landowner in northern Hungary, he had several fortresses under his command. In 1549 he became captain of the one at Eger. He recognised the danger posed by the Turks – who were steadily extending their empire further into Hungarian territory – and the need to reinforce the town's defences. Although the Turks were defeated, and in spite of the news of his victory spreading beyond the frontiers, he received neither glory nor honour. On the contrary, he resigned from his post, disappointed that the expected relief forces had not come to the rescue. He accepted the post of *voïvode* (commander) of Transylvania. Frustrated by the Habsburg attitude and the weakness of the military forces, an opinion he freely and loudly expressed, he was rapidly suspected of conspiracy and thrown into prison in 1569. He was freed only a short time before his death.

FORTUNE AND MISFORTUNE

Man has always been attracted to this region; the first known traces go back to the Neolithic period. Later, the ancestors of the Hungarian people, who occupied the Carpathian Basin, settled in this valley with its small river known today as the Eger. King Stephen (István), who organised Hungarian territory around the churches in the 11C, made it a bishopric. The Mongol invaders in 1241 destroyed the town and massacred or carried off the inhabitants, leaving it empty. The region was eventually repopulated by families from Western Europe. People from France, Italy and Northern Europe contributed to making Eger a cultural centre influenced by Renaissance ideas. It could be said that Eger's resistance to the Turks delayed the Ottoman expansion, even if the later defeat in 1596 allowed them to establish themselves in Hungary. It should be noted that at this time the town was defended by foreign mercenaries who offered to give themselves up without resistance, provided they were spared and set free. The promise was not kept, however, and some of them were massacred, others thrown into prison. From this time and for the next 90 years, the Turks dominated Eger, altering the city to suit their customs and needs as they saw fit. They built mosques and baths, of which little trace remains, except for a minaret and a few ruins.

The city of wine that honours its women

The Turks laid siege to Eger in 1552. Over 100 000 were said to have attacked the town defended by 2 000 soldiers. Dobó, captain of the Hungarian troops, opened the wine cellars and broke open the casks for his bearded men. The red from the wine so coloured their beards and lips that the sultan's men believed that the Hungarians drew their strength from drinking bull's blood. They thus called the Eger wine *egri bikavér*, or Bull's Blood, a name it has retained.

However, the 2 000 soldiers could do little against the 100 000 Turks, but the women of Eger rushed to their aid. Not only did they prepare their food and serve them wine but they also boiled oil and pitch to pour on the attackers. A very beautiful painting, *The Women of Eger* by Bertalan Székely, can be found in the castle's painting gallery.

The year 1687 saw Eger's liberation; this time it was 4 000 Turks who put up resistance for four months, and were then authorised to leave the town freely. In 1690 Eger had between 3 000 and 4 000 inhabitants. Emperor Leopold I of Habsburg had the castle blown up at the beginning of the 18C, fearing that this fortified town would become a resistance centre for Hungarian independence. Ferenc Rákóczi II was to be the unfortunate hero of this battle, which in hindsight would later confirm Austrian fears *(see Sárospatak)*.

★★VÁR (CASTLE)

The simplest way to get to know Eger is by going to the castle. This is easy to find as it overlooks the city. Take Dózsa György tér to the foot of the ramparts; from there a short, steep rise leads to the south gate and the interior of the fortifications.

Tour

Along the watch path, there are magnificent **views★★** of the city. On the way there is **Gárdonyi Géza's tomb** (Gárdonyi Géza sírja), with an inscription that warns the reader: "Only the body lies here". Gárdonyi Géza is the famous author of a book about the siege of Eger, which is very often studied in Hungarian schools: *The Eclipse of the Rising Crescent Moon*, sometimes translated as *The Stars of Eger*.

Szent János ruins – **St John's Cathedral**, begun in the 11C, was to mark the importance of Eger diocese. The Romanesque construction was destroyed by Mongols, and work resumed at the end of the 15C; fire put a stop to the Gothic style reconstruction. Later, the stones were used to reinforce defences and, in 1552, a gunpowder store exploded and blew up what remained of the cathedral.

★★ **Kazamaták** ⓥ – Under the cathedral's foundations several levels of **underground galleries** and **casemates** can be visited. There is an impressive network of corridors, rooms and storerooms where guides will explain how the Turks' attempts to bore tunnels to insert explosives and blow up the castle were foiled. A few

Revault/PIX

Eger – Former Bishop's Palace

humble chick-peas were put on a taut drum skin, which reverberated with the movement of the air caused by each blow of the assailants at work, giving them away to the besieged.

Dobó István Múzeum ⓥ – This is located in the old Bishop's Palace. Visitors can pay homage to the valiant captain by visiting the castle museum named after him. There is a statue of Dobó on the ground floor, in the Heroes' Hall. Castle furniture, objects and tapestries are upstairs, as well as models illustrating the various phases of the history of the cathedral hill.

★ **Egri Képtár** (**Painting gallery**) – This is in the building to the left of Dobó Museum, and is well worth a visit, and not just for Bertalan Székely's famous painting, *The Women of Eger* but also the collection of Italian and Dutch school 16C, 17C and 18C canvases, as well as Hungarian paintings of the 18C, 19C and early 20C, including some very beautiful works by Mihály Munkácsy.

EGER

Ady Endre u	BZ	2
Almagyar u	BZ	4
Bajcsy-Zsilinszky Endre u	BZ	5
Cecey Éva u	BY	8
Dobó István u	BY	10
Egészségház u	BZ	14
Frank Tivadar u	BZ	15
Gerl Mátyás u	BY	18
Harangöntő u	BY	19
Koháry István u	AZ	20
Markhót Ferenc u	BY	26
Mecsét u	BY	28
Mekcsey István u	BZ	30
Petőfi Sándor tér	BZ	32
Rákóczi Ferenc	AY	34
Sándor Imre u (Dr.)	AYZ	36
Szarvas tér	BZ	38

Érseki Főszékesegyház	AZ
Ferences templom	BZ
Gárdonyi Géza sírja	BY
Görögkeleti templom	AY
Kispréposti palota	BZ
Líceum	BZ
Megyeháza	BZ
Minaret	BY
Minorita templom	BZ
Nagypréposti palota	BZ
Palóc Múzeum	BZ
Török Fürdő	BYZ
Vár	BY

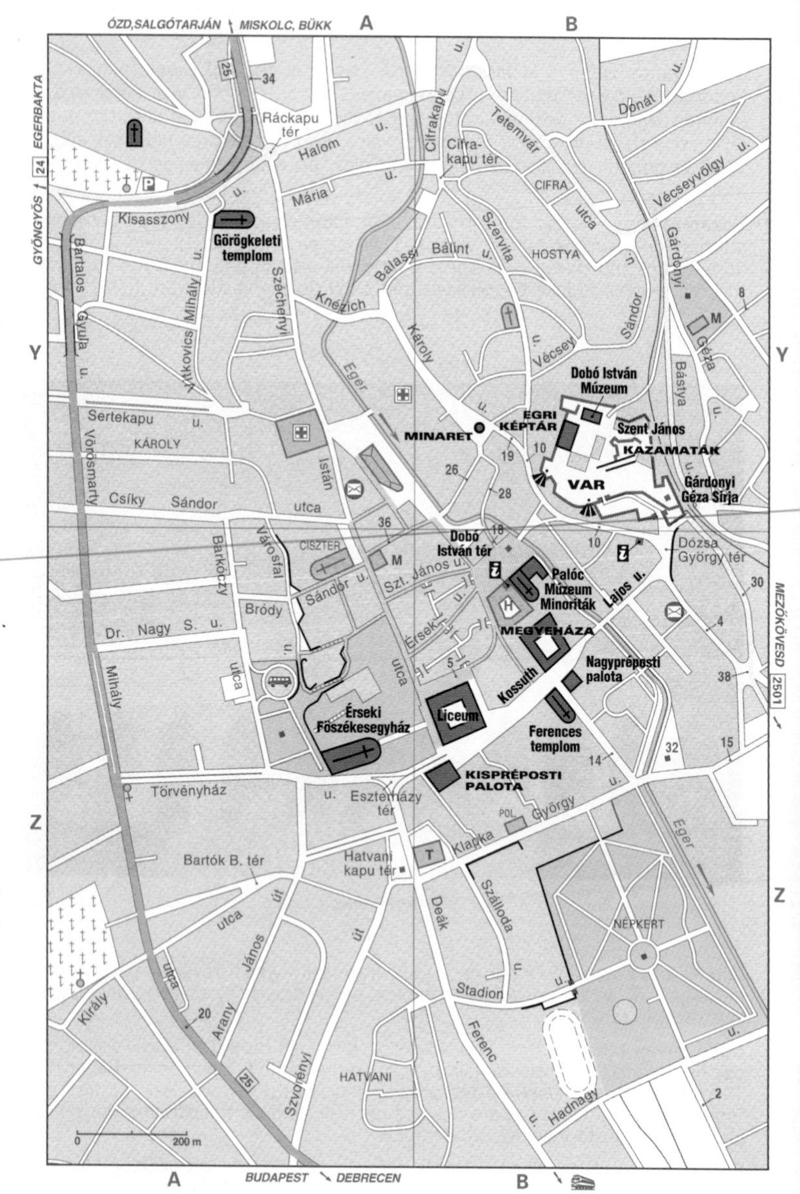

CITY CENTRE

Return from the castle via Dózsa György tér; at n° 1 you will see the **ruins of a Turkish bath** (Török Fürdő maradványai). Then take Kossuth Lajos utca and cross **Eger patak** (Eger brook).

Kossuth Lajos utca – It is worth stopping to have a look at the fronts of several of the houses in this street.

★★ **Megyeháza** – *N° 9.* The **County Hall** dates from the 1750s and was designed by a Viennese architect. Admire Heinrik Fazola's work, especially the ironwork over the main gate with its representation of Faith, Hope and Charity. In the passage there are two other wrought-iron **grilles**★★ that are justifiably the most famous examples of Hungarian ironwork.

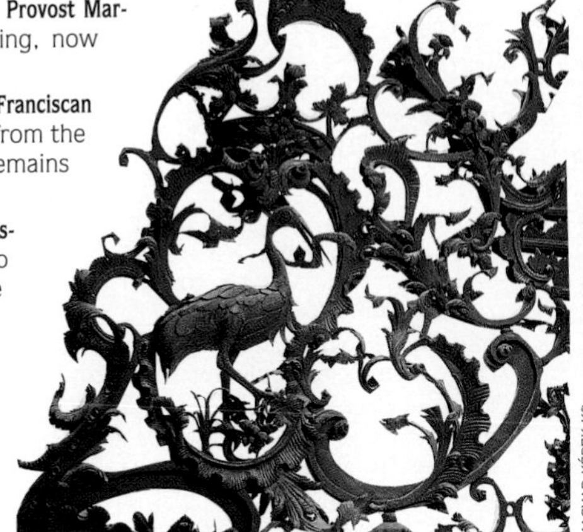

MAGYAR KÉPEK Kft

Nagypréposti palota – *N° 16.* The **Provost Marshall's house** is a Baroque building, now home to the province's library.

Ferences templom – This **Baroque Franciscan church** has a single nave dating from the mid-18C, together with the remains of a Turkish mosque.

★★ **Kispréposti palota** – *N° 4.* The **Assistant Provost's house** is a Rococo building dating from 1758. The façade is of hewn stone, with cleverly assembled curves. The wrought-iron balconies are by Fazola.

Érseki Főszékesegyház – The **basilica** is an enormous neo-Classical building created by the architect who built Esztergom's basilica. Access is by a monumental staircase edged with statues (St Peter and St Paul are on the left, St Stephen and St Ladislas on the right). A wide portico, with six Corinthian columns and a pediment, makes an impressive entrance. The decor inside is subdued.

Líceum ⓥ – The Líceum, the former teachers' training school, was the Ho Chi Minh grammar school for a while. Its library and observatory are worth a visit.

★★ **Library** – *First floor, door n° 48.* Founded by Bishop Charles Eszterházy, the archbishopric library opened its doors on 28 December 1793. Its extremely varied collection of 130 000 volumes includes medieval manuscripts, incunabula, works from the 16C, 17C and 18C, and the only letter written by Mozart on Hungarian soil. The Regency oak bookshelves were carved by a local craftsman. The library also has an interesting **painted ceiling**, considered a masterpiece of Hungarian fresco art. Johann Kracker represented a session of the famous Council of Trent (Italy) which was held between 1545 and 1563, and which changed the nature of the Church. It was Kracker's last work, created with his son-in-law's help: 132 characters are represented, most of them famous people. The painter also depicted himself: he is the man with a moustache holding a lance and standing to the left of the bishop.

Observatory – *Sixth floor.* This small astronomy museum has a collection of measuring instruments.

Camera obscura – *Ninth floor.* The mystery of the "dark room" will be revealed to you in a darkened chamber where a panorama of the city is reflected by a play of mirrors.

On leaving the school take Bajcsy-Zsilinszky utca on the right.

★ **Dobó István tér** – This is the city centre's main square, where a statue of the local and national hero stands, the defender of Eger and victor over the Turks.

Minorita templom ⓥ – The **Friar Minors' Church**, standing among the other façades along the south side of the square, is a beautiful example of Baroque architecture. Started in 1758, it took 15 years to build. There is a painting by Johann Kracker, representing the Virgin and St Anthony, hanging over the main altar.

Palóc Múzeum – This **exhibition of Palóc folk art** is in a building next to the Friar Minors' church. Several masterpieces by *Palóc* people, mostly from the region west of Eger, can be seen: fabrics, bedspreads, painted furniture, carvings by shepherds.

Leave the square by heading north, and take Gerl utca then Mecset utca.

★ **Minaret** ⓥ – This is the only well preserved trace of the Turkish occupation; it has 14 sides and is 40m/131ft high.

A place to stay

La Casa Panzió – *Cecey Éva u. 32. ☎/Fax 36/413 573. 5 rooms at around €28.* In the upper part of the town, a prettily decorated *panzió*. Charming rooms. Breakfast served in the garden.

Just nearby, the Cecey *panzió* is more modern, with a similar degree of comfort and price.

Panoráma Panzió – *Joó János u. 9. ☎/Fax 36/420 531. 7 rooms between €35 and €40.* A *panzió* with a panoramic view of the town. Clean and modern rooms. Sauna and fitness room. Just nearby the Siesta Panzió is a little less expensive but without the view!

Minaret – *Knézich Károly u. 4. ☎ 36/410 020, Fax 36/410 473. 38 rooms between €35 and €40.* A very comfortable hotel located in front of the minaret. Quality restaurant in the cellar.

Senator Ház – *Dobó tér 11. ☎ 36/320 466, Fax 36/320 466. 11 rooms between €35 and €55.* Our best address. On the town's main, historic square. A charming little 18C house. Quality service.

Offí Ház Hotel – *Dobó tér 5. ☎ 36/311 005. Rooms between €65 and €75.* Near the Senator Ház, a little hotel with old-fashioned charm.

A place to eat

Fehérszarvas Vadásztanya – *Klapka György u. 8. ☎ 36/411 129.* The most famous and popular restaurant in town. Traditional decor. Specialities: grilled food and Hungarian music.

HBH Bajor Sörház – *Bajcsy Zsilinszky. ☎ 36/316 312.* In Eger's historic town centre; excellent restaurant specialising in Hungarian and Bavarian cooking.

Ködmön Csárda – *Szépasszony-völgy. ☎ 36/413 172.* In the Woman's Valley, where a great many restaurants and wine cellars are to be found, a large traditional inn offers many Hungarian dishes and wines. Folk music and dance. A tourist haunt in summer.

Jóbarát Kisvendéglő – *Bródy S. u. ☎ 36/410 496.* Traditional restaurant; simple and inexpensive.

Where to get a drink?

Dodos – *Széchenyi u. 6. ☎ 36/413 335.* A very popular tea shop. A large, luxurious room with chandeliers and mirrors. A pleasant afternoon stop.

Balla Család – *Szépasszony-völgy, 18-as pince. ☎ 36/313 297.* In the Woman's Valley. You can taste the famous Egri Bikavér or Bull's Blood. You can have something to eat at the small Balla bar.

ADDITIONAL SIGHTS

Görögkeleti templom – *Szécheny utca 55 is about 1km/0.6mi from the city centre, on a rise.* The **Orthodox church**, also called the Serbian church, dates from the late 18C. Its construction was controversial and it was only completed thanks to the authorisation of Emperor Joseph II. A beautiful carved wooden **iconostasis★**, decorated with painted images, makes the visit worthwhile.

EXCURSION

★★ **Bükk** – *See this name.*

ESZTERGOM★★

Komárom–Esztergom province – Population 33 789

Michelin map 925 C 7 – 66km/40mi northwest of Budapest
Local map see DUNAKANYAR

Esztergom, a former royal seat, is the queen of the Danube. The Danube, after Vienna, barely touches Győr, crosses Komárom, avoids the northern part of the Gerecse Mountains, and then quietly traces its bed from west to east, sketching out the northern border of modern Hungary. It runs below Esztergom, cuts a passage between the Pilis and Börzsöny hills, collides with the Cserhát Hills, then, having lost energy, turns in a right angle to form the famous **Danube Bend** (Dunakanyar) before flowing south. Esztergom is the last big town before Budapest on the right bank. Set on two hills separated by a small tributary of the Danube, Esztergom looks down regally on the river flowing at its feet.

The birth of the State – A royal residence for three centuries and Hungary's religious capital, the town was the seat of Hungarian Catholicism for over 1 000 years, and is still the seat of Hungary's Archbishop Primate.
Castle Hill has been inhabited since 350 BC. The Celts established a community here and the Romans occupied the site until the 4C, in large camps that were part of the Roman walls. This Roman colony was called Solva Mansio, and was visited by Marcus Aurelius; the emperor-philosopher stayed there several times and wrote a part of his *Thoughts* there. Most importantly, however, the town has preserved the memory of Prince Géza (pronounced Gay-za), a descendant of the Magyar conqueror Árpád. After raising an army, he established the seat of power at Gran, which later took the name Esztergom. He reigned there from 972 to 997. His son Vajk, baptised István (Stephen) was prince from 997 to 1000 and crowned king on Christmas Day of that year. He reigned until 1038.
Assuming the crown placed on his head by Pope Sylvester II, Stephen I affirmed his authority; he made a part of the hitherto nomadic population sedentary, obliging the villages to federate into groups of 10 to build a church and support a priest. He founded two archbishoprics and built a basilica. He imposed the notion of welcome and tolerance since he felt that the real wealth of a people lay in exchange and the meeting of differences. Since he chose the western form of Christianity, as opposed to the Greek Church, Géza, followed by his son Stephen I, set Hungary at the centre of Europe as one of the advanced strongholds of western civilisation.
Esztergom, called Strigonium during the Middle Ages, developed and lived its golden age from the end of the 12C to the mid-14C. The king received a great many visitors including Godefroy de Bouillon, Louis VII, and Frederick Barbarossa, King of Germany and Holy Roman Emperor. In the mid-13C, however, following the Tartar invasions, King Béla IV moved the royal seat to Buda.
The archbishop remained in the town and settled in the royal palace. The succession of archbishops received visits from famous European scholars and artists, making Esztergom a major cultural centre rivalling the capital.

A bridge in waiting – Originally Esztergom was on both banks of the Danube. Slovakia and Hungary were separated here by the river, and could not come to an agreement on the rebuilding of the Mária Valéria Bridge linking Esztergom and Štúrovo.
The Turks had already built a boat bridge here, later constructing a bridge supported by piers. In 1762 a ferry pulled by a cable, nicknamed the flying bridge enabled people to cross the river. In 1842 a boat bridge was used again before the Mária Valéria Bridge was built; the widest point between two piers was 120m/394ft. In 1919, the Czechs demolished one of the arches, and the bridge was not restored until several years later. Destroyed by German troops over Christmas 1944, the bridge remained in a state of ruin for more than fifty years. There was a ferry over the river. After many years of discussion between Hungarians and Slovaks, an agreement was finally reached, and now, a bridge with several brand new arches is in place, and has been linking the two countries since October 2001.

A place to stay

Alabárdos Panzió – *Bajcsy u. 49. ☎/Fax 33/312 640. Rooms between €23 and €29.* Located in the town centre, this *panzió* can be recognised by its yellow façade, and offers rooms that are clean and modern.

Ria - *Batthyány u. 11-13. ☎ 33/313 115. Fax 33/401 429. 13 rooms between €23 and €36. 100m/110yd* from the basilica, *panzió* with simple and well-kept rooms.

Esztergom – *Nagy-Duna Sétány. ☎ 33/412 883. Fax 33:412 853. 34 rooms between €35 and €51.* Modern hotel well situated next to the Danube.

A place to eat

Prímás Pince – *Szt. István tér 4.* A tourist restaurant. In the 500-year-old ramparts surrounding the basilica. International cuisine.
Szalma Csárda – *Nagy-Duna Sétány.* On the banks of the Danube, a traditional inn in a quiet street away from the centre.
Anonim Restaurant – *Berényi u. 4.* Below the basilica; a restaurant in a picturesque, paved street. Hungarian and international cuisine.
Arany Elefánt Étterem – *Petőfi u. 15.* Popular and friendly little restaurant. Simple but decent food. Local customers. Very inexpensive.

Esztergom Basilica

SIGHTS

The location – The town is in an area with distinctive geographical relief: Two hills, **Vár-hegy** (Castle Hill) and **Szent Tamás-hegy** (St Thomas' Hill) provide contrasts in appearance, making it a pleasant place to visit. An arm of the Danube, **Kis Duna** (the Little Danube) cuts off a peaceful little island, a place to relax and take a stroll alongside the so-called Water District. It takes 10min to walk from the basilica to the bridge linking **Primás-sziget** (Primate Island) to the riverbank.

★ **Szent Adalbert Főszékesegyház (Basilica)** – In the 19C this imposing building replaced the church originally founded by King Stephen I. That edifice, called the beautiful church, was devoted to **St Adalbert**. It was destroyed during the battles against the Turks. Only the chapel, built by cardinal **Thomas Bakócz**, constructed to serve as his sepulchral chapel, survived the vicissitudes of the wars. This cardinal is famous not only for building himself a chapel, but also because he transformed a Crusade into a revolt in 1514; it is said that he was disappointed he had not been made Pope. The remains of this chapel were taken apart into 1 600 pieces in the early 19C and moved from the original site, and then put together again and fitted into today's basilica. The Bakócz Chapel, made of red marble and carved by Tuscan sculptors, is one of the oldest vestiges of the Renaissance in existence outside Italy. The new basilica built according to plans by Pál Kühnel and János Packh was finished in 1869 by Joseph Hild, the architect of Eger Cathedral, in the neo-Classical style that can be seen today. The first stone was laid in 1822. The work lasted for close to 50 years and the building was finally consecrated in 1856. **Franz Liszt** directed the **Esztergom Mass** (or Gran Mass; Gran is the German name for Estergom).

The cathedral's outline forms an integral part of the Esztergom landscape. Its imposing measurements (118m/387ft long, 47m/154ft wide, a façade 97m/318ft high for a total height of 100m/328ft) and its impressive location make the structure stand out. The basilica does not have any real architectural value in itself, but it is very much a presence, owing to its sheer mass, on a cliff overlooking the Danube. Several artists participated in its ornamentation, which is not particularly noteworthy either, apart from its sheer size. A copy of Titian's *Assumption* could appear in the Guinness Book of Records; it is said to be the largest picture ever painted on a single piece of canvas. Hungarian cardinals since Cardinal **Ambrus Károly** have been buried in the **crypt**. Cardinal **Mindszenty**, the Primate of Hungary, who took refuge in the American embassy after the 1956 uprising, died in Vienna in 1971, and was eventually laid to rest here. His remains were moved to Esztergom in 1991 because he had expressed the wish to be buried in Hungary only after the last Soviet soldier had left. There is an impressive atmosphere in the candlelit crypt, guarded by statues representing Mourning and Eternity.

A. Mudrak/MAGYAR KÉPEK Kft

The **Danube Bend** (Dunakanyar) can be seen from the cupola, cutting a passage between the Pilis and Börzsöny hills before flowing on towards Szentendre and Budapest.

Treasury – Numerous sacred objects used for religious services are exhibited here. This rich collection comprises ecclesiastical vestments, chalices, pyxes, crucifixes and patens. Among the objects, pay special attention to the **Baroque Maria Theresa chalice**, the **Garamszentbenedek monstrance**, the gold **Matthias Calvary cross** encrusted with enamel, and numerous Italian, Byzantine and Hungarian pieces of historical interest. A more selective presentation, emphasising the most beautiful elements, would avoid visitors having the impression that this treasure, with its 350 objects made of gold, precious stones and metals, resembles a high-class collection of bric-a-brac.

★ **Királyi palota** – The **royal palace**, built in the late 12C during the reign of Béla III, is on the southern part of the plateau. Covered with earth by the Turks, the castle was only rediscovered in 1930 when the archaeological digs began, now making it possible to visit certain rooms. From being a royal residence, it became a bishops' residence when King Béla IV moved the royal seat to Buda after the departure of the Mongols.
The restoration of the palace has brought interesting architectural elements to light, including the 12C vaulted room, considered the oldest room in Hungary. It is to the **Queen's Room** that the second wife of King Matthias Corvinus, Beatrice of Aragon, used to withdraw. The royal audiences took place on the first floor in the **Double Room** also called Primate **János Vitéz' Study**. This 15C room is also known as the **Room of Virtues**, as it is decorated with frescoes, attributed to a Florentine master, which depict the four cardinal virtues: Prudentia (prudence), Temperentia (temperance), Fortitudo (courage) and Justitia (justice).
The vaulting is decorated with signs of the Zodiac. From this room visitors go into the older royal chapel (11C-12C); the artists reputedly came from Normandy and Burgundy for the marriage of **Béla III** and **Marguerite Capet**. The early Gothic columns of this building are decorated with characters symbolising the battle between Good and Evil. The Byzantine frescoes may have been commissioned by Béla III, who was educated at the Byzantine court.

★★ **Keresztény Múzeum (Archbishop's Palace** or **Christian Museum)** ⓥ – *Berényi Zsigmond utca 2.* This was founded by Cardinal Archbishop **János Simor**. The museum exhibits some very interesting 14C and 15C works from various European schools. The tour takes at least 2hr. Those who are particularly interested may take their time, as the rooms are quiet and fairly empty.
The founder was formerly bishop of Győr, where he began his collection. He brought 80 paintings with him and was moved by the idea of inspiring and promoting contemporary religious painting. At the same time he wanted to restore Esztergom to its former glory, as demonstrated by his other great projects including the creation of the cathedral portal, the restoration of the Bakócz Chapel, the opening of the basilica treasury, the construction of the new archbishop's palace and the creation of the library. In 1874 János Simor received the cardinal's hat and, during his stay in Rome, bought 50 paintings from antique dealers. Continuing his search for and purchase of artworks, it became apparent that the cardinal archbishop intended to create a museum. From this time on, he received numerous donations. His most important purchase was undoubtedly the acquisition of the **Bertinelli collection**: 63 Renaissance paintings seen for the first time when the Pope was elected in 1878. Simor's successor, Cardinal Kolos Vaszary, did not pay any particular attention to the Episcopal treasure. The church's general situation, as well as the archdiocese's financial ruin, did not encourage him to continue the project.
1913 was a new beginning. **János Csernoch**, a former collaborator of Cardinal Simor, undertook to bring the collection back to life with the assistance of his young secretary Dr **Antal Lepold**; this was done primarily by recruiting a young art historian, **Tibor Gerevich**.
The collection left by **Arnold Ipolyi**, bishop of Besztercebánya (now Banská Bystrica in Slovakia) was later added, increasing the number of works belonging to the museum. Lastly, when Hungarian-born Princess San Marco, **Nako Mileva**, died in 1926, she left the Esztergom Museum her collection as a legacy.

Ground floor – Three rooms are devoted to temporary exhibitions of contemporary religious craftsmanship.

First floor – Notice the bust of János Simor on the first-floor landing.

Room I – In the centre of the mural panel on the left is a triptych by a 15C Hungarian master, **Tamás Kolozsvári**, dating from 1427. It comes from what was one of Hungary's oldest Benedictine abbeys, located in Garamszentbenedek (now Horský Benadik in Slovakia). The artist is considered the finest Hungarian painter of works of this scale. It is also thought that he was a talented miniaturist. He most likely directed a large studio.

The **Garamszentbenedeki Úrkoporsó** (the sepulchre of Garamszentbenedek) in the centre of the room, another important piece in the museum, comes from the same abbey. Set on a coffer decorated with wooden sculptures (soldier-guardians of the tomb), the sepulchre, which rolls on four wheels, was used to carry a wood carving of the body of Christ, (a statue which is now in Garamszentbenedek church) during Easter season processions. This beautiful carving is 3.25m/11ft high, 2.26m/7.4ft long and 1m/3.28ft wide; it has been restored several times and is thought to have been created in 1840 in an artist's studio in a mining town north of Garamszentbenedek.

The statues of the four Evangelists and the Madonna of the Visitation are also worthy of note.

Room II – Above two panels by a painter known only by the initials BE, who is thought to have painted these works in 1494, is a 1510 wooden sculpture of God and angel musicians; it is a charmingly fresh, simple composition, representing God the Father.

Nearby a forcefully realistic carved statue of the Madonna (1500) gives a spiritual, holy dimension to the image of an ordinary mother.

On the same mural panel in the centre of the room, four great paintings date from the beginning of the 16C; they represent the *Agony in the Garden*, *Christ Bearing His Cross*, the *Crucifixion* and the *Resurrection*, and are attributed to **Master MS** who would seem to have been influenced by Dürer.

Room III – This is the largest room, where paintings and canvases from the Italian schools are exhibited: Florence, Siena, Venice and Bologna. Virtually all the works should be mentioned, the most beautiful being those from the studio of **Taddeo Gaddi**; two small paintings by a Venetian artist, *Virgin with Child bearing a Crown* together with a *Crucifixion*, and *Christ on the Cross* (1320) from the Sienese school; the Paolo di Giovanni Fei (1380) triptych; the Martino de Bartolomeo (1400) triptych; a composition on lines and diagonals by a Florentine artist, *Life of Hermits at Thebes* (1400), and *Young Girl with a Unicorn*, painted between 1440 and 1470.

The **Austrian school** is represented among others by **Franz Anton Maulbertsch**; *The Last Supper* (1770) is apparently the sketch for a fresco by this artist whose works embellished the walls of numerous churches in 18C Hungary. There is a beautiful painting by **Joseph Winterhalter**, *Allegory of Faith, Hope and Charity* (1780).

From the **Spanish school**, the portrait entitled *St Peter of Alcantara in Meditation*, attributed to **Ribera**, should not be missed.

Between Room IV and the great tapestry exhibition hall, do not miss the small room that houses one of the marvels of the museum and the **Dutch school**: An *Ecce Homo*, painted between 1470 and 1480 by **Hans Memling**. Christ shows His wounds and seems to be glowing serenely as He compassionately contemplates the world. Some doubt exists as to whether the painting should be attributed to Memling but it is the actual work which is meaningful and, despite its small size, this painting stands out, inviting visitors to contemplate it unreservedly.

The **tapestry room** exhibits Flemish and French works.

★ **Duna Múzeum (Danube Museum)** ⓥ – *Kölcsey utca 2.* The Hungarians, faced with the capricious behaviour of the Danube and the Tisza, had to solve many difficult problems. They were also able to take advantage of the two rivers by making an ally of the power of the water and its supply. This country's engineers are among the best hydrologists in the world. The Danube Museum explains, without pretension, the presence of water in nature and exhibits a great many inventions devised throughout the centuries to make intelligent use of it. Use of hydraulic power, irrigation and transport is demonstrated in the little museum by a number of excellent, highly educational models that explain how man has used water throughout the ages. This museum will interest adults, but will be particularly exciting for children. Even without understanding Hungarian, visitors can follow the essential story by just looking and by pressing on a button: the model comes to life, the water runs, and the boat-watermills on the Danube turn their wheels. Allow 1hr for the visit.

Széchenyi tér – This large square is bordered with interesting buildings. Several have already been restored, and various periods can be recognised. The largest one at the far end of the square is the **town hall**, a 17C Baroque private residence that was occupied at the end of the century by Vak Bottyán (One-Eyed Bottyán), one of Ferenc II Rákóczi's generals during the War of Independence. On the balcony, as a reminder of the right to justice in the town, is the hook where the executioner's sword hung. All the buildings are to be restored. The **Rococo style** can be recognised in the buildings at n°s 7 (1768) and 24 (1780); the early **Baroque style** (late 18C) at n° 15; the **Classical style** (1802) at n° 19; the **Romantic style** at n°s 3 (1862) and 21 (1860). There is a monument to the Holy Trinity in the middle of the square.

FERTŐD

Győr-Moson-Sopron province – Population 2 800

Michelin map 925 D 2 – 24.5km/15.3mi to the east of Sopron

In Hungary, the castle built at Süttör for Prince Miklós Esterházy is referred to as the Little Versailles or the Hungarian Versailles. **Fertőd** is the name of the new municipality, formed in 1945 by the joining of Süttör to Eszterháza, the estates bought by Prince Pál Esterházy in 1681. At that time, the Esterházy family's property in the region stretched for almost 150 000ha/370 000acres.

A man of culture, writer, poet and musician (one of his musical compositions, the *Harmonia Cœlestis*, is still played today), but with heavy debts, Prince Pál was obliged to rent out his estates to the Bishop of Esztergom. Nevertheless, in 1720, Prince Joseph Esterházy recovered the estate and started to build a residence, assisted by an architect of Italian origin, Anton Martinelli. It was Pál's grandson, Miklós the Magnificent or the Lavish, who really made headway with the present-day castle from 1762, with the help of the architect Melchior Hefele. He wanted to build a palace to prove that he was a match for the Habsburgs.

The musician prince - A man of taste and culture, Prince Miklós wanted to have an orchestra permanently to hand, to play at the castle's celebrations and festivities. He had an opera house and a chapel built and music had to be constantly present. He took a Kapellmeister into his service, under contract, in the person of Joseph Haydn, as well as musicians to form an orchestra.

A very severe, draconian contract obliged Haydn to take on full responsibility, not only for the music but also for the equipment and practical aspects. When he entered the Prince's presence, Haydn had to wear a blue costume with gold braid. He had to oversee the conduct of the musicians and male and female singers, who also wore a uniform, since any unseemly behaviour on their part was out of the question. In deference to the Prince's wishes, he was obliged to compose to order, and exclusively for him. As a devoted servant, he was responsible for scores, instruments and rehearsals. Nevertheless, Haydn was able to work in security, and, in spite of everything, with a certain independence, shrewdly protecting his freedom.

"Servant? Yes, but free": Joseph Haydn – Haydn (1732-1809) himself described his situation at Eszterháza and the benefits of this apparent dependence on the Prince better than anyone. He wrote, "...my Prince was satisfied with all my work, and I received his approval. Put in charge of an orchestra, I could alter, make additions or omissions, and be as bold as I pleased. I was cut off from the world, there was no one to confuse or torment me, and I was bound to become an original."

The 30 years spent in the service of the Esterházys in no way hampered Haydn's enthusiasm or creativity. A few months after the Prince's death, he left for London, then returned to Vienna, let his imagination run riot and wrote the London symphonies, quartets, masses and oratorios... His spirit was so prolific that Mozart said of him, "he can do everything, jest and upset, cause laughter and deep emotion."

Papa Haydn, an instigator of strikes? – Haydn knew how to look after his musicians and protect them, to the extent that they affectionately called him Papa. He demonstrated the interest he showed in them and often defended them in front of the Prince. In the winter of 1772, the Prince refused to allow them to visit their families in Vienna for a few days. At that time, Haydn was composing the *Symphony in F sharp minor*.

R. Matès

Fertőd – Former Esterházy Castle

He gave it an original fifth movement, written so that the musicians could blow out their candles one after the other and leave the orchestra. The Prince accepted the lesson and granted them leave; the symphony has since had the additional title of *Farewell Symphony*.

★★ESTERHÁZY-KASTÉLY (FORMER ESTERHÁZY CASTLE)

This Rococo Baroque building with 126 rooms is symmetrical on both the courtyard and garden sides. Three monumental wrought-iron gates open onto the main courtyard. Two ochre-coloured buildings form a semicircle.
Opposite the entrance gateway, the main body of the castle can be reached via two staircases that meet to form a large balcony, on the *piano nobile*. The courtyard is in a perfect line, facing north-south, with the castle's south façade giving onto the park and gardens.
After the Second World War, major restoration work was undertaken to renovate the castle's rooms from which most of the furniture had disappeared. The original stoves and a few pieces of furniture can still be admired.

The Prince's chinoiserie – The fashions of the day left their mark on Esterházy Castle and pseudo-Chinese decoration can still be seen on the ground floor. The **Sala Terrena** was the summer dining hall, cooled by the brilliant white Carrara marble floor, with flowered frescoes on the ceiling signed with Miklós' initials.

Contested luxury – On the first floor, the **ceremonial hall** and the **concert hall**, often used today, demonstrate the luxurious lifestyle of the time, particularly if you imagine the dazzling festivities that Prince Miklós knew how to organise. These events were a combination of music, dancing, games, hunting, ballet and copious meals. They continued into the night, lit by thousands of lanterns held by peasants and the sparkle of fireworks. Miklós welcomed illustrious guests who included Empress Maria Theresa and the German writer, Goethe. These invitations emphasised the privileges and the wealth of the host but also gave rise to jealousy and censure, to the extent that, in 1766, the women from the estate surrounded the castle to protest and demand the abolition of tithing.

ADDITIONAL SIGHT

Muzsika-ház – *Madách sétany 1*. This house was the residence of Haydn and the musicians. To visit the house, take the pathway leading in front of the south façade of the castle. The three-roomed apartment occupied by Haydn for 30 years has been turned into a small museum.

GÖDÖLLŐI KIRÁLY-KASTÉLY★★

GÖDÖLLŐ royal castle – Pest province

Michelin map 925 D 8 – 28km/17mi north-east of Budapest

Access: leaving from Budapest, take the M 3 motorway north-east. The motorway runs close to Mogyoród and **Hungaroring** where the annual Formula 1 automobile Grand Prix takes place.
For those who do not have a vehicle: M 2 underground line (red) to Örs vezér tere terminus, then the HÉV suburban train to Gödöllő.
While the town of **Gödöllő** (pronounced Geuh-deuh-leuh) itself is of no particular interest to visitors, it attracts tourists and Hungarians from Budapest because of its royal castle, a major historical site linked to the memory of Emperor Franz Josef and Empress Elizabeth, better known as Sissy. The greater part of the castle has been restored, and the overall restoration plan spread over several years even includes the construction of a hotel in the park, near the dressage arena. While the royal castle is open to visitors as a historic site, some of its rooms are also used for receptions, banquets, concerts etc.

A SHORT HISTORY

The Grassalkovichs – It was the great Hungarian lord, Count **Antal Grassalkovich I** (1694-1771), who had this castle built. He entrusted the plans to architect András Mayerhoffer. The first stage of construction from 1741 to 1749 saw the completion of the chapel, the two corner towers that finished the façade, a riding arena and five wings. The front part took on its current form in the following period, from 1752 to 1759. In 1751, **Maria Theresa**, Empress of Austria and Queen of Hungary, visited Antal Grassalkovich I and stayed at the castle. Work on the completion of the last two wings and several rooms in the living quarters was started in 1760. The count's son, Antal Grassalkovich II, made several modifications from 1782 to 1785. He replaced the corner towers with the two projecting mansard-roofed pavilions that can be seen today.

He also had a theatre built. Antal Grassalkovich III then undertook other transformations. His death in 1841 marked the end of the male branch of this family. The female line inherited the property, which was bought in 1850 by Baron György Sina, and then, in 1864, by a Belgian bank.

The grand era of Franz Josef and Sissy – The Hungarian State became owner of the castle in 1867. Renovated in six months under the direction of architect Miklós Ybl, the castle was given to the Emperor of Austria, Franz Josef, and Empress Elizabeth, for their coronation as sovereigns of Hungary. The royal family liked to come to Gödöllő to rest in the spring and autumn, far from the protocol and formality of the Vienna court. Elizabeth particularly loved this place; she was an excellent horsewoman and could go riding in the surrounding woods. With fox-hunting, greyhound and horse racing, parties, receptions and concerts, these were undoubtedly happy years at Gödöllő. The local people soon came to adore Sissy. "During her stays at Gödöllő, the court that formed around the Empress was very different from the one at Vienna. Here, Elizabeth did not have to submit to the much-detested constraints of protocol. Moreover, as Franz Josef was present only for brief stays, she was the star around which everything radiated." (Jean-Paul Bled, *Rudolph and Mayerling*, Fayard). After Sissy's assassination in Geneva in 1898, Franz Josef spent less and less time at the castle. The last visit was in 1911. His successor, Charles I of Austria, King of Hungary under the name of Charles IV, who reigned from 1916 to 1918, only stayed here once.

Sissy

J.-L. Charmet/MAGYAR KÉPEK Kft

Decadence, renewal and decline – In 1919 the castle became the seat of the high military command of the Council Republic before being occupied by Romanian troops. In 1920, when Regent Miklós Horthy came into power, the property again became the summer residence of the head of State and relived glorious years of splendour during which receptions, parties and hunts were offered to high-ranking guests. During the Second World War the German troops sacked the castle. The Soviet troops burned all the furnishings and transformed it into a military hospital and camp. The Russians left it for good in 1990.

TOUR ⓥ

Exterior – Gödöllő royal castle, with a surface area of 1 700m²/2 033sq yd and a park of 28ha/67 acres, is Hungary's largest Baroque castle. Beyond the stone bridge, the main façade has a projecting part, crowned with a dome; it has a beautiful wrought-iron balcony resting on four twin red-marble Ionic columns. The Grassalkovich arms are in the centre of the balustrade. One of the unusual features of the castle is the fact that its seven wings overlap at right angles behind the building, one after the other. This becomes evident if you cross the entrance hall and go into the inner courtyard, framed by two U-shaped wings.

Interior – The double **main staircase** has stone balustrades.

Small Dining Room – A Rococo stove in faience decorates one of the corners. There is a painting on the wall of Empress Maria Theresa with her family.

Pantry – In a showcase, you can admire a beautiful Herend porcelain dinner service, used by the royal family.

Aide-de-camp's Bedroom – Telegraph apparatus at the disposal of the royal family is exhibited in this room, together with a few authentic telegrams.

Small Coronation Room – Monumental painting by Edward von Engerth, depicting the coronation of Franz Josef. Near the stove is a portrait of Ferenc Deák, one of the creators of the 1867 Compromise that brought about the Austro-Hungarian monarchy.

Franz Josef's Study – Objects belonging to the Emperor, including a clock and candlestick, are arranged on the neo-Baroque desk from the royal castle at Buda. There is a portrait of Archduke Rudolph, who committed suicide at Mayerling (Austria).

Franz Josef Salon – Austro-Hungarian history is recalled by the engravings and paintings. There are primarily pictures of the royal couple at public events, such as their welcome at the Pest Concert Hall.

Great Hall – This formal room has stucco walls with gilded highlights. Five golden chandeliers hang from its ceiling.

Queen Elizabeth's Salon – Portraits of Elizabeth and several influential politicians, including Count Andrássy.

Queen Elizabeth's Study – Sissy learned Hungarian here, as did her children. Portraits of their tutors.

Queen Elizabeth's Dressing Room – Hung in violet, the Queen's favourite colour. Several stages of Elizabeth's life are evoked here with portraits, books by authors she loved and objects such as a wooden casket that belonged to her.

Queen Elizabeth's Bedchamber (Maria Theresa's former bedchamber) – This bedchamber was especially redecorated for Maria Theresa's visit in 1751. Unfortunately, it is totally unfurnished today.

T. Hortobagyi/MAGYAR KÉPEK Kft

Gödöllő - Royal Castle

ADDITIONAL SIGHT

Mezőgazdasági Gépmúzeum (Agricultural Machine Museum) ⓥ – *Páter Károly utca 1.* This museum in the university complex is worth a visit for those interested in agricultural development (despite the explanatory signs being only in Hungarian). The collection of tractors, agricultural equipment and machine tools is particularly impressive.

GORSIUM/TÁC★★

Fejér province

Michelin map 925 E 6 – 15km/9mi south of Székesfehérvár

About 2km/1.2mi from Tác, the remains of the Roman town of Gorsium appear amid an enchanting, green setting. The trees and the birdsong give an almost Mediterranean feel to the site.

THE ROMAN CAMP ⓥ

In the middle of the 1C AD a Roman camp was established here to oversee the road and the ford across the River Sárvíz. The camp soon became a colony of over 7 000 inhabitants, which Emperor Hadrian raised to the status of town. This community became both the seat of the Lower Pannonia Provincial Assembly and of the cult of the emperor.

In AD 260, barbarians destroyed the town. It was rebuilt 30 years later and named Herculiana.

The town's layout, brought to light by archaeological digs begun in 1958, is perfectly visible today. Visitors can see the main central civic buildings, walk along the paved main street bordered with shops, and see the vestiges of two basilicas and the town governor's palace.

Gorsium – Roman camp

Slightly to one side is the 1 200-seat **theatre** and the remains of a cemetery from the same period.
The town was abandoned after the Romans left. Stones from various buildings were then reused to construct a great many houses in the surrounding area, particularly in Székesfehérvár.
The park is well laid out, and the atmosphere is so calm and serene that the short tour can be looked on as a relaxing walk.
The **Festival of Flowers** takes place in the spring; in summer, plays by long-dead authors are performed.

GYÖNGYÖS

Heves province – Population 35 000

Michelin map 925 C 9 – Local map see BÜKK

While the name means pearl, the town has unfortunately lost some of its lustre. It has maintained an artisanal and industrial activity, and above all has remained a trade centre. In the heart of the wine-growing region, Gyöngyös has confirmed its role as a commercial centre by adding tourism to its activities.

Fő tér – Two statues embellish the square. The statue of **Róbert Károly** (Charles Robert of Anjou) (1288-1342) who gave the status of town to Gyöngyös, was erected in 1984 for the 650th anniversary of the royal decree. The other statue, called **Huszárd** was erected in memory of the sixth Hussard regiment.
North of Fő tér on the right is **Szent Bertalan Church** (St Bartholomew's). It is thought to be the largest Gothic church in Hungary, despite the Baroque decoration added in the 18C.
Just behind the church, **Zeneiskola** is an interesting Baroque building. Formerly a school run by the Jesuits, it is now a conservatoire.
Take the pedestrian street from the church and continue to the Szent Bertalan/Szalléz u. crossroads. You will come to **Szent Korona Ház** where the Szent Bertalan church treasure is kept. A hewn stone porch supporting a balcony marks the entrance to this little museum. Among the objects exhibited are 43 gold coins and 18 coins dating from the Middle Ages.

A place to stay, a place to eat

Mátra – *Mátyás Király u. 2. ☎/Fax 37/313 063. 40 rooms between €28 and €45.* The best-known hotel, warm welcome.

Gyöngyös Borozó – *Bugat Pál tér 2. ☎ 37/300 019.* Unusual restaurant-wine bar, where you sit on chairs made of poplar and eat off tree trunks. Worth seeing!

Mátra Múzeum ⌚ – *Kossuth Lajos utca 40.* The former **Orczy Castle** (Orczy-kastély), in a park, is the setting for the Mátra Museum, which is a good introduction to a visit to the mountain range.

Seven rooms on the **ground floor** present Roman remains and Gothic objects, wine-growing, economic life, the guilds, daily life and household objects (furniture, tools). Room 5 is a reminder of the terrible fire of 1917 that destroyed the town (8 000 of its 20 000 inhabitants were left homeless).

Eleven rooms **upstairs** are devoted to the Mátra massif: mineralogical wealth, the nature of the soil, flora and fauna, hunting etc. In Room 5, the Bruno Room, there is the skeleton of a young mammoth found in 1947.

Exotic animals and fish are on show in the aquariums in the **basement**.

EXCURSIONS

★★ **Mátra** – *See this name.*

★★ **Hollókő** – *See this name.*

GYŐR★

Győr-Moson-Sopron province – Population 130 000

Michelin map 925 C 4

Győr, the town of three rivers, is located at the confluence of a branch of the River Danube, the Mosonyi-Duna, the River Rába and the River Rábca. Full of life, these waters bathe the lower parts of the old town, the true centre of interest in Győr, adding to its charm.

Like many other Hungarian towns, Győr does not flaunt its riches. It is said that, after Pest and Sopron, it is the Hungarian town with the highest number of old buildings. After the unexpectedly ugly outskirts, it is refreshing to see the town centre. Visitors coming from Vienna or Budapest generally arrive in Győr on Szent István út, where, if you are coming from the direction of Vienna, you turn left along Czuczor Gergely utca, beyond the town hall.

THE OLD TOWN

Széchenyi tér – In the centre of this large square stands the Holy Virgin's column, dating from 1686, and raised to give thanks for the liberation of Buda and the departure of the Turks.

Patikamúzeum ⌚ **(Pharmacy Museum)** – On the square at n° 9, on the corner of Czuczor Gergely utca, is a chemist's shop which used to belong to the Jesuits. You can go inside and admire the built-in furniture and vaulted ceilings, decorated in the Rococo style, dating from the end of the 17C.

Szent Ignatius templom – The **church of St Ignatius** was built by the Jesuits between 1635 and 1641. It was later given to the Benedictines. The Italian architect, Baccio del Blanco, took his inspiration for the plans of the building directly from the Church and Convent of Jesus in Rome. The decoration inside the church is impressive.

Apátúr-ház (Abbot's House) – Opposite the church, on the other side of the square at n° 5 is the house of the members of the abbey of Pannonhalma, now the **Xantus János Múzeum** ⌚, with an exhibition relating the history of the town and, for philatelists, a collection of all the postage stamps printed in Hungary.

Vastuskós-ház ⌚ – At n° 4 on the square, the **house with an iron stump** derives its name from a tree stump with nails hammered into it, visible in a corner. There used to be an old custom whereby any craftsman visiting the town would hammer a nail into the stump. The **Imre Patkó collection★** in this house is really worth a visit. There is a collection of works by 20C Hungarian artists, and visitors can also peacefully admire works by Chagall, Rouault, Braque, Picasso and numerous objects that the journalist Imre Patkó brought back from his travels.

Magyar Ispita – *Rákóczi Ferenc 6.* The **Hungarian hospice** and its chapel can be seen from the small porch looking onto the street. The former hospice now houses the Town Museum.

Városi Művészeti Múzeum (Town Museum) ⌚ – *Entrance Nefelecs utca 2.* The interior spaces are opulent, in particular the patio supported by the sturdy Tuscan pillars. This museum houses the collection of fine Baroque and Renaissance furniture put together by Péter Váczy.

Napóleon-ház (Napoleon's house) – If you go back along Széchenyi tér and then take Király u., you will go past n° 4 where, on 31 August 1809, Napoleon Bonaparte spent the night after the battle of Raab (mentioned on the Arc du Carrousel near the Louvre in Paris. Raab is the German name for Győr). The first floor is home to the art gallery of the Xantus János Múzeum.

★★ **Káptalan-domb (Chapter Hill)** – This is a street which runs from Dunakapu tér to Bécsi-kapu tér. It goes over the confluence of the River Rába and the Mosonyi-Duna branch of the Danube.

GYŐR

Street	Grid	No.
Apáca u.	ABY	2
Apor Vilmos püspök tere	AY	4
Arany János u.	AZ	6
Gárdonyi Géza u.	BZ	7
Gutenberg tér	AY	8
Hédervári u.	AY	10
Káptalandomb	AY	12
Kazinczy u.	AYZ	13
Király u.	AY	14
Kossuth Lajos u.	AZ	16
Lépcső köz	AY	17
Nefelejcs köz	BY	18
Pálffy Miklós u.	BY	20
Rónay Jácint u.	AY	22
Sarkantyú (Sark) köz	AY	23
Schweidel u.	BYZ	24
Széchenyi tér	BY	

Sight	Grid
Apátúr ház	BY
Római Katolikus Hittudományi Főiskola	AY
Karmelita templom	AZ
Magyar Ispita	BY
Napóleon ház	AY
Patika Múzeum	BY
Római Katolikus Hittudományi Főiskola	AY
Székesegyház	AY
Szent Ignátius templom	BY
Városi Müvészeti Múzeum	BY
Vastuskós ház	BY

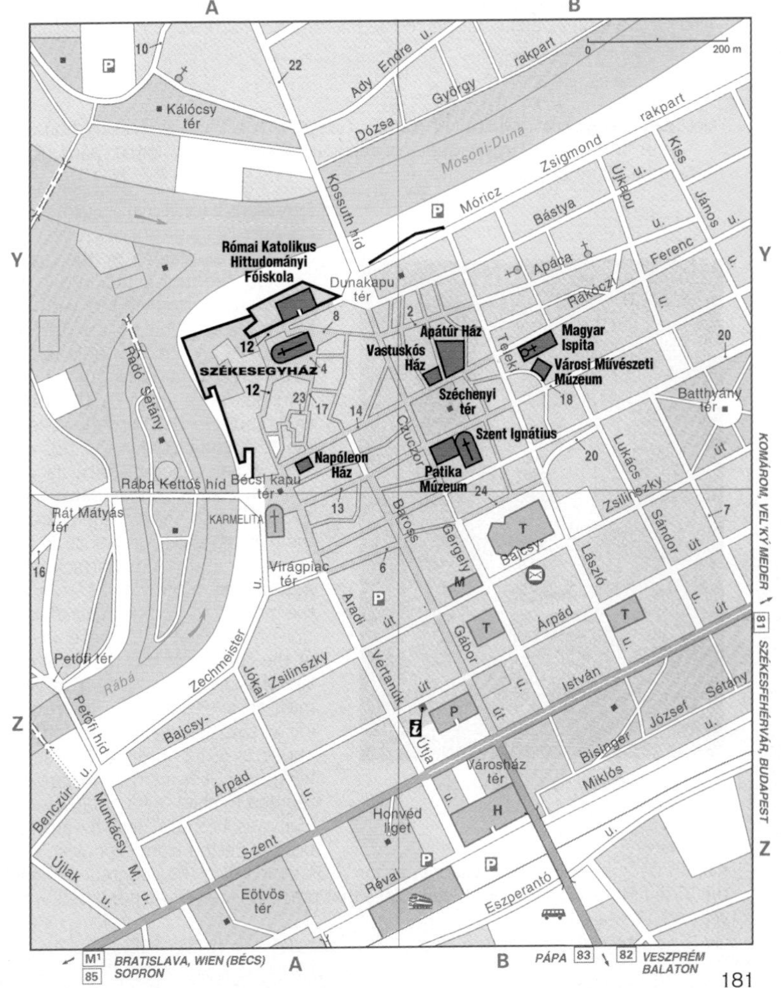

A place to stay

Pető Panzió – *Kossuth L. u. 20. ☎ 96/313 412. Rooms at around €29.* Away from the town centre; *panzió* with clean and well-kept rooms.

Gróf Cziráky Panzió – *Bécsi-kapu tér 8. ☎ 96/310 688. 11 rooms at around €32.* In Győr's historic district, *panzió* in a picturesque house.

Klastrom – *Zechmeister u. 1. ☎ 96/315 611, Fax 96/327 030. 42 rooms at around €61.* Magnificent 18C Carmelite cloisters serve as the setting for this hotel. The rooms are rather simple, however. In summer there is a restaurant in the garden.

Schweizerhof – *Sarkantyú köz 11-13. ☎ 96/329 171, Fax 06/96/326 544. Rooms at around €85.* An extravagance! High-class hotel in a house dating from 1765. Fitness room, sauna, pool, solarium.

A place to eat

Schweizerhof – *Sarkantyú köz 11-13.* Hotel-restaurant. Quality international cuisine.

Vaskakas – *Bécsi-kapu tér.* Inside the old castle walls, a tourist restaurant of an impressive size. Hungarian cooking.

Várkapu Vendéglő – *Bécsi-kapu tér 7.* In the town centre, restaurant with outside tables in the small pedestrian square. Simple and somewhat worn decor (animal photos and lithographs). Hungarian specialities.

Sárkánylyuk – *Arany János u. 29.* Typically Hungarian restaurant, very high quality.

Matróz Csárda – *Dunakapu tér 3.* In two cellars; very popular little bar-restaurant with a seaside decor. Worth a look even if you do not eat here.

Kishalász Vendéglő – *Apáca u. 4.* Fish restaurant with simple decor. In summer, there are tables outside in the pedestrian street.

Római Katolikus Hittudományi Főiskola (Catholic College) – The Diocese treasury-house is located on this site. A large number of religious objects are exhibited, particularly illuminated manuscripts.

F. Szelényi/MAGYAR KÉPEK Kft

Reliquary bust of St Ladislas

★ **Székesegyház (Cathedral)** – Further up, on Apor Vilmos püspök tere, the district is dominated by the cathedral. Started in the 11C in the Romanesque period, it has suffered the ravages of time. It was partially destroyed by the Mongols in the 15C. Restored in Gothic style, it was damaged once again by the Turks and rebuilt in the Baroque style in the 17C; completed in the 18C and 19C, it has a neo-Classical façade and the main doorway dates from 1938. Despite this strange mixture, the building is still grandiose. There are frescoes by Maulbertsch, *The Assumption of the Virgin Mary*, over the main altar, and the *Transfiguration* on the vault of the nave. In one of the chapels of the cathedral is a **bust of László I★★** (Ladislas I) as Hermes, an extremely fine, impressive early-15C reliquary. In addition, above another altar in the north wing is an icon of the Virgin Mary reputed to shed tears of blood. The icon was brought here by an Irish bishop, fleeing from Cromwell, who died in Győr in 1663. Four years later, on St Patrick's day, the congregation saw the Virgin Mary shed tears of blood. Since that time, her memory is honoured every year on 17 March.

On Bécsi kapu tér, the church of the Carmelites dates from the 18C.

GYULA♆♆

Békés province – Population 35 000

Michelin map 925 G 13

Gyula (meaning chief warlord and judge) is the name of respect given to the military chiefs of the Magyar tribes. It has been suggested that the town was given this name to honour the grandson of one of the chiefs of the seven tribes of Árpád. Three towns in this part of the province, Békés, Békéscsaba and Gyula, each stand at the tip of a triangle with sides of around 15km/9mi. For several centuries, Gyula was the province's principal administrative centre until the function was transferred to Békéscsaba in 1950. Gyula was obliged to relinquish this honour to Békéscsaba because of its location, close to the Romanian border, and also due to the fact that, in 1860, it refused to allow the railway line to pass through its territory.
Of the three towns, Gyula has maintained a reputation on a national and international scale, due to its history, castle and baths.

The town – This is set in the midst of marshland, and is crisscrossed by canals. The famous 17C Turkish traveller, Evliya Chelebi, who left numerous accounts and descriptions of Hungary on his journeys through the country, compared Gyula with Venice. Established in the Middle Ages, Gyula Castle and its moat were built in the 14C. In 1566 the castle was taken by the Turks, who remained there until 1694. Despite successive restoration and renovation, it has retained the appearance of a massive fortress with thick brick walls.

A water town – The marshes were drained in the 19C and the water-flow controlled. However, Gyula is still a water town, thanks to its thermal springs that supply 11 indoor and nine outdoor swimming pools. Water temperatures range between 22 and 39°C/71 and 102°F. The baths are very popular and are internationally renowned. Several good hotels provide accommodation for people taking spa treatment and tourists, many of them foreign. **Várfürdő** (the castle baths) forms a vast complex, comprising spa establishments and hotels, and surrounds the castle situated in the north. On the south side, a small river runs along the side of this park. **Élűvíz-csatorna** (the spring-water canal). Along this wide stream, spanned by a few bridges, there are also a few *panziók* (guest-houses) and the possibility of accommodation in private houses.

SIGHTS

★★ **Százéves cukrászda (Century-old tea shop)** – A visit to this shop has two rewards, as it is both a pastry shop and a museum piece. Located on the corner of *Jókai Mór utca* and *Béke sugárút*, it is outstandingly special: the shop has kept its decor, composed of 18C wall decorations and Rococo furniture, interspersed with elements from the 19C. Visitors can take a seat beneath pleasant arches, decorated with garlands and painted scenes. In addition to the decor, there is a small exhibition of equipment and objects used by pastry chefs. This feast for the eyes is followed by a feast for the palate; try a succulent cake (or even several) to a backdrop of Edith Piaf songs.

★ **Vár (Castle)** ⓥ – Your visit takes you right to the tower platform where you can appreciate the surroundings and, in particular, the sheer size of the baths complex. Still in the process of restoration, the building's parallelepiped shape, dominating the tower with the same shape, is simply astonishing. Only the central part of a much larger edifice, which used to have several walled enclosures, now remains of the castle.
In the summer, the castle is used as the background for numerous performances of plays, music or dance.

Erkel Emlékház ⓥ – *Apor Vilmos tér 7.* **Ferenc Erkel**, the composer of the national anthem, was born in Gyula. His **birthplace** has been turned into a museum where a few hand-written scores are exhibited. Ferenc Erkel was the author of the famous opera *Bánk Bán*. It is said that inspiration for the opera came to him as he was resting under a tree in the castle park. In the museum, photos of his life as a musician and of his friends and family, illustrate Hungarian society in the middle of the last century. Ferenc Erkel was also one of Béla Bartók's teachers.

Dürer Terem ⓥ – *Kossuth Lajos utca 17.* The **Dürer room** is used for temporary exhibitions. Albrecht Dürer's father was a local artist. His first name was Anton and his last name was spelt Thürer. He emigrated to Nuremberg in 1465.

★ **Kohán György képtár** ⓥ – *Béke sugárút 35.* This small building set in the midst of a park of tall trees, houses paintings donated to the town by the painter György Kohán (1910-66). Some 600 paintings, inspired by the Impressionists, and 2 000 drawings illustrate Hungarian provincial art.

★ **Ladics-ház** ⓥ – *Jókai Mór utca 4.* This house used to belong to the Ladics family, a well-to-do bourgeois Gyula family. Guided tours are in Hungarian (you may be given a text in English) but, even without understanding the commentary, this well-furnished house will give you an idea of the everyday living space of a bourgeois family.

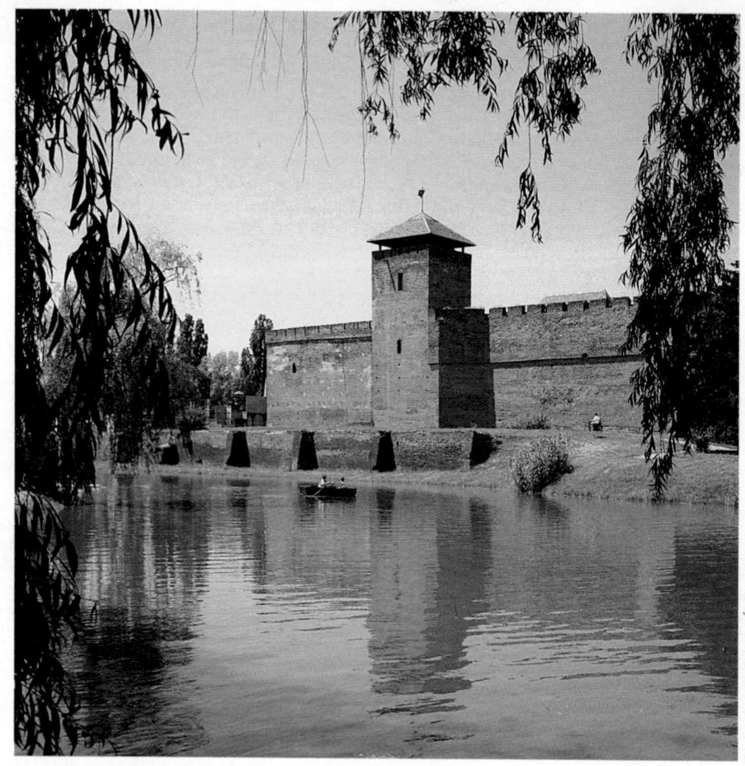
T. Hortobagyi/MAGYAR KÉPEK Kft

Gyula Castle

EXCURSION

Békéscsaba – *15km/9mi to the west along road n° 44.* The administrative centre of Békés province is a quiet town and justifies the first part of its name, *békés* (peaceful), despite the fact that people still remember that the region used to be called the site of conflict, due to its tormented history. In the 18C, János György Harruckern, a Habsburg envoy encouraged German and Slovak immigration in order to repopulate the region. They settled in separate districts of Békéscsaba and Gyula and lived on good terms with one another. The Slovak language is still in use. Békéscsaba is also the birthplace of the great 19C painter, **Mihály Munkácsy**.

★ **Munkácsy Mihály Múzeum** ⓥ – *Széchényi utca 9.* In addition to works by the artist, the museum has an exhibition describing the region's various ethnic groups. You will discover the richness of Slovak, Romanian, German and Hungarian handicrafts.

★ **Munkácsy Emlékház** – *Gyulai út 5.* In a villa belonging to Munkácsy's uncle, where the painter spent part of his childhood, is an exhibition of around 20 paintings by the artist, together with a few pictures by his contemporaries.

★★ **Szlovák Tájház** ⓥ (Slovak house) – *Garai utca 21.* A fine example of a traditional Slovak house. A tour of the three rooms will probably give you a few ideas for painted furniture decoration...

★★ **Meseház** ⓥ (House of Fairytales) – *Békési út 17.* In a world of puppets, total enchantment for children and adults alike.

HÉVÍZ ✝✝✝

Zala province – Population 6 000

Michelin map 925 F 3 – Local map see BALATON

The literal translation of *Hé-víz* is hot water which, by extension, comes to mean thermal water. It is difficult to calculate the population of this small town; its only centre of interest is the warm-water lake with recognised therapeutic properties which attract an impressive number of people. This should be seen and above all put to the test, irrespective of the season.

A short history – Hévíz waters were first used in the Middle Ages to tan skins; their curative powers were quickly recognised, however.
About 200 years ago Count Festetics of Keszthely, the owner of Keszthely and Hévíz, made the town into a spa; it gradually grew in popularity, especially after a few miracles helped its reputation.
The daughter of a lord of Tátika was very beautiful, but her legs were paralysed. After bathing several times in the lake, she recovered the use of her legs and resplendent health, and married Sándor Rezy, Lord of Csobánc. They lived happily ever after and undoubtedly had many children. A Finnish writer compared Hévíz to "a small piece of the Mediterranean in the middle of Transdanubia".

THE LAKE

The lake covers a surface area of 5ha/12 acres. It is fed by a spring that produces about 80 000m³/282 685cu ft of water every day, and is 38m/125ft deep, with a variant temperature of 38-42°C/100.4-107.6°F. Given the lake's capacity, the water is completely renewed every 28hr. The surface temperature varies from 23-24°C/73.4-75.2°F in winter and 33-35°C/91.4-95°F in summer. In winter there is a light cloud of steam over the lake that can be seen for several miles and the local residents say that the lake is smoking its pipe.
Waterlilies grow and bloom in these waters all year. In winter and spring you can bathe in the company of the wild ducks that stop off at Hévíz.
The small houses built around the lake contribute to the other-worldly atmosphere of the lake. When the crowds go, they create an impression of a little fairy-tale palace. One wonders where the princess is, what the water elves are up to, and whether a fairy will rise out of the steamy vapours. Relax, and dream... But for all that, you are strongly recommended not to forget your inflatable rubber ring. You will notice that a number of strollers, who have long grown out of children's games, are carrying all kinds of inflated objects. To take advantage of the tepid water and be completely relaxed, without having to move or use any energy to keep your head out of the water, this little air-cushion is essential. You can borrow one from your children or grandchildren, rent one at the entrance to the park when obtaining your ticket, or even buy one from the innumerable shops. Frequent visitors to the lake have perfected various accessories, from floating chessboards to floating lecterns to support a book or magazine above the water, and so enjoy reading in an unusual setting!
Hévíz developed between the two World Wars, but its expansion really took off in 1970 when the construction of a number of hotels started; the majority offer treatment based on thermal baths as well as dental and eye care.

R. Palotas

Hévíz – Thermal lake

A place to stay, a place to eat

Saint Hubertus – *Móricz Zsigmond utca.* ☎ *83/340 502. Rooms at around €28.* A *panzió* with clean and well-kept rooms, one with a balcony. Restaurant strikingly decorated with boar and deer heads.

Helios – *Vörösmarty u. 91.* ☎ *83/342 895, Fax 83/340 525. Rooms between €55 and €70.* High-class hotel consisting of three buildings: two modern ones and a castle. We recommend the castle but avoid rooms near the elevator. Pool.

Park Szálló – *Petőfi Sándor u. 26.* ☎ *83/341 190, Fax 83/341 193. 26 rooms between €59 and €79.* Town centre, a friendly little hotel with a view of the lake. High-quality restaurant.

Erzsébet – *Erzsébet királyné u.* ☎*/Fax 83/342 035. 47 rooms between €73 and €80.* Right in the town centre, near the thermal lake, a delightful hotel that can be recognised by its sky-blue façade.

Hűvösvölgyi Csárda – *Ady Endre u.* On the edge of the town in the direction of Alsópáhok, this large and attractive, typically Hungarian inn regularly puts on folk events.

Magyar Csárda – *Tavirózsa u. 1.* In a small street with a row of about half a dozen restaurants (so you have a choice), an inn with an established reputation. The cooking could be better however. Hungarian specialities.

Korona – *Széchenyi u. 43.* ☎*/Fax 83/340 839.* Good-quality restaurant. Chicken, turkey and beef specialities. The establishment also has a few rooms (€18 to €36).

Miraculous water? – All this is very fine, you may think, but what kind of treatment is offered at Hévíz, and where do people stay? Hévíz is more than a romantic and poetic venue, it is also a place where people come to take the waters as these have a dual effect, both physical and chemical.

Physical effect – As the water is hot, the body can plunge in without contracting and without a drop in temperature. This means that the muscles can relax. The hydrostatic pressure is excellent for the venous and lymphatic systems, and swellings and oedematous conditions diminish.

Chemical effect – The water has a balanced composition of negatively and positively charged ions and various soluble substances that are all recommended for rheumatism, bodily movement disorders etc.

The mud – The mud covers the bottom of the lake and is used for the thermal baths. Slightly radioactive, it contains various components whose organic elements have a light bactericidal effect. As a consequence, no pathogenic agent can live in the lake water.

HOLLÓKŐ★★

Nógrád province – Population 650

Michelin map 925 B 9 – 100km/62.5mi north-east of Budapest – Local map see BÜKK

In the heart of the Cserhát massif, the village is located on a hill in the midst of a landscape of vineyards. Classified as part of Unesco's world heritage, it should be emphasised that the village of Hollókő is not a *skanzen*, that is to say, a village that has been constructed or reconstructed to become an open-air museum. Although Hollókő suffered damage on several occasions, it is composed of houses built by the inhabitants, or rather their ancestors, which they have rebuilt, restored or restructured, keeping the original appearance.

A LITTLE-KNOWN ETHNIC GROUP: THE PALÓC

This region was inhabited by a minority of Slovak origin, the **Palóc** (pronounced palots). In the 1930s, the village was not very accessible; at that time, a Hungarian sociologist, Viola Tomori, made a study of the inhabitants of Hollókő who were obliged to draw their resources from nature. Her observation led to strange conclusions. For example, in the relationships between men and women, it was considered that marriage and love were two distinctly separate things. The conflicts between feelings and interests were among the most serious problems that a family had to face. Nearly all the songs would speak of love and contain a wealth of expressions associated with love. The way costumes were worn, interior decoration and ornamentation were all aimed at drawing attention: for example the number of embroidered petticoats beneath women's skirts was also an indication of their wealth. The variety and colours of women's headdresses were also part of their awareness of their appearance and a means of seduction.
A collective body was in charge of organising work and festivities. The family structure was extremely important and the hierarchy was asserted in the location of their houses. A family's first house would be located on the edge of the roadway; the descendants subsequently built their houses on the same plot, which stretched at right angles to the

roadway, forming a line. The oldest and most senior family in the hierarchy always occupied the house closest to the roadway. Village dignitaries were elected and paid by the villagers. The inhabitants have mostly abandoned these traditional customs and costumes, which are now hardly ever seen except for festivities and on 15 August.
Located well away from any development sector, the village has certainly been protected from transformation. This has enabled it to keep itself almost intact, resulting in the Unesco classification and its listing among the sites and treasures whose original appearance is to be preserved. A few hundred inhabitants live here in about 50 peasant-style houses, some of which have been turned into small museums or accommodation for visitors.

★★THE VILLAGE

Leave your car in the car park at the entrance to the village and go down Kossuth Lajos utca, the paved main street that leads to the church.

Church – This is a small white building with a wooden bell tower covered in shingles. If you are in the vicinity on a Sunday when a service is being held, you may well come across village woman in traditional costume, a blouse and skirt embroidered with multicoloured flowers, a pink waistcoat edged with green or green edged with pink. The headdresses are always very colourful, with different designs, comprised of a white embroidered bonnet, possibly with a scarf in the form of a crest or a fan-shaped crown on the top. It is more rare to meet a man wearing a black embroidered suit, a white shirt also embroidered and a black hat, decorated with an embroidered ribbon.

Take Petőfi Sándor utca to the right of the church, which lower down joins Kossuth Lajos utca. Go up this street.

As you walk through the streets – As mentioned above, all the houses are built at right angles to the street. A succession of three fires destroyed part of the village in 1874, 1886 and 1896, but each time the inhabitants rebuilt the houses identically, using the same techniques. The thick walls are built on a stone base. The structural framework is made of wood, including the gables which are decorated and have a sort of small protruding canopy. The passageway leading from one room to another along the side of the house is protected by a roof overhang. The gardens are separated by interwoven wooden fencing which is also used at the front of the house. The appearance of the village is certainly not the same as in times past; the roofs were originally thatched and now there are no animals roaming along the pathways. Geraniums and baskets of flowers decorate façades and gardens. However, the interiors that you can visit are decorated as in days gone by. The furniture is decorated with hand-painted garlands; numerous accessories such as embroidered cushions, tablecloths and duvet covers, create a warm, cheerful atmosphere.

★Postamúzeum ⏱ **(Post Office Museum)** – *Kossuth Lajos utca 80.* Despite being small, this museum is worth a visit to learn about how the distribution of mail has developed, and about communication techniques.
The **first room** shows objects and equipment, such as the LB III/30 telephone exchange, which enabled eight conversations to carry on simultaneously, on the same line.
The **second room** is given over to the major moments and various periods in the history of the post office and communications in Hungary. Displays feature mail delivery on foot or by horse in the Middle Ages, country delivery boys during the Turkish occupation, post carts under King Matthias, post inns in the 18C etc.

A place to stay, a place to eat

If you like sleeping under an eiderdown in an old house with rather short beds, embroidered cushions and fabrics, reserve well in advance at: *Nógrád Tourist, Salgótarján, Erzsébet tér 3,* ☎ *32/310 660.*

Panorama Campsite and Panzió – *Orgona u. 31.* ☎*/Fax: 32/379 048. 22 rooms at around €20.* Overlooking the little village and offering a beautiful view of the valley; this little complex is well located. Bungalow rental. Open all year.

Muskatli vendéglő – *Kossuth Lajos utca 61.* ☎ *et fax 32/379 262.* In this beautiful, typical house with its simple, traditional decor, the meals are cheap and very acceptable. Very lively on winter evenings. Small terrace with wooden benches and tables.

★VÁR (CASTLE)

Access to the castle is either from the car park on arrival in the village, or from the lower part of the village via a small path – signposted Vár – leading off Kossuth Lajos utca.
Built in the 13C and destroyed in the early 18C, the partially restored castle is one of the best preserved in Hungary. It is particularly interesting for its **viewpoint** over the neighbouring slopes and sheltered vines.
The ruins are surrounded by verdant countryside. A peaceful spot where you can picnic.

HORTOBÁGY-PUSZTA★★★

HORTOBÁGY Puszta –Hajdú-Bihar province

Michelin map 925 D 12 – 40km/25mi to the west of Debrecen

Hortobágy-puszta is part of the **Hortobágy National Park** (Hortobágy Nemzeti Park), 80 000ha/192 000 acres (some people estimate it at 100 000ha/247 000 acres) forming a protected nature reserve. **Hortobágy** village (approximately 2 000 inhabitants) is located in the centre of this park. A visit to this region, or even better a longer stay, will leave visitors with fond memories, even if you are not fortunate enough to see the *délibáb* or mirage. Dark clouds seem to appear suddenly, hiding the sun and dimming the sky.

The wet Puszta – The Great Plain stretches as far as the eye can see, with no obstacles bar a few slight inclines with *tanyas* (homesteads) and their wells which seem to have been installed here to add to the decor. This impressive expanse can, to some extent, be compared with the sea or other extensive areas that seem never-ending and where the sky and the earth join at the horizon.
The environment here, a type of *puszta*, is more in keeping with the image most people have of Hungary. Several events have disturbed the region with the passage of time. In the Middle Ages, 52 villages disappeared off the map, destroyed by the Mongols and the Ottomans. Devoid of inhabitants, the plain was used as pasture and was the domain of the *pásztor* (shepherds), *csikós* (herdsmen on horseback), *gulyás* (cattlemen) and *kondás* (pig-keepers). Then, in the 19C, the flow of the Tisza was regulated, causing changes to the distribution of water; as the land dried up, it was transformed into a salty, sterile plain. Irrigation work has now allowed part of the land to be restored to the cultivation of crops and the raising of livestock.

★**Hídivásár** – Hortobágy Bridge, with its nine arches, that shepherds call *kilencyukú híd* (*kilenc* meaning nine and *lyuk* meaning hole), is the heart of Hortobágy. It is Hungary's best known and longest stone bridge (92m/280ft). Numerous photographs have

A place to stay

Pásztortanya – ☏ *52/369 127. Rooms at €20. 14km/8.4mi from Hortobágy, on road n° 33 heading for Tiszafüred.* Traditional *panzió*-restaurant with about a dozen decent rooms.

Hortobágy Hotel-Campsite – ☏ *52/369 071. Open April to November. Rooms at €24.* In a small modern building, a hotel with pleasant rooms.

Epona Rider Village – ☏ *52/ 369 020. Rooms between €85 and €95.* Immense Club Med-style resort. For horse lovers and sports enthusiasts.

A place to eat

Hortobágyi Csárda – *Petőfi tér 2.* ☏ *52/369 139.* Not to be missed in Hortobágy National Park, this is a traditional inn in a pretty thatched house. Musical entertainment all year round (except January).

Patkós Csárda – *Road n° 33, Tiszafüred.* ☏ *52:378 605. Between Tiszafüred (8km/4.8mi away) and Hortobágy (30km/18mi away).* A traditional inn.

been taken of it and it illustrates the pages of a multitude of books and magazines. It is a kind of symbol of the wet *puszta*. Built between 1827 and 1833, it replaced a small wooden bridge and gradually became so famous that a **Bridge Festival** is held every year on 20 August. This major folk art event brings back to life the old traditions of fairs of the last century. Horses also play their part.

★**Hortobágyi Pásztormúzeum** ⌚ **(Shepherds' Museum)** – This museum is devoted to the life of shepherds and the inhabitants of the region. There are interesting embroidered felt clothes, as well as various objects invented and made by these men who used to spend months at a time with their animals on the plain. The objects are similar to those made by the men of the dry *puszta* to make their nomadic life easier.

Körszínmúzeum (Round Museum) – This exhibits the park's natural resources, the fauna and flora. Twice a year, Hortobágy becomes the resting-place for thousands of migrating birds. More than 330 species of birds have been recorded in the various milieus of the park. Some areas are closed to the public and others visited only with authorisation, granted to researchers and specialists. You need to know your birds well to put names to all the species, from shrike to bustard, spoonbill to warbler.

Go over the Kilenclyukú híd and turn right towards Máta.

Máta – This is where the **Nonious**, the Hungarian draught horses, are bred. An International Horse Festival is held here every year in July. A real opportunity to spend a few days looking at equestrian shows and splendid teams in harness.

M. Guillou/MICHELIN

KALOCSA★

Bács-Kiskun province – Population 20 000

Michelin map 925 G 7 – 119km/74mi to the south of Budapest

Kalocsa is the **capital of sweet paprika**, which is grown on over 3 000ha/7 400 acres around the town. This may be the origin of the fondness of the women of Kalocsa for floral ornamentation, expressed in mural paintings and embroidery. You will have an opportunity to appreciate the quality and delicacy of their work, and perhaps buy some, in particular at the Regional Folk Art Centre.

An eventful history – Like Esztergom, the town was founded in the 11C by Stephen I who made it a bishopric; raised to the rank of archbishopric, it was granted a cathedral. The Danube, whose bed was shifted by 6km/3.7mi, and the surrounding marshland, have long assured its protection. The town suffered from Turkish oppression and was destroyed by fire in the 17C.

Kalocsa's religious past, despite the modest size of the town and the destruction it suffered, justifies the presence of two important buildings in the centre of the town, the Archbishop's Palace and the Baroque cathedral. These two edifices are located on Szentháromság tér at the far end of Szent István király út, Kalocsa's main street.

SIGHTS

Magyar Fűszerpaprika Múzeum ⓥ **(Paprika Museum)** – *Szent István király utca 6.* The museum relates the history of paprika, its arrival in Hungary, how it is grown, transformed into powder and used. In September the harvested paprika is dried and the countryside is then covered with magnificent red carpets. The museum also presents the life of the Hungarian Nobel prize-winner, Albert Szent-György, who discovered vitamin C from research using paprika. The same building houses Kalocsa Korona Tours Kft., a company which arranges boat trips on the Danube, visits and shows on the Puszta.

★ **Érseki palota** – The **Archbishop's Palace** dates from the late 18C. It was built to plans drawn by a friar in the Baroque style. The symmetrical, massive façade gives onto the square; a section projects forward with an ornamental pediment framing the entrance. On the opposite side, the building is also both symmetrical and impressive, facing a large park. It is interesting to visit. There is a library containing precious volumes, including a Bible that belonged to Martin Luther with notes on the text in his own handwriting. It contains a total of 120 000 volumes some of which date back to the 13C. The main room on the upper floor (when it is open), and the chapel have frescoes by the Austrian painter and fresco artist, Franz Anton Maulbertsch, who decorated numerous churches and religious buildings in Hungary.

Főszékesegyház – The **Cathedral** is Baroque. Three other churches had already been built on the same site. The foundations of the first (11C) and the second (13C) have been discovered, but no traces remain of the Gothic church built in the 14C. The cathedral you see today is the work of Mayerhoffer and was built between 1735 and 1754.

In the interior, the pale pink, combined with the golden stucco decoration, gives a serenely radiant atmosphere. The archbishop who brought the crown presented by Pope Sylvester to King Stephen was buried in this crypt. The crown was given in recognition of the King's conversion and to ensure his authority over Christianity in Hungary. The **Archbishop's Treasury** contains an exhibition of vestments, liturgical objects and a bust of St Stephen (1896) weighing 50kg (48kg of silver and 2kg of gold).

A place to stay, a place to eat

Béta Hotel Kalocsa – *Szentháromság tér 4. ☎/Fax 78/461 244. 30 rooms from €21.* A fine hotel. Good value for money, simple but tasteful decor, and pleasant, well-equipped rooms with arches.

Piros Arany – *Szent István király út 37. ☎ 78/462 220. Rooms at €26.* A small hotel in the town centre; it has no particular charm but the rooms are clean and not overpriced.

Kalocsa – *Szentháromság tér 4. ☎ 78/461 047. Rooms between €31 and €46.* In a beautiful building 200 years old; the town's main hotel is well located near the castle and the cathedral.

Csajda Csárda – *Csajda u. 2. ☎ 78/462 670.* In the middle of the town's housing estate, a traditional inn where you are not likely to meet tourists! One of Kalocsa's main restaurants. Hungarian cooking.

The surrounding area

Bárka-Csárda – *Road n° 5301. ☎ 60/452 531. At least 10km/6mi from Kalocsa; on road n° 5301 to Kiskőrös, at the junction with the River Maloméri.* A small unpretentious restaurant with fish specialities (perch, catfish, pike) caught before your very eyes.

In the immediate vicinity of the palace and cathedral, there are two monuments, one in honour of the Holy Trinity and the other in memory of Pál Thomory, the Archbishop of Kalocsa and leader of the army that fought at Mohács.
More recently, after the 1956 Uprising, the Bishop of Kalocsa replaced Cardinal Mindszenty, Archbishop and Primate of Hungary, confined in the American Embassy, and led discussions with the Communist government to preserve the Church's right to exist.
Szent István király leads directly from the Archbishop's Palace and makes for an interesting stroll.

★ **Viski Károly Múzeum** ⓥ – *Szent István király 25.* The Viski Museum, with its wealth of exhibits, shows the life of the various communities who lived in the region: Hungarian, Swabian and Slovak. This is illustrated by a reconstruction of the various milieus and lifestyles, from houses to fields, and from everyday events to the more important ones that mark a life from cradle to grave. Visitors will see the change in habitat and in clothes, which over time became decorated and embroidered, an art for which the women of Kalocsa became renowned. A collection of old coins will interest numismatists.

Schöffer Miklós Múzeum ⓥ – *Szent István király 76.* Was Nicolas Schöffer, the sculptor born in Kalocsa and a great name in kinetic art, a revolutionary or a reactionary? A visit to the museum may well provide an answer.
If you are undecided as you leave the museum, turn left, go as far as the crossroads and stop at the **Schöffer Fénytorony** (Light Tower). This metal tower, made of steel struts and beams, decorated with mirrors, lit up and animated, will, for a while, be among the symbols and images of revolutionary avant-garde art. Should we read into this a reactionary demonstration by a native of these parts against all the garlands of flowers decorating the town?

Népművészeti Tájház ⓥ **(Regional Folk Art Centre)** – *Tompa Mihály utca 7.* Embroidery, decorated objects and walls painted by true artists are on display. Kalocsa shirts are famous for their embroidery.

Vasútállomás – *Mártírok tér.* This small building with doors and windows decorated in blue is Kalocsa **station**, which offers the charm of a different age. There are painted decorations around windows and doors and the walls are crowned with drawings of garlands of flowers and leaves.

KAPOSVÁR

Somogy province – Population 74 000

Michelin map 925 H 5

The name of Kaposvár, the province's administrative centre, means the castle on the Kapos. The castle is no more: like many others it was destroyed by the Turks and later by the Habsburgs. The town is located to the south of Lake Balaton between the lake and Pécs. It stands on the stretch of the River Kapos that runs from east to west before it turns north and joins the Sió. The latter then flows parallel to the Sárvíz and their waters join forces before flowing into the Danube.
Kaposvár is associated with two great names in the history of Hungarian painting: József Rippl-Rónai and János Vaszary.
Kaposvár is also the birthplace of Imre Nagy whose tragic destiny moved the entire world. A statue has been erected to his memory in a small square named after him. It was placed there on 23 October 1996 as a reminder of the 1956 Uprising and also to celebrate the 100th anniversary of his birth (1896).

Imre Nagy

The son of a Budapest metalworker, Imre Nagy was called up to fight on the Russian front during the First World War. He was imprisoned and set free during the October revolution. Imre Nagy joined the Soviet revolutionary movement and did not return to his native land until 1921. Under the regime of Horthy, he was again forced into exile, spending some time in Vienna before returning to Moscow where he was to engage in self-criticism. He was arrested there in 1938. When freed he ran a *kolhoz* (collective farm) in Siberia. From the outset of the Second World War, he was put in charge of broadcasts in Hungarian for Radio Moscow International. At the end of the war, he returned to Budapest, became Home Secretary and then took charge of agricultural policy. After a period of disgrace, he was called back into power in 1953 as Prime Minister. In 1955, he was in disgrace once again and excluded from the Party; the Party called him back once more on 23 October at the time of the uprising. In the confusion of events, Nagy took decisions that shook the Kremlin's authority and policy. On 3 November, Russian troops entered Budapest. Nagy was arrested and deported to Romania. Repatriated six months later, he was sentenced in secret and executed on 16 June 1958. Exactly 31 years later, day for day, he was given an official burial and rehabilitated.

The stork region – A population of white storks *(Ciconia ciconia)* returns to the region in March every year and leaves for distant skies towards the end of August. They steadfastly return to this spot and, because of the interest the birds arouse, they give a certain character to the region and their presence adds to its fame. In actual fact, it is not Kaposvár but a neighbouring village, undoubtedly more peaceful, which the storks prefer. **Nagybajom** is located 25km/16mi from Kaposvár and the storks come here to lay their eggs and raise their fledglings. In 1996 Nagybajom was given the title of European Stork Village. To the satisfaction of these large white birds, the village's proximity to an area of marshland provides them with an abundant supply of frogs and small fish. Moreover locals have been so understanding and thoughtful that even the electricity board has prepared and installed special supports for their nests.

★**Somogy Megyei Múzeum** – *Fő utca 10.* The provincial museum houses an exhibition of paintings from 1860 to the present time, as well as a local history exhibition, a section on natural history and a display showing what the region was like at the time of the Magyar conquest. There is also an exhibition of handicraft and folk art (wood and horn carved by shepherds and swineherds, as well as printed indigo cloth).

The art gallery includes works by János Vaszary, Mihály Zichy, Ferenc Martyn, Aurél Bernáth etc.

Csíky Gergely Színház – *Rákóczi Ferenc tér.* The immense cake-like structure set in the square is the **theatre**, which is reminiscent of the kind of buildings put up in spas or holiday resorts in the 1930s. Pale yellow, with numerous windows with white wooden frames, this building dating from 1911 is certainly not obviously a theatre.

A place to stay, a place to eat

Borostyán Vendégház – *Rákóczi tér 3. ☎ 06/82/512 475, Fax 82/310 123. 9 rooms between €32 and €44.* Almost opposite the theatre, a cosy house with tasteful rooms. Restaurant with Hungarian and international specialities.

Kapos – *Ady Endre. u. 2. ☎/Fax: 82/316 022. 67 rooms between €31 and €47.* Main hotel in town offering every comfort. Restaurant with Hungarian specialities.

Diófa – *József A. u. 24.* One of the town's main restaurants. Hungarian specialities: liver and meat. *Rooms available (8 rooms between €20 and €35).*

★**Rippl-Rónai József Emlékmúzeum** Ⓥ – *Rómahegy 88.* A wooden gate on a bend, barely the width of a car leads, at the end of a pathway, to a large yellow house in the middle of a park. The paintings of Rippl-Rónai are exhibited here in his birthplace.

József Rippl-Rónai – Born in 1861, the son of a schoolmaster, Rippl-Rónai studied pharmacy. He obtained his diploma and spent several years as a private tutor before taking up painting. He enrolled at the Munich Academy and then became Mihály Munkácsy's assistant in Paris and fulfilled the numerous orders received from all over the world. In Paris, he met other artists such as Aristide Maillol and a Scotsman, James Pitcairn-Knowles. Rippl-Rónai disregarded detail, rejected chiaroscuro and processes that had a tendency to assert realism. He refused what he called the hierarchy of detail and claimed to take inspiration from egalitarianism. "All the details in my pictures have the same importance and are painted in the same manner," he wrote. He thus arrived at a style of painting that he described as the corn grain technique, which consisted in not blending colours on the canvas but in making little patches like a grain of corn, either of pure colour or of a mixture made on the palette. A good illustration of this technique is the painting on show at the Hungarian National Gallery in Budapest, *Lazarine and Anella in the park.*

MAGYAR KÉPEK Kft

Portrait of Zorka Bányai by Rippl-Rónai

Starting in 1890 Rippl-Rónai began to take part in numerous exhibitions. At the Champs de Mars Exhibition in Paris in 1894, his painting entitled *My Grandmother* won him the recognition of Parisian critics. By 1895, he was holding regular exhibitions with the Nabis group. In 1901, he returned to Kaposvár to live. In 1914, in France with his family, he was taken unawares by the declaration of war. He was arrested and interned with his wife and adopted daughter. Freed following the intervention of Maillol and Maurice Denis, he was able to return to Budapest. He died in 1927.

EXCURSIONS

★★ **Szenna** – *16km/10mi to the south-west. Leave Kaposvár on Berzsenyi Dániel utca, road n° 67 towards Szigetvár. Cross over the railway line, then turn right after the bridge.*
This modest town has one of Hungary's finest **open-air museums** ⓥ **(Szabadtéri Néprajzi Gyűjtemény)**. The most interesting feature is the **Reformed Church** (Református templom) which dates back to the 18C. Inside the church, which is still being used, there is an admirable crowned pulpit and painted coffered ceiling. The other buildings in the village enclosure are from other places in the region. They were dismantled and rebuilt on the site.

★ **Somogyvár** – *28km/17.5mi to the north-west on road n° 6701.* For six centuries, Somogyvár was the province's administrative centre. In 1091, Ladislas I called on Benedictines from the abbey of St-Gilles in France (Gard *département*) to establish a monastery here. The vestiges uncovered have allowed the church's dimensions to be measured, 60m/196ft long by 24m/78ft wide. The outline of the cloisters can be distinguished from the foundations. The site is impressive.

KECSKEMÉT★★

Bács-Kiskun province – Population 110 000

Michelin map 925 F 9 – 83km/52mi to the south of Budapest

Kecskemét is a town of song and music, located in the heart of the vast *puszta* between the Danube and the Tisza. It is a charming town, and the cherished birthplace of the musician Zoltán Kodály. In summertime, the paprika fields bring colour and sparkle to the countryside echoed by the grapes on the vines and the apricots and apples in the orchards.

A food production centre – Kecskemét's agricultural origins go back to the 15C when the breeding of cattle was one of the principal activities on the Alföld, or Hungarian Great Plain. From the archives, we know that between 1560 and 1570 one-third of the cattle that crossed the Danube to Vác (to the north of Budapest) belonged to Kecskemét farmers. The town suffered in the fight for independence but the 18C saw the development of crops, fruit, vegetables and grapevines which brought prosperity to the town resulting in the building of schools, churches and houses.

A town famous for foie gras and the home of barackpálinka – In 1950 Kecskemét became the administrative centre for the new Bács-Kiskun province, Hungary's largest, named after the surrounding region. The food processing industry has continued to expand, driven by the development of agriculture. Cattle, sheep, horses and poultry thrive in this region which is also renowned for the production of **foie gras**. Nowadays, clusters of greenhouses, with their diaphanous plastic domes for growing early fruit and vegetables, form part of the landscape composed of vast expanses of cereals, vineyards and orchards. Although the Kecskemét region produces around one-third of Hungary's wine, the best Hungarian wines do not come from this area. The local wine is light with little character. The town is nicknamed the town of great repute because of the excellence of its products, which include spirits and liqueurs such as the renowned apricot brandy *(barackpálinka)*. A visit to the Zwack distilleries *(Matkói u. 2)* is recommended.

A FEW MUSICAL NOTES

"Song brings beauty to life and singers bring beauty to the lives of others"– Kodály's words make it clear that song and singing were his principal vocations. With his friend, Bartók, he was one of the first collectors, if not the first, of the tunes and words of folk songs which gave rise to the creation of ethnomusicology. As a composer, his work is a classical combination of Hungarian folk music and the European heritage. As an ethnomusicologist, Kodály was to travel beyond the frontiers of Europe carrying out research and working in North Africa, in Algeria in particular. He wrote a number of works for the Kecskemét Choral Society, *(The Old People, Anna Molnár,*

The Latecomers, Jesus and the Merchants in the Temple). His great classical work is the *Psalmus Hungaricus* which dates from 1923. The text comes from a 16C poem by Mihály Vég who used to append the words "from Kecskemét" to his name. Kodály was also a great teacher; he taught and trained a number of musicians, composers and conductors. He is particularly well known for the teaching method he developed, known today as the Kodály method which is used in Hungary. If you have been fortunate enough to visit the little-known parts of Hungary, meet people, be invited to family celebrations and folk gatherings, you will have had an opportunity to see and listen to spontaneously formed singing groups, of astounding quality. All the participants know the songs and their voices all come into the music at the correct pitch to produce a harmonious sound forming a veritable choir. The Japanese who have adopted the Kodály method train excellent musicians, and other countries have drawn inspiration from Hungarian musical education.

A captivating town, a musical town – **Zoltán Kodály**, one of the great names in Hungarian culture and 20C music, was born in Kecskemét. Although he did not stay there, Kodály was particularly attached to the town and declared, "I have always felt deep down that I belong to Kecskemét, like a plant that grows in sandy soil whose roots grow down beneath the layer of sand to reach the sap so vital to their existence." Since his death in Budapest in 1967, the birthday of this great musician and teacher has been celebrated every year with an International Choir Festival and an International Music Festival, held on alternate years.

MAGYAR KÉPEK Kft

Zoltán Kodály

Kodály Zoltán Zenepedagógiai Intézet (Kodály Institute) – *See also following page.* Founded in 1975, the Institute is housed in a former monastery of the Franciscan order, built on medieval ruins in the 18C. It has been restored and converted for its current purpose and in its peace and spiritual dimension has become a monastery of musicians. A modern part was added in 1980: squeezed between two buildings constructed in the worst period of the Communist era it could not be considered an architectural success. Kodály International Seminars are arranged every two years, usually in July and August, with an International Choir Camp held in parallel.

SIGHTS

As a market town and a place of trade, Kecskemét had open spaces and squares specifically for these activities. Over time, a number of buildings were constructed on or around these sites beautifully illustrating various styles of Hungarian architecture.

This is why the town centre seems like a large park: you cross it to go from the town hall to the Kodály Institute, to the Cifrapalota passing by the New College... the town centre is delightful at any time of year. In one of his Lieder, **Brahms** called it **"the most charming town in the world"**.
With a view to improvement, the town authorities have decided to re-pave many of the streets. The concrete slabs are not, unfortunately, as attractive as the old surfaces. In spite of this, however, several places have retained their charm.

Nagytemplom (Great Church) – The view from this yellow-ochre church is marred by the Aranyhomok *(Golden Sands)* Hotel built in the 1960s. Inaugurated in 1806, the late-Baroque Great Church has two plaques on the façade, the first commemorating the victims of the 1848-49 War of Independence and the second a distinguished First World War cavalry regiment. The Great Church's chimes regularly play a Hungarian folk tune turned into a song to the glory of the recruitment of soldiers for the independence movement, the song of the soldiers of Lajos Kossuth. It also plays tunes by Kodály, Mozart, Erkel and Handel.

★ **Városháza (Town Hall)** – This pink building is by Ödön Lechner and Gyula Pártos. Building was started in 1893 and municipal employees moved in 28 months later. Its architecture is beautiful, in the Art Nouveau style, with restrained decoration. The architects decided to add Kecskemét's motto or battle cry to the building: "Fear not height nor depth." Inside the town hall, the staircase leading to the Council

A place to stay

Fábián Panzió – *Kápolna u. 14. ☎ 76/477 677. Rooms between €30 and €33.* In the town centre, this charming family-style *panzió* has about a dozen rooms and an inner courtyard.

Három Gúnár – *Batthyány u. 1-7. ☎ 76/483 611. 45 rooms between €36 and €42.* Comfortable hotel. Restaurant and bar (billiards and video games).

Aranyhomok Szálloda – *Kossuth tér 3. ☎ 76/486 286. 111 rooms between €50 and €55.* The town's biggest hotel, very well located on the main square with its many monuments.

A place to eat

HBH – *Csányi u. 4. ☎ 76/481 945.* Restaurant with dark wood decor; specialises in Bavarian and Hungarian cuisine. Speciality: Bavarian knuckle of ham. Terrace in summer.

Mágnás – *Csongrádi u. 2. ☎ 76/417 640.* Slightly away from the centre, a restaurant with tasteful decor. Speciality: haunch of venison. Wide choice of Hungarian wines.

The surrounding area

Wéber Tanya – *Lűwy dűlű 14, 6034 Helvécia. ☎ 76/429 848. Family apartment for around €55. 6km/3.6mi from Kecskemét.* A farm-inn with three thatched cottages. Meals possible. Horse breeding.

Cifra Csárda – *Ceglédi út. 21, 2750 Nagykőrös. ☎ 53/351 212. About 15km/9mi from Kecskemét, on road n° 441.* A charming traditional inn offering Hungarian cuisine and wines. Gypsy music is a regular feature.

Room is particularly interesting. It is composed of two flights of stairs that lead across a series of decorated arcades and arches. The guided tour of the Council Room is worth taking. Commentaries are available in Hungarian or German but a text in English is provided to allow other visitors to follow the presentation. This room was decorated by **Bertalan Székely**, a painter of historical scenes in an academic Romantic style. His work can be seen on monuments and other buildings in Hungary.

Ferences templom (Franciscan Church) – On Kossuth tér on the right, the Franciscan church, or St Nicholas' Chapel, is the oldest building in Kecskemét and dates from the 13C. Although built in the Gothic style, it was renovated in the Baroque style in the 18C. A few vestiges of St Michael's Chapel, which preceded the Franciscan church, can still be seen to the left of the church.

Go around the garden, and on the left you will see Kéttemplom köz (a blind alley between the two churches) and a small bridge leading from it to the entrance of the Kodály Institute.

Kodály Zoltán Zenepedagógiai Intézet – This temple of music is unfortunately not open to the public as it is permanently in use. However, it is interesting to have a brief look inside. One side of the cloisters is open to the public and there is a small exhibition on Kodály. The reception/information desk sells a leaflet in various languages on the life of the musician and his work, together with information on the Institute's activities. This limited contact at least gives visitors an idea of the size of the Institute where the young and not so young from all over the world come to learn choral singing and Kodály's method of training. Apart from practice rooms and the library, the Institute also has a boarding scheme for foreign students some of whom are also accommodated in private homes. Your visit may coincide with one of the numerous, regular musical performances given by the Institute. If so, this is an opportunity not to be missed, as you will not only be able to see part of the inside of the building but also enjoy an exceptional musical event. There is a shop selling all sorts of high-quality Hungarian objects and products opposite the small bridge leading to the entrance of the Institute.

Kossuth tér – Returning to Kossuth tér after leaving Kéttemplom köz, visitors will see the 17C **Reformed Church**, built during the Muslim occupation with the authorisation of the Sultan which was purchased for the sum of 669 pieces of gold. It was subsequently modified on several occasions. The church is built against a building

Kossuth tér

that separates the main park into two squares, Kossuth tér and Szabadság tér, and which houses the **Liberté** restaurant. A visit to this restaurant is to be recommended first and foremost for the superb Art Nouveau setting which has been tastefully restored.

Continue your walk along this side of the square and, leaving Kalvin tér on the right, you will see a building with extremely fine, unpretentious architecture of great merit, the New College.

Új Kollégium (New College) – A mayor of Kecskemét, Péter Lestár, who played a major role in the town's development said, "Even if we live in huts, we must build palaces for our schools." And this is what they did in Kecskemét. The New College, built between 1911 and 1913 has a façade constructed like a piece of music, with a sense of harmony between occupied and empty spaces, with corresponding relief and ornamentation. It is unfortunate that the building is not open to the public because, behind the façade is a variety of interior spaces where everything is in its right place. If you open the door, perhaps the staff will kindly allow you to look beyond the entrance hall. The architects Valér Mende and Lajos Dombi deserve a mention. The New College was home to Kodály's music and singing school for a long while. After the break with the Communist regime, it was returned to its former owners and is now a secondary school belonging to the Reformed Church. There is also a small Reformed Church **museum**, Református Egyházművészeti *(in Csányi János utca)*, in the same building.

Cifrapalota ⌚ **(Ornamental Palace)** – *On the corner of Csányi János and Rákóczi út.* The name Cifra conjures up a world of folk tales, decoration, hand embroidery and illuminated design. Once again an example of fine architecture, in a consistent style, its extravagance is controlled and presented in a joyous, fresh approach. The shapes, relief or coloured decoration and carefully sculpted woodwork of this building give it a contemporary and up-to-date feeling, despite its age. The interior is of the same standard as the façade and even the central courtyard forms part of the same harmonious unity. If you visit the art gallery, you will discover some fine paintings by 20C Hungarian artists. You should also visit the Great Hall which used to be a gaming room, a fact emphasised by its rather provocative decoration. The Cifrapalota, with its enamelled tiles, paintings and colourful designs, is a perfect illustration of the intelligent use of folk themes and forms of expression in architecture, giving it sufficient character to successfully withstand the passage of time.

F. Szelényi/MAGYAR KÉPEK Kft

Tudomány és Technika Háza ⓥ **(House of Science and Technology)** – This is the former synagogue. The building is important for historical reasons. Like other places of worship in the town centre, the synagogue was damaged during an earthquake in 1911. It was rebuilt and later desecrated during the Second World War. It subsequently fell into disuse and was later turned into a conference centre. It is now in continual use and medical congresses are regularly held here.

The town centre – Architecture of high quality flourishes in the town in a variety of forms, with buildings from different eras that have been integrated to form a harmonious unity. The contemporary period is represented by buildings constructed according to technical and economical criteria, such as the Aranyhomok Hotel or the numerous housing developments that are no credit to architecture. There is, however, a pleasing exception to this on the edge of Szabadság tér, the **Luther palota** on the corner of Luther köz (Luther Passage) and Hock János utca, built at more or less the same time as the hotel mentioned above.

Other recent buildings include the library, which can be reached from Szabadsag tér by taking Arany J. u. The **Evangelical Church** designed by Ybl is also located here, and is worth a visit for the simple, restrained atmosphere of a place of worship. The **library**, inaugurated in 1998, is a peaceful place to think and study. The interior is spacious and varied and the library contains information on culture, communication, information technology, multimedia, audio-visual products, books, the press etc. It is an impressive place to visit, in silence.

Other recent buildings illustrate the richness of Hungarian architecture, for example the **Budapest Bank** building on the corner of Nagykűrösi u. and Koháry István u. with its forms inherited from the Baroque period, reproduced using modern materials and techniques.

Still in the town centre, take Kossuth tér, leaving the town hall and the Franciscan Church behind you, and you will come to the **Katona József Színház** Theatre in Katona József tér. Built in the 19C by Austrian entrepreneurs, it gave rise to controversy. Numerous performances are now given in the theatre, including excellent concerts by the Kecskemét Symphony Orchestra. It is worth a visit. Behind the theatre, in Bajcsy-Zsilinszky is the **Hungarian Photography Museum** (Magyar Fotográfiai Múzeum), housed in the small synagogue. It puts on temporary exhibitions and is worthy of interest since the Hungarians have produced great photographers such as Brassaï and Capa.

Bozsó Múzeum ⓥ – *Klapka u. 34, on the corner of Vörösmarty u.* In Hungary, museum gallery collections are often bequeathed to local municipalities by private individuals. In Kecskemét, the most interesting of these collections is in the Bozsó Museum. In this magnificent old house, where the painter János Bozsó (1922-98) used to live, visitors pass through a series of rooms in which a few good examples of his paintings are exhibited as well as a large collection of domestic objects. The last rooms, one on the upper floor, contain a splendid collection of sculpture and religious objects.

Leskowsky Hangszergyűjtemény ⓥ **(Leskowsky Museum of Musical Instruments)** – Mr Albert Leskowsky has donated his collection of musical instruments to the town. As the museum's director, he maintains it, adds new items to the collection and gives a guided tour. There is an unusual assortment of instruments, from regions near and far, all invented to produce noise and sound, beat out rhythm, charm and captivate – when you are in Kecskemét music is never far away.

Magyar Naív Művészek Múzeuma (Museum of Naïve Art) and **Szórakaténusz Játékmúzeum és Műhely (Toy Museum and Workshops)** – *Gáspár András u. 11.* There are two museums in this building. The first houses a series of canvases by Naïve painters and a few pieces of sculpture; it is said to be one of the strangest collections in

Europe. The second is more of an arts workshop for children and young people, and has an exhibition of toys. For those who are interested, it is a means of discovering how this social/educational activity functions.

Magyar Népi Iparművészeti Múzeum ⓥ **(Museum of Hungarian Folk Art)** – *Serfűzű u. 19/A.* This museum is bound to interest folk art enthusiasts since it contains most of the models for the handicrafts produced in various regions of Hungary – pottery, weaving, saddlery, cloth printing etc. You will also see how contemporary artists and craftsmen have adopted these old crafts to design objects more in keeping with modern life or simply to find an enhanced means of expression.

KESZTHELY★★

Zala province – Population 22 000

Michelin map 925 F 3 – Local map see BALATON

This is one of the cities in the Lake Balaton area that does not depend solely on tourism. It was in 1739 that the Festetics family became the owner of several properties on the extreme west of Lake Batalon, including the lake itself and the land surrounding it, as well as the Keszthely area.
Linked with the Széchenyi family of Nagycenk, whose father István laid the foundations of the National Library and the Academy of Sciences, the Festetics family, through Count György, founded the first agricultural school in Keszthely, the Georgikon.
This busy town stands in a dominant position overlooking Lake Balaton. The castle terrace has a fine balcony from which the north and south shores of the lake can be admired.
A **Roman road** used to go north to Szombathely and Sopron. The town's main streets now follow its route.
Along the south side of the lake stretches the spa resort, which comprises three hotels, Helikon Park (15ha/36 acres), the landing-stage, the avenue along the shore and Helikon Beach.

★FESTETICS-KASTÉLY ⓥ (FESTETICS CASTLE)

This is located at the end of the street that is an extension of Kossuth Lajos utca. There are paying parking facilities nearby.

The construction of the castle was begun in 1745; the northern parts were finished in 1887. The Festetics family owned the castle until 1945. If we can still admire the library and its contents, it is certainly due to the intelligence of an officer in the Soviet Army, a professor of French origin, who, at the moment of the Liberation, protected the castle from being ransacked by his own troops by sealing certain doors. The library and numerous pieces of furniture were saved in this way.
The castle is home to a music school and a group of rooms reserved for official receptions or seminars. Some of the rooms still contain many of the original pieces of furniture, brought from England by the English wife of a member of the Festetics family.
There is also a well-presented collection of arms and a few hunting trophies. A great many chamber music concerts are given in the **main hall**.

A place to stay

Párizsi Panzió – *Kastély u. 5. ☎ 83/311 202. Rooms between €29 and €40.* In the castle's former outbuildings, *panzió* with clean and modern rooms looking directly onto the courtyard.

Hullám – *Balatonpart. ☎ 83/312 644, Fax 83/315 950. Open April to October, 50 rooms between €40 and €61.* On the shores of Lake Balaton, beautiful 19C house with direct access to the beach.

Abbázia Club Hotel – *Erzsébet királyné u. 23. ☎ and fax 83/312 596. Rooms between €31 and €48.* This hotel in the town centre can be recognised by its yellow façade. All necessary facilities.

A place to eat

Hungária Gösser – *Kossuth u. 35.* In the town's shopping and pedestrian street, a central, popular restaurant. A sort of pub serving Hungarian dishes and beer. Large outside tables in summer.

Bacchus – *Erzsébet Királyné u. 18.* A lovely restaurant in the hotel's cellars. Terrace in summer. Hungarian specialities, and as the name indicates, a wide choice of wine.

Hungaricum Borház – *Helikon u. 4.* A delightful place! A veritable little museum, this picturesque cellar has a wide selection of Hungarian wines. In summer there is a pleasant inner courtyard where meals are also served.

R. Palotas

Keszthely Castle

★★ **Helikon Library** – Founded in 1790, the library contains some 52 000 books. The oak furniture and shelving were made by a local craftsman, János Kerbl.

Agrártudományi Egyetem (Agricultural Sciences College) – The college was founded by Count Festetics. In his day, the count, who was fond of Greek literature, set up the **Helikon** festivals. He held gatherings of the most eminent writers and poets in Transdanubia in his castle.

The English-style garden – Designed by an Englishman, this is a very pleasant garden for a stroll. On your way around the castle, you can stop and look at the statues on the south wing, symbolising the Festetics family's activities: horse-breeding, farming and shipbuilding.

THE TOWN

Walk to Kastély utca and take Kossuth Lajos utca.

Fő tér – The town hall, **Polgármesteri Hivatal** on the main square dates from the late 18C.

Magyarok Nagyasszonya templom (Our Lady of Hungary Church) – This Gothic church was built out of stone recovered from the nearby Roman camp at Keszthely and probably from the chapel that stood here before. Some 14C and 15C frescoes were discovered during recent restoration work. The church's founder and two members of the Festetics family are buried here. Kristóf Festetics' funerary monument may be seen, and Count György is buried in the crypt.

Georgikon Majormúzeum ⓥ – *Bercsényi Miklós utca. 64-65.* The **Georgikon** Institute functioned until 1848. Some of the buildings were restored in the 1970s and now house the **museum** devoted to the Institute's history, wine-growing and work on the land.

Balatoni Múzeum ⓥ – *Múzeum utca 2.* This neo-Baroque building was built in 1928 and is now a museum devoted to the Balaton region's geological and ethnographic history. Roman and medieval relics are exhibited. A slide slow illustrates the **Kis-Balaton** (Little Balaton), a protected marsh area extending southward.

EXCURSIONS

Hévíz – *See this name.*

Fenékpuszta – *7km/4.2mi south along road n° 71.* Relics from a 4C Roman forum have been uncovered on the edge of Kis-Balaton.

★ **Kis-Balaton** – *See Balaton.*

KISKUNFÉLEGYHÁZA

Bács-Kiskun province – Population 35 000

Michelin map 925 F 9

This small, quite charming country town is the subject of controversy. Is it the birthplace of Sándor Petőfi? The story goes that the poet said that he was born in Kiskunfélegyháza, but this is strongly contested by the small town of **Kiskőrös**, around 50km/31mi away, to the south-west. In any event, you can visit the house where Sándor Petőfi was supposed to have been born and where he certainly lived, and also visit another house, in Kiskőrös, which claims to be the poet's real birthplace, along with the small adjoining museum.

Városháza (Town Hall) – *Kossuth Lajos utca 1.* Built between 1910 and 1912 by Nándor Morbitzer and József Vass, this is a fine example of Art Nouveau. It has a brick façade, decorated with earthenware tiles with plant and floral designs. The interior of the building is a model of the art of overlapping and interweaving space and decoration. The stucco has painted garlands reminiscent of embroidery and the chandeliers echo the structure. It is possible to visit the great hall which has a tremendous sense of harmony achieved by the space, decor, furniture and lighting. The pastel shades throughout, dominated by pinks, yellows and blues, might have been faintly incongruous and certainly took some audacity to conceive. Visitors should take a look at the fine detail: capitals, stained-glass windows, door surrounds, integrated columns, carved balustrades – not forgetting the frieze crowning the exterior façade which spreads out like an embroidery in majolica.

Kiskun Múzeum Ⓥ – *Dr Holló Lajos út 9.* A police barracks dating from the time of Maria Theresa (a few cells still exist) houses the province's Town and Regional History Museum. The museum's founder, Gyula Szalay, was the person who continued the work of Ferenc Móra, the author of children's stories. One room is devoted to archaeology exhibits, jewellery and objects used by the peoples who lived in the region. The Sarmatians and Avars supposedly invented shoes with flexible soles. One of their distinctive characteristics was to inscribe people's hierarchical ranks on their belts. Note also the first ice-skates made of bone and a picture-showcase which gives three different images, depending on the way you look at it.
Decorated gingerbread was once made in Kiskunfélegyháza, with designs, shapes and colours reminiscent of the majolica adorning the town hall.
There is an exhibition showing the inside of a peasant shelter and the shepherd life of yesteryear: clothing, equipment for the nomadic life, a screen for hanging up tools, a notched stick for recording the number of animals and a staff to ward off wolves. In the museum courtyard stands a mill, which was brought here in 1960 and was in operation until 1945.

KISKUNHALAS

Bács-Kiskun province – Population 32 000

Michelin map 925 G 9

This average-sized town, commonly known as Halas, is famous for its **lace**. This is not a very old tradition since it was only at the start of the 20C that an art teacher, Árpád Dékány, and a lacemaker, Mária Markovits, started the activity, which expanded to the extent that it acquired international renown. This needlepoint lace uses 40 to 50 different stitches.

★ **Csipkeház** Ⓥ – *Kossuth utca 39.* The **Lace Centre** is also the Arts Centre, and exhibits the riches of the handicraft with simplicity, showing the various stages of execution for the tablecloths, doilies and other articles. All of these works are a combination of patience, professional expertise, imagination and invention.

Artreference/MAGYAR KÉPEK Kft

Kiskunhalas Lace

Thorma János Emlékmúzeum Ⓥ – *Köztársaság út 2.* The museum has work on show by a local painter and a large archaeological collection.

Végh-kúria – *Bajcsy-Zsilinszky utca 3.* An exhibition of paintings by Balázs Diószegi, a little-known contemporary painter.

EXCURSION

Kiskőrös – *30km/19mi to the north-west along road n° 53.* You can visit **Petőfi szülőháza** Ⓥ, Sándor Petőfi's birthplace (see above), a modest, thatched house. Set in the garden is another house with souvenirs of the poet and his family on display.

KOMÁROM

Komárom-Esztergom province – Population 20 500

Michelin map 925 C 5

This town, on both banks of the Danube, was cut in two by the Treaty of Trianon. The northern part, which consisted of the old centre and is of greater interest, became Slovakian and is now called Komárno. The Hungarian part to the south has grown and is now an important river port.

A town for taking the waters – Komárom is also a thermal spa, with sulphurous and carbonated waters to relieve pains of the joints and rheumatism. The waters are recommended for post-operative care. This spa is available to individuals through *Komthermal*, a hotel with two suites and 35 rooms, and a campsite open all year round with 450 spaces for tents or caravans. These two establishments and local residential hotels are linked to the baths. The medical services are good and the cost reasonable.

A SHORT HISTORY

A fortress town – About 3km/2mi from Komárom, on the same site as **Szőny**, once stood *Brigetio*, one of the first and most important Roman fortifications in Pannonia. A great many relics have been brought to light (fresco remains, sarcophagi, as well as a collection of gold pieces) that can be seen at the National Museum in Budapest or the Kuny Domokos Museum in Tata.

Komárom was a fortress serving as an advance defence post for Vienna. When Napoleon occupied the Austrian capital, it was also the fallback position for Emperor Francis I of Habsburg and his court in 1809. It was at this time that the decision was made to build a series of fortifications capable of lodging 200 000 people. The northern part is in Slovakia at the junction of the Danube and the Vág. Komárom has three forts on its territory: to the east beside the Danube, Csillag-erőd (Star Fort), to the south of the city, Igmándi-erőd (Igmándi Fort) and to the west Monostori-erőd (Monostori Fort). Csillag-erőd is used as a storage facility and Igmándi houses the city museum artworks (mainly copies of Roman statues).

J.-Ch. Gérard/MICHELIN

View of the fortress

★★ MONOSTORI-ERŐD ⓥ

The building of this immense **fortress**, classified as a historical monument, lasted 21 years. Built on a 58ha/139acre site it is composed of a single building of 34 000m²/366 000sq ft with 640 rooms and units split into 14 parts. Some 2 000 masons and over 10 000 workers participated in its construction.

During the Second World War, the Germans put Jewish prisoners here prior to their deportation. The Soviets used it as a munitions depot. As many as 14 000 tip trucks are said to have been loaded here when they left Hungary in the 1990s. Some even say that rockets and nuclear warheads were stored here.

A great name in operetta

Franz (Ferenc) Lehár, one of the great names in Viennese operetta, was born in Komáron in 1870. At this time Vienna and the Imperial court waltzed to the music of Johann Strauss, father and son. Operetta, inspired by the waltz, lived its golden age with *Der Fledermaus* and *The Gypsy Baron (Der Zigeunerbaron)* by Johann Strauss (the son). Franz Lehár, originally a violinist, then a conductor of military orchestras, continued the tradition and was hugely successful with *The Merry Widow*, played for the first time in 1905. He then composed *The Count of Luxemburg* (1909) followed by *Land of Smiles* (1929), also great successes. In his works Lehár was innovative and introduced touches of the folk music of the country in which the operetta was set.

The fortress, sunk into the sand along the Danube, is practically invisible from the outside. The visit, provided the appropriate time is taken, can be impressive and is reminiscent of descriptions in Dino Buzzati's novel, *The Desert of the Tartars.* It really takes at least 3hr to visit the site and imagine the lives of the occupants, from the simple soldier to the commanding officer.

The work of the bricklayers, said to have come from Italy, can also be admired. Spiral vaults, cellar vaults, enormous mushroom posts – all the possible variations made from that little rectangular block of baked clay known as a brick have been used here.

Monostori Fortress has been open to the public for a few years now, and is a probable candidate for the Unesco World Heritage List. There are also plans to turn it into an international military museum as well as an information centre and a venue for discussion in the service of peace.

The place makes for an extraordinary visit that is worth the trip. However, to fully appreciate the tour, visitors who do not speak Hungarian should either come with a guide speaking their language or an interpreter.

A place to stay, a place to eat

Tulipán – *Kelemen L. u. 1. ☎ 34/342 604. Rooms at around €29.* Small hotel that can be recognised by its unusual pink façade. Simple, modern rooms. Fitness centre and solarium.

Karát – *Czuczor Gergely u. 54. ☎ 34/342 222, Fax 34/344 500. Rooms at around €49.* A quiet hotel with pleasant rooms.

Kocsis – *Táncsics M. u. 79. ☎ 34/342 400.* This restaurant is universally appreciated in the town.

KŐSZEG★★

Vas province – Population 13 500

Michelin map 925 D 2

Kőszeg, sometimes called the jewel box, is about 3km/2mi from the Austrian border. You will not find gold or glittering gems here, but a healthy, lively, unpretentious town. As a mark of its simplicity, in the streets you will come across little bags of fruit and tomatoes set atop a crate, a stool or a small table, with a sign indicating the price. Just leave your money in the box and help yourself. Trust reigns.

The town is very attached to its past as well as to its present. This is illustrated by one of the jewels of the town, a simple sketchbook called the *Growth of the Vine Book*. Every year since 1740, on St George's Day (23 April), the eve of St Faith's, a clever artist has made a very realistic drawing of the largest shoots of the Kőszeg grapevines. Seven to eight colour-wash drawings have been added year after year for over two and a half centuries, a brilliant addition to the history of wine-growing.

A memorable "victory" over the Turks – In 1532 the Turks, heading for Vienna, stopped in front of the castle, which was under the command of Miklós Jurisics, a courageous captain with, according to legend, only 50 men. The Turks greatly outnumbered them (some say there were 60 000, others say 100 000). Kőszeg held out for 25 days, before Captain Jurisics made an agreement with the heads of the Ottoman army. He was to raise a Turkish flag over the castle to symbolise their victory, while, in exchange, the Ottoman soldiers would break camp. Thus the Turks abandoned their march on Vienna. Ever since, Kőszeg's bells have chimed every day at 11am, in memory of this "victory".

SIGHTS

The entrance into the heart of the old town is through a vaulted passageway built into a tower, the **Heroes' Gate** (Hősi Kapu), constructed in 1932 to mark the 400th anniversary of the victory over the Turks.

MAGYAR KÉPEK Kft

Jurisics tér

★★ **Jurisics tér** – Several buildings of different styles line this square, making an interesting architectural group.

★ **Szent Jakab templom – St James' Church** was built in the early 15C. A few frescoes from that time show an immense St Christopher carrying Christ, Mary and the Wise Men. The carved-wood benches and altars are worthy of note.

★ **Szent Imre templom – St Imre's Church** is Baroque in style. There is a Dorffmeister fresco inside as well as a Maulbertsch altarpiece representing Mary visiting Elizabeth.

★ **Tábornokház** (**General's House**) – *N°s 4 to 6.* Of medieval origin, this building has a 17C twin-arched loggia. An interesting **crafts museum** can be visited, where several crafts are explained (saddler, watchmaker, photographer) guided by Marcus Aurelius' motto, *"Love your craft and enjoy practising it".*
After the visit, you can climb to the top of the tower for a **view** over the town.

Sgraffitós-ház (Graffiti House) – *N° 7.* There is a pleasant tearoom called **Garabonciás** (The Sorcerer's Shop) on the ground floor of this house with its unusual façade.

Patikamúzeum – *N° 11.* Jars, tubes and instruments are exhibited in this old pharmacy, turned into a museum. You can see medicinal plants being dried upstairs.

Take Chernel utca.

Jurisics-vár – Entrance to the **castle** is by a little bridge crossing over the old dried-up moats. In summer the courtyard is the stage for live performances: plays, concerts etc.
The **Knights' Hall** is used as a theatre and concert hall, and as a ballroom in winter. Temporary exhibitions are also held here starting in springtime. Climb up one of the towers for a **view** over the town.

A place to stay, a place to eat

Aranystrucc – *Várkör 124. ☎ 06/94/360 323. 18 rooms at €30.* The rooms have a certain charm. The sound of bells could be annoying. Restaurant.

Szarvas – *Rákóczi u. 12.* Good food and pleasant service.

Kulacs – *Várkör 12.* Honest local fare. Choose a table in the courtyard in summer. The place is delightfully cool with splendid geraniums.

Jurisics Múzeum ⌚ – This is devoted to the history of the town.

Room 1 – Here the castle's history is presented, notably with models and maps illustrating the building's structural development. Pottery and weapons in the museum showcases.

Room 2 – Town history. Beautiful semicircular desk.

Room 3 – Wine-growing history. Every year since 1740, on 23 April, drawings are added to the extraordinary sketchbook illustrating the growth of vine shoots. It fell to the mayor to cut the shoots of vine to be drawn.

Room 4 – Room devoted to schools and the Concordia choir.

Room 5 – Bourgeois family furniture. Note the wardrobe and a sacristy piece in marquetry.

Room 6 – Pipe chest and a copy of a faience stove dating from the Maria Theresa period.

Room 7 – Faience and jewels, with a pretty little Herend porcelain rabbit.

Room 8 – Contemporary history, with a special focus on Scout camps.

Room 9 – History of the castle's archaeological digs; a 1730 Lutheran Bible in a showcase.

Kálvária-hegy – *West of the town along Hunyadi János utca.* View of the town from Calvary Hill.

Csónakázó-tó – *North of the town along Sziget utca.* A **lake** for boating, and a pleasant picnic spot.

MAJKPUSZTA REMETESÉG★★

MAJKPUSZTA hermitage – Komárom-Esztergom province

Michelin map 925 D 6

Access – Although it is not always indicated on maps, Majkpuszta is well signposted and is located between Oroszlány and Vértessomló.

Leaving from Csákvár, head towards Vértessomló and turn off left to drive alongside a small lake. A very good restaurant overlooks it and welcomes both hermitage visitors and families who come here to relax with their children or fish on the lakeside.

From here a passable road through the forest leads to the Camaldolese hermitage.

TOUR ⏱

An oratory to the Virgin Mary existed at Majk as early as the 13C. The lands and forest came into the possession of the Esterházy family through the wife of Prince Miklós (the prince who built Fertőd Castle).

The founding of the hermitage was signed in 1733 at Tata Castle. The donation included part of the forest, and hunting and fishing rights. The hermitage that can be visited today was designed by an architect named Franz Arton Pilgram. There are a few frescoes painted by Maulbertsch.

The Order's rule imposed silence on the monks. They could only speak two or three times a year. Each monk had a cottage, or cell, its modest comfort financed by the family whose arms were carved over the door. This door looked out onto a small garden where the monk grew flowers and herbs. The cottage would be entered from the garden, and consisted of four spaces: an ornamented oratory chapel, a study and workshop where the monk could classify and dry herbs, sleeping quarters and, finally, a corner to eat and store food. The monk lived according to the rule in this enclosed space. Most monks devoted part of their time to studying the medicinal characteristics of plants.

The property was bought back by the Esterházy family, who used it as a hunting lodge until 1945.

In 1980 the restoration of the property was begun. The hermitage is really worth the trip, especially for those who enjoy peace and quiet. Some cottages have facilities to accommodate guests and even for seminars or conferences.

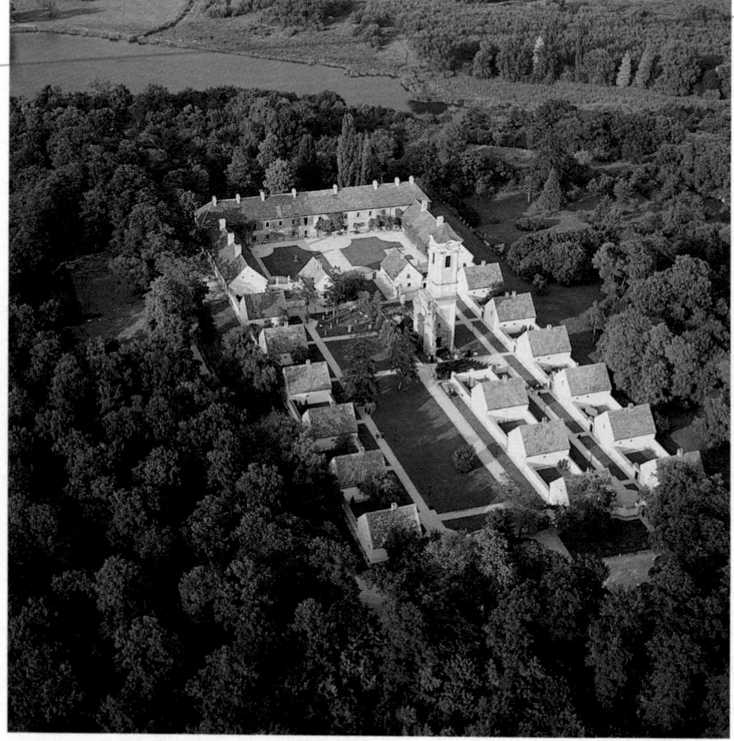

Majkpuszta Hermitage

The Camaldolese Order

The Camaldolese Order was founded in Italy in the 11C, by the hermit St Romuald. Born in Ravenna in 952, Romuald was abbot of the monastery of St Apollinare-in-Classe in AD 998 before founding a hermitage at Camaldoli in the Arezzo province. Romuald imposed a severe rule on the contemplative order, based on the rule of St Benedict, combining the life of a hermit with community life.
The Order's seat has remained at Camaldoli with the monks of the congregation living either in monasteries or in hermitages, depending on the lifestyle they have chosen.

A part of the main body of the hermitage still awaits restoration. There are several interesting frescoes of hunting scenes in the rooms open to the public.
The only part of the chapel that remains is the bell tower, also open to the public. From its heights visitors can look out over the treetops to admire the surrounding landscape.
Summer concerts take place in this marvellous, peaceful setting.

MARTONVÁSÁR★

Székesfehérvár province – Population 4 500

Michelin map 925 E 7

Count **Antal Brunszvik** built the family residence in Martonvásár in 1785; in 1870 it was made into the small neo-Gothic castle you see today.

The memory of Ludwig van Beethoven – The great composer stayed here often. The cultured Brunszvik family was open-minded and quite progressive. One of the count's children, Ferenc, became a close friend of Beethoven to the point of being among the rare few who could speak with him using the familiar form of speech. It is said that Beethoven was taken with Ferenc's sister Jozefin, and composed the *Moonlight* and the *Appassionata* sonatas for her.
Friends of Ferenc asked Jozefin to intervene on their behalf and this is how Beethoven came to write *St Stephen the King* and *The Ruins of Athens* for the opening of the German theatre in Budapest.
Theresa, another of Ferenc Brunszvik's sisters met the famous Swiss teacher Pestalozzi, and became interested in his work. She founded Budapest's first kindergarten. A statue was erected in her memory and the National Primary Teacher Training School bears her name. She also exchanged correspondence with the sociologist and reformer Robert Owen.
Today the castle is home to the Institute of Biological Research for Agriculture. Two rooms, called the **Beethoven Emlekmúzeum** ⌚, have been set aside to illustrate the great composer's stays here. A pleasant stop.

The park – The concerts given each summer on Lake Island, which is part of the park, are worth attending, although occasionally a train whistle may join in with the woodwind instruments unannounced.

MÁTRA★★

Heves province

Michelin map 925 C 9 and 10 – Local map see BÜKK

The Mátra massif ranks with the Balaton area as one of Hungary's prime sightseeing regions: spa treatment, tourism and hunting are the region's main activities.

HILLS OR MOUNTAINS?

The great Hungarian thermal fault, stretching from the northern shores of Lake Balaton to Budapest, reaches as far as the southern slopes of the Mátra Mountains. It runs along a series of massifs, which, in the north, form Hungary's backbone. To the east of the Danube, this backbone takes on mountainous proportions and forms Upper Hungary.
From the Börzsöny massif to the Bükk Mountains, passing through the Mátra Mountains, the chain rarely exceeds an altitude of 1 000m/3 280ft. Mt Kékestető (1 014m/3 326ft high), in the heart of the Mátra Mountains, is Hungary's highest peak. Upper Hungary is composed of massifs of either sedimentary or volcanic formations. The Mátra Mountains belong to the volcanic category.
A road runs through the middle of the massif from Parád and Galyatető to Gyöngyös, and makes for an easy journey. The Mátra Mountains are covered with magnificent beech groves.

STAYING IN THE MÁTRA

Before leaving

Before starting out it is advisable to get a map from:

Tourinform – *3200 Gyöngyös, Fő tér,* ☎ *37/311.155.* Gyöngyös Tourist Office.

Avar Hotel – Túraszervező Iroda (Tourism Agency), *3200 Gyöngyös, Városkert út 22,* ☎ *20/410 102.* This office organises trips by bicycle or on foot.

A place to stay

At Mátrafüred

Hunguest Hotel Hegyalja – *Béke u. 7.* ☎ *37/320 027. 79 rooms at around €33.* An old hotel dating from the 1930s, where workers used to stay during their holidays.

At Kékestető

Hegycsúcs – ☎ *and fax 36/367 086. 17 rooms between €20 and €53.* A night in the highest place in Hungary is quite a high point on the itinerary. This unusual hotel is the old radio relay tower. The view is exceptional.

At Galyatető

Nagyszálló – *Kodály Z. u. 10.* ☎ *37/376 011, Fax 37/376 015. 111 rooms between €30 and €35.* Old-fashioned charm. All the rooms have a balcony opening onto the countryside and the mountains. Pool. Peace and quiet guaranteed.

At Mátraszentistván

Jäger – *Virág u. 3.* ☎ *37/376 424, Fax 37/376 577. 24 rooms at around €31 half-board.* A charming chalet hidden in the pines.

A place to eat

At Mátrafüred

Benevár – *Parádi u. 10.* Pleasant and friendly.

Fekete Rigó – Pleasant welcome and local cuisine. *Fekete rigó* means blackbird.

At Mátraháza

Borostyán Vendéglő – *On road n° 24, which runs through the village.* ☎ *37/374 090.* A large tourist inn with a welcoming terrace and decor.

Mátraházai Honvédüdülő – ☎ *37/374 036. 59 rooms between €35 and €48.* On the road to Parád, a castle is the setting for this restaurant offering copious Hungarian dishes. The dining room, with traditional decor and wood beams, is very spacious. Ideal for lunch, and also for spending the night.

DISCOVERING THE MÁTRA

At 80km/50mi from Budapest, the Mátra can easily be reached by the motorway, bus or train.

The massif has good facilities for tourists and enables visitors to come into contact with unspoilt nature.

Round trip from Gyöngyös – 80km/50mi – about 4hr.

Gyöngyös – *See this name.*

Take road n° 24 in a northbound direction.

★ **Mátrafüred** – *Altitude 340m/1 115ft.* This holiday and health resort attracts large numbers of people from Budapest in winter, as well as Germans and Austrians. It is the departure point for excursions and walks in the forest. There is a wide choice of different, well-marked walks and ski trails, of varied lengths.

Mátraháza – Mátraháza is higher than Mátrafüred, and, at an altitude of 740m/2 430ft really resembles a health and winter sports resort, with good hotel, guesthouse and restaurant facilities. There are a large number of trails for walking and skiing. Provided they take the usual precautions, enthusiasts will also be able to satisfy their liking for mushroom picking. Ski lifts and alpine ski slopes open with the first snowfalls.

★★ **Kékestető** – Hungary's highest peak at an altitude of 1 014m/3 326ft is marked by a rock painted in the Hungarian national colours.

Two ski slopes snake downwards from the summit, one towards Mátraháza which ends near the Pagoda Hotel and the other to the north which is said to be faster and more difficult.

Go up to the top of the television tower platform to take full advantage of the **panorama** over the region. The view stretches as far as the Great Plain in the south and, in fine weather, to the Tatras in the north.

Continue in a northerly direction and turn left 3km/1.9mi further on.

Galyatető – Another resort ideal for excursions and skiing. You will see a few *büfé* (snack-type restaurants) and a strange construction, the **Nagyszálló★** (Grand Hotel) which has a swimming pool. The Grand Hotel, made of stone, is a sight in itself. A luxury residence before the Second World War, the Grand Hotel was reserved for union officials and for foreign comrades under the Communist regime.

Numerous pathways for excursions and walks leave from Galyatető.

The trip continues beyond Galyatető and follows a picturesque forest road that runs close to the village of Mátraszentistván.

J.-C. Saturnin/MICHELIN

Hungary's highest point

Mátraszentimre – This highly popular winter sports resort, located at an altitude of 810m/2 657ft, has accommodation available in private homes and in a few hotels or guesthouses. In the summer, this modest resort is a base for hikers setting off into the surrounding area.

Continue towards Hasznos then Pásztó. In the village turn southwards and, at Szurdokpüspöki, take road n° 2406 towards Gyöngyös.

Gyöngyöspata – A visit to the village church is a must. A unique piece of Hungarian art, the **Tree of Jesse★★** (Jessze fája) is located behind the altar. This exceptional sculpture dates from the mid-17C. Jesse is represented lying down. Two branches of a tree rising from his body encircle a picture illustrating the birth of the Virgin Mary and support 18C busts representing Mary's ancestors. A tree-trunk with the Crucifixion has two guardian angels on either side.

PARÁD AND THE NORTH OF THE MÁTRA

See Parád.

MISKOLC

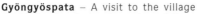

Borsod-Abaúj-Zemplén province – Population 182 000

Michelin map 925 B 11 and 12 – Local map see BÜKK

Numerous abandoned or under-exploited industrial sites explain why Miskolc is beginning to attract foreign investment. Indeed the region, once known as the Hungarian Ruhr, has a wealth of natural resources, gypsum, limestone and silica. Miskolc is also a major university town, much appreciated in the domains of research and development.

A town founded as a consequence of the Treaty of Trianon – Miskolc did not exist at the time of the Austro-Hungarian Empire. There used to be five villages on the area now covered by the town in the Sajó Valley. The Treaty of Trianon gave Czechoslovakia the industrial sites and railways. The Hungarian authorities, therefore, developed an industrial area in this sector between the two World Wars, which the Communist period expanded further. The town of Miskolc is now described as a town on the decline. It is true to say that when you enter this urban area, the long avenues lined with dismal blocks of flats are somewhat depressing. Nevertheless, there are a few sights worth seeing and, as the town is at the foot of the Bükk massif, excursions are possible and there are places to stay.

THE TOWN CENTRE

Leave from Városháza tér.

Városháza tér – A small tree-lined square, cool in the summer. On the corner of Hunyadi utca are two old buildings, the **town hall** (Városháza) and, a few metres further on, the **administrative headquarters** (Megyeháza) of the province.

A place to stay

Talizmán – *Vár u. 14. ☎ 46/378 627. Rooms between €20 and €24. 50m/55yd from the castle ruins.* Quiet rooms. Traditional restaurant.

Székelykert – *Földes F. u. 4. ☎ 46/411 222. Rooms at €30.* In a little alleyway, *panzió*-restaurant with simple, clean rooms.

Pannonia – *Kossuth u. 2. ☎ 46/329 811. 34 rooms at around €80.* The only high-class hotel in the town centre. Pastry shop and restaurant.

A place to eat

Krupla József – *Erdő sor 15.* One of the oldest restaurants in town. Several rooms: one upstairs with medieval decor (lances, iron chandeliers and a central fireplace) and downstairs, long cellars that are more rustic with wooden tables and benches. A delightful place!

Vigadó – *Görgey Artúr u. 23.* Large restaurant near the beautiful merry-go-round dating from 1888. In summer, large terrace overlooking Népkert park. Hungarian cuisine. Folk music almost every evening.

Széchenyi István utca – This can be considered the main street. Reserved for pedestrians and the tramways, it is particularly lively during the daytime, due to the shops and cafés.

Erzsébet tér – This square is surrounded by buildings, one of which is the typical domed baths establishment. In the centre is the first statue of Lajos Kossuth, erected in Hungary four years after his death. On the same side, a little further on is the **Sötétkapu** (Dark Gate), a covered way which leads to Rákóczi utca. At n° 2 on this street, is the house known as Rákóczi's house *(see Sárospatak)*. This was his headquarters during the fight for independence. The Habsburgs took their revenge by burning the town in 1706.

All along Széchenyi István utca you will see a succession of private residences in various styles. On the corner of Déryné utca stands the **National Theatre** (Nemzeti Színház) which was built to replace the first Hungarian-language theatre, built in 1823 and destroyed by fire. The present building was constructed between 1847 and 1850.

Take Kossuth Lajos utca on the left, leading to Deák tér.

Magyar ortodox templom (Hungarian Orthodox Church) – This church was built between 1785 and 1787 by Greek immigrants who had fled from the Turks. It is in the late-Baroque style. The principal feature is the 16C **iconostasis★★★**, 16m/52ft high, which is comprised of about 100 icons, and includes Kazan's ***Black Virgin***. This painting was a gift from Catherine II of Russia when she visited Miskolc on her way to Vienna. Visitors should also see the Mt Athos Crucifix (1590) brought by Greek immigrants.

Return towards the centre and after Deák Ferenc tér, turn left along Horváth Lajos utca. You will come to Hősök tere where two Baroque style buildings are located, the **Minorite Church** (Minorita templom), and the old presbytery, now a student hostel, on the left as you face the entrance to the church.
To the south of Széchenyi utca via Erzsébet tér, take Kálvin J. utca on the left. The Ottó Herman Museum is located at n° 1 on the corner of this street and Papszer utca.

★ **Herman Ottó Múzeum** – This museum is worth a visit for its collection of prehistoric objects, principally discovered in the region, its collection of stones and minerals, presented tastefully and with intelligence, and a collection of paintings and folk art.

Avas-hegy – Avas Hill can be distinguished by its **television tower** (Kilátó). Nearly 800 wine cellars have reputedly been dug out of the hill, between 50-100m/55- and 105ft in length. Some are over 500 years old.
Avasi reformatus templom, the Reformed church, was originally a Gothic church. Burned down by the Turks in the middle of the 13C, it was rebuilt in 1560. It has a painted wood interior and seats decorated with Rococo floral designs. A separate bell tower, dating from 1557, has a Renaissance gallery.

THE SURROUNDING AREAS

★★ **Diósgyőri Vár** – The castle was built for Louis the Great in the second half of the 14C. Imagine what it was like when it was built in the middle of the woods in a forest landscape; it was called the **Queens' Castle** at that time. It was a holiday residence much appreciated for the surrounding area, well stocked with game. Louis the Great of Anjou used it for diplomatic negotiations. During the War of Independence under Ferenc Rákóczi it changed hands several times, was later abandoned and gradually fell into ruin. It was restored between 1950 and 1960. Built in a square, it is flanked by a square tower on either side. In the summer, in the centre of what now forms a courtyard, numerous shows are put on. Visitors can climb to the top of one of the towers for a view of the town. The castle museum is located in one of the lower parts of another tower.

At the foot of the castle, there is a small museum to the memory of an opera singer who died in Miskolc in 1872. This was Róza Széppataki, known by the name of Déryné, Mrs Déry, an extremely popular actress and singer. **Déryné-ház** (Mrs Déry's House), with furniture and objects of the time or which belonged to her, makes a pleasant visit.

Lillafüred – There is a small train from Miskolc to Lillafüred, which crosses the west of the town and zigzags through the forest almost touching the trees. You leave from Kilián-észak station in Miskolc at Dorottya utca 1. Trains from here head for two destinations, one of which is Lillafüred. You will see people making charcoal in the forest and, in the season, you can pick mushrooms.

Lillafüred is located where two valleys, the Szinva and the Garadna, meet. It gets its name from the first name of the wife of a Minister of Agriculture, András Bethlen, who enjoyed excursions in the area. The lady's name was Lilla Vay and this place was named **Lilla's Baths** at the end of the 19C.

Hotel Palota and the surrounding area - Hotel Palota is a strange place, with a special atmosphere perhaps arising from the memories it holds. The history of this hotel is worth relating. Its slightly disturbing appearance alone arouses curiosity and makes you wonder about it. Could it be Sleeping Beauty's Castle? Or rather, Dracula's? It was built between 1927 and 1930. After the Treaty of Trianon (1920), Hungary, and this northern region in particular, lost much of its territory. The major city in the area used to be Kassa (now Košice in Slovakia). Miskolc, which took over Kassa's industrial activity, started to expand. Alongside this rather uninspiring activity, it was felt that a reminder of the splendour of days gone by, the legacies of Matthias Corvinus and Louis the Great, needed to be introduced. It was decided, therefore, to build a luxury residential hotel on this site. The project was an important one for the Horthy period, between the two wars. All Hungary's great past is recounted in the pictures and stained-glass windows where the country's famous can be recognised. The Communist regime took over the hotel, including these nationalist images, some of which were replaced, and made it into an establishment for union members.

Hotel Palota is now open to all and it is well worth coming here for a drink, a meal or to stay.

PICTOR

Lillafüred – Palota szálló (Palace Hotel)

A place to stay, a place to eat

Palota – *Erzsébet sétány 1.* ☎ *46/331 411. 133 rooms between €66 and €87.* One of the most beautiful hotels in Hungary, in a neo-Baroque mansion. The rooms are sumptuous! Pool, fitness centre, bowling alley and billiards.

Matthias – Within the walls of the Palota Hotel, a unique restaurant with Gothic-church decor complete with vaulting and stained-glass windows. It is worth a visit for the setting alone but it is even better if you have a meal! Hungarian and international specialities.

Located at the far end of **Hámori-tó** (Hámor Lake), the hotel also makes a good centre for the numerous walking possibilities in the area. In the close vicinity of the hotel are some **caves**: Anna-barlang, István-barlang and Szeleta-barlang. The **István cave** is a few hundred metres from the hotel and is considered to be the most beautiful. From the hotel, visitors can go for a walk along Hámori-tó, on the right shore. After 7-8km/4.5-5mi, you will come to a foundry that was at the origin of the Miskolc iron and steel industry. An iron merchant from Eger, Henrik Fazola, built a foundry that produced the cast iron that was transformed in the Hámor workshop. This first furnace was built in 1770 and was enlarged by the founder's grandson between 1810 and 1813. Lastly, a small museum was inaugurated in 1952, next to the old foundry.

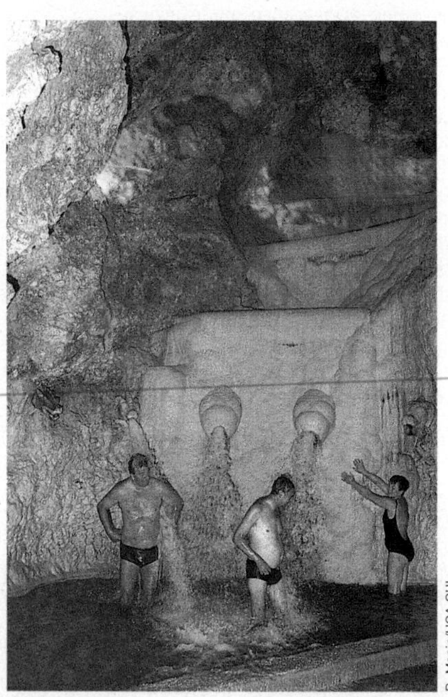
R. Manin/HOA QUI

♨♨**Miskolctapolca** – The waters of this holiday resort and spa are renowned for their therapeutic properties. Located at the south-eastern extremity of the town, the baths have been used since the Middle Ages. The springs rise from a depth of 900m/2 952ft and the slightly sparkling water spurts out in a cloud of bubbles at a temperature of around 30°C/86°F. It is used to treat disorders of the neurovegetative system, cardiac neuralgia, stomach and intestinal complaints of a nervous origin, and physical and mental exhaustion. The baths have a particularly interesting feature, fairly unusual in Europe, the **Termál-barlangfürdő** (spa bath caves). A swimming pool has been made in a cave, hewn out by the water, which can be accessed from the spa pavilion. The extremely humid air in the cave is beneficial for the treatment of respiratory complaints and, more specifically, for treating asthma and bronchitis. The outside pool is very popular in fine weather.

MOHÁCS

Baranya province – Population 22 500

Michelin map 925 I 7

There is nothing particularly exciting about this little town on the Danube except for the **Mohácsi busójárás★★**, the annual carnival held in February *(see Calendar of Events at the beginning of this guide)*.

The great Battle of Mohács, which the Hungarians lost in 1526, almost five centuries ago, still seems to cast a shadow over the town. On 29 August of that year, Mohács took its place in history.

T. Hortobagyi/MAGYAR KÉPEK Kft

A NATIONAL TRAGEDY

Mohács, the scene of Hungary's demise... At the beginning of the 16C the world was undergoing dramatic change and Hungary had its own pain and troubles. The 1514 Peasant's Revolt was particularly violent and was severely repressed: **János Szapolyai** (John of Zápolya), Transylvania's *Voïvode* or governor, had leader **György Dózsa** put to death by forcing him to sit on a red-hot iron throne and wear a burning iron crown. His companions were made to eat his flesh. The uprising of the miners who had not been paid was equally significant. The country, poorly governed, was prey to battles between overlords and no longer had the resources to prepare its defence against the Turks. In 1526 the young Hungarian king Louis (Lajos) II Jagiello, then 20 years old, barely managed to assemble an army of 25 000 men to oppose the Turkish invader, the army of Sultan Suleiman I (the Magnificent or the Great). He counted on János Szapolyai's reinforcements, about 12 000 men. With no knowledge of military tactics, he was led into a direct conflict with Suleiman's forces, who were better armed and four times as numerous. The battle took place on the plains near Mohács, on 29 August 1526, where Louis II's army was cut to pieces and destroyed in record time. There is still discussion as to whether János Szapolyai deliberately arrived too late to ensure the young king's fall, in order to take the throne himself.

It was a crushing defeat and the losses were immense. Over 10 000 soldiers perished. The archbishops of Esztergom and Kalocsa, five other bishops, and a great number of landed lords, nobles and aristocrats also lost their lives. The king himself drowned as he tried to cross a swollen river in his flight. Another version says that he was murdered by his own lords. His widow escaped from Hungary, taking with her everything that she could save from her husband's treasure. Hungary was divided into three, and the Turks occupied the central part, which included Buda, for one and a half centuries.

On 11 November 1526 János Szapolyai was made king, under the name of János I, preceding Ferdinand I, the first Habsburg king.

SIGHTS

Kanizsai Dorottya Múzeum – This museum is housed in two different buildings. The first *(Szerb utca 2)* is devoted to the Battle of Mohács, while the second *(Városház utca 1)* is a Folk Art Museum.

Battle site – *8km/5mi south. Take road n° 56 for 6km/3.6mi and turn right.*

The **Mohácsi Történelmi Emlékhely** ⓥ, a memorial to the Battle of Mohács, was created in **Sátorhely** in 1976, on the site of a mass grave discovered in 1960. Visitors can walk across this large area of lawn, with its strange carved wooden posts, and read the inscription on an immense piece of wrought ironwork: *Here began the decline of a powerful Hungary.* There is also an exhibition with a description of the battle in Hungarian, from both the Hungarian and Turkish viewpoints.

NAGYCENK

Győr-Moson-Sopron-Sopron province – Population 1 700

Michelin map 925 D 2 – 15km/9mi south-east of Sopron

A beautiful castle, a charming little train, horses, an interesting museum, a good restaurant, a castle-hotel and above all an appointment with the man called the Greatest Hungarian, István Széchenyi.

THE GREATEST HUNGARIAN

Count **István Széchenyi** (1791-1860) was given this name because he put all his energy and part of his fortune into serving his country, launching its economic growth and placing it among the world's developed nations. It becomes evident that the title is well deserved when something is known of his life and life's work. His father created the National Museum and the National Library, and he was a worthy heir. He launched the Hungarian nobility's liberal movement at the start of the century, and, as a soldier, took part from 1809 in the wars against Napoleon. In 1826 he was an officer in the army of the Emperor of Austria and a Habsburg partisan.

Horse-breeder – Among his greatest passions was horse-breeding. As early as 1822 he organised horse races because he thought this would promote horse-breeding, and so in 1825 he founded an association. In 1828 he published *About Horses*.

Politician and patron – At the same time, he participated in the activities of the National Assembly from 1825 to 1827, where he gave a year of his income to set up an association of scientists, of which he became president. He financed this work, which later became the institution of the Academy of Sciences, and he constructed the building that is still its home in Budapest, at the foot of Chain Bridge on the Pest side. At Pozsony (formerly Presbourg and now known as Bratislava, the capital of Slovakia) he founded the Casino, the predecessor of the National Casino of Hungary.

Szelényi/MAGYAR KÉPEK Kft

István Széchenyi

Engineer – Part of Hungary, between the Danube and the Tisza, was a flood area, entirely subject to the whims of the two rivers. At the same time, the Danube, a splendid transport waterway, was not yet being used to its full potential. And so István Széchenyi launched two important projects: the control of the flow of the rivers and protection of the flood areas. He also devoted himself to other means of transport, improving the roads, which he began to have surfaced with macadam, a technique brought back from his trips to England. He also created the first railway line, and it is perhaps the spirit of Széchenyi that was behind the first underground train line to be built on the European Continent, which still functions in Budapest.

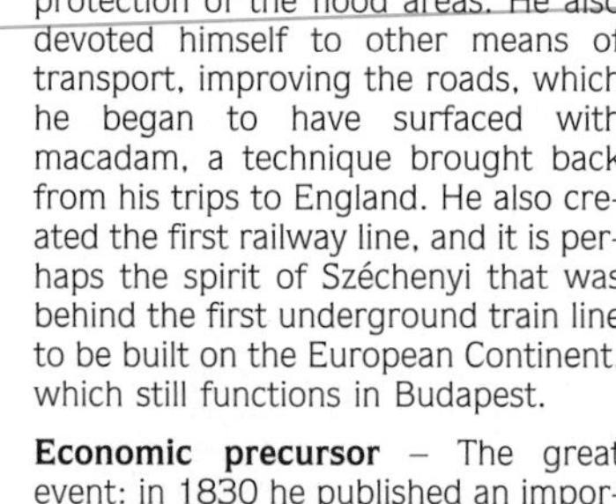

Economic precursor – The great event: in 1830 he published an important economic book, *Hitel (Credit)*, which was crucial to Hungary's future. In this book, he denounced feudal law on inheritance and presented the advantages of the credit system for development and investment. What he was proposing, in fact, was the organisation of the modern banking system. To respond to criticism, he published *Világ (The World)* in 1831 and *Stádium* in 1833.

A man of business and of action – Starting in 1830 he created several companies: the Steam Navigation Company on the Danube in 1831, the Pest Cylinder Mills in 1837 and the Commercial Bank of Hungary in 1841. He directed the work to control the flow of the Danube and the Iron Door dam from 1833, the construction work for the Chain Bridge between Buda and Pest from 1836, and the National Theatre and the tunnel through Castle Hill in Budapest.

A man of sentiment – This man battled throughout his life against conservative and narrow-minded people who were unable to grasp and understand his visions for Hungary's future. He spent every ounce of his strength and energy; yet unfortunately in affairs of the heart he had neither peace nor rest. Very early on he fell in love with his brother's wife, an Englishwoman whom he could not marry until after the death of her husband. This union, so long awaited, sadly did not live up to his expectations.

Smuggler? – In the course of his many travels, he came to understand the extent to which Hungary lagged behind other countries in all domains. One day he risked a conviction or at least a very serious diplomatic incident by smuggling out a protected gas appliance, after bribing a customs officer, an act that was liable to the death penalty.

A revolutionary and victim of persecution – A former Habsburg partisan, long opposed to Lajos Kossuth, he joined forces with him in 1848 after reluctantly laying his reservations aside, and became part of the revolutionary government. In this new government led by Count Lajos Batthyány as Prime Minister, he was Minister of Public Works and Transport, and Lajos Kossuth, Minister of Finance. The worrying situation greatly upset him, the fear of armed conflict overwhelmed him, and he retired to a psychiatric asylum in Döbling where he remained until the end of his life. Towards the end of the 1850s he wrote a satirical work on the Habsburg occupation's authoritarian and repressive system, which was published anonymously in London in 1859. After this publication he was threatened and persecuted, and finally committed suicide in 1860. Up to the very day of his funeral he was a worry to the Austrians. Brought from Döbling to Sopron, his coffin was then carried by a group of men for 15km/9mi from Sopron to Nagycenk. The Viennese police, fearing protests, ordered that the ceremony take place a day earlier than announced. Despite this measure, 6 000 people were present. The next day the crowd was even greater. Among the participants was a delegation from the Academy of Sciences, and in three days over 50 000 people came to honour the man that Lajos Kossuth, despite the differences that had set them in opposition, called "the greatest Hungarian".

A place to stay, a place to eat

Kastély Szálló– *Kiscenki út 3. ☎ and fax: 99/360 061. 19 rooms between €35 and €74.* Pleasant, quiet, with a very good restaurant. From April onwards, difficult to find a room at the weekend without prior reservation. Most of the regulars are Austrians. The courtyard and the former hothouse are marvellous settings for dinner. The rooms are comfortable, but slightly dark and characterless. Bicycle hire. Tennis possible, including an indoor court.

★★ SZÉCHENYI-KASTÉLY ⓥ

The village of Nagycenk owes its fame to the Széchenyi family who built the family **manor** here at the end of the 18C. It was extended in 1838, and István Széchenyi often came here to work in peace. This is where he was buried, and his **mausoleum** is continually visited by Hungarians and foreigners alike.

The manor was seriously damaged during the Second World War, but it has been rebuilt. Today it is the **Széchenyi Museum**, along with the Transport Museum, a stud farm, a restaurant and a hotel. Nearby you can see the church designed by Miklós Ybl, one of the great 19C Hungarian architects, and a little steam train will take you for a ride through the country.

★ **Széchenyi István Emlékmúzeum** ⓥ – If you know something about István Széchenyi, the visit to the museum will be more interesting. At the entrance, you can choose a cassette player and a cassette in your own language, which will tell you about the exhibits in each room, as the labels are only in Hungarian.

The home – This is the setting of a 19C family of Hungarian aristocrats. The ground floor rooms and the period furniture relate to the different periods in Széchenyi's life. A far cry from the splendid Esterházy Castle, here you will see the strict, reserved luxury of a family concerned about the future of the country, more preoccupied with action than appearances. István Széchenyi's father had already founded and participated materially in the National Library and National Museum and this work was continued by his son. In 1820 he took possession of the family property, very much decided, as he wrote at the time, "to give an example, and work for the happiness of the people and not only for profit". He wanted to make the place a model farm, and distributed part of the land to the serfs.

István's public and private works – Upstairs the museum presents and illustrates all the great projects undertaken, launched and directed by István Széchenyi. While visitors can understand the size and importance of these public works, it is difficult to conceive what they represented in social and economic terms. In this house which at the time already had gaslights, Széchenyi installed a modern bathroom as well as flush toilets.

The horse – The fact that the western part of the castle is now a stud farm open to visitors with possibilities for horse-riding bears witness to István Széchenyi's interest in horses. Open daily from 10am to 4pm, it offers coach rides and even driving horses in harness.

MAGYAR KÉPEK Kft

Nagycenk – Széchenyi Castle

ADDITIONAL SIGHTS

Múzeumvasút (Steam Train Museum) – This little open-air museum also bears witness to another of István Széchenyi's interests. Steam locomotives are exhibited here, including some that still function, pulling a few carriages for 3.5km/2.2mi to Fertőboz. Once there, there is a magnificent **view**★★ over Lake Fertő. Most of this stretch of water is on Austrian soil (Neusiedler See). You can even hire the little train if you wish to travel alone. The lake is classified as a national park in both countries. The Hungarian side to the south is part of Fertőtavi Nemzeti Park.

Szent István-templom (St Stephen's Church) – St Stephen's church in the middle of the village was designed by Miklós Ybl, and is worth a visit. It has fine proportions, and its simplicity and restraint contrast pleasantly with the extravagance of Baroque. It is considered an example of the Hungarian Romantic style.
A few metres further on, in the village cemetery, the Széchenyi **mausoleum** contains the remains of István, as well as other members of the family.

NYÍRBÁTOR

Szabolcs-Szatmár-Bereg province – Population 13 000

Michelin map 925 C 15 – 36km/22mi to the south-east of Nyíregyháza

This small town on the Nyírség plain was endowed with two churches by István Báthori, Prince of Transylvania, one in the late 15C and the other in the early 16C.
In the summer, in August, the **Nyirbátor Music Festival** is attended by Hungarians from all over the country.

★★ **Református templom** – This Gothic Calvinist church, located on a grassy mound, is easily recognisable by its wooden bell tower, quite separate from the building itself. The late-Gothic nave possesses a **vault** with finely drawn ribs which extend to form elegant columns. One side of this vault is lit by very high ogival windows with pointed arches. The carved pulpit, *prie-dieu* kneeling-desks, all perfectly aligned, and the background of white walls give the building as a whole an atmosphere of rigour, simplicity and serenity.
The church serves as a burial place for the Báthori family and István lies in the church in a Gothic tomb. Another monument marks the burial place of a translator of psalms.
At the side of the church stands the bell tower with four pinnacle turrets and a shingle roof, forming a contrast with the lightness and slim lines of the church. *Do not attempt to climb to the top.*

★★ **Harangláb (Former Minorite Church)** – The original building was also built on the initiative of István Báthori. Damaged several times, then laid waste by the Turks, the church was rebuilt in the 18C in the Baroque style. A particular feature of this church is the five altars and the pulpit, all richly carved, and commissioned from a local sculpture workshop. The sculptures express profound sincerity, with a great deal of simplicity and sometimes naïvety. To the left of the entrance to the church is the astonishing **altar** known as the Passion Altar or Krucsay Altar because it was erected at the request of János Krucsay in memory of his wife whom he had executed on his own orders.

T. Hortobagyi/MAGYAR KÉPEK Kft

Vaulted arch of the Reformed Church

Báthoryi István Múzeum – Located in the former monastery, the museum has a collection of fossilised animals from the Ice Age, discovered in a Bátorliget marsh, as well as exhibitions of local history.

EXCURSION

Máriapócs – *11km/7mi to the north-west along road n° 4911, then take a small road on the right.*

This town received a visit from Pope John-Paul II in 1991. It is an extremely popular place of pilgrimage. People come from far and wide to pray to the weeping Black Virgin, represented on an icon that can be viewed in the church. This icon is only a copy of the original, exhibited in St Stephen's Cathedral in Vienna. Since she has been in Vienna, not one tear has escaped her eyes. However, the eyes of the Virgin of Máriapócs are said to have shed a few tears. The iconostasis in the present-day church dates from the 19C.

NYÍREGYHÁZA

Szabolcs-Szatmár-Bereg province – Popualtion 113 000 inhabitants

Michelin map 925 B 13 – Local map see BÜKK

Nyíregyháza is in the centre of the **Nyírség** plain (land of the silver birch) which occupies the northern part of Hungary in a corner formed by the River Tisza. After crossing Romania and the town of Satu Mare, the river turns up along the province's eastern boundary, touches the frontier with Ukraine and, after a hairpin bend, flows back downwards towards the south-southeast and disperses into the pools and lakes of the Hortobágy region. The Nyírség plain was cleared in the 9C and 10C by the first people to arrive here, who cut down around 600ha/1 482 acres of forest for crops and livestock. In the 15C the region was the second most developed area in the country but it has now well and truly lost this position. The climate is cooler than on the Great Plain but has more sunshine, making the region ideal for market gardening and raising livestock. Sunflowers, fruit, potatoes and tobacco are all grown here. The Nyírség is one of Europe's largest apple-growing regions.

Its history – Already mentioned by this name in the early 13C, Nyíregyháza and much of the land hereabouts belonged to the Báthori family. In 1627, it became the property of István Bocskai. Bocskai, Prince of Transylvania who, with the assistance of the Turks, was the pretender to the throne, was supported by the military force of the Hajdúk. They settled in the region and strongly defended their freedom. Numerous quarrels between the various communities sprang up and the town of Nyíregyháza declined to the extent that there were only about 50 families at the end of the 17C. It only began to develop again in the late 19C.

A place to stay, a place to eat

Bencs Villa – *Sóstói u. 54. ☎ 42/402 004. Rooms between €35 and €60.* Charming villa dating from the late 19C, with a few rooms.

Tölgyes – *Sóstói u. 40. ☎ 42/410 590.* A bar-restaurant with a saloon decor on one of the town's main thoroughfares. Good for a quick lunch. International cuisine.

Nyíregyháza – View of the town centre

The town – This unpretentious town seems to be self-sufficient. A long circular ringroad runs around an airy, open centre with large avenues with trees and plants, squares and gardens, giving it the appearance of a large city. Although it does not have any extraordinary sights, Nyíregyháza is a good place to stay, close to Ukraine and Romania. The town centre is formed of several squares that are linked by shop-lined streets and buildings from various eras. Kossuth Lajos tér, Hősök tere, Szabadság tér, Jókai tér and Kálvin tér form a series of squares, which make for a pleasant trip through the town.

Jósa András Múzeum és Megyei Levéltár ⓥ – *Benczúr Gyula tér 21.* The Jósa András Museum houses a fine collection of paintings, including a large number of works by **Gyula Benczúr**, who was born in Nyíregyháza, and exhibits commemorating Gyula Krúdy, one of Hungary's greatest poets. As in most Hungarian museums, there are exhibits relating the history of the town and an old collection of objects from the era of the Magyar conquest.

SURROUNDING AREA

Sóstófürdő – *5km/3.1mi to the north. Leave Nyíregyháza along Kossuth Lajos utca then take Sóstói út.*

Originally there were two 14ha/34.5-acre lakes in Sóstófürdő which, by the 19C, had become a place for excursions and walking. Sóstófürdő has since become a residential area, spa and place for leisure activities. It has a wide avenue with abundant vegetation and is a pleasant place to relax in the summer heat. It is surrounded by 500 ha/1 235 acres of forest. Water gushes from the springs at a temperature of 50°C/122°F, supplying the thermal swimming pools with alkaline water, containing sodium, recommended for various body movement disorders. Six huge swimming pools are open to the public. Visitors can also go boating and hire bicycles.

The **museum-village★** (Skanzen) located in Tölgyfa utca, provides good illustrations of the old types of dwellings that can still be seen in country areas. A large number of ethnic groups immigrated to this region bringing their customs and traditions with them.

Hajdúság and the Hajdúk

The name Hajdúk is of Slav origin. It does not refer to an ethnic group as sometimes suggested, but to a community of a social, political or military origin. Some people believe that the Hajdúk descended from a body of cattle drovers, involved in livestock trading. In their midst were also highwaymen, fiercely attached to their freedom and formidable warriors. The only point which they conceded in exchange for this freedom was the support of their force. If they promised their assistance, those receiving it knew they had fearsome military support at their disposal. The Hajdúk had supported Dózsa. It was these warriors who helped István Bocskai to defeat the Habsburgs. In gratitude, Bocskai allowed them to settle on his land. This is why the names of the places occupied by the Hajdúk were preceded by the word *hajdú*. These towns became local communities with special privileges whose inhabitants had the benefit of a special status. The privileges of the Hajdúk were ended in 1876. Nowadays there are a large number of towns in the great Nyírség plain whose names start with Hajdú.

ÓPUSZTASZER★★

Csongrád province

Michelin map 925 G 10 – 32 km/20mi to the north of Szeged

The park is located in the south of Hungary between Szeged and Csongrád. It is marked with seven huge arrows driven into a mound, representing the original Magyar tribes. This composition, named "The Seven Hungarian Arrows" is by a Hungarian artist, László Morvay.

The Memorial itself is located at a site that was called "Szer" when, as history records, Árpád received the pledge of loyalty there from the seven chiefs of the tribes that founded Hungary. It commemorates the conquest of the Carpathian Basin by the Magyars: the episode was recorded by Anonymus, Béla III's anonymous chronicler, who wrote the *Gesta Hungarorum* (a 24-sheet document preserved in the National Library). This was also the place where, after the Second World War, Imre Nagy, the Minister of Agriculture at that time and a convinced communist just back from Moscow, attended the first symbolic ceremony of distribution of land to Hungarian peasants.

Vestiges – The park is on a mound, elevated a few metres above the Great Plain. In fact, wherever visitors look, they can see these hillocks of varying sizes that in places seem to be lifting the great flat expanse. These are the vestiges left by the region's inhabitants who, in the Bronze Age, used to burn the chiefs of the tribe when they died and bury them under mounds of earth with their possessions, horses etc. The number of mounds spread over the Great Plain is estimated to be three or four thousand. Many of them have disappeared, obliterated by the development of agriculture. It is an impressive place. The 55ha/136-acre Memorial park is only a part of the National Nature Conservation Park. It offers a complex area of archaeological, cultural, artistic and ethnographical riches, combining exhibitions with events and shows that have the *puszta* as background.

A famous panorama – In the 19C, in Europe, a number of panoramic paintings became famous. These consisted of a 360° image viewed by spectators seated in the centre. A Hungarian, Feszty Árpád was particularly taken with what he had seen in Paris and decided to make one in Budapest to illustrate the Bible. His father-in-law, the famous romantic writer, Mór Jókai, advised him to make one on the theme of the arrival of the Magyars, particularly as the Millenary anniversary was imminent.

The idea was accepted and Feszty Árpád ordered a canvas from Belgium measuring 120m/365ft by 15m/46ft high, which was stretched to a circumference 38m/115ft in diameter. The sketch was based on a specially selected part of the countryside, the Valóci Valley in the Carpathians, now in Ukraine. Two great Hungarian painters were among those who made this immense fresco: Lászlo Mednyánszky painted the landscapes and Pál Vágó, the equestrian scenes and figures. An anecdote relates that Feszty Árpád offered to be the model for Árpád.

A building was constructed in Budapest to create and house the work of art and enable people to admire it. After an exhibition in London, the Panorama returned to Hungary and was set up in Budapest's City Park, in a permanent building, made specially for the canvas. Second World War bombing damaged the Panorama. Wishing to save the picture, some well-intentioned but inexperienced people cut it into 8m/24ft strips which were then rolled up, badly stored, transported from one museum to another and damaged in all manner of ways for 30 years. To restore the canvas, of which 60% had been destroyed, a Polish team, hired after a competitive recruitment process, used 2 500litres/550gal of solvent, and 7t of sawdust. This much revered work has been on show again since 1995, and Hungarians have flocked to admire it.

TOUR ⏱ *2hr*

You should be aware that excursions to the park and Panorama are highly popular with Hungarians and they are particularly crowded at weekends.
Entrance to the Panorama is every 30min. Cafeteria.

On show in the **Rotunda**, a building shaped like a yoghurt pot, the **Panorama** is an impressive, magnificently executed sight. Without spectators realising, it combines a painted part with a realistic foreground, which gives the various scenes an astonishing sense of depth. It reveals the qualities of the great landscape artist, Mednyánszky, and Vágó's talent for painting horses, cattle and figures.

The image unfolds in front of the spectators who are in the centre of the picture. A commentary on the show is given successively in different languages (indicate the language required for the commentary at the entrance), accompanied by music, the noise of battle and the cries and moans of the warriors. The most significant scene is where Árpád, on a white horse, surrounded by the seven tribal chiefs, is contemplating his victorious troops as they advance across the plain. On his left, his wife is enthroned on a wagon drawn by four grey oxen with broad horns. She is protected from evil spirits by the skulls of two bulls placed on either side of the wagon.

Further on, a scene shows the Magyars settling at the edge of a forest, setting up their tents. It is the Panorama's most densely populated scene with the largest number of figures of the 2 000 represented on the fresco.

In complete contrast to the figure of Árpád, on the summit of another hill overlooking the plain and the valley of the Danube, men are approaching the sacrificial white horse, the Táltos, where the man who is in charge of the ritual sacrifice of the animal, the Kádár is standing. Young girls are dancing around him while white smoke announces good omens.

In fact, victory is almost nigh, the valley's inhabitants have been defeated and the Magyars can settle on the land of Szvatopluk, chief of the Moravian Slavs, who, beaten and cast out, threw himself into the Danube. Without tarnishing Prince Árpád's glory, the story might suggest that Szvatopluk was simply cheated and betrayed by Kusid, the messenger sent by Árpád.

Kusid, filled with wonder at the lands he had just visited and much impressed by the banks of the Danube, paid a visit to the sovereign of this area, Szvatopluk (Attila's successor), to greet him in the name of Árpád. Szvatopluk rejoiced at this visit believing that Kusid represented the chief of a peaceful tribe of people, simply wishing to cultivate some of Szvatopluk's land.

Satisfied with the welcome he received, Kusid mounted his horse once more, taking with him a flask of water, a bag of black soil and a sample of the grass and returned to Árpád and his companions. After listening to Kusid's tale, Árpád filled his drinking horn with the water from the Danube, imploring God's blessing and begging Him to grant him this wealth for ever. He sent Kusid back to Szvatopluk to offer to "trade his soil, grass and water" for a white horse in harness. Szvatopluk joyfully accepted the magnificent horse with its decorated harness, thinking that it was a mark of gratitude on the part of the settlers and told Kusid that he and his companions could take as much soil, grass and water as they wished. Kusid departed to carry the news. Árpád, accompanied by his seven tribal chiefs, rode into Pannonia as master of the territory. When Szvatopluk protested, Árpád sent the reply, "Don't stay a moment longer. You sold your soil for a horse, the grass for a harness and the water for a bridle."

Szvatopluk protested, ordered the horse to be put to death, the bridle to be cast into the meadow and the saddle into the Danube. He heard Kusid reply: "If you kill your horse, you feed the dogs, if you cast your bridle into the meadow, the reapers will find it, if you drown your beautiful golden saddle, the fishermen will take it out of the water." Szvatopluk took up arms in his defence, but the Magyars were stronger and he was obliged to flee, pursued until he cast himself into the Danube which bore him away.

MAGYAR KÉPEK Kft

ADDITIONAL SIGHTS

A walk through 1896 – *1st floor of the Rotunda.* A set of mirrors plunges you into a street with shops among models representing all the social classes of the era. Wealthy gentlemen and their ladies, the length of their dresses denoting their fortune, maidservants whose dresses had to reach just above their ankles, rich and poor children, soldiers of all ranks, shops, trades and services, many of which have now disappeared. At that time, black clothes for women were a sign of elegance, with white and purple worn as a sign of mourning.

Panopticum – *On the top floor of the Rotunda.* This is a realistic presentation of the principal rulers of Hungary. While the gallery enables visitors to admire the costumes, which can be assumed to be authentic, it is a pity that the models seem to have been taken directly from a clothes shop window, thus lessening the effect.

Árpád's Memorial - This classical-style monument was erected in 1896. Many Hungarians have their photographs taken in front of it.

Dike-keeper's house – Near the lake is a model, with sound and light, showing the occasions when the dikes holding back the River Tisza burst their banks. In one single night in 1876, the bursting of the dikes caused terrible flooding which almost totally destroyed Szeged.
There are a number of other exhibitions for visitors: excavations of the ancient Szer Abbey, farm buildings from the Szeged region and a presentation of local specialities.

PANNONHALMI-FŐAPÁTSÁG★★

PANNONHALMA Abbey – Győr-Moson-Sopron province

Michelin map 925 D 5 – 18km/11mi south of Győr

For security reasons we strongly recommend you to leave your car at Szt. Márton-hegy, just before you get to the abbey. Car park and café-restaurant.

Since AD 996, the date of its foundation by Prince Géza, Pannonhalma Abbey, one of the world's largest Benedictine abbeys, has stood majestically at the top of a hill overlooking the plain. It is on the Unesco World Heritage list of sites.

A SHORT HISTORY

Géza, the first Magyar prince converted to Christianity, called on the Benedictine monks to help convert the country to Christianity. They came from Cluny, the seat of monastic life at the time; it was the Cluny Order that spread throughout Europe. The monks established an abbey on Pannonhalma Hill, which was governed according to the Order of St Benedict and dedicated to St Martin, born in Savaria (Szombathely) and later to become the famous Bishop of Tours.

King Stephen (István, Géza's son) granted a great many privileges to the abbey, which he visited frequently. With his aid, it was able to grow and assert itself.

The monks resisted the Mongols in the early 13C, and then, governed by abbots who were more interested in wordly things than spirituality, the abbey declined.

It found a certain lustre again in the early 16C, but the Turkish invasion drove away the monks who were, nevertheless, able to save books, documents and precious objects. The Turks, however, who occupied the monastery, destroyed paintings and sculpture, and converted the church into a mosque, since it faced towards the east. After their departure, monks returned to the site and had to invent a new mode of existence.

No longer having the same privileges, they offered their services to society, which they continue to do today.

Like all monasteries in Hungary, Pannonhalma was closed by Joseph II in 1786. It was reopened in the early 19C. The monks then devoted themselves to education, teaching and the training of teachers.

Pannonhalma Grammar School was created in the abbey just before the Second World War and currently has 350 students.

Pannonhalma Abbey, apart from the actual monastery, which houses about 70 monks, also has a boarding school as well as the St Gelbert Theological Academy, a seminary and a home for the aged.

A place to stay, a place to eat

Pax – *Dózsa György u. 2. ☎ 96/470 006, Fax 96/470 007. 25 rooms at around €38.* A pleasant hotel with a view of the valley. Restaurant.

Pannon – *Hunyadi u. 7. ☎ and fax 96 - 470 041. 6 rooms between €25 and €27.* A simple *panzió* with a view of the monastery. Small restaurant with unpretentious cuisine.

TOUR ⌚

Central courtyard – In the central courtyard stands a statue of the first abbot, Asztrik, who brought the Pope's gift to King Stephen of the famous crown with the crooked cross. There is also a bas-relief of the king presenting his son Imre to St Gellert. Go under the grammar school building and climb up to the raised strip of earth overlooking the Kisalföld (Small Plain). From this balcony you can contemplate the very same landscape as the monks.

From here you will be led to the **cloisters**, where the sundial reminds visitors that one of its hours will be their last, before entering the church.

Church – The entrance is by the **Porta Speciosa**★ with its red marble columns; the capitals and bases are carved out of white limestone. This ensemble was created by Ferenc Storno, as was the tympanum fresco which represents St Martin in the famous scene where he shares his cloak with a beggar.

The Storno family – whose house can be visited at Sopron *(see this name)* – came from Italy and left their mark on a great many of western Hungary's late-18C buildings. They were made responsible for planning the cloisters and the abbey church. The Storno family also created the pulpit and the red-marble neo-Romanesque altar.

★★ **Library** – Its foundation goes back to the 11C, to the time of Ladislas I (St Ladislas). Today's library dates from the 19C, and bears the mark of one of Esztergom Cathedral's architects, János Páckh. Its wood is painted to look like marble, and the clever lighting uses a system of mirrors to redirect daylight and the rays of the

MAGYAR KÉPEK Kft

Pannonhalma Abbey

sun. Thought to be Hungary's largest library, it has a collection of 300 000 works, some unique, such as the oldest manuscript in the country: the early-11C Tihany Abbey Deed of Foundation.

Painting gallery – The visit concludes with the painting gallery that exhibits a great many Dutch, Italian and Austrian works of art, especially from the 16C, 17C and 18C. Visitors can also see ecclesiastical objects and vestments.

PÁPA

Veszprém province – Population 34 000

Michelin map 925 E 4

This Baroque town in Transdanubia is a short distance from the Bakony Mountains. It is best known for its famous blue cloth, inherited from a long tradition.

THE BLUE CLOTH OF PÁPA

The Kluge family settled in Pápa in the second half of the 18C, where they started their *kékfestő* (blue dyeing) works.

At that time the cloth trade was in the throes of a serious crisis in Western Europe. Europeans had been familiar with blue dye since before the 16C. Cultivated in Germany, *Istais tinctoria* was the base for dyeing fabric blue. The long, complicated process added to the price of the cloth, which found few buyers. In the 16C Dutch merchants imported a magical plant, indigo, from India and Bengal. Dyeing cloth blue suddenly became easier. Production rose sharply, prices dropped, and buyers became plentiful. With more cloth at a lower price, the German dyeing trade was endangered. The fashion could not be stopped. The governments of the period took action against the weavers' workshops that made the cloth with imported indigo, and in certain towns the dyers of the new blue cloth were even threatened with death. These craftsmen emigrated to more wel-

MAGYAR KÉPEK Kft

coming countries, forming the so-called blue dye diaspora. This is how Johann Friedrich Kluge came from Sorau in Saxony, at the invitation of Maria Theresa of Habsburg, stopping first at Sárvár before settling with his family in Pápa. The Kluge workshop was the first created in this town, in 1786 and in the following century two more workshops were also set up.
As the years passed, the Kluge family enlarged its business, developing it in line with customers' requirements, scientific discoveries and new techniques, and expanding what at that time was a leading industry. This industry continued to function up to 1956, when it was nationalised.
There are still about a dozen towns in Hungary today which continue to use the same processes, producing the magnificent cloth with a blue background, printed with light-coloured patterns.

SIGHTS

★★ **Kékfestő Múzeum** ⓥ **(Blue Cloth Museum)** – *Március 15 tér 12.* To celebrate the 200th anniversary of its establishment, the Kluge works were turned into a museum and classified as a historic monument. A visit is well worth while. Everything has been preserved and seems ready to operate. What is missing is the steam, the fabrics dripping with dye, the smell, and, naturally, the workers who kept an eye on all the stages of manufacture for the blue cloth of Pápa. You can see the factory's chemistry laboratory, which already combined research and development. At the end of the visit, there's a display of Irén Bódy's creations, demonstrating magnificent use of this printing technique. A shop at the museum entrance sells the fabrics, either in lengths, or made into clothing. The guided tour is in Hungarian, but you will quickly understand the manufacturing process and easily follow the various stages of production.

A place to stay, a place to eat

Arany Griff – *Fő tér 15.* ☎ *89/312 000, Fax 89/312 005. 25 rooms between €20 and €36.* A very fine hotel with spacious, light rooms. Good food, copious helpings. Tennis and horse-riding available.

Vadásztanya Étterem – *Rákóczi u. 21.* Restaurant slightly out of the town centre, specialising in game.

★ **Esterházy-kastély** – Pápa's Baroque appearance is attributable to Count Károly Esterházy, bishop of Eger and Vác. He had this castle built by Jakab Fellner and József Grossmann. It is now used by cultural institutions and for teaching. The chapel has been turned into a **library**. The ceiling frescoes are the work of Ignác Mildorfer, an artist at the court of Vienna.

Fő tér – Several Baroque houses grace the square. Note, in particular, n°s 12 (Tourinform), 21 and 23.

Római katolikus templom – The two castle architects also designed this church, known simply as the big church. Inside, there are Maulbertsch frescoes, representing St Stephen, Christianity's first martyr, a rarity in Hungary, since representations of St Stephen are generally those of King Stephen I.

PARÁD and the north of the MÁTRA

Heves province

Michelin map 925 C 10 – Local map see BÜKK

In the Mátra Mountains, on road n° 24 leading to Eger, Parádsasvár, Parád, Parádfürdő Recsk and, finally, Sirok, there is a series of interesting places, set like pearls in a necklace of greenery. The route through these various places is, in fact, along the country road that continues the trips through the Mátra massif with Gyöngyös *(see Mátra)* as as the departure point.

Before you arrive in Parád, half way between the crossroads with the Galyatető and the Parád road (around 5km/3.1mi) on the left, the sulphurous springs of **Parádsasvár** can be distinguished by their smell. This mineral water is bottled and used to treat digestive disorders and stomach-ache. The Parádsasvár glass factory here has been producing *objets d'art* and sets of glass and crystal tableware for two centuries. These are on sale at the factory.

★★ **Kocsimúzeum** ⓥ **(Carriage Museum)** – This museum, located in **Parád**, is the only large museum of its kind in Hungary. The Carriage Museum is housed in the stables of Count Károlyi's castle. As well as the museum, this fine building, with

Gabler/MAGYAR KÉPEK Kft

Parád – Carriage Museum

foundations made of red Cifra marble, is home to the horses which, from time to time, pull the carriages or work in the nearby dressage arena.
The museum is worth a visit; visitors can follow all the stages in the manufacture of a horse-drawn vehicle. All the trades are represented. Wheelwrights' and saddlers' tools are on show. The smithy has not been forgotten, neither have the decorator, carpenter or cabinetmaker. Beyond the presentation of the various trades there is an exhibition of country wagons, carts, charabancs, and luxurious and not so luxurious carriages, including sleighs used for work or rides in wintertime. Well-presented models give an insight into all the tricks of the trade used to make these vehicles, built for travelling, for a discreet, romantic ride or for ceremonial processions.

Parádfürdő – Parád and Parádfürdő form one town. When you leave the Kocsimúzeum you are already in Parádfürdő. There is a **sanatorium** in this spa which provides accommodation and restaurant facilities. This spa establishment functions as a hotel and in no way resembles the typical image of a sanatorium, the name formerly given to a hospital treating people suffering from tuberculosis.

Palócház – *Sziget utca*. This wooden, thatched **Palóc House** illustrates the everyday life of the Palóc, a Mátra ethnic group *(see Hollókő)*.

Recsk – The small town of Recsk is of no particular interest in itself. Leave the town centre heading right and follow the signposts to a camp, located 5km/3.1mi further on. This camp was used to house political prisoners during the Stalinist period under the Rákosi regime. A monument to the memory of the **prisoners of the camp**, closed by Imre Nagy in 1953, was erected in 1991.
About 5km/3.1mi to the north of Recsk, is the spa centre of **Mátraderecske**. Its four outdoor swimming pools with water at a temperature over 30°C/86°F are popular from May to September.

Sirok – This town is worth a visit for the ruins of its 14C **medieval castle**. Those who are able to make the climb will discover a **panorama**★★ over the Mátra with the Késkestető peak, the Bükk Mountains and, to the north, the mountains in Slovakia.
Some 8km/5mi north, **Bükkszék** is another spa. It produces a mineral water, *Salvus*, recommended for people with gastric disorders or respiratory complaints. Its open-air swimming pools are located in a pleasant green setting.

PÉCS★★★

Baranya province – Population 168 000

Michelin map 925 I 6

Nestled in a hollow in the Mecsek Hills, Pécs, protected from the chilly north winds and warmed by the sun, has a soft, pleasant, and colourful atmosphere. It has a Mediterranean flavour, a hint of an Oriental perfume. This atmosphere existed during the Ottoman occupation and undoubtedly inspired the Turks, who had taken the city without resistance, to make it into a Turkish city, a centre of culture and education, to the extent that Turkish literary history refers to the Pécs School of poetry.
The hillsides surrounding the city have favoured viticulture and the production of highly reputed wines. The region's sparkling wine is aged in the city-centre wine cellars, built underground on five levels. In September the festive season begins, and in early October the Pécs **Grape and Wine Festival** celebrations are held with great merriment, music and dancing.

A SHORT HISTORY

The Romans replaced the Celts in the 3C and made this site the administrative centre for their Valeria province. The town was then known as Sopianae (today the name of a Hungarian cigarette brand). After the arrival of the Magyars in the 9C, King Stephen made it into a diocese by a charter dated August 1009. A series of bishops and archbishops followed, encouraging cultural development in Pécs, which led to the foundation of Hungary's first university in 1367. The most famous of the bishops to govern the diocese was **Janus Pannonius,** who held this position from 1459 to 1472. He wrote numerous Latin poems that were esteemed throughout Renaissance Europe. After initially supporting King Matthias, he rose against him when he attacked Austria and Bohemia. Janus Pannonius the priest was more concerned about the people and their immediate condition than eternity, as expressed in his words, "Look around you and do not forget to be a true man of the present, here and now."

The Ottoman period – Seventeen years after the defeat at Mohács, in 1543, the Turks took possession of the city after driving out all the inhabitants from the centre. They turned the churches into mosques or destroyed them, and made Pécs into an administrative and cultural centre. In 1686, Louis of Baden liberated the city. It was abandoned until immigrants came from Germany and Bohemia, bringing it slowly back to life. It was another bishop, György Klimó, who supported the town's cultural development during the 18C. Indeed, the Pécs library, created in 1774, was Hungary's first public library; today it holds 300 000 books. In 1921, after the Treaty of Trianon was signed, Pozsony (Bratislava) University was moved to Pécs.

SIGHTS

★★ **Szent Péter Székesegyház (St Peter's Basilica)** – The basilica stands on 11C foundations, over a crypt dating from the same period. Its base is 27m/88ft wide and 77m/252ft long, and the building is flanked by four corner towers. The church was converted into a mosque by the Turks and has greatly changed over the ages. It took on its present appearance at the end of the 19C. The most interesting parts include the **crypt**★★, the chapels under each of the towers, and all of the paintings and frescoes, mainly by Hungarian artists. In the north-west, the chapel is dedicated to the Virgin Mary and in the north-east to the Heart of Jesus, both decorated by Bertalan Székely (the painter of a great many frescoes and paintings including *The Women of Eger*) and Károly Lotz. The Corpus Christi Chapel to the south-west has a beautiful altar made of the same red marble as the one in Esztergom's Bakócz chapel. Lastly, to the south-east, the Mór chapel bears the name of a bishop of Pécs.
Going down from the basilica towards Szent István tér, music-lovers may note a statue of Franz Liszt at the window balcony in the south part of the **Bishop's Palace** (Püspöki palota). Liszt, his likeness captured in bronze, braves the weather and contemplates Szent István Square.

★★ **Ókeresztény Mauzóleum** ⏲ – This strange mausoleum dating from the year AD 350 was discovered accidentally in 1975. In the crypt you may see a sarcophagus and well-conserved frescoes representing *The Fall of Adam and Eve*, and *Daniel in the Lions' Den.*

★★★ **Csontváry Múzeum** ⏲ – *Janus Pannonnius utca 11.* Tivadar Csontváry Kosztka's main works are exhibited in this former grammar school. Born in 1853, the same year as Van Gogh, Csontváry, who was originally an assistant pharmacist, also had a tragic life. He died in 1919, and his work has only recently been recognised. Picasso, on discovering his work at a Paris exhibition, is said to have commented with his usual modesty, "I didn't know that there was another great painter in this century besides me." There are eight great paintings by Csontváry in the museum, including *The Solitary Cedar* and *Baalbek*, together with very interesting graphic work.

Return to Dóm tér.

Káptalan utca – This street (Canon Street) has several museums and art galleries.

Endre Nemes Múzeum ⓥ – *At n° 5.* Works by Endre Nemes (1909-85), a painter born near Pécs but who lived in Sweden. This museum is also home to works by another Hungarian painter, Zlatko Prica, who lived in Zagreb (Croatia).

PÉCS

Batthyány u	BY	3
Ferencesek utcája	AX	
Garay u	AXY	7
Hungária u	AX	8
Jókai tér	ABX	
Káptalan u	AX	9
Kazinczy u	BX	12
Király u	BX	
Kodály Zoltán u	AX	13
Majorossy Imre (Dr.)	BX	14
Mátyás király u	AX	16
Móricz Zsigmond tér	ABY	17
Széchenyi tér	BX	21
Szepessy Ignác u	ABX	23
Teréz u	BX	24
Váradi Antal u	AXY	25

Belvárosi Templom	BX	
Ferences Templom	AX	
Jakováli Hasszán Dzsámi	AX	
Museums		
Csontváry Múzeum	AX	
Martyn Ferenc Múzeum	AX	M[1]
Modern Magyar képtár	AX	
Nemes Endre Múzeum	AX	M[2]
Régészeti Múzeum	AX	M[3]
Zsolnay Múzeum	AX	
Ôskeresztény Mauzóleum	AX	N
Pécsi Nemzeti Színház	BX	
Püspöki palota	AX	
Szent Péter Székesegyház	AX	
Szerecsen Patika	ABX	
Zsinagóga	BX	

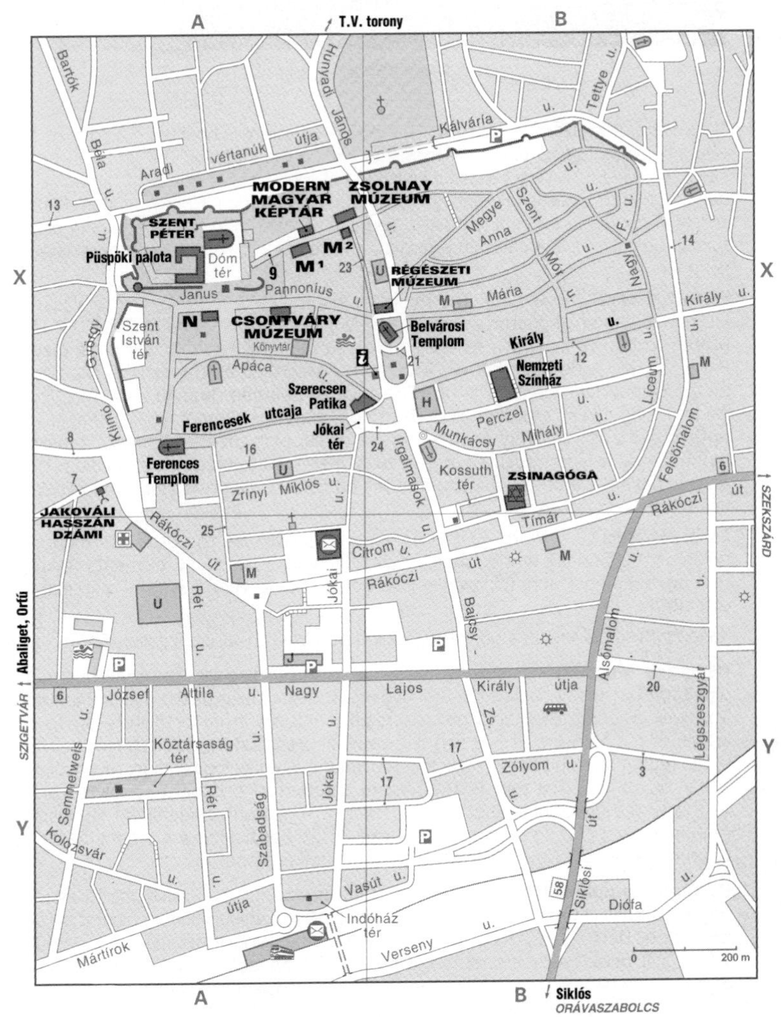

T. Hortobagyi/MAGYAR KÉPEK Kft

Pécs – Former mosque

★★ Modern Magyar Képtár ⓥ – *At n° 4.* This **modern art gallery** is housed in a former 19C villa and only displays paintings from the end of the 19C and the first half of the 20C. You will find a very beautiful collection of the works of the most famous Hungarian painters: Károly Ferenczy, László Gulácsy, Simon Hollósy, Ödön Márffy, József Rippl-Rónai and many others. You can often admire the paintings in peaceful solitude. There is a charming garden, a haven of coolness, much appreciated in summer.

★ Vasarely Múzeum ⓥ – *At n° 3.* The museum was created in 1976. Győző Vásárhelyi, better known as Victor Vasarely, was born in the Pécs area in 1908. He emigrated to France in 1930, where he created most of his life's work (he died in Paris in 1997). Perhaps his work could be described as the artistic expression of the Hungarian scientific mind. This type of painting, known as op art (optical art) long after Vasarely's first paintings, played with geometrical shapes and optical illusions. Vasarely used all kinds of support media – canvas, tapestry, monumental mosaics such as at Carracas, metal, glass etc. In the museum Hungary is paying tribute to the artist in his homeland. Downstairs there is another exhibition devoted to mining.

★★ Zsolnay Múzeum ⓥ – *At n° 2.* It is here that you will see the products manufactured at the Zsolnay works, which makes artistic objects and elements for decorating buildings, and for use in the home. Some very beautiful porcelain is exhibited.

Take Hunyadi János utca on the right and go down towards Széchenyi tér.

★ Régészeti Múzeum ⓥ – *Széchenyi tér 12.* This building was once the home of a dignitary, but today houses the archaeological department of the Janus Pannonius Múzeum. The museum presents the region's history from prehistory up to the arrival of the Magyars. It is a very educational presentation that retraces daily life in the region by using either objects discovered in archaeological digs, reconstituted items, or models. The tour is arranged in an interesting manner enabling visitors to follow the development of society, even if they don't understand Hungarian. Among the models to be admired is one of St Bartholomew's (Szent Bertalan) Church made from tiny pebbles carved to resemble stone.

Belvárosi templom (Dzsámi) – The former mosque of the Pasha Ghazi Kassim is now a Catholic church. This is the town's largest remaining building from the Turkish period. Built shortly after the beginning of the Turkish occupation in 1580, it was constructed with stones recovered after the demolition of the medieval St Bartholomew's Church. When the Turks left, it was taken over by the Catholics and used for worship. The minaret was knocked down in the 18C.

Szerecsen Patika **(Saracen Pharmacy)** – Still on the square, to the south-west, on the corner where Apáca utca leads off, is the pharmacy. It has beautiful Zsolnay ceramics. There is a small exhibition of ceramics next to the dispensary.

Király utca – This is a pleasant pedestrian street where tourists like to stroll, stopping at a terrace café or having a snack in one of the many restaurants. The **Palatinus Hotel** at n° 5, the city's smartest hotel, was built in 1913 and has been well renovated. Its Art Nouveau lobby is worth a look.

Pécsi Nemzeti Színház **(Pécs National Theatre)** – Constructed at the end of the 19C, this Rococo building is a pleasant stop on the walk down Király utca.

Take Kazinczy utca on the right, then Perczel utca.

Jókai tér – Small square lined with shops, cafés and restaurants.

Ferencesek utcája – Students, tourists and Pécs residents intermingle in this busy pedestrian street.

Ferences templom – The **Franciscan Church**, built in the first half of the 18C, has a finely worked Baroque interior created by monks.
There is a statue of St Francis near the Pigeon Fountain (Galambos kút).

Return to Széchenyi tér and take Irgalamasok utcája on the right.

Go past the **town hall** (Polgármesteri Hivatal) and, a little further on, you will see a small **enamelled fountain** made at the Zsolnay works.

★ **Zsinagóga** – *Kossuth tér.* The first synagogue was built on this spot in 1843. It was destroyed and replaced by the present building, constructed in 1869. There is an Angster organ in the synagogue, as well as carved furniture and painted decorations. Nearly 3 000 Jews were deported from Pécs; barely 10% returned.

Take Citrom utca.

At the end of the street, the **Post Office** (Posta) façade can be seen on the other side of Jókai utca. The building is a beautiful example of Art Nouveau.

A place to stay

Fónix – *Hunyadi u. 2. ☎ 72/311 680, Fax 72/324 113. 15 rooms between €18 and €33.* Close to a former mosque, a pleasant little hotel with an unusual entrance. Simple, clean rooms.

Toboz Panzió Falatozó – *Fenyves sor 5. ☎ 72/325 232, Fax 72/210 631. 11 rooms between €29 and €138.* Set among the pines, a family *panzió* in the upper town.

Aranyhajó Fogadó – *Király u. 3. ☎ 72/310 263, Fax 72/212 733. 11 rooms between €36 and €46.* Certainly the oldest hotel in town, if not in Hungary. It was founded in 1802 and the building dates from 1695. Spacious rooms. Restaurant, billiards, bar.

Palatinus – *Király u. 5. ☎ 72/233 022, Fax 72/232 261. 100 rooms between €72 and €82.* Smart, Art Nouveau hotel. Beautiful, airy dining room. Bowling alley and sauna.

A place to eat

Cellarium Étterem – *Hunyadi u. 2. ☎ 72/314 453.* Next to the mosque, this restaurant is in a large, prettily decorated cellar dating from the Turkish period. Hungarian specialities and an enticing wine list.

Bagolyvár – *Felső Havi dűlő 6.* Restaurant with a very beautiful view of the valley. This establishment produces its own wines (vines on the lower slopes). Quality Hungarian cuisine.

Aranykacsa Étterem – *Teréz u. 4.* Restaurant with modern, slightly cold decor, but with refined cuisine. There is also a wine cellar several hundred years old and a bar.

Kalamáris Étterem – *Rákóczi út 30. ☎ 72/312 573.* Good food and wide choice of wine.

Tettye Vendéglő Gasthof – *Tettye tér 4. ☎ and fax: 72/310 438.* A good place, highly prized by the local inhabitants. Slightly old-fashioned decor. Very pleasant terrace. Frequent musical entertainment.

Afium – *Irgalmasok u. 2.* This bar-restaurant in a cellar with old-fashioned decor is a meeting place for artists. Friendly atmosphere.

A good café to set you back on your feet – If you need to rest and relax after visiting the museums, a good place to go to is the **Morik Café** *(Jókai tér)*. Inside or out, coffee-lovers will have a choice of 40 sorts of coffee. Other equally good quality refreshments, such as pastries, are also served. You could also try the **Capri Café** *(Citrom utca 7)* or the **Dante Café**, in the same building as the Csontváry Museum.

★ **Jakováli Hasszán-dzsámi** – *Rákóczi út.* This is the best-preserved mosque in Hungary still to have its minaret. Some elements of Turkish art are on show.

TV-torony (Television Tower) – *Access by bus n° 35 leaving from Indóház tér south of Nagy Lajos király útja.* This is worth the effort. The television tower (176m/577ft high) is on Misina Hill (535m/1 755ft), overlooking the town and its surroundings. A lift will take you to the first level where there is a café and a restaurant. Splendid **panorama★★**.

EXCURSIONS

The Mecsek Hills – The Mecsek Hills stretch south-west and north-east of Pécs. The massif consists of hills and forests that form a protective barrier against the north winds. This massif's highest point is a modest 680m/2 230ft, but there is such a contrast between the hollow where Pécs is located and the Mecsek Hills that they appear mountainous in comparison. This rather well protected area offers beautiful walks for those seeking peace and country air.

Orfű – *12km/7.5mi to the north-west. Leave Pécs by taking successively Nagy Lajos Király útja, József Attila utca, Athinai utca and Nendvitch Andor utca, then just before Makai István utca take Páfrány utca on the right.*

The **drive★** is very pleasant. Sometimes in the forest you go through a veritable tunnel of greenery.
The holiday resort of Orfű has all the facilities for holidaymakers of all ages. Several small lakes have been laid out for swimming, fishing or boating. A large campsite has pitches or bungalows for hire by holidaymakers. Swimming is safe, the water is filtered. Orfű is very popular with Hungarians as well as tourists mainly from Germany, Austria and Holland.

Abaliget – *4km/2.5mi from Orfű.* It is possible to visit a cave here. For about 500m/550yd, there is a succession of stalactites and stalagmites, where the temperature is constant and humidity high. Finding accommodation in this small village of 600 inhabitants is not difficult. There is a hotel, as well as a horse-riding centre, a campsite and a few rooms in private homes.

Siklós – *See this name.*

Zengővárkony – *11km/7mi north-east. Take road n° 6 towards Bonyhád.*

At the entrance to this charming little village you will see the **Museum of Painted Eggs★**. The wonderful collection of several hundred eggs, donated by a German woman of Hungarian origin, is displayed in a small building surrounded by a lawn. Other means of decoration, apart from painting, have been applied to the fragile shells, which, thanks to the patience and talent of the unknown artists doing this delicate work, have become works of art. The weaving workshop nearby brings old looms to life and offers lengths of cloth and table linen for sale.

PUSZTA

See BUGAC-PUSZTA and HORTOBÁGY-PUSZTA

SÁROSPATAK★

Borsod-Abaúj-Zemplén province – Population 15 000

Michelin map 925 A 13

The "Hungarian Cambridge" and "Hungary's Athens" are expressions that perfectly describe Sárospatak, more so than the "town of muddy torrents" which is the literal translation of its name.
The town, which overlooks the River Bodrog and its branches, stretches along one of the river banks, with nothing on the other side but a small residential area called Kis Patak.
Access to the main points of interest is via a long avenue successively called Arany János út, Rákóczi út and finally Kazinczy Ferenc út.
Sárospatak is well known as the town of the Rákóczi family, the most famous member being Ferenc II. It is also the birthplace of St Elizabeth (Szent Erzsébet), who is still very much revered in Hungary.
The town fell into Magyar hands in the late 10C-early 11C, and was incorporated into the royal domain in the 1050s. In the 12C the immigration of Italian families gave new impetus to the town's development. It became a royal town once more, thanks to Sigismund of Luxembourg, and King Matthias allowed the *Pálóczi*, the lords of Sárospatak, to build a castle here.

Ferenc Rákóczi II, Prince of Transylvania – The Rákóczi family possessed land with a surface area of more than one million hectares. Ferenc was born in 1676 shortly before the death of his father Ferenc I. With his mother he spent three years in a besieged fort in Mohács.

A place to stay

Dóra Vendégházak – *Dózsa György u. 13. ☏ 47/312 365. 4 rooms between €15 and €25.* A little family *panzió* in a quiet street.

Bodrog – *Rákóczi u. 58. ☏ 47/311 744. 50 rooms between €39 and €50.* The only hotel in town. Not particularly attractive from the outside, but the rooms are spacious, clean and comfortable. The service is very good. Sauna and fitness centre. Restaurant.

A place to eat

Vár Söröző Vendéglő – *Árpád u. 35.* Locals consider this the best restaurant in town. The helpings are generous and the dishes full of flavour, and the view of the River Bodrog with the castle is a definite plus.

Rákóczi Étterem – *Szent Erzsébet tér 10.* This restaurant, not far from the castle and set in a beautiful vaulted cellar, serves traditional food.

After his marriage in 1694, he returned to his native region and, despite pressure, refused to enter into rebellion against the Austrians. However, once faced with the violence of the repression and the peasants' suffering, he resolved to head the revolt against the Habsburgs.

Ferenc II Rákóczi was a gentleman, and also something of a character. Cultured and curious, he divided his time between business obligations and the pleasures of life. His thoughts and writings reflect a leaning towards meditation and a concern for social relations.

An aesthete and gourmet, he put the wines from his Tokay vineyard to the forefront. He also put them on the table of Louis XIV who described Tokay as "the king of wines and the wine of kings".

For a time Ferenc Rákóczi attracted the attention of Russia's Peter the Great and France's Louis XIV, but he did not hold their interest very long. He found himself alone in the fight against the House of Austria. His army was gradually broken up, and the fifth prince of Transylvania was forced to go into exile. His destiny led him to Russia, Poland and then to France.

In 1717 Ferenc Rákóczi went to Turkey to solicit the sultan's aid. He was given asylum and accommodation in a little town on the Marmara coast. He died there in 1735 after devoting his time to theology, reflection, writing... and woodwork.

SIGHTS

★★ **Rákóczi-vár (Rákóczi Castle)** ⓥ – *Kádár Kata utca.* The restored part open to visitors is only one element of the fortress. The place is surrounded by walls within which are a park and a few buildings.

The oldest part of the structure, modified through the centuries, is the **Vöröstorony** – the **Red Tower** – a former medieval keep dating from the 15C. The name Red Tower is thought to stem from the red-tinted plaster with which it was originally coated.

Szelényi/MAGYAR KÉPEK Kft

Sárospatak – Rákóczi Castle

At the beginning of the 16C the owners, the Perényi family, rebuilt the castle in the Renaissance style, adding a walled palace in the Italian style. The palace was later remodelled and occupied by the Rákóczi family until 1711.
A wooden bridge leads to the entrance at the foot of the tower. As soon as you enter the castle, three vaulted rooms set the scene. In one of them, utensils, containers and old kitchen crockery are exhibited. The Renaissance elements in the castle are especially noteworthy, and are the best preserved in Hungary. The **great hall** or **Nagy Palota**, decorated with sculpted elements, is reached via a narrow staircase, leading to a platform that today forms the roof of the **Red Tower**. There are beautiful **views** of the city, the surrounding countryside and the River Bodrog.
Still in the Red Tower, there is a **room with a Renaissance-style fireplace**. Lastly, in the corner tower there is another room of great symbolic significance, in the form of a semicircular closed balcony. The ribs of the small vaults join in a keystone in the form of a rose, under which the supporters of the fight for national independence secretly swore their allegiance. The expression *sub rosa* (under the rose) has remained to designate any agreement concluded in secret.

★ **Szent Erzsébet-templom** – *Szent Erzsébet tér*. This dates from the end of the 15C. Originally a Roman Catholic church, it was taken over by the Calvinists and turned into a Reformed church. Inside, a painting evokes the memory of St Elizabeth. An immense Baroque altarpiece dedicated to the Virgin Mary decorates the main altar. Outside the church there are two bronze sculptures by Imre Varga. One is of St Elizabeth who made the journey on horseback between Sárospatak and Varburg Castle several times. The other statue is of her husband Louis.

Református Kollégium – *Rákóczi út, 1*. This college founded in 1531 is part of the reason why Sárospatak is sometimes called Hungary's Athens. In 1650, György Rákóczi's wife Zsuzsanna Lorántffy, invited a Czech humanist, **János Amos Comenius**, who was renowned as a teacher, to come to the college. He organised teaching at the college and stayed there for four years. The Rákóczi family put their printing shop at his disposal. Comenius was able to publish a large number of works in Latin and the first illustrated teaching manual for children, ***Orbis Pictus***. King George II of England saved the college following Counter-Reformation persecution, by intervening at the court of Vienna. Famous Hungarians who studied here include: Ferenc Kazinczy, who reformed the Hungarian language; Mihály Csokonai Vitéz, one of Hungary's greatest poets; Lajos Kossuth, the statesman; Zsigmond Móricz, the writer; and many others who, like them, have their bust or statue in the park, commonly known as the Iskolakert (the school garden).
A small building in the courtyard is home to two permanent exhibitions: one offering a collection of applied art, and the other on the history of the college.

★★ **Library** – About 200 000 works (in Greek, Hebrew, Latin and Hungarian) are kept here. In this long room, the cupola usually found in great libraries has been replaced by a *trompe-l'œil* painting. A wooden gallery resting on oak columns runs round the room. Paintings representing the Arts and the Sciences are at either end.

Take Rákóczi út towards the town centre, then turn right into Eötvös utca after about 250m/275yd.

Comenius Tanítóképző – Jenő Lechner designed this **teacher training college**. The beautifully proportioned structure dates from 1912, and is a mixture of Art Nouveau and the Renaissance style from Upper Hungary .
Opposite stands the **Cultural Centre** (Művelődési Ház), a building by **Imre Makovecz**, the master of what is known as Organic architecture.

Szent Erzsébet

Born in 1207 in Sárospatak, Erzsébet (Elizabeth) was a descendant of the Árpáds, the daughter of King Andrew (Endre) II. At the age of 14 she married Louis of Marburg, Count of Thuringia. They loved each other dearly, but in 1227 Louis died. Erzsébet remained in Marburg with her children, and her charitable nature led her to help the poor, despite her mother-in-law who reproached and watched her constantly. One winter's day in the middle of February, Erzsébet climbed down a little staircase carrying some food in her apron for the poor. When her mother-in-law stopped her and demanded to know what she was carrying, the frightened Erzsébet was at a loss for words. Without thinking, she opened her apron and said, "I was gathering roses"... and it was indeed an apron full of roses that she revealed to the shrew. Erzsébet died in 1231 at the age of only 24. She was canonised in 1235. Every year the country remembers her on 19 November. Many Hungarians bear her name.

SIKLÓS

Baranya province – Population 11 000

Michelin map 925 I 6 – Local map see BALATON

Hungary's southernmost town is famous for its hilltop castle, dating from the 15C, its imposing mass seeming to defy time. Another form of wealth not only for Siklós but for the region, is wine. Here in the south, the **Villány** fought with the **Szekszárd** for the title of best red-wine producing area in Hungary. It was the Romans who brought grapevines and wine to this region; they occupied the area and called it Serea.

★VÁR (CASTLE) ⏱

The earliest relics here go back to the 13C, but the present building, which has always been occupied, comprises the 15C medieval part, with the additions made in the 16C and 18C.

This is the only castle in Hungary where the old part is so well preserved. Its most famous owner was Kázmér Batthyány, the hero of independence, who had already freed the serfs on his own lands. Lajos Kossuth appointed him Minister of Foreign Affairs in the government founded at Debrecen. From 1959-60 the castle was restored and fitted out to receive exhibitions as well as a tourist hotel and a restaurant.

You enter over an old drawbridge, after crossing a courtyard defended by arrow slits. From the **watch-path**, there is a view of the beautiful landscape encompassing the Villány hillsides. The 15C **Gothic chapel** with its delicate arcades has conserved a few fragments of frescoes and a Renaissance window. The **Knights' Hall** should also be visited, along with the **former prison** and the **torture room**, presented here in its terrible starkness where the methods of torture are described.

ADDITIONAL SIGHT

Malkocs Bej dzsámija – *Vörösmarty utca.* **Bey Malkoch mosque** was reconstructed using the remains of a mid-16C building. Sections of wall were taken and reconstituted according to engravings and descriptions of the time. The monument deserves particular attention, especially its wooden ceiling.

EXCURSIONS

Nagyharsány – *3km/1.8mi east along road n° 5701.* This village is very well known in Hungary. It is the place with the highest temperatures in the country. In 1967 a park was set up for use by sculptors from all over the world, and it serves as a meeting place for artists. All the works are carved from stone and bear the name of their creator.

Harkány – *5km/3mi west along road n° 5804.* Harkány is a well-known thermal spa with waters that spring from the ground at 60-62°C/140-143.6°F. The water contains fluoride and sulphur, and the smell lingers to remind you! The mud baths

MAGYAR KÉPEK Kft

Siklós Castle

offered here are effective in treating rheumatism, joint ailments and certain gynaecological infections. The hotels for tourists and spa guests are virtually all on Bajcsy-Zsilinszky, opposite the main entrance to the baths. As in all spa towns, there are small restaurants, cafeterias and pastry shops, in this case all along Kossuth Lajos utca.

Máriagyűd – *5km/3mi north-west.* Half way up the Tenkes Mountains and a few kilometres north of Harkány, the pilgrimage site of Máriagyűd is the oldest in Hungary. In 1006 Benedictines from Pécsvárad built a chapel housing a statue of the Virgin Mary which later disappeared. In 1687 the Virgin appeared to two peasants. In 1698 a new statue was erected. During the struggle for independence from 1703 to 1711, it was moved to Siklós and then to Esztergom, where it still stands. In 1713 another statue was given by the Bishop of Pécs, and the church was enlarged. From 1723 to 1799, 302 miracles occurred. In 1802 Pius VII consecrated Máriagyűd as an official place of pilgrimage.

The wine road – *13km/7.8mi to the east along road n° 5701.* **Villány** is a market town of 2 500 to 3 000 inhabitants where a small wine festival is held each Friday evening in summer. There is a **wine museum (Bormúzeum)** ⌚ that can be visited and which sells wines, just as the surrounding shops and wine cellars do. In the area around Villány, which has given its name to the wines of the region, other towns have wine cellars and producers, such as **Palkonya**. In **Villánykövesd**, you can go down into the cellars cut into the ground along Petőfi utca. Open from May to October, they offer visitors tastings of Kékoportó, Oportó, Cabernet, Cabernet Sauvignon, Merlot and also some whites, including Olaszrizling and Hárslevelű. Be careful, however. While it is pleasant to have a drink, the level of alcohol tolerated when driving in Hungary is 0%.

SOMLÓ

Veszprém province

Michelin map 925 E 4 – 45km/27mi west of Veszprém

Mt **Somló**, on the plain not far from Somlójenő, is also commonly known as God's hat, and is 432m/1 416ft high. It is said to be a magical place, with high-quality grapevines producing a very good wine, the Somló white that goes well with fish dishes. Nevertheless, the wine's greatest virtue is ensuring that the wishes are fulfilled of mothers-to-be who want to have a son. The legend does not say when it is to be consumed to accomplish this, nor how much should be drunk.

During the Communist period wine production was seriously hampered. An association has now been formed in support of Somló wines and to reconstitute the vineyard that was destroyed when authorisation was granted to build holiday homes for workers from the nearby aluminium mines.

Climb to the top - Climbers brave enough to scale the mountain will be rewarded by the beautiful **panorama**★★ from the Szent István viewpoint. On the way down, they can visit the wine cellars, the largest being at **Somlói Borok Háza** (Somló wine production centre) where visitors can taste the local wine.

On the way down, turn right towards Somlószőlős, then right again and you will be able to see the 19C **Doba Castle**, built on a small promontory. It is surrounded by a botanical park (80ha/192 acres).

SOPRON★★

Győr-Moson-Sopron province – Population 55 000

Michelin map 925 C 2

Sopron or Little Prague, the former Ödenburg of the Austro-Hungarian Empire, is a charming town with almost all the sights in the centre, in what is known as the old town. Sopron still has virtually all its historical buildings. Those damaged during the Second World War have been restored thanks to a single man, Endre Gatsk, who worked for more than half a century to save and preserve Sopron's architectural heritage. In Sopron, the Baroque mixes with the medieval, and the dimensions are so much smaller here, that the buildings have a special charm.

The weekends have an Austrian flavour. Many inhabitants from the neighbouring country cross the border just to do their shopping, buy clothes, wines, meat and pastries, all cheaper and of very good quality. They also come to relax for a couple of days.

Civitas fidelissima, the most faithful town

Sopron is in Hungary because its citizens wanted it to be. Indeed, in 1921, by referendum, they refused to accept the conclusions of the Treaty of Trianon that had put Sopron in Austria. They asked to remain Hungarian. This is why, on the map, Sopron seems to have been detached from Austria with the frontier running around it and placing it in Hungary only 6km/3.6mi from the neighbouring country. The inhabitants show a certain pride in the choice made by their former mayors, yet their town expresses a kind of wistfulness and the overall atmosphere gives the visitor the impression that, the choice having been made, nostalgia still remains.

Sopron wines – Red wine accounts for 75% of total wine production in the Sopron region: a great deal of Cabernet Sauvignon, some Merlot, Cabernet and a little Pinot Noir. The red wines here are slightly acid and rich in tannin. To try this out, taste a 1995 Sopron Cabernet Sauvignon, and a Sauvignon Blanc from the same year.

Does everyone in Sopron have eye and tooth problems? – It would be easy enough to think so given the number of dental surgeries, opticians, eye doctors and clinics. But no, the people in town have not been struck with any particular curse. It is just that Austrians come to Sopron, as they do to many of the towns in western Hungary, to be examined and to receive treatment, because Hungarian practitioners are excellent, and have the very latest equipment. The savings on the cost of healthcare seemingly compensate for the hotel stay.

A SHORT HISTORY

The Celts were apparently the first to settle in the region, on the site of present-day Sopron. The Romans came in the first century, and built a camp called Scarbantia on the site of the old town. They stayed there for more than three centuries. Scarbantia was raised to the rank of municipality, that is to say, its inhabitants benefited from Roman citizenship. Sopron was put on the Amber Route from the Baltic to Italy. Central Europe's transcontinental north-south line also went through the town, and its situation as a crossroads made it a strategically important and wealthy town. Towards the end of the 4C Emperor Valentinian reinforced the defences, but they were soon to be destroyed. From the 5C there was a succession of occupants; Avars, Germans, Slavs and, finally, the Magyars who settled here, rebuilt its defensive walls (5m/16ft thick, 15m/49ft high) and fortified the town which, in the 11C, withstood the Crusaders led by Peter the Hermit.

In 1277 Sopron received the status of a royal city, which gave it the freedom to carry on trade without having to submit to seigniorial rights and pressure. It reinforced its defences again, built ramparts around the town and erected 34 towers and keeps to protect its 22 000 inhabitants. In the shelter of all these fortifications, all sorts of business activities developed which fostered prosperous trade. Sopron, with its large merchant and craftsman class, became an active centre for the expanding sophisticated society, welcoming artists and scientists from abroad.

In 1557 Sopron's first secondary education establishment was created, in 1762 Haydn's *(see Fertőd)* works were printed in Sopron and, in 1769, a theatre opened. Meanwhile, the town had increased the number of elementary schools and, in particular, had created a college for forestry management that still operates today in the middle of a splendid botanical garden.

A WALK IN THE OLD TOWN

The old town is surrounded by Várkerület to the east and north, Színház utca and Petőfi tér to the west and Széchenyi tér to the south.

★★ **Fő tér** – *Illustration p 74*. On this square, the most airy open space in the old town, visitors can stop for a few minutes' rest at the foot of the Plague or Trinity Column (1701) to take in a few of the characterful buildings.

Várostorony (Town Tower) ⌚ – This is the tallest building, standing 61m/200ft high and is commonly referred to as **Tűztorony** (Fire or Watchtower). The tower's watchman used to stand on the balcony to give warnings of fire. The place is now open to visitors, who can see the roofs and layout of the old town, as well as a **panoramic view**★ of the surrounding area and the foothills of the Austrian Alps. The tower stands on a Romanesque base and foundations and consists of several different styles. The square ground floor, with walls 2m/6.5ft thick, dates from the 12C. A cylinder rests on this base, around which the arcaded balcony is placed. Both were made in the 16C. The Baroque crest at the top was set there in 1680. From this balcony, if you turn towards Fő tér, there is a view over the town hall's roofs.

B. Koch/PHOTONONSTOP

Sopron – Lion Pharmacy

Városháza (Town Hall) – This was built in the eclectic style at the end of the 19C. Apart from the municipal services, the town hall contains 15 000 books and 5 000 medieval documents, charters, royal bulls and manuscript fragments, accumulated since 1381.

Storno-ház ⓥ **(Storno House)** – *Fő tér 8.* Built in the 15C, this was remodelled several times and rebuilt in the 18C in the Baroque style. Among the many famous people who stayed here were King Matthias in 1482 and Franz Liszt in 1820 and 1881. Today, apart from an exhibition on Sopron from the 16C to the present, the house has preserved part of the Storno inheritance, which is exhibited here and gives an idea of the 19C middle class. The Storno family was a family of Italian immigrants who restored a great many buildings and monuments in the region.

Fabricius-ház (Fabricius House) ⓥ – *Fő tér 6.* Like most of the buildings in the town, this stands on Roman foundations, and its present appearance dates back to the 18C. Fabricius House shows three exhibitions, among which, on the first and second floors, is a history of the Amber Route that may be of interest to historians.

The exhibition on 18C daily life in Sopron is more interesting owing to its setting and especially for the quality, quantity and presentation of everyday household objects (valuable furniture, trunks containing trousseaux, faience stoves and, among the kitchen objects, a strange multi-speed spit).

★ **Roman Museum** – Downstairs there is a splendid space with Gothic vaults in brick. This is the setting for an exhibition of Roman tombstones as well as three large statues representing Jupiter, Minerva and Juno, found when the town hall was being built.

Patikaház Múzeum (Pharmacy Museum) ⓥ – *Fő tér 2.* This pharmacy, the first in Sopron, is called the **Angel Pharmacy** and dates from 1595, although some people give the date as 1601. In 1623 the second one, the Lion Pharmacy, opened its doors. By the end of the 19C there were 11 pharmacies in Sopron, one for every 6 000 inhabitants. There is still a **Lion Pharmacy** today at n° 29 Várkerület.

The Angel Pharmacy exhibits many objects from the time of its foundation, such as pots of blue glass or enamelled faience to preserve ointments, pomades and potions from the light. There are also drawers for arranging things in alphabetical order by their Latin name, such as dried plants, instruments, tools, containers for making preparations etc. The pots are decorated with an angel or a lion, depending on which pharmacy they came from. The Bayer company book containing the formula for aspirin is displayed here.

Turn your back to the Fire Tower and leave Fő tér on the right to tour the old town via Templom utca (Church Street).

Kecske templom (Goat Church) – *Templom utca 1.* According to legend, goats are said to have discovered a treasure, which the goatherd then kept for himself. However, overcome with remorse, the goatherd later built this church with part of his fortune. Others think that the church bears its name because of the sculptures visible in various places, including that of a goat's head and a kid, which might be part of the coat of arms of the anonymous donating family. In any case, the legend still thrives.

The Franciscans started building the church at the end of the 13C and work continued into the early 14C. Then the monastery was occupied by Benedictine nuns, which is why the church sometimes bears their name. The main altar painting is by Dorfmeister, whose works can be found in many Hungarian churches. This artist, who lived at Sopron, is one of the great masters of Baroque painting. There is also a late-15C tabernacle as well as a pulpit from the same period.
The **chapter room** is a beautiful Gothic room with vaults whose ribs run to the bases of the columns. In the 17C, this church was the seat of five Diets, and three queens were crowned here.

Központi Bányászati Múzeum (Mining Museum) ⓥ – *Templom utca 2.* The Mining Museum is opposite the Goat Church in a Baroque building that was the former residence of the Esterházy family. The family crest is over the door. Hungary's oldest mines, opened in the 18C, are in the Sopron region. The museum makes for an absorbing visit, with explanations on all the old and new underground mining techniques. Large live models illustrate the operation of the impressive mechanical monsters that bore into coal veins.
It was in the neighbouring residence at n° 4, in 1921, that the Allies checked the results of the Sopron referendum requested by the citizens.

A place to stay

Palatinus Hotel – *Új utca 23. ☎/Fax 99/311 395. 32 rooms between €41 and €57.* The rooms are small. The advantage of this hotel is that it is situated in the heart of the old town.

Sopron Hotel – *Fövényverem utca 7. ☎ 99/312 184, Fax 99/311 090. 112 rooms at around €104.* A sunny, pleasant hotel even if the 1970s architecture is a bit heavy. The rooms look out onto the old town, and also offer a beautiful panorama of the Lővér Hills. Outside pool, tennis court, fitness centre, restaurant, bar and the old town minutes away.

Pannonia Med Hotel – *Várkerület 75. ☎ 99/312 180, Fax 99/340 766. 60 rooms between €49 and €102.* On the inner boulevard that runs around the old town, this is a very comfortable establishment. Good quality cuisine.

Outside of town on the green part of the Lővér Hills, there are a number of hotels, some of which have not yet lost their Communist-period decor.

Szieszta Hotel – *Lővér krt. 37. ☎ 99/314 260, Fax 99/316 923. 280 rooms between €43 and €72.* A mass of concrete but surrounded with greenery and at advantageous prices. The renovation of the rooms and the public areas is being done floor by floor.

Maroni Hotel – *Lővér krt. 74. ☎ 99/312 549, Fax 99/341 182. 180 rooms between €22 and €47.* Well situated among the greenery.

Szilenció Hotel – *Lővér krt. 33. ☎ 99/314 033, Fax 99/314 265. 64 rooms between €22 and €37.* As its name suggests, the hotel is in a peaceful setting.

Panoráma Hotel – *Panoráma út 38. ☎ 99/312 745, Fax 99/322 745. 18 rooms at around €23.* Has a good location in the hills and offers good services: car park, garden, TVs in rooms. The restaurant prepares meals to order.

A place to eat

In town you will find good restaurants in very different settings, at the far end of a courtyard or in a passage enclosed by medieval walls. There are also excellent ice creams and pastries and marvellous coffees, for instance at **Carpigiani** *(Szent György utca 12)* or at the **Stefánia** pastry shop in the same street.

Pannonia Med Hotel – *Várkerület utca 75.* The hotel has a very pleasant restaurant with good cuisine.

Gambrinus – *Fő tér 3.* In the old town, on the ground floor of Gambrinus House or on the terrace. Meals or drinks at any time of the day. Copious servings.

Corvinus –*Fő tér 4.* Welcoming, more for a quick, simple meal.

Gyógygödör Borozó – From the Corvinus, go down into a cellar where you will find this restaurant. Excellent local wines accompany the dishes.

Halászcsárda – *Fövényverem utca 15. ☎ 99/338 403.* This pleasant fish restaurant – the **Danube** and **Lake Fertő** are nearby – is a few minutes from the town centre, just below the Sopron Hotel whose massive form can be recognised north of the old town. The prices are reasonable. Note that in the evening the place closes at 9pm.

Gabriel Étterem – *Előkapu 2-4. ☎ 99/340 311.* Modest and inexpensive. Frequented by the local inhabitants.

Cézár Pince – *Hátsókapu 2.* South-west of the old town near Orsolya tér. A cellar where you can try decent local wines.

Evángélikus templom (Lutheran Church) – The church was built between 1782 and 1783, but the bell tower was only added 80 years later, because Josef II, Emperor of Austria, had forbidden the building of bell towers on Lutheran churches. The church can hold a congregation of 4 000, on three levels. The organ, the largest in Hungary, has three keyboards, 52 registers and 1 860 pipes. The main altar was bought at auction in Vienna. At the top there is God the Father and St Michael surrounded by six angels carved out of the wood. There are four bells in the tower. The biggest one weighing 3 400kg/7 480lb is called the Heroes Bell and is engraved with the names of Lutherans who died during the First World War. On the second one, called the Peace Bell, a portrait of Luther is engraved. The third and smallest bell is only rung when the pastor recites the *Pater noster* (the Lord's Prayer in Latin), which is why this one is called the Pater Bell. The fourth one rang out when the results of the referendum were proclaimed, and is called the Loyalty Bell.

Go down Templom utca and take Fegyvertár utca on the left.

Orsolya tér – On this small square are the **Church of the Virgin Mary** and an old arcaded house called **Lábasház (House on Stilts)** ⓥ where temporary exhibitions are held. The Mary Fountain in the centre of the square dates from the 16C, although it was only placed here in 1930.

★ **Zsinagóga** ⓥ – *Új utca 22-24.* This street was once called Jews Street, after the community that settled here in the 9C. The Jews were driven away in 1526. In the early 14C they built a synagogue, which was turned into a private residence after their expulsion. No Jew was mentioned as a citizen of Sopron from 1526 to the middle of the 19C. The synagogue, rediscovered in 1967, has since been restored with great care and is worth a visit.

At n° 28 is a plaque informing passers-by that in 1944 this street was a ghetto for Sopron Jews, and that they were confined here until they were taken to the death camps.

Liszt Ferenc Kultúrház – The **Franz Liszt Cultural Centre** stands south of the old town, along Fő tér. Note that it should not be confused with the Franz Liszt Museum. The Cultural Centre does not hold any souvenirs of Liszt. Rather, it houses the Tourinform, the official tourist agency, as well as a library, a theatre etc.

Néprajzi Gyűtemény (Ethnographic Collections) ⓥ – *Deák tér 1.* This is still often called the **Liszt Ferenc Múzeum** (Franz Liszt Museum) as a tribute to the great composer, whose memory was honoured here until 1990. Today it contains a magnificent collection of craft objects, rustic instruments and tools.

German is the language used for fines in Sopron. If you find a parking ticket under the windscreen wiper, it will be in German. Sopron, with its medieval centre, has made a particular effort to welcome the Austrians, as if to apologise for leaving them. This can be seen in day-to-day dealings, and here, more than elsewhere, the sad memory of the Treaty of Trianon, which reduced the Austro-Hungarian Empire to a shambles, is omnipresent.

ADDITIONAL SIGHT

Pékmúzeum (Baker's Museum) ⓥ – *Bécsi út 5.* This former bakery has been turned into a museum, which still smells of baking.

EXCURSIONS

★★ **Lake Fertő** – *15km/9mi north-east. Take the road to Tómalon, cross Sopronkőhida.* A stop in the village of **Fertőrákos** is called for, to visit the **quarries**★ reminiscent of France's Baux-de-Provence. There is a spectacular, almost bird's-eye **view** from the path along the upper part of the old stone quarry. In summer, concerts are given among the rocks.

The road goes down to Üdülőtelep through fields of rushes that grow on either side of the lake. The actual shores of this protected nature reserve – the greater part of which is in Austria (Neusiedl Lake) – have been turned into a pleasant and refreshing resort that is very popular in summer. The **lake**, whose waters disappeared mysteriously in the 19C only to reappear again just as mysteriously, is also a paradise for birds and ornithologists. Note also the nearby lakeside dwellings linked by wooden bridges on piles. The lake is now completely navigable. Boat rides are organised, providing an added attraction. In the tourist season a border post operates from 9am to 6pm enabling people to cross from Hungary into Austria and vice versa.

Fertőd – *See this name.*

Nagycenk – *See this name.*

SZEGED★★

Csongrád province – Population 170 000

Michelin map 925 H 10

A town near the border where three countries join, Hungary, Romania and Yugoslavia, Szeged is a charming, beautiful city, a small Paris. It has boulevards and avenues, wide squares, parks and gardens, and is watered by the River Tisza that was once its misfortune. The flow of the river is now fully under control and contributes to the charm of Szeged. The city seems to enjoy life in the same way as someone who has had a close brush with death and savours every instant of life as a precious gift. One of its specialities is the making of women's slippers or *papucs* (pronounced pa-pootch). It is also the city of sun, the Hungarian city with the most hours of sunlight.

THE CITY SAVED FROM THE WATERS

Before the catastrophe – Its name is supposedly a corruption of the Hungarian word *sziget* (island), which already gives an indication of the city's close links with water. After the founding of Hungary, Szeged was a centre of salt distribution for about 200 years, a product over which it had a royal monopoly. The city's growth was halted with the arrival of the Mongols, who virtually destroyed it. Szeged was beginning to recover when Turkish invaders pillaged and ransacked the city again, although later on, it was able to win the sultan's protection. Indeed, he made it his personal domain up to 1686. After the departure of the Turks, it was not until the end of the 18C that prosperity returned to the city.

The catastrophe – A century later, on the night of 12 March 1879, at 2.30am, the dikes holding back the River Tisza broke in several places. The waters rose in a few hours to 8.06m/26.5ft above the reference level. Some districts remained under 3m/10ft of water for two months. Szeged almost disappeared off the map. Out of the city's 5 785 houses, only 265 withstood the flooding. Many thought that Szeged would never come back to life (the catastrophe's sequence of events is perfectly illustrated by an illuminated model in the Ópusztaszer memorial, in the dike caretaker's house). Another, even higher rise in the water level occurred in 1970. The Tisza's waters rose to 9.60m/31.4ft, but with different results. The dikes held this time, as the new Szeged had been rebuilt to a higher standard than the old city.

The promise – Five days after the dikes broke, Emperor Franz Josef came from Vienna, promising that Szeged would rise up again, more beautiful than ever. He dispatched a royal commissioner, Lajos Tisza, to oversee and co-ordinate the work.

The resurrection – The reconstruction of the city began according to Lajos Tisza's plans. A great many European cities helped Szeged in its reconstruction, and today Szeged is the most European of cities. In appreciation of the aid and donations, the city's outer boulevards were named after the donating cities and capitals: Brussels, London, Paris, Rome and Vienna. Moscow appeared after the Second World War for political reasons. Odessa was replaced in 1989 by Temesvári krt.

THE CITY – RIGHT BANK

★**Széchenyi tér** – Despite its size, this square covering over 5ha/12 acres in the heart of the city does not look at all out of place. It is planted with all kinds of trees (plane trees, hazelnut trees, sycamores, maples and magnolias), decorated with statues and fountains and ornamented with flower beds. Among the statues are those of the people who saved the city, as well as some paying homage to a few anonymous people, and the River Tisza is personified in both its characters, one destructive and the other generous. Széchenyi tér is a street in perpetual motion, where passers-by sit, stroll and dream. People of all ages come here throughout the year. In springtime they come for the fragrant evening air, in summer for the afternoon shade and the evening cool, in autumn for the enchanting colours and in winter for the invigorating snowball fights on a magnificent white carpet.

Városháza (Town Hall) – This is one of the largest buildings on the square. The beautiful yellow Baroque building is flanked by a watchtower whose bells ring every 15min. The inner courtyard is a pleasant place in summer, when the **Városházi Esték** chamber music concerts are given (town hall, evenings).
The Mayor's office is at n° 11 next to the town hall. The building was constructed before the flood and the two structures are linked by a closed passage called the **Bridge of Sighs** (Sóhajok Hídja), an allusion to the world-famous original in Venice. The building itself is called the **Bérház**. The little bridge was built in 1883 on the occasion of King's Day, enabling Emperor Franz Josef to go directly from where he and his courtiers had their apartments, to the town hall.

A place to stay

Tisza Hotel – *Széchenyi tér 3. ☎ 62/478 278. 48 rooms and 6 apartments between €29 and €80.* Private garage or secure parking place. The hotel has been renovated and has a fine position right in the centre of town. What is more, the area is quiet. The breakfast room is magnificent, and the service pleasant.

Royal Hotel – *Kölcsey u. 1-3. ☎ 62/475 275, Fax 62/420 223. 95 rooms at around €58.* One of the rare hotels in the town centre, near Klauzál tér. Decent.

Mátrix Hotel – *Zárda u. 8. ☎ 68/556 000, Fax 68/556 010. 10 rooms. at around €39.* A little hotel that is clean and well kept.

Marika Panzió – *Nyíl u. 45. ☎ 62/443 861. Rooms between €23 and €34.*

Csirke Panzió – *Bocskai u. 3/B. ☎ 62/426 188, Fax 423/367.*

A place to eat

Halászcsárda – *Roosevelt tér 12-14. ☎ 62/424 111.* A very good fish restaurant. Prices rather high.

Botond Restaurant – *Széchenyi tér 13. ☎ 62/312 435.* Warm welcome. Good cooking. Hungarian specialities.

Székely Étterem - *Thököly u. 41. ☎ 62/401 791.* Traditional dishes and quick service.

★★ **Klauzál tér** – On leaving Széchenyi tér and taking Kárász utca for about 50m/55yd, you come to Klauzál tér, a long square at right angles to the pedestrian street running to Árpád tér. Klauzál tér is a classic, with a balanced layout that contributes to Szeged's elegance. In the middle is a statue of Lajos Kossuth who gave his last speech here before going into exile. As a point of interest, if you are a gourmet or simply enjoy food, forget about history and everything else and stop at the **Virág** pastry shop (Virág Cukrászda) to the south of the square. You can choose between cakes, ice creams and other delicacies. Depending on the season or your taste, you may decide to sit under one of the large umbrellas or settle on the benches or steps.

Korzó – This is what the people of Szeged call the city's lively main street. It begins at Széchenyi tér and continues along Kárász utca. Walk about 300m/330yd away from Klauzál tér, and then cross Kölcsey utca on the right as far as Kálvin tér. Once there take a step backwards to admire the surprising **Reők palota**★. This well renovated building is a fine example of Baroque art. Its proportions, the diversity of its doorways and windows and ornamentation give it undeniable elegance.

★ **The university district** – It is worth spending some time in this true Latin quarter recalling its Parisian counterpart, for its personality, colour and atmosphere. Leave Kálvin tér, passing Reők palota on your left. Take Tisza Lajos kőrut on your left and cross a large square, Dugonics tér. On the city centre side, at the far end of the gardens, is **József Attila University**, named after the great poet. When he was a student he was expelled from the University for writing these words in 1924 (under Regent Miklós Horthy):

> "I have neither father, nor mother,
> I have neither God, nor country."

Another celebrity, **Albert Szent-Györgyi**, also worked in this eclectic building. He received the Nobel Prize in 1937 for his work conducted in Szeged on the vitamin C contained in paprika.

It was in this university that Szeged students held a meeting in 1956 to have Russian removed from the curriculum and to set up a students' organisation that would be independent of the Communist Party.

In the middle of the square stands a **musical fountain** that was built to mark the 100th anniversary of the great flood. In spring and summer, it plays a few melodies several times a day. Many artistic performances take place here, including music and dance, during Szeged's festival.

Hősök kapuja (Heroes' Gate) – Continue along Tisza Lajos Boulevard until you reach the arch where Boldogasszony sugárút (Avenue of the Blessed Virgin) meets **Aradi vértanúk tere** (Arad Martyrs Square. This refers to the 13 Hungarian generals executed in 1849 on the orders of the Austrian general Haynau, also called the Brescia Hyena on account of his cruelty). The gate is guarded by two impressive and almost terrifying statues of soldiers. They represent Horthy's white guards who were responsible for annihilating the reds after the defeat of the Council Republic headed by Béla Kun.

Two monuments on the square recall the battles against the Habsburgs: an equestrian statue of Ferenc II Rákóczi and a memorial column to the Szőreg battle victims (5 August 1849), with a *turul* at the top. From Aradi vértanúk tere, go through a metal gateway to Rerrich Béla tér where a copy of a medieval statue (1373) stands. The original is in Prague and represents St George and the Dragon.

Fogadalmi templom – Szeged Cathedral, also called the votive church, is on **Dóm tér**, a square measuring 12 000m²/14 350sq yd that is surrounded by university buildings. The square becomes wildly animated during the summer festival *(see Calendar of events)*. A stage and stands for 6 000 spectators are erected here for this great cultural event.

The church was built between 1913 and 1930 in accordance with wishes expressed after the 1879 flood. There are two neo-Romanesque towers on either side of the façade, which is decorated with a mosaic of the Twelve Apostles.

A tour of the square under the arcades will allow you to discover the **National Pantheon** and meet more than 80 Hungarian celebrities (men only) in the domains of Art, Culture and History. Among these illustrious individuals is the British engineer Adam Clark who was responsible for the construction of the Chain Bridge in Budapest.

Dömötör-torony (St Demetrius' Tower) – This medieval building stands in front of the cathedral. The square base dates from the 12C and the three octagonal upper floors are from the 13C. The tower came close to destruction to make room for the votive church, however it withstood the dynamite, which was viewed as a miracle, and so was restored.

Szerb ortodox templom – *Somogyi utca*. The 18C **Serbian Orthodox Church** deserves a visit for its golden tree, a very beautiful **iconostasis**★ created in the mid-18C. Eighty icons hang from the branches of the tree.

If you go down Somogyi u. in the direction of the River Tisza you will come to the embankment and, on the right, a pleasant walk along the river where many people take a stroll. You can have a rest on a bench beside a bronze statue.

★ **Móra Ferenc Múzeum** ⓥ – Ferenc Móra was the museum's director from 1917 to 1934. There is an ethnographic collection, an archaeological collection and a painting gallery. The exhibition illustrating the **life of the Avars**★ (a people of Mongolian origin who invaded part of Europe in the 8C) is very interesting. Inside a large yurt (nomad's tent) visitors can admire splendid jewels, discover everyday utensils and understand the relationship these people had with animals.

Opposite the entrance, a room is devoted to paintings based on the 1879 flood. They were executed by early 20C Hungarian masters, Pál Vágó, Mednyánszky, Munkácsy and Nyáry. One of them represents Emperor Franz Josef who had come to see the extent of the catastrophe. In the other rooms you will find paintings by István Csók and Rippl-Rónai.

Upstairs there is an exhibition on old Szeged, folklore, handiwork, clothing decorated with crewel embroidery, and painted, ornamental chests, all local specialities. Various trades are illustrated including beekeeping, saddlery, embroidery, and the making of the famous **papucs**. This word refers to the women's slippers made in Szeged. There are several sizes but only one form, which adapts to the shape of the foot. Colourful and embroidered, *papucs* were certainly inherited from the Turks. You will see them on women's feet at folk dance performances, but they are generally worn indoors as house slippers. You may buy some at the shop of Sándor Rátkai, the city's best craftsman and manufacturer *(Munkácsy u. 5)*.

Várkert (Castle Garden) – Here you may see a few vestiges of the old 13C castle that served as a prison before being destroyed after the flood. A collection exhibited in the museum was moved to what remains of the ruins. The Castle Garden overlooks the river embankment on one side. On the other side, it is bordered by Stefánia, which later runs into Dózsa Gy. u. The former Kass Hotel, now the Deutsch residence, rises up between two buildings. It is not just a legend: the Kass Hotel really did once offer the very best Hungarian and French speciality food.

There is a statue of a man with a long moustache standing in front of the hotel. He is holding a violin, and is probably the only existing statue of a gypsy musician. This is Pista Dankó, who travelled throughout the world, bewitching all those who had the good fortune to hear him play.

Szegedi Nemzeti Színház (National Theatre) – *Deák Ferenc utca 12*. Built after the 1883 flood, it burned down in 1885 and reopened the following year. The National Theatre appears in all its splendour when it is lit up. It has been used as the decor for a number of films.

On Szent István tér stands the first reinforced concrete construction in Szeged. **Víztorony**, (literally water tower), is a reservoir 91m/298ft high.

Gróf palota – *Tisza Lajos krt. 18-20.* This is a fine example of Art Nouveau.

★★ **Új Zsinagóga (New Synagogue)** – *Gutenberg utca 20.* While Budapest's synagogue is larger, the one in Szeged is considered the most beautiful in Hungary, and possibly even Europe. It was built between 1900 and 1903 under the direction of Chief Rabbi Emmanuel Loew, and was designed by Lipót Baumhorn in the Art Nouveau style with Moorish elements. An immense dome, symbolising the world, is supported by 24 columns representing the hours of the day. The dome is decorated with white roses for faith and blue stars to evoke the infinite nature of the universe. A Star of David blazes like the sun at the summit. Miksa Róth, a celebrated glassmaker, who decorated numerous buildings, including Budapest's Academy of Music, created the stained-glass windows. Many concerts are given in the New Synagogue, which has excellent acoustics.

The names of 1 874 Jews who died in the Second World War are engraved on white marble plaques in the entrance hall and there is a niche containing a symbolic tomb for those lost in the War.

The old synagogue is used as a theatre.

A legend says that during the 1879 flood the waters reached the synagogue and rose dangerously close to the Ark of the Covenant protecting the Torah, when suddenly the waters stopped and the sacred scroll was saved.

Alsóvárosi templom (Lower Town Church) or **Havi Boldogasszony-templom (Church of Our Lady of the Snows)** – From Vértanúk tere, facing the two sentinels flanking Boldogasszony sgt., take Szentháromság u. on the right up to Mátyás tér. This **Franciscan church** dates from the end of the 15C, whereas the bell tower was constructed in 1772. The pulpit and altars are Baroque. The main altar harmonises perfectly with the apse, and is symmetrically supported by two more restrained side altars which set off the splendour of the main altar. The **Franciscan monastery** adjoins the church. In this district, which has kept an almost countrified appearance, old houses can still be seen with planks on the gables set in the form of sunrays.

MAGYAR KÉPEK Kft

Szeged – Franciscan Church

THE CITY – LEFT BANK

Szeged has shown little development on the other bank of the Tisza. Take Belvárosi híd to cross the river. On the left as you leave the bridge, there are several hotels starting from Szent-Györgyi Albert u., as well as a baths complex.

Ligetfürdő – Sports and leisure complex. Swimming pools of different sizes.

Partfürdő – *Közép Kikötő.* Hot and cold thermal baths. Large water slide. Beaches and pools along the River Tisza.

Népliget – In line with the bridge, the **People's Wood** is a park that includes an amusement park, called Vidámpark.

SZÉKESFEHÉRVÁR**

Fejér province – Population 110 000

Michelin map 925 C 4 – Local map see BALATON

Székesfehérvár is the pearl in the oyster. Do not miss it, many foreign visitors by-pass the city without seeing it. From the motorway between Budapest and Lake Balaton, or road n° 8 to Veszprém, all you can see of Székesfehérvár is the industrial zone and blocks of residential flats squashed up against the horizon. Chance a detour and you will discover an old town full of unexpected charm.

THE ROYAL SEAT

After Esztergom, Székesfehérvár – Székes (seat or throne), Fehér (white), Vár (castle) – or Alba Regia was the most important town in the kingdom of Hungary. Kings, from Stephen in 1038 to János Szapolyai (John I) in 1540, were crowned and buried here. Stephen built his palace and cathedral here, both created by Italian architects. The crown jewels were kept at Székesfehérvár as well as the national archives. Built in the middle of marshland, the town was easy to defend although this did not prevent it falling into Turkish hands in 1543. Like many other places, the occupation left its mark on Székesfehérvár, and the cathedral and palace were pillaged and destroyed. The royal tombs were profaned. On their departure, the Turks left behind a heap of ruins. Although Emperor Leopold restored to the town its privileges and rank as a free royal town, this was little more than wishful thinking. It was following Maria Theresa's decision to found the diocese of Székesfehérvár that reconstruction slowly began to gain momentum at the end of the 18C. The marshes were drained, living conditions improved and the railway line became one of the major reasons for its growth. However, during the Second World War, the city, which was an important railway junction, was the site of heavy fighting. German troops fought bitterly here; the town changed hands several times, and suffered serious damage (although the old town was not so severely affected). After the war and during the Communist period, the diocese was looked on with suspicion. Nevertheless, given its strategic position, its economic growth was clearly so important that the aluminium industry, the manufacture and assembly of buses and the production of televisions were located in the town. The population doubled in less than a decade, which explains the presence of the large housing estates on the outskirts of the town.

The first bill of human rights? – On a hill near Székesfehérvár, King Andrew (Endre) II put his seal to the Golden Bull that he proclaimed in 1222. Some call this the first Hungarian constitution. It can also be considered as an outline for the bill of human rights. Written and proclaimed opportunely to respond to pressure by the Empire's barons, whose support the king needed, it recognised their right to rebel against their sovereign if he abused his power. It also forbade any form of abuse of power.

MAGYAR KÉPEK Kft

Székesfehérvár – View of the town centre

A STROLL THROUGH THE OLD TOWN

Leave the car in one of the car parks (fee) to be found around the centre of the old town. This roughly triangular area is defined by three streets: in the north and west by Mátyás Király körút, which extends southwards for a few metres along Piac tér, and in the East, Vár körút, which extends southwards along a short stretch of Budai utca and closes the triangle.

This approximate triangle enclosing the centre is divided by two long squares which run into one another: Városház tér (Town Hall Square, to the south) and Koronázó tér (Coronation Square, to the north). It is difficult to dissociate these squares. They are overlooked by a gable of the Bishop's Palace and, very near it, by the Franciscan church, opposite the **Polgármesteri Hivatal**, the town hall. The **Püspöki palota** (Bishop's Palace) was built in the Copf style (also called Zopf, *see Introduction: Hungary and the arts*) at the start of the 19C. It was made using stones from the royal palace and the remains of the medieval basilica.

Nemzeti Emlékhely (National Memorial) – Also known as the Garden of Ruins. Visitors can see the foundations of the basilica, which was destroyed in 1601, when the Turks' gunpowder store exploded. Some 37 kings of Hungary have been crowned and 17 buried in this sacred place. It was also here that the tombs of Béla III and his wife were found. In the garden, Roman, Gothic and Renaissance masonry is exhibited. The white marble sarcophagus near the entrance contains the remains of Géza, Stephen or Imre, Géza's younger son.

★ **Kossuth Lajos utca** – This charming and lively street, with its adjoining passages and inner courtyards, intelligently integrates contemporary concrete architecture into an old and varied environment.
The **Árpád Fürdő** baths are located at the junction of Táncsics Mihály u. and Kossuth Lajos u. There is a pink Secessionist (Hungarian Art Nouveau) style building nearby. As you walk along this street, do not hesitate to go through the porches and visit the courtyards to discover marvellous urban spaces.
Go down Kossuth Lajos u. to Szent István tér, a sort of public garden where the **equestrian statue of St Stephen** can be seen in front of the Provincial Hall. Turn right, go along Petőfi u. and up Arany János u. **Maulbertsch fountain**, on the corner of these two streets, bears the name of the Austrian artist whose Baroque frescoes decorate a large number of churches and castles.

Megyeház utca – This is an interesting street although not as animated as Kossuth Lajós utca, and without the same range of architecture. You can continue along it and admire the houses at n°s 7 and 11, which are examples of late-18C neo-Romantic construction. Take advantage of a few open doors looking onto inner courtyards to appreciate the charm and the peace. At n° 17 the **Town History Museum** ⓥ **(Várostörténeti Múzeum)** is joined to the **Doll Museum**★★ **(Baba Múzeum)** ⓥ which will charm both parents and children, especially little girls.

Budenz-ház ⓥ – *Arany János u. 12.* This house is where József Budenz (1836-92), a specialist in Finno-Ugric languages, once lived. It is now home to a permanent museum exhibiting a collection of 19C and 20C fine and applied art, a legacy from Miklós Ybl, the most famous of the late-19C Hungarian architects.

Szent István székesegyház – *Arany János u.* The present **Cathedral** was built in the 18C aided by Maria Theresa. It is in the Baroque style and was designed by Franz Anton Hildebrandt, court architect. Johann Cymball painted the ceiling frescoes. Outside, on the north wall, Christ on the Cross is dedicated to victims of the 1956 insurrection.

A place to stay

Magyar Király – *Fő u. 10. ☎ 22/311 262. Rooms at around €47.* The façade and stairs are eye-catching. The rooms are rather simple.

Alba Regia – *Rákóczi u. 1. ☎ 22/313 484, Fax 22/316 292. 104 rooms at around €41.* In a good position a stone's throw from the pedestrian centre. A building with no particular charm, but the rooms are very comfortable.

A place to eat

Szárcsa Csárda – *Szárcsa u. 1. ☎ 22/325 700.* On the outskirts of the city. The restaurant is currently in vogue. The dishes and decor are refined. There is also a *panzió* (rooms between €36 and €44).

Vastija Vendéglő – *Kossuth u. 3. ☎ 22/315 091.* In a picturesque pedestrian street. This little restaurant (beautiful dining room with vaulted ceiling) offers local specialities: filet mignon and chicken livers.

Ősfehérvár Étterem – *Koronázó tér 3.* The best-known restaurant in town. Restrained, carefully done decor. Speciality: Hungarian filet mignon.

Szent Anna-kápolna – **St Anne's Chapel**, the only surviving medieval building (1470), is a small and very sober structure that modestly affirms its presence opposite the cathedral. There is a statue of Domonkos Kálmáncsehi in front of the chapel. Of peasant origins, he became Bishop and Provost of Székesfehérvár, and then Chief Justice. The 18C Baroque altar inside is noteworthy.

★ **Fekete Sas patika** **(Black Eagle Pharmacy)** – *Fő utca 9.* This former Jesuit pharmacy was bought in 1773, at the time when the Order was being suppressed, and was given this name by the new owner. It was in operation until 1971. The interior is very beautiful, with carved and fitted furniture made by a Jesuit brother, where all the instruments and containers used by pharmacists in the past to make their preparations are now exhibited.

MAGYAR KÉPEK Kft

★ **Szent János Nepomuk templom** – **St John of Nepomuk Church** was built by the Jesuits between 1745 and 1751, and was taken over by the Cistercians. Frescoes inside decorate all the surfaces of the walls and vaulting. Note the 18C carved and gilded wood pulpit. A visit to the **sacristy★★** is a must, to see the set of Rococo furniture, made by a Jesuit brother in oak and lime, and perfectly appropriate for the size of the room.

★★ **Király István Múzeum** – *Országzászló tér 3.* On the ground floor, the museum exhibits a collection of Roman masonry and sculptures, including the most important part of the display, those from the Roman village of Gorsium *(see this name)*. The first floor upstairs is devoted to the region's archaeological history from prehistory up to the Turkish occupation.

A few steps northwards on the corner of Fő utca and Ady Endre utca, stands **Mátyás Király Emlékműve**, a monument inaugurated in 1990 to commemorate the 500th anniversary of the death of King Matthias Corvinus. The **Vörösmarty Theatre** (Vörösmarty Színház) at the far end of Fő utca illustrates the eclectic style. **István Csók Galéria** (*Bartók Béla tér 1*) presents temporary exhibitions illustrating current trends in Hungarian painting.

ADDITIONAL SIGHTS

Former Serbian quarter – *Take Ady Endre utca until it turns onto Tobak utca, and continue to Rác utca.* The Serbs settled here in the 16C, during the Ottoman occupation. **Rác utca** (Serb Street) is a reminder of this era, with a row of 12 magnificently restored traditional houses that constitute a veritable **open-air museum** **(Palotavárosi Skanzen)**. The **church** (Rác templom) has a very beautiful 18C **iconostasis★★**.

★ **Bory-vár (Bory Castle)** – *Go north from the centre, take Szekfű Gyula then Berény út and continue on Béla út and turn right along Bicskei u. after the cemetery, then take Máriavölgy u. to Bory tér.*

This curious construction, a castle with a mixture of architectural styles, was created by Jenő Bory (1879-1959), an architect and sculptor who was born in Székesfehérvár. For 40 years of his life he used his vacations to build this extraordinary structure with his own hands.

EXCURSIONS

★★ **Gorsium** – *See this name.*

★ **Velencei-tó (Lake Velencei)** – *10km/6mi east along road n° 70.* This rush-covered stretch of water extends over $26km^2$/10sq mi, and is a remarkable nature reserve, part of the Balaton region tourist circuit. The south-west shore is a paradise for nature lovers and ornithologists alike. The southern shore has been developed to welcome holidaymakers.

Várpalota – *9km/5.4mi west along road n° 8.* The curious mass of **Thury-vár** dominates the centre of the town. The **castle** stands at the end of a small square. It has a type of pediment at the top of the wall reinforced on either side by two enormous square towers. Nicknamed Peter Courage in former days, it was destroyed and rebuilt in about 1445. On the fringes of the advance of the Turkish armies, it withstood numerous sieges. One of its captains, György Thury, is still famous.

The castle's history can be relived by a tour of the various rooms.

SZENTENDRE★★

Pest province – Population 19 000

Michelin map 925 C 8 – Local map see DUNAKANYAR

Szentendre is a must for visitors staying in the Hungarian capital. Despite the constant crowd of tourists and numerous cafés, restaurants, boutiques and souvenir shops emphasising its commercialised aspect, this little town on the so-called Danube Bend tour is well worth a visit.
Stretching along the right-hand bank of the river, Szentendre has a romantic appeal. Indeed it is not surprising that late-19C artists sought inspiration and even settled here in an artists' colony (today north of Ady Endre utca, in an open-air sculpture park).
Szentendre is also a place for relaxation and leisure. Visitors can unwind on the banks of the Danube, go canoeing or enjoy the man-made beach.

A SHORT HISTORY

Szentendre was undoubtedly inhabited in prehistoric times. Nevertheless, the first inhabitants of which we have definite proof were the Celts (4C BC) and the Illyrians (people who lived in the northern part of the Balkans). The Romans in Augustus' reign established military camps and fortifications to defend the Roman walls. Traces of the Roman period are still visible in Római sánc utca, where the Ulcisia Castra military camp was located.

The Serbian community – The Serbian population goes back for the most part to 1690, when the Turks, thirsting for conquest, occupied today's Serbian capital. Protected by Emperor Leopold, a community of about 6 000 Serbs settled in Szentendre with a privileged status. Joined later by other compatriots, the Serbs formed a veritable enclave in the city, preserving their customs and their religion, that is to say Orthodox Christianity. The 18C was Szentendre's golden age. The Hungarians, Serbs, Greeks and Dalmatians who lived here made it a flourishing trade centre. Each community created and embellished its own homes and places of worship. The latter resembled Western Baroque churches from the outside, but remained faithful to their religious denomination. That is why several Orthodox churches can be found in this small city in a Catholic area.

THE OLD TOWN

In the tourist season the old town hums with activity. Lone travellers and guided groups – cameras at the ready as they docilely follow their guide – walk along the streets and alleys while the shopkeepers stand guard at their doors, trying to persuade passers-by to come in and have a look. For shopping, there is ample choice in **Bogdányi utca**, **Bercsényi utca**, **Alkotmány utca**, **Szerb utca**, or **Dumtsa Jenő utca**.

A place to stay

Horváth Fogadó – *Daru Piac 2. ☎ 26/313 950. 7 rooms between €27 and €35.* *Panzió* with plain and quiet rooms.

Bükkös Hotel – *Bükkős part 16. ☎ 26/312 021, Fax 26/310 772. 16 rooms between €36 and €41.* This hotel is the most popular in town. Reservations are a must.

A place to eat

Aranysárkány – *Alkotmány u. 1. ☎ 26/301 479.* In a little, uphill street. The dishes are delicious and prices reasonable. The venison with blueberries, grilled foie gras and lamb with tarragon is food fit for a king!

Rab Ráby – *Péter Pál u. 1. ☎ 26/310 819.* With its unusual, friendly decor, this is one of the town's best-known restaurants. A meeting place for artists.

Bárczy Fogadó – *Bogdányi u. 30. ☎ 26/310 825.* A restaurant in an 18C house specialising in Serbian and Hungarian cooking. Unusual decor with its white walls and blue tablecloths reminiscent of the houses on the Greek islands.

Korona – *Fő tér 18-19. ☎ 26/311 516.* This charming restaurant is on the town's main square, and has a pleasant terrace. However, prices are high and it is very tourist oriented. Speciality: goulash.

Labirintus Étterem – *Bogdányi u. 10. ☎ 26/317 054.* A voyage to the land of wine. This bar offers a taste of most of the nation's wines as well as a chance to visit its little museum describing the various wine-growing regions. Be careful not to drink too much! Adjoining restaurant.

★★ **Fő tér** – Classified as a historic monument, Szentendre's main paved square is triangular in shape with several streets leading off it – some go down to the Danube, others up the hill. In the centre stands a **Plague Cross**, a frequent sight in Hungarian towns. The Serbian Merchants' Association erected this monument in 1763 to commemorate the fact that the town was spared from the plague, and to give thanks to God. The cross is made of intricate wrought iron. It stands on a marble pillar decorated on each side with icons.

All around the square a series of shops and restaurants spill out onto the pavement in summer. Near the monument, hop into a carriage to tour the city. This is the departure point for carriages drawn by a pair of very gentle horses, driven by a coachman in period uniform. The ride is thoroughly enjoyed by children, and is a good opportunity to take photographs for the holiday album.

Kmetty Múzeum ⓥ – *Fő tér 21.* This museum, in a former merchant's home, is entirely devoted to the painter **János Kmetty**, who was born on 23 December 1889 in Miskloc and died on 16 November 1975 in Budapest. During his first trip to Paris in 1911 he was influenced by masters such as Cézanne, an influence that was to be apparent in his early landscapes. He then joined Lajos Kassák and the group of activist artists. From 1930 he spent his summers in Szentendre and in 1945 became a member of the local artist colony.

His life's work consists principally of self-portraits and still-life paintings. A selection of these is exhibited here (painting titles in English and Hungarian). Noteworthy on the ground floor are *Self-portrait with a Beard* (1912), and *Self-portrait with Blue Eyes* (1919-20) in which the artist fixes his intense expression on the spectator. *Still Life with a Yellow Vase* (1930) and *Still Life with Fruit in a Blue Vase* (1930) are, together with *Still Life with Self-portrait*, highly coloured. Paintings from the 1960s can be seen downstairs, and show a complete change in the expression of the same subjects. The lines are straight, the forms more schematic.

Blagoveštenska – From the outside, the 18C **Church of the Annunciation**, built by András Mayerhoffer (a Hungarian architect of Austrian origin) does not give the impression of being a Serbian Orthodox church. Visitors need to go inside the church to realise this. The entrance is via the portal located on the small neighbouring street, Görög utca. On reaching the bottom of the steps, visitors can hear Slav chants rising from the sanctuary and are struck by the Rococo **iconostasis**. Its panels mainly represent saints painted on a colourful, animated background.

The tall carved-wood seats resembling choir stalls have particularly high arms; this meant that worshippers could lean on them while standing during services.

★ **Kovács Margit Múzeum** ⓥ – A very well restored 18C former merchant's home is the setting for ceramist **Margit Kovács'** (1902-77) works. After studying graphic arts and painting on porcelain, she made several trips to study in the great European cities (Vienna, Munich, Copenhagen, Sèvres...). In 1937 she received a first prize at the Paris World Exhibition. Twenty-one years later, she again won first prize at the World Exhibition in Brussels. The compositions of this talented and prolific artist are highly varied: glazed clay, terracotta or pottery painted with a white or coloured glaze, with themes ranging from *genre* figures to folk traditions, religious or mythological subjects, decorative objects... All these compositions vary from the sombre to the naïve or gay, even humorous. The exhibition, of a highly personal art and vision of the world, can only charm the visitor. To quote a few examples of the various themes: a delightful *Family Album*, composed of a radiant mother with her two children (Room 1); *The Madonna of Kugelhopf*, a beautiful turned terracotta figurine (Room 2); *Country Wedding*, a mural depicting peasant life, and *The Fates*, infernal goddesses who metamorphose into graceful young women in Margit Kovács' hands – or at least two of them do (Room 3); *Fishermen's Wives*, anguished women wrapped in long cloaks, waiting for their husbands' return (Room 4). The visit continues in the barrel-vaulted wine cellar: *The Evangelists*, represented in an unusual way, through their associated symbols and in the shape of jugs (the man for Matthew, the lion for Mark, the bull for Luke, the eagle for John); *Angel Playing the Harp*, a painted and glazed sculpture with remarkably fresh colours (Room 5); decorative objects (Room 7); unglazed sculptures,

Family Album
by Margit Kovács

MICHELIN

including *Pottery with Bagpipe Player* (Room 8); the troubling *Magician* and the *Good Fairy and Bad Fairy* (Room 10). It should also be noted that there are a few pieces of the artist's furniture along with photos of her at work.

Marcipán Múzeum – *Dumtsa Jenő utca 7.* Children will certainly love this little museum, reached by passing through a pastry shop and tearoom. While marzipan, that soft and sweet almond-paste delicacy, is a popular treat for the young and sweet-toothed, it is nevertheless surprising to find it here in the form of what could be termed artistic compositions. Master confectioners have created several colourful tableaux of varying dimensions, showing an eye for detail as well as extraordinary patience and perseverance. The Budapest Parliament, the Chain Bridge, Franz Josef I and Sissy, Michael Jackson (life-size, made of white chocolate!), Mozart, Snow White and the Seven Dwarfs, Vienna's Spanish Riding School, Muppet Show characters and many others will amaze you. As you return through the shop, beware – the counter and shop window are very tempting!

Nemzeti Bormúzeum ⊙ – *Bogdány utca 10.* Linked to the neighbouring restaurant, this **wine museum** houses an exhibition on the 20 Hungarian wine-producing regions in a beautiful vaulted wine cellar. Some 170 types of wine and 5 000 bottles are here, to the joy of connoisseur and simple wine-drinker alike. A jewel in the collection: a 1936 Tokay made with 6 *puttony (see Tokaj).*

Várdomb (Castle Hill)

Take Alkomány utca, a small street that climbs and joins Fő tér.

Templom tér – On this tiny square where there are craftsmen during the holiday season stands a **Catholic church** dedicated to St John the Baptist. The most visible parts on its outside date from the early 14C. The Baroque interior includes painted wood altars decorated with wooden statues, of folk inspiration. The frescoes in the chancel are modern and were painted by members of the Szentendre artists' colony.
On the other side of the church, the **Czóbel Múzeum** ⊙ is devoted to **Béla Czóbel** (1883-1976), a Hungarian painter who was a member of the Paris School and divided his time between Budapest and the French capital. Several paintings represent views of Paris or the Seine. A talented portraitist, Czóbel gave particular attention to women. His portraits are varied, the colours brilliant.

Szerb Egyházi Múzeum ⊙ – The **Serbian Museum of Sacred Art** (explanations in English and Hungarian) has very interesting collections on two floors. The most important exhibits are the 19C iconostasis from the Serbian Orthodox church in Buda, an 18C carved-wood Entombment by Teodor Phelonin Grunkoviæ, several large 18C mantles worn by Orthodox priests during services, Serbian and Russian icons, and an incunabula in four volumes (under glass) dating from the late 15C.

Belgrád templom (Beograda) – Near the museum, the **Serbian Episcopal Cathedral** took the name of Belgrade, because it was built by Serbian refugees from that region. This fine reddish edifice, its steeple thrusting heavenward, is entered by a carved-oak Rococo portal. The interior is awe-inspiring. The iconostasis is resplendent with gilding, and is decorated with two rows of paintings, the upper representing the Life of Jesus, the lower the saints.

J.-C. Saturnin/MICHELIN

Szentendre – Hungarian open-air museum

SURROUNDING AREA

★★ Szabadtéri Néprajzi Múzeum (Open-air Ethnography Museum) ⊙ – *4 km/2.4mi north in the direction of Skanzen. By bus, leaving from near the HÉV station.*
Founded in 1967, this museum reconstitutes rural interiors, from modest or rich homes, as well as workshops of different trades from several Hungarian regions. The exhibits illustrate 18C and 19C regional life. Each region, whether Northern Hungary, Upper Tisza, Middle Tisza, North-east Hungary, the Great Plain, southern, central or western Transdanubia, or Kisalföld has a map *(explanations in English)* to help visitors find their bearings.
In the Upper Tisza, villages had a main street that became wider in the centre of the community. Take a look at the Calvinist church with its painted interior and wooden belfry, as well as the mill driven by horses walking round in a circle.
In the Hungarian Great Plain the houses had everything under one roof – the living quarters, storehouses and stables. In the Kisalföld region, the homes ran along each side of the main street, with a votive chapel marking the beginning of the street. The grocer's is noteworthy. Further along in the area devoted to eastern Transdanubia, recognisable by the wooden campanile in the middle of the road, visitors can stop to look at the thatched schoolhouse. The neighbouring room is where the schoolmaster, his wife and new-born baby lived. There is also a forge, and a Baglad house where well-off peasants lived.

SZIGETVÁR

Baranya province – Population 12 000

Michelin map 925 H 5

This quiet provincial town preserves the memory of a 1566 siege that marked Hungarian history.

One against forty – More than 20 000 men lost their lives, including the leaders: Zrínyi on the Hungarian side and Suleiman the Magnificent on the Turkish. Szigetvár, or the castle on the island, was built on an island in a marshy part of the River Almás to the west of Pécs.
In their plan to take Vienna and pursue their conquest of Europe, the Turks could not leave a single fortress untouched. They attacked Miklós Zrínyi's castle in 1566, where, from 8 August to 6 September, 2 500 Croatian and Hungarian soldiers held out against 100 000 Turks. For a month Miklós Zrínyi and his men refused to surrender to Suleiman the Magnificent, the victor of Mohács. It was only when the food and water ran out that they vainly attempted to escape. Maximilian I, Emperor of Austria, had refused to send reinforcements. In a bloody, hand-to-hand battle the soldiers abandoned the burning castle to fight the Turks. Miklós Zrínyi was killed in the fighting. It is said that a quarter of the Turkish soldiers were killed in this battle, meaning that each soldier from the castle killed 10 men. Suleiman also died, but of a heart attack. During the battle, the Turkish commander's body was strapped to a throne in his open tent, so his soldiers would still feel they had a leader. Suleiman's son was informed in plenty of time to come and take over command.
The battle of Zrínyi's castle was celebrated by Bertalan Székely (who illustrated the bravery of Eger's women in painting) and by the hero's great-grandson, with the same name as his ancestor, Miklós Zrínyi (1620-64). A man of letters and a strategist, he wrote *The Siege of Sziget* to the memory of his great-grandfather, a text that is still studied in schools.

SIGHTS

Vár – The **castle** that was abandoned to the flames and the Turks was transformed and used by the Turks themselves. They reinforced it and built a mosque in the courtyard. It was reconstructed by the Hungarians in the 18C and restored in 1960.

Zrinyi Miklós Múzeum ⊙ – This is in the former mosque. The story of the 1566 siege is told here, and an equestrian statue of the hero can be seen in the park near the museum.
A statue of the poet and lute-player Sebestyén Tinódi, singer of the castle's epic, stands outside, near the castle's main gate. This visit makes for a restful stop while travelling through southern Transdanubia. Inside the walls, the peace and cool atmosphere in the shade of the trees is a far cry from the tumult of ancient battles.
A **memorial** to the Soviet troops who liberated Hungary stands next to the castle.

Tinódi (Cultural centre) – *Olaj Lajos utca 8.* Built in 1985, it was created by **Imre Makovecz**, master of Organic architecture.

Római katolikus templom – The former Ali Pasha mosque, built in 1567, was turned into a Baroque church. The frescoes illustrate the 1566 siege, and are the work of István Dorfmeister.

EXCURSIONS

Ormánság – *25km/15mi south.* This part of the Dráva Valley is a marshy area that is often flooded. In the areas liable to flooding, the houses were built on rollers so that they could be moved to higher ground to escape the water. An example of this kind of house, called *talpas házak*, can be seen at the Ormánság Museum in **Sellye** where a great many household objects as well as folk costumes and decorated furniture are also exhibited. In **Vajszló**, on road n° 5804, several houses on stilts can be seen between Sellye and Harkány.

SZOLNOK

Jász-Nagykun-Szolnok province – Population 83 000

Michelin map 925 E 10

Szolnok (formerly Zounouk), on the right bank of the River Tisza, is the main city in this part of the Great Plain, called the Central Plain. It is an industrial centre and, above all, a thermal spa that draws numerous visitors. The Tisza, the areas for leisure and rest, and the thermal baths as well as a very strong cultural life all make the city very attractive.

Szolnok in the past – Although the traces of the past are not immediately obvious, a look at the town's history will confirm its importance. King Béla IV sought support in the region, occupied at the time by the Jász and Cuman people, who were respectively shepherds and horsemen. The Turks, who occupied the city for 130 years, made it one of their main administrative centres. Szolnok was won over to Ferenc II Rákóczi's cause, and, in retaliation, the Habsburgs blew up the castle. It was only in the 19C that Szolnok actually found the conditions necessary for its development. Trade, control of the flow of the Tisza and the construction of the railway line linking the town to the capital all contributed to its expansion and enrichment. Szolnok has remained a railway junction where passengers can take trains direct to various towns in Hungary as well as foreign capitals such as Warsaw or Bucharest.

Damjanich János Múzeum ⓥ – *Kossuth Lajos tér 4.* This old restored inn is now a museum that presents several exhibitions *(you have to buy a separate ticket for each exhibition)*. Three main sections make the visit worthwhile: the exhibition on the archaeological digs has some beautiful pieces; the exhibition on the province is an educational presentation of the various peoples who successively lived in the region: the third section is devoted to painters from the Szolnok School. This school, or artists' colony rather, to use the literal translation of the Hungarian word, was established in Szolnok in 1902 in studios financed by the city. The artists lived and worked on the other side of the bridge over the Zagyva on Gutenberg tér. They included some painters of great merit whose works hang in the museum for you to admire: Adolf Fényes, István Nagy, László Mednyánszky.

There is a pleasant walk along the Tisza, between the river, Templom utca, **Tisza Park** and **Verseghy Park**.

Szolnoki Galéria – *Templom utca 2.* The former synagogue has been turned into a painting gallery where temporary exhibitions are held. The architecture of the building is interesting.

Tisza Hotel és Gyógyfürdő – *Verseghy Park 2.* The **decor★** and atmosphere of this thermal spa and hotel will take you back a few decades or remind you of certain cinema decors. The waters here treat rheumatism among other ailments.

János Damjanich, a hero of the War of Independence

János Damjanich, after whom the museum is named, died the victim of a broken promise. He is one of the 13 martyrs executed by Austrian general Haynau at Arad on 6 October 1849, for having resisted the Habsburgs. In the spring of the same year, Hungarian troops were in full control of the military situation as they faced the Austrians. Emperor Franz Josef asked Tsar Nicholas I for help. The Russian and Austrian forces, with greater numbers and arms, rapidly took the situation in hand, and given the unequal battle, the Hungarians were forced to capitulate. General Haynau, nicknamed the Hyena for his cruelty, became Hungary's absolute master. He promised the Tsar he would avoid all bitter vengeance against the vanquished. Breaking his word, however, he had the Hungarian generals shot by a firing squad. On the same 6 October Haynau also had the moderate Prime Minister, Lajos Batthyány, as well as several other ministers executed. It is a day of mourning commemorated in Hungary every year.

Tiszaliget –This district is on the other bank of the Tisza. There is a pool and baths to relax in around the small **Lake Csónakázótó**.

A place to stay, a place to eat

Tisza Hotel – *Verseghy park 2.* ☎ *56/371 155, Fax 56/421 520. 33 rooms between €46 and €49.* Good level of comfort at affordable prices.
It is worth having a meal in the hotel restaurant because of its setting, atmosphere and the quality of the food.

Roza – *Petőfi Sándor u. 34.* The best Hungarian cuisine in town.

EXCURSION

Cegléd – *35km/21mi to the west along road n° 4.* This little town has a discreet, almost timid charm. It honours the memory of **György Dózsa**, the great defender of liberty. This rigorous man with his exemplary courage perished in atrocious pain and suffering. György Dózsa (1470-1514) was a soldier, ennobled after several military exploits. In 1514 the archbishop of Esztergom called on him to command the peasant army raised to fight the Turks. Dózsa, however, finding it exceedingly difficult to organise the battle and, sympathising with the peasants' grievances and complaints, took their side against the nobles. He was defeated at Temesvár (Timišoara in present-day Romania). Taken prisoner, he was tortured to death by the nobles he had fought against. In the middle of Kossuth Lajos tér a statue – the work of József Somogyi – has been raised in his memory.
The other significant event linked to Cegléd was **Lajos Kossuth**'s call against the Habsburgs on 24 September 1848. **Kossuth Múzeum** ⏲ *(Múzeum utca 5)* illustrates his life through paintings and personal effects.

SZOMBATHELY

Vas province – Population 85 000

Michelin map 925 E 2

This active university town, teeming with life, is quite different from tourist centres such as Sopron or Kőszeg. Founded by the Romans, it developed in the Middle Ages. The Mongols, Turks and Habsburgs successively either destroyed the town or hampered its development. In the 18C the place expanded in all fields and, later on, the railway favoured trade with southern Austria.
The town's name is a reference to its past commercial activity. In the Middle Ages, Saturday *(szombat)* was often a market day, and *hely* means site, or place.
The writer **James Joyce** made Szombathely the birthplace of the father of one of the characters in his novel, *Ulysses*.

A Roman soldier, venerated up to the present day – The man who, on a winter's night, cut his cloak in two and gave half to a poor man who was cold, was born in Szombathely (then called Savaria) in AD 316. This young Roman legionary had an amazing destiny. He subsequently converted to Christianity, became the Archbishop of Tours, founded a number of monasteries and was canonised. He is now known as **St Martin**.

SIGHTS

Püspöki palota – *Berzsenyi tér.* The Bishop's Palace and the Cathedral are the town's main sights. Like most of the other buildings in the district, these two, commissioned by Archbishop János Szily in the late 18C, were designed by a Viennese architect, Melchior Hefeli, thus giving the district a certain harmony.
On the ground floor of the Bishop's Palace, the **Sala Terana** has frescoes of Roman ruins by Dorfmeister. Also on show are liturgical objects and vestments, missals and Bibles as well as photographs of the Cathedral before the bombing.

Romkert – In a park behind the Cathedral is a **garden with Roman ruins**.
Colonia Claudia Savaria, the colony founded by Emperor Claudius in AD 43, was the principal city of Upper Pannonia. Several roadways crossed at Savaria. The discoveries exhibited in the Romkert were brought to light in 1938. A basilica dedicated to St Quirin was built here, of which a few mosaics can still be admired.

Iseum ⏲ – *Rákóczi út.* A concrete reconstruction of a temple to Isis, with some of the original elements incrusted in the concrete. It is somewhat dismal but should not be missed. Every year, operas and concerts are held here.

Dominating this sanctuary at n° 12 Rákóczi utca, is an **art gallery**★ that will give visitors an insight into 20C Hungarian art. In the same street is the old **synagogue** with its two onion-shaped towers, another of the town's sights.

Savaria Múzeum ⌚ – *Kisfaludi S. utca 9.* The museum gives onto a pleasant garden. It is a folk art museum with a number of works by shepherds: a collection of objects and domestic utensils dating from the Roman era, as well as glass flasks and receptacles. A local history museum gives visitors an idea of the damage caused during the Second World War.

Arborétum – The Kámoni arboretum to the north of the town lies between two large avenues, Paragvári útja and 11-es-huszár u. You access the arboretum from the latter. There are over 2 000 varieties of plants, and the surroundings are particularly cool in summer.

Vasi Múzeumfalu ⌚ – *Árpád út 30.* Open-air ethnographical museum illustrating regional life from the 18C to the 20C.

There are two lakes in the vicinity, **Horgász-tó** and **Csónakázó-tó** where visitors can go boating.

EXCURSIONS

Ják – *12km/7.5mi to the south.* This small municipality has a splendid Romanesque **abbey church**★★ which, with Zsámbék and Bélapátfalva, is considered to be a magnificent example of this type of architecture, rare in Hungary. The building of the church, commissioned by the Márton Nagy family began in 1220. It was dedicated to St George in 1256. The establishment of a monastery and construction of a church was a reflection of the power and might of the families who commissioned the building. This power and might was also expressed in the design and execution of the buildings, a gallery between the two bell towers being reserved for members of the nobility. Although it escaped destruction by the Mongols, the church has suffered from various restoration efforts. The most recent restoration work was undertaken between 1896 and 1904 by the architect, Frigyes Schulek, who built the Fishermen's Bastion in Budapest. Most of the **doorway** sculpture and the tympanum sculpture in particular, was replaced, stained-glass windows added and some of the Baroque elements removed.

Szelényi/MAGYAR KÉPEK Kft

Ják – Church door

Close to the abbey church is St James' Chapel.

Bük – *23km/14mi to the north-west.* This highly renowned spa has springs considered to be the most abundant in Hungary if not in Central Europe. Water gushes out at a temperature of 58°C/136°F. It is alkaline and is used for the treatment of gynaecological and muscular problems. Taken as a course of treatment, it is used to relieve biliary and gastric ailments. An 18-hole international golf course and a number of other leisure activities are available for people taking the waters.

Sárvár – *26km/16mi to the east along roads n° 86 and n° 88.*
Sárvár is a spa, fed by water which shoots up from a depth of 2 000m/6 560ft at a temperature of 83°C/181°F. The water contains alkaline bromide chloride, iodine, sulphates and trace elements. Asthma, respiratory tract disorders, rheumatism and painful joints are treated here.
Sárvár is also the town where the castle of the vampire princess, Erzsébet Báthori, is located. The princess was the wife of Ferenc II Nádasdy, Prince of Sárvár and a military hero known as the Black Captain, who won fame in the war against the Turks. Erzsébet was a diabolical woman who tortured her maidservants to death. She was taken to Transylvania and shut up in a castle where she died. They say that her story inspired the author of Dracula. Her portrait, exhibited in the gallery at Nádasdy Castle, gives no indication of her evil nature.

★★ **Nádasdy-vár** ⌚ – The present-day pentagonal castle dates from the 16C and used to belong to the Nádasdy family. This open-minded, cultured family set up a printing works in Sárvár, which printed the first books in Hungarian, a Latin grammar book and a translation of the New Testament.

The Magyar Cavalry

The Hussars were a tradition in the army and in the units made up of Hungarian troops. The Magyar cavalry's reputation goes back to the 10C and 11C. Its excellence was linked to the sturdiness of its steeds, which were tough and fast. The horsemen who came from Hungary to terrify the peasants in the far south of Italy, in the distant Iberian Peninsula, and on the shores of the Baltic Sea, enriched stories and legends with their exploits. There is the story of Lehel, a Hungarian chief who, when made prisoner, stunned the prince who was holding him captive, by saying, "You will go before me to the place where you want to take me, and where you will be my servant." The belief was that anyone who had killed another man with his own hands became his slave in the life beyond.
The strength of the cavalry and its supremacy lay in its nimbleness, rapidity and the accuracy with which the Hungarians could shoot arrows. The Hungarians had invented a recoil bow made of bone and wood stuck together. This bow was small and easy to handle and the horsemen could shoot without reining in their mount. Its shape and design made it as sturdy as a large bow. It had one weakness, water and rain would slacken the strings and cause the parts of the bow to come unstuck.

Nádasdy Castle is now home to a museum. On the 1st floor, the main part of this museum illustrates the life of the Hussars (uniformed models, weapons and breastplates etc).
Also on the upper floor, do not miss the richly painted and decorated great hall, known as the **Knights' Hall★★**. The ceiling frescoes, representing scenes of battles against the Turks, date from the mid-17C and were painted by Hans Rudolf Miller. The paintings on the walls are 18C and the scenes from the Bible were painted by Dorfmeister.

Arboretum – On the other side of Várkerület is the arboretum, which was laid out by the Bavarian royal family. The last member of the family occupying the castle died in 1921. The arboretum is a peaceful and relaxing place to walk through. It is also informative for those who wish to read the Latin and Hungarian names of the plants and trees growing there.

TAPOLCA

Veszprém province – Population 18 200

Michelin map 925 F 4 – Local map see BALATON

Tapolca, a small town with little character, nevertheless has a pleasant, well laid out town centre. Its small open-air lake, Malom-tó (Mill Lake), fed by water from underground springs, is surrounded with little squares and outdoor dining areas that are very lively in summer.

★Tavas-barlang (Lake Cave) ⌚ – *Kisfaludi utca 2.*
The extraction of bauxite from neighbouring mines involved drying up underground water layers. Pumping this water caused the underground Lake Tapolca to dry up and disappear for seven years.
Discovered accidentally in 1902 by a mason drilling a well, Lake Tapolca lies in a series of cavities worn into the mass of subterranean limestone rock. It is located about 18m/59ft below the surface and is easily reached down 72 steps and a few gentle slopes. This well-maintained, underground site makes for an interesting visit that takes about 45min.
There are two options: a simple descent to the caves, allowing visitors to understand and observe the site, or the descent plus a trip on the lake in a little metal boat that seats three people, one of whom is put in charge of it.
The air in these caves is completely pure, and contains 95% humidity. The temperature is a constant 25°C/77°F.

Tapolca "cures" – *Ady Endre utca 3.*
The hot springs and air with over 95% humidity provide efficient treatment, notably for bronchial conditions and asthma.

Iskola Múzeum ⌚ –
The **School Museum** may well surprise younger people and bring back childhood memories for older visitors.

A place to stay, a place to eat

Gabriella Hotel – *Batsányi tér 7.* ☎/*Fax 87/412 642. E-mail: mludasz@mail.elender.hu. 14 rooms at around €38.* The former mill has become the Gabriella Hotel, a small, very inexpensive and family run establishment with a restaurant. Reservations necessary in summer.

EXCURSION

★★ **Sümeg** – *18km/11.2mi to the north-west.* Whichever route you take to Sümeg, you will be drawn by the sight of the **castle**★★ (Sümegi-vár), perched imposingly on its promontory. Its silhouette outlined against the sky arouses curiosity. The castle was built in the 13C and had parts added over the ages. The Turks never succeeded in capturing it. It was, in fact destroyed by the Austrians in 1710.
The tour of the castle is compensation for the effort required to reach it, if only for the **views**★ on the way up. In the east are the extinct volcanoes of Tapolca and the Bakony Mountains. There is an exhibition of furniture, weapons and armour in the 13C tower.
At specific times, equestrian shows and pony rides for children take place in the courtyard.
In the town, the **parish church** (Római katolikus plébaniatemplom) on Deák Ferenc tér was built by Bishop Márton Padányi Bíró, one of the city's benefactors. It is worth visiting for its **frescoes**★★ by Franz Anton Maulbertsch, an Austrian painter whose works cover the walls of a large number of 18C Hungarian churches. This church is sometimes called the Rococo Sistine. The metaphor is somewhat excessive.

TATA★

Komárom-Esztergom province – Population 25 000

Michelin map 925 D6

This is a water town rather than a watering place, although, like many Hungarian towns it has thermal baths. The draining of the marshes and river flow control led to a water management programme, and water is all-important. Canals were created, two lakes, Öreg-tó (Old Lake) and Cseke-tó (Small Lake) add to the town's charm, and numerous springs, some of them warm, spurt out here and there. This perhaps explains the presence here of the training centre for the Hungarian swimming team.
Tata, set between the Vértes and Gerecse mountains, captivated kings very early on, and they made it their residence. In the 14C, King Sigismund built a castle on the spot now known as Öregvár (the Old Castle). Before attending the coronation of her son Lajos, the king's daughter Erzsébet hid here after she had carried off Szent István's crown. King Matthias Corvinus added Tata Castle to his Visegrád residence to make a royal hunting domain. During the Great Plague in Buda, Ladislas moved the Diet here.
Tata is a wonderful resort, leisure and walking centre. In the last week of June, the town puts on a richly diversified festival with shows, special events and craft exhibitions.

SIGHTS

Tata has two lakes: **Öreg-tó**★★ (the Old Lake), covering more than 250ha/600 acres, surrounded by the town, and Cseke-tó, the small lake, which is in Tata itself.

★★ **Öregvár** – The origins of the **Old Castle** go back to the 14C. A tower remains from this period. The castle now standing is a 19C neo-Gothic construction which houses the **Domokos Kuny Museum** ⏲★, named after a master ceramist from Tata. The museum exhibits archaeological discoveries, Roman and medieval masonry. On the first floor, life in the castle is illustrated, with a very beautiful stove in the form of a Gothic church. On the second floor, there is an exhibition of porcelain. You will also see a full-size snooker table, imported at the end of the 19C by an Englishman who came to train horses here when horse racing was beginning to develop.

The mills – Water is also a source of energy. Tata, a town of mills, has had numerous watermills. The last one was built in 1587 and functioned until 1968.
Several mills are still visible, among them that of **Cifra-malom** of which only ruins remain *(Bartók Béla u. 3)* and **Nepomucenus-malom** *(Alkotmány u. 2)* which has been well restored and converted into a Museum of the German Minority, once a large community in Tata.

A place to stay, a place to eat

Tóvárosi Fogadó – *Tópart u. 11. ☎ 34/381 599. Rooms between €28 and €36.* Panzió in a beautiful traditional house, overlooking the lake.

Kristály – *Ady Endre u. 22. ☎ 34/383 577, Fax 34/383 614. 25 rooms between €30 and €45.* A beautiful 200-year-old house converted into a hotel. The rooms are simple. Restaurant.

Gottwald – *Fekete u. ☎ 34/381 760. 15 rooms at around €51.* A fine hotel in the woods, with a restaurant.

Zöld Lovag Étterem – *Ady Endre u. 17.* This bar-restaurant is worth a visit for its setting (vaulted cellar) and its decor. Waitresses in traditional costumes.

Országgyűlés tér – The wooden 18C octagonal **clock tower** reveals the varied talents of Jakab Fellner, who also built the Esterházy-ház, now a hospital in the western part of the town on Hősök tere. It was in this house that Francis I, the heir apparent to the emperor of Austria, sought refuge before signing the Schönbrunn Treaty with Napoleon on 14 October 1809.

Nagy templom – Still in the same district, on Kossuth tere, the great church was also built by Fellner.

Kálvária-domb (Calvary Hill) – Fellner built a chapel and a tower 45m/148ft high on the top of this hill. The **view★** of the town is worth the climb. The panorama extends over the Gerecse Hills, and sometimes as far as the Danube and Slovakia.

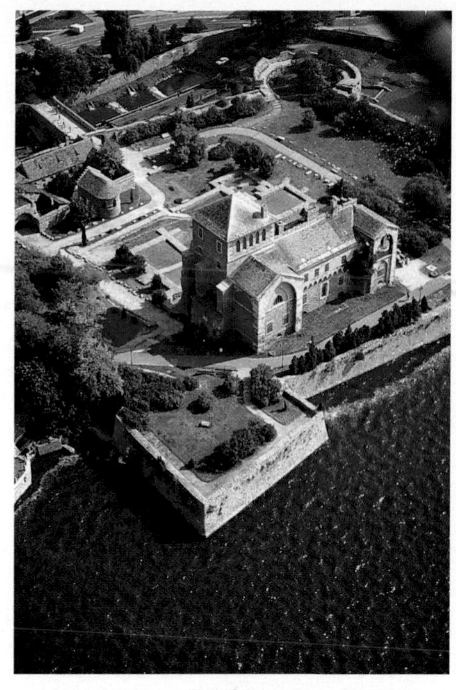
R. Palotas

Tata Castle

Cseke-tó – The smaller lake (about 12ha/29 acres) is in the north-east of the town, in woods, surrounded by a landscaped garden (200ha/490 acres). It is peaceful, cool and shady, with the light reflecting off the water. There is a strange church in the park, consisting of faux ruins erected by a French architect, Charles Moreau, who reused the stones from an old abbey together with Roman tombstones. The national swimming team's training centre is near the south entrance to the lake.

ADDITIONAL SIGHTS

Vértesszőlős – *5km/3.1mi south-east along road n° 100.* It was in this region that one of our ancestors, *Homo erectus sapiens*, once lived. His remains were discovered by László Vértes in 1960 on St Samuel's Day. This distant relative, christened Samuel, is thought to have been one of the first human bipeds capable of reasoning. Parts of the finds have been preserved at Budapest's ethnographic museum; a few traces remain in situ at Vértesszőlős, where they are protected.

Kocs – *8km/5mi south-west.* Kocs (pronounced Kotch) is famous as the place where the coach was invented. Originally, it was entirely closed in and drawn by three horses, two in the front and the third pulling from the back axle. Initially there was no suspension or shock absorbers between the body and the axle, so the *kocsi* inventors used down-filled cushions and covered the passenger part with an awning to make the trip more comfortable. The name of this vehicle was exported throughout Europe, becoming *coche* in French and coach in English... one of the contributions of the Hungarian language to world linguistics.

TIHANY★★★

Veszprém province – Population 1 700

Michelin map 925 F 5

The amazing setting owes its attraction to the wildness of the landscape and the 5km/3.1mi long peninsula jutting out into Lake Balaton as if trying to reach the other shore. Although it is busy on summer days, the approach to the village and the abbey still give the impression that the place is extraordinary. The peninsula is a nature reserve with a large population of birds and has been protected since 1952.

THE PENINSULA

If you go to the peninsula overland you will naturally take road n° 71. You can, however, reach it in a more original way by crossing the lake by ferry, leaving from Szántód on the south shore of Lake Balaton. The access road runs alongside an area of marshland called the outer lake (Külső-tó). Tihany village is situated on a hillside. Lower down, there are lavender fields that encircle the inner lake (Belső-tó), a 30ha/74-acre expanse, 25m/82ft above the level of Lake Balaton.

Visitors should allow a full day to walk around the area, taking the time to dream, meditate and admire the natural setting. Pathways, usually well signposted, run around the peninsula, and the abbey located on higher ground is a permanent landmark. There is a magnificent **view**★★ over Lake Balaton from the viewpoint to the left of the church.

★★ APÁTSÁG (ABBEY ⓥ)

In the middle of the 11C, King András I, who had married the daughter of King Jaroslav the Wise of Russia in Kiev in 1060, founded the Benedictine abbey of Tihany. András was the elder son of Vazul, Stephen's cousin, who had his eyes gouged out and his sons expelled by the king, to remove the family line from power.

Fortified in 1267, the site withstood successive attacks from the Turks but was finally destroyed by the Habsburgs in 1702 and now only a few ruins of the castle remain.

★★ **Abbey church** – This was built in the middle of the 18C on the site of the first church. The **interior** is the work of a friar who laid out, carved and decorated it in the Baroque and Rococo style of the time. The altars, the abbot's throne, the choir balustrade and the organ were made by Sebastian Stuhlhof. Some of the ceiling frescoes were painted by Bertalan Székely, one of the painters of the Panorama at Ópusztaszer *(see this name)*, Lajos Deák-Ebner and Károly Lotz in the late 19C. The baptismal fonts and the Lourdes altar are 20C.

The original organ is by the German organ-builder, Silbermann. It was severely damaged by a grenade in 1945, then restored. In 1993 a Hungarian organ-builder from Aquincum fitted a new mechanism. The organ concerts put on in the summer have been extremely successful.

G. Durand/PHOTONONSTOP

Tihany – Abbey church

Crypt – This is all that remains of the Romanesque abbey. It has fine groined vaulting supported by massive pillars. In the crypt is the tomb of the founder, King András I who died in Zirc in 1060. This is the only tomb of a Hungarian king that is still in its original state. On the wall you can see a copy of the abbey's Deed of Foundation (the original is in Pannohalma Abbey).

Museum – Housed in an 18C building beside the church, the museum puts on temporary exhibitions as well as an exhibition on Charles IV of Habsburg, the last King of Hungary (1916-18), who waited in vain at Tihany to be restored to the throne. Finally, there is a *lapidarium* with stones and sculpture of Roman and medieval origin.

ADDITIONAL SIGHTS

In the vicinity of the abbey, there are two streets popular with tourists, **Árpád utca** with the inevitable souvenir shops and **Pisky István sétány**.

A place to stay

Kántás Panzió – *Csokonai u. 49. ☎/Fax 87/448 684. Rooms at €39.* A good address in the heart of the little village.

Panoráma – *Lepke sor 9-10. ☎/Fax 87/448 494. 30 rooms at around €39.* This hotel on the lakeside truly deserves its name. The rooms are comfortable and peaceful.

Tihanyi Kastélyszálló – *Fürdőtelepi u. 1. ☎/Fax 87/448 611. 25 rooms between €23 and €73. Open May to 15 October.* On the shores of Lake Balaton, this luxury hotel, set in a 5ha/12-acre park, used to be Archduke Joseph's manor. An extravagance!

A place to eat

Fogas Csárda – *Kossuth Lajos u. 9.* The town's oldest inn serves mostly Lake Balaton fish. Allow yourself to be tempted by the celebrated *fogas*, a kind of pikeperch. In summer choose the terrace with a view of the valley.

Echo Étterem – *Visszhang u. 23, 8237 Tihany. Open April to September.* The restaurant offers a breathtaking view of Lake Balaton. It is also distinguished by being on the top of Echo Hill.

Pál Csárda – *Visszhang u. 19.* A small traditional inn with a terrace and an outdoor refreshment stall. Hungarian specialities.

Tihanyi Babamúzeum – *Visszhang u. 4.* Have a drink at the charming Doll Museum café.

Halászház (Fisherman's House) – This records the traditional life of a Balaton fisherman, with an exhibition of folk art.

Csúcs – There is a superb **viewpoint★★** from the top of Csúcs Hill (alt 232m/760ft) on the north-west side of the peninsula.

The small caves – Dug out by Russian monks at the time of King András I, these caves are still visible, including a well that remains from the time of the monks.

Echo Hill – The hill is renowned for its echo, which could once send back up to 16 syllables.

★**The former geysers** – In this volcanic landscape, more than 100 cones mark the sites of geysers that spouted up on the peninsula and were later petrified by volcanic eruptions. The most impressive is located behind the **Aranyház** (Golden House).

TISZA-TÓ

Lake TISZA – Jász-Nagykun-Szolnok province

Michelin map 925 D 11

The River Tisza was a source of wealth for the land it irrigated but also a source of danger *(see Szeged)*. The flow of the river was regulated by work initiated by István Széchenyi in the first three decades of the 19C.

After the Second World War, the need for power led local authorities to examine a project to construct a dam on the Tisza with Tisza-tó, Lake Tisza, as the **retaining reservoir**. The other purpose of this retention dam was to irrigate the land that had dried up and was covered in salt, due to the regulation of the flow of the river.

Nowadays, the retention dam covers 127km^2/49sq mi in a succession of lakes of different shapes. They are shallow, with islands and creeks – a fisherman's paradise – with zones allocated to motor craft not necessarily appreciated by everyone.

Holidays and nature conservation are, however, the key words in the region. When the flow of the Tisza was regulated, a bridge was built, setting Tiszafüred on the road from Debrecen to Budapest. To the north of this bridge is a nature conservation area only accessible with a permit specifically for studying and monitoring plants and animals. To the south there are various facilities, from campsites to luxury hotels, including spa treatment. Various types of accommodation are available together with entertainment and water leisure activities.

⚓ TISZAFÜRED Population 15 000

Tiszafüred is the area's main holiday resort. Numerous foreign visitors come here for the peace and quiet and to take advantage of the water sports activities. Fishing, swimming, boating, water-skiing or simply sunbathing after a swim in the warm water (as the lake is shallow, it warms up quickly in the summer sun) make for activity-filled days. Fishing permits, boat hire or tickets for trips on the lake can be obtained from tourist agencies located in the resort.

If you take a stroll in the southern part of the town, you will discover several traditional houses and potteries. You can also visit the **Kiss Pál Múzeum** ⏲ *(Taricsky sétány 6)*, a sort of fisherman's museum which also has a display of rider's saddles – a link with the nearby Hortobágy region *(see this name)*.

Lakeside towns *145km/91mi round trip – allow a full day.*

Leave Tiszafüred along road n°34 heading south.

Berekfürdő – A pleasant spa, mostly frequented by Hungarians.

A place to stay, a place to eat

In Tiszafüred

Vadász – *Szöllősi u. 4.* ☎/Fax *59/351 910. Rooms at €10 without breakfast.* A small, simple and charming hotel.

Fidibus – *Near Horgász campsite.* This boat anchored to shore can make you dream even if you will not be sailing off into the horizon.

Füzes – *Húszöles út.* Specialised in *langós*, savoury fritters coated with garlic and filled with meat.

Karcag – The town of wrought iron has a few interesting sights. The **Győffy István Múzeum** *(Kálvin u. 4)* not only has a display of craft objects but also wrought-iron work made by local craftsmen. **Kántor Sándor Fazekasház**, the Pottery Centre *(Erkel Ferenc u. 1)* and **Nagykunsági Tájház**, a regional house with traditional furniture *(Jókai u. 16)*, are also of interest.

Take road n° 4 south towards Kisújszállás and Szolnok.

Kenderes – This small town is well known as the place where Admiral Miklós Horthy was born and lived. As Regent, he was the Head of State from 1920 to 1944. People say he built a 30km/19mi water supply pipe linking the Tisza to his family home. He was exiled to Portugal and died in 1957. His ashes were brought back to his birthplace for burial in 1994.

Take road n° 3404 then n° 3221 in a northerly direction to return to the lake.

Kisköre – This small resort south-west of the lake, near the dam, has a family atmosphere and is therefore not as busy as Tiszafüred, but it offers exactly the same facilities and activities.

Return to Tiszafüred along the road that runs beside the dam and the east shore.

TOKAJ

Borsod-Abaúj-Zemplén province – Population 5 500

Michelin map 925 B 13 – Local map see BÜKK

The name of this small town brings to mind one of the most famous of all wines, which Louis XIV called "the king of wines and the wine of kings".
Tokay wine owes its reputation to its quality, but the Sun King's recognition gave it, and still gives it, a certain cachet. Tokaj itself is small and the town gives its name to the various wines of a region of some 6 000ha/14 800 acres of vines and a large number of great wines. The wine that enchanted the King of France was brought to him by Ferenc Rákóczi who was seeking his protection. The best-known wine today is the **Tokaji aszú** *(see Food and drink)* which has a unique taste, due to the special way it is prepared.

Tokay wines –Tokay wines, which go back to the Middle Ages, have been exported since that time. They have never lost their popularity. A Polish saying goes, "If it isn't Tokay, it isn't wine", which would make certain wine-growers turn pale. The great of this world, including kings, loved the wine, even Pope Pius IV used to say, "This wine is fit for a Pope". Peter the Great of Russia bought a vineyard in the region. Beethoven, Voltaire and Schubert used to drink Tokay and highly praised its quality. Greeks fleeing from the Turks settled in and around Tokaj in the 17C and 18C and took an active part in the development of the wine trade.

SIGHTS

Tokaj is a small town where two rivers meet, the Bodrog and the Tisza. The town centre has been renovated, giving it the appearance of a happy provincial town that is particularly good at welcoming wine enthusiasts. Although it is far from the capital (233km/146mi), the region offers a multitude of tourist attractions and draws visitors throughout the year. At weekends, it is not rare to see groups of around 20 people, company executives and their wives, on a training course involving culture and the knowledge of wine, so they will then be able to discuss Hungarian produce and carry its reputation far and wide. Some wine cellars such as **Rákóczi Pince**

Vines in the Tokaj region

(Kossuth Lajos tér 13) organise tastings for visitors. Rákóczi Pince is located at the entrance to an old cellar hollowed out of the ground, which stretches for several kilometres. Barrels and bottles are stored here, maturing as they await buyers.

Tokaji Múzeum ⓥ – *Bethlen Gábor utca 7.* The **Tokaj Museum** is housed in the residence of a wine merchant of Greek origin. The cellar and attics are devoted to wine. The cellar displays wine baskets, Gönc barrels, bottles of various ages from different types of vines, and objects and instruments used for making and bottling wine. The exhibition in the attics is devoted to the growing and preparation of vines. On the ground floor there is a collection of religious objects, including a *prie-dieu* kneeling-desk incrusted with ivory, a monstrance, several carved and painted wooden crucifixes and a collection of icons including a small triptych. On the first floor is a reconstruction of the apartment of the Greek wine merchant who took part in the settlement of a number of contracts in the region regarding the winegrowers and wine producers' corporation.

ZEMPLÉN MASSIF

Round trip of 172km/107mi – allow a full day

Leave Tokaj along road n° 3615 towards Tarcal, then take road n° 37 on the left.

Szerencs – Inhabited since the great invasions, Szerencs – like all old Hungarian towns – has seen many successive occupants. A Benedictine abbey was built on the site in the 13C but Szerencs became well known for its **castle** in the 16C. The fortress was built on the abbey ruins in the 16C and became the property of the Rákóczi family. It was in this castle that István Bocskai was elected Prince of Transylvania and then prince of the whole of Hungary. He received a royal crown from the sultan but, since he was prudent, did not commit himself and did not wear it. The Rákóczi family succeeded István Bocskai and it was in this castle that Zsigmond Rákóczi acceded to the throne. After the fight for independence failed and, despite the good relations established with Louis XIV and the Tsar, Ferenc Rákóczi had to resign himself to exile. He was taken in by the sultan and was to remain in Turkey until he died. An honest man, he devoted his time to studying, writing, handicrafts and hunting. His ashes were returned to Hungary in 1906 and buried at Kassa, a town that has been on the other side of the border since the Treaty of Trianon, in today's Slovak Republic. The castle was recovered by the Habsburgs and offered as a reward to servants of the court.
The castle was restored after the Second World War, and its function changed. It now houses various municipal departments, a library, a small theatre, a local history museum and a hotel (Huszárvár, the Hussar's Castle).

Leave Szerencs heading northwards along road n° 3712.

The countryside is green and hilly all along the road around the Zemplén massif.

★ **Vizsoly** – The first Bible printed in Hungarian was produced at a printer's shop in this village in 1590. It was translated by Gáspár Károlyi who was a clergyman from Gönc. This was an important event, the book being the first ever printed in Hungarian. On the other side of the wide street that crosses Vizsoly is the **Reformed Church** (Református templom), which has been perfectly restored. The specially designed lighting reveals splendid **frescoes**★★, some of which date from the 13C, and the most recent having been painted before the late 15C. When Calvinist reform dominated, these frescoes were covered over with a white coating. They only came to light in 1940. An inscription says, "If you are not here to pray, do not tarry." Nevertheless, do take the time to stop and have a look.

A place to stay, a place to eat

Makk Marci – *Liget köz 1. ☎ 47/352 336. Rooms at around €25.* A pleasant family *panzió* in the town centre. Warm welcome. Pizzeria.

Toldi Fogadó – *Hajdú köz 2. ☎ 47/353 403. Rooms at around €35.* Tokaj's best-known restaurant, in a pedestrian street. Friendly atmosphere. Hungarian and international cuisine. A few rooms.

In the surrounding area

Tokaj Disznókő – *☎ 47/361 371. About 10km/6mi from Tokaj, on road n° 37, at the junction with road n° 3615.* This vineyard can be visited and tastings had of the famous Tokaji aszú. It has been in existence since the 18C and was taken over by the French firm AXA-Millésime in 1992. There is also a well-known restaurant in the cellars of the beautiful 17C castle. High quality international cuisine.

Gönc – It is in this village of coopers that the barrels used as a unit of measurement for Tokaji aszú are made.

Continue as far as Bózsva and turn left a little further on, then go through Nyíri and Füzérkomlós.

Hollóháza – A famous porcelain factory (vases decorated with flower patterns) whose reputation stretches beyond the borders.

Go back the way you came and take a small road on the left at Füzérkomlós.

You will clearly see **Füzér Fortress** which belonged to the Rákóczi family, sitting on a hillock.

Pálháza – The **Reformed Church** (Református templom) is a Baroque building with a wooden bell tower. If you have time, take a pleasant trip through the woods on the small, narrow-gauge forest train which takes you as far as Kőkapu.

Széphalom – **Ferenc Kazinczy** (1759-1831) lived in this village. He reformed the Hungarian language in the 18C.

From Széphalom to Sátoraljaújhely, the road runs along the border between Hungary and Slovakia.

Sátoraljaújhely – This border town was also part of the Rákóczi family estates.

★ **Sárospatak** – *See this name.*

Road n° 37 brings the trip around the Zemplén massif to a close.

VÁC

Pest province – Population 35 000

Michelin map 925 C 8 – Local map see DUNAKANYAR

This relatively quiet town on the Danube, perhaps less brilliant and opulent than Esztergom and perhaps less picturesque and less visited than Szentendre, is nevertheless worth visiting. Its location on the left bank already differentiates it from the other towns.
An important river junction in the 2C, with the Roman name of *Uvcenum*, Vác became a bishopric during the reign of Stephen I. The bishops gave the town its Baroque appearance in the 18C.

SIGHTS

Danube Promenade – From north to south, Liszt Ferenc sétány, Ady Endre sétány and József Attila sétány follow one another forming a long promenade that is very popular in fine weather. It is a pleasant place for a stroll or a picnic and for children to play. In the summer, the river makes the atmosphere cooler and it seems as if there is a light breeze along the Danube, much appreciated by those out walking. There is a landing-stage between Liszt Ferenc sétány and Ady Endre sétány where you can take the car ferry to Szentendre Island.
A little further on, it is worth stopping to have a look at the **Franciscan Church** (Ferences templom). This small Baroque church and its surrounding square (Géza király tér) mark the centre of the medieval town. King Géza I is buried in the church. The pulpit was carved by a friar and represents the four cardinal virtues, Justice, Prudence, Temperance and Fortitude.

Take Budapesti Fő út on the left.

Konstantin tér – This large rectangular square was laid out by a succession of different bishops. The entrance to the imposing neo-Classical **Cathedral** is through a portico with six Corinthian columns. The cathedral is attributed to a French architect, Isidore Canevale, who, in fact continued the work begun by two Austrian architects, Franz Anton Pilgram and Johann Hausmann. Inside the building, the dome is decorated with a fresco by Franz Anton Maulbertsch, representing the Virgin Mary meeting St Elizabeth. In the crypt can be seen the remains of the medieval cathedral.

Opposite the cathedral, surrounded by a park, is the **former Bishop's Palace** (Püspöki palota). If you continue along Köztársaság út, you will go past **Trinity Column** (18C) and the **Piarist Church** (Piarista templom) beside a covered market, executed in the Organic style by László Saros.

Március 15 tér – This square is entirely lined with single-storey Baroque houses. The **town hall** (Városháza) is at n° 11. Construction began in 1736 but was only finished for Maria Theresa's visit in 1764. The building has fine proportions and is decorated with a wrought-iron balcony and sculptures representing Justice and the coats of arms of Hungary and the Miggazzi family.
Köztársaság út ends in a **Triumphal Arch** commissioned by Archbishop Miggazzi for Maria Theresa's visit. This arch adjoins a building given to the town of Vác by Maria Theresa, hence its name, Theresianum.

Theresianum – Now a prison, this was originally an academy for young Hungarian nobility. It was in use until 1855. With the failure of the 1848 revolution, the building was converted into a prison. The Regent, Miklós Horthy, made it the toughest and safest prison in the country between the two World Wars. Political prisoners were kept here. The Communist regime used it for the same purpose without relaxing the discipline. Among the guests in forced residence was a certain Abraham Lajbi Hoch, who escaped. Better known as **Robert Maxwell**, he became a press magnate and came to a tragic and somewhat mysterious end. He fell overboard from his boat and drowned in 1991.

EXCURSION

Vácrátót – *10km/6.2mi to the south-east along road n° 2104.* The **arboretum** ⏱★★ can be considered a botanist's paradise and a sheer marvel for plant lovers. Founded by Count Sándor Vigyázó in 1870, this park was originally a large landscape garden covering 29ha/72acres. Vilmos Jámbor, a landscape gardener and botanist, turned it into a place of scientific research without detracting from its charm. More than 12 000 species have been preserved in conditions close to their natural milieu.

VESZPRÉM★

Veszprém province – Population 64 000

Michelin map 925 E 5 – Local map see BALATON

North of Lake Balaton, the university town of Veszprém is built on several hills, and has a thoroughly unusual look to it. The most pleasant and picturesque part is the old town, or castle district.

The city of queens – King Stephen I founded the Veszprém bishopric and had the fortress built in the 11C. From the coronation of Gizella, Stephen I's wife, all the queens of Hungary were crowned by the bishop of Veszprém. The sovereigns were very attached to the city, and made it one of their preferred places of residence.
History has not spared Veszprém. Before the Turkish invasions, rivalry between Ferdinand of Habsburg and János Szapolyai resulted in the first destruction of the city. Later battles and fighting between the Austrian armies and the Turks caused the Viennese to destroy the fortress in 1702. The War of Independence supported by Rákóczi meant the destruction of what was left of Veszprém.
As the site remained of interest, the Church participated in its reconstruction and most of the buildings that we can admire today date from the late 18C and early 19C.

★THE OLD TOWN

Leave the car on Óváros tér.

The entrance to the old town is through **Hősök Kapuja**, Heroes' Gate. Just before you reach this gate, it is worth going to the top of **Tűztorony** (Fire Tower) for the beautiful panoramic **view**★★ of the city and its surroundings, including the Bakony Mountains.

Vár utca – The only street in the old town begins at Heroes' Gate, and is lined with buildings from different periods. The **Piarist Church** from 1836 is at n° 14 while the **Piarist Grammar School** at n° 10 was constructed in 1740. At n° 21, across the road, is a building by Jakab Fellner, the architect from Tata who also built the **Bishop's Palace** at n° 16 as well as the building for bishopric personnel at n° 14.
For the most part, these buildings offer little more than their façades in terms of interest, although this partially contributes to the special atmosphere of the street. The wind often blows along it and the Fire Tower chimes ring on the hour, so they say that at Veszprém either the wind blows or the bells ring.

Ph. Roy/HOA QUI

Veszprém – In the old town

★ **Gizella-kápolna** – The **Gizella Chapel** was discovered in the 18C when building began on the Bishop's Palace. It probably dates from the 13C, as suggested by the Byzantine-inspired frescoes decorating its walls.

St Michael's (Szent Mihály) Cathedral – Its origins go back to the 11C, after which it was destroyed and rebuilt several times. Only the Gothic **crypt**★ has survived. It is the original and is worth visiting. During the summer months temporary exhibitions are held here.

Nearby, several ancient vestiges can be seen under a transparent dome. They are from **St George's Chapel** (Szent György-kápolna), founded in the 10C.

Gizella Múzeum ⓥ – *Vár utca 35.* Objects of worship from the bishopric treasury, as well as Christian works of art.

St Stephen's (Szent István) Church belonging to the Franciscans adjoins the museum.

Vár utca ends at the far end of the ramparts and is nicknamed World's End. From here, there is a **view** as far as Benedek-hegy (Benedictine Hill) and to the viaduct across the River Séd. Statues of St Stephen and Queen Gizella were raised for the 900th anniversary of the death of Hungary's first king; they seem to watch over the city.

ADDITIONAL SIGHTS

South, at the foot of Castle Hill.

Megyeház – *Megyeház tér.* The seat of the Provincial Council is an eclectic, late-19C building.

Petőfi Színház – *Óvári Ferenc utca 2.* **Petőfi Theatre** deserves a look, for those interested in Art Nouveau.

Laczkó Dezső Múzeum ⓥ – Costumes of the various communities that lived in parts of Slovakia, Germany and Hungary are on display, together with everyday household objects. There is also an archaeological exhibition on the Roman occupation of the region.

Coming out of the museum, you will see **Bakony-ház** on the left. This 18C peasant home has been rebuilt and turned into a glass-blower's workshop.

EXCURSIONS

The tableware route: porcelain and crystal – *Circular tour 65km/39mi. Leave Veszprém westward along road n° 8.*

Herend – Fragile as they are, Herend porcelains have been placed on prestigious tables for more than one and a half centuries. The Victoria flowers and butterflies pattern is still manufactured. A stop at Herend is a must, to visit the **Porcelain Museum (Herendi Porcelánmúzeum)** ⓥ, which presents the most beautiful **pieces**★ in the collection. A modern complex has been built to show the products of the Herend works to best advantage. Three brick buildings closing off a square with a pool and fountain contain the workshops that demonstrate the making of porcelain. At the end of the tour, it's well worth having a look in the shop: very beautiful pieces, with matching prices.

In 1826 a citizen of Sopron who was working in a porcelain factory settled in Herend. Unfortunately, he accumulated a few debts, and in 1839 was obliged to relinquish his business to one of his creditors, Mór Fischer, a Tata porcelain maker.

MAGYAR KÉPEK Kft

Mór Fischer developed the business both technically and commercially, improving the products to the point of achieving the quality of Viennese porcelain. He had foreign technicians come, and drew inspiration from the Meissen style and technique (Meissen is where a chemist had discovered the secret of white porcelain and the possibilities of decorating it). At that time, Japanese and Chinese porcelains were being bought at high prices, so Herend porcelain was well placed to compete. The first plates were put on offer, decorated with flowers and butterflies. In 1851, Herend products were presented at the Great Exhibition in London, among the 19 most important manufacturers. Queen Victoria herself was charmed by the flowers and butterflies and ordered a complete service for the royal table.

A few years later, on the occasion of a New York exhibition, the President of the United States bought all the available production from the past 15 years. Mór Fischer, however, more concerned with the artistic aspect than the commercial, saw the company decline. It went bankrupt, and the man who created it died.

To avoid closing completely, new directors launched into intensive production. From 1870 they began manufacturing little statues, hunting scenes etc. In 1936-37, the factory was given a boost after winning gold medals at the Brussels and Paris exhibitions. Nationalised in 1948, the factory was bought by its employees in 1992 and is once more a flourishing enterprise.

Take the minor road towards Szentgál and Úrkút.

Ajka – Good wine blossoms in crystal. To complement the porcelain, a beautiful set of crystal glasses makes it possible to appreciate wines and other drinks. And so, you should make a second stop, this time at Ajka, if only to wander through the numerous shops selling sets of glasses and other objects in crystal.

This forest region belonging to the royal estate was gradually parcelled out to feudal lords. This was how the Ajkay family settled at the confluence of the River Torna and the River Csinger.

The glass industry came to Ajka in 1878, introduced by the Zichy family. Settled in Úrkút, this family moved its workshop to Ajka, where it operated until 1918. Relaunched in 1921, it has not stopped growing ever since.

The techniques used today are traditional ones, including hand blowing. Products are distributed in Western Europe and North America.

The **Banyászati Múzeum (Mining Museum)** ⌚, is in the forge.

Magyarpolány – In this charming village, 36 houses dating from the late 19C and the early 20C are part of the Hungarian national heritage. In one of them you will find a little folk art museum as well as a craftsman's workshop.

Return to Veszprém along road n° 8.

Öskü – *14km/9mi to the north-east. Take road n° 8 towards Székésfehérvár.* Set in the countryside is a large and quite unique mushroom, which should stir your curiosity. This is not a Walt Disney creation but simply a round **chapel** capped with a hemispherical roof. The walls date from the 11C and the roof and chancel from the 15C.

VISEGRÁD★★

Pest province – Population 2 100

Michelin map 925 C 7 – Local map see DUNAKANYAR

As you drive along the Danube Bend, the high fortress is an obligatory stop for visitors to look down on the legendary river. It is not by chance that kings and queens built their castles and residences here. There were, of course, strategic reasons, but above all there was the beauty and opulence of the landscape. Numerous European sovereigns paid visits to Visegrád through the ages.

A SHORT HISTORY

Before the 10C the Romans, in their advance, stopped at the Danube. They occupied the right bank of the river and built a fortress on the site which was then inhabited by Slavs who called the place **Visegrád** (high fortress). Two and a half centuries after the foundation of Hungary, King Béla IV ordered a residential castle to be built at the foot of the mountain, and a citadel at the top. The Angevin king Charles Robert, who reigned from 1307 to 1342, decided to build the Royal Palace; its ruins were discovered only in 1934. In 1335, at Visegrád, the king received the King of Poland, King John of Bohemia, Prince Rudolf of Saxony, the Prince of Lower Bavaria, Henrik de Wittelsbach and representatives of the Teutonic Order of Knights. This meeting lasted two months and enabled the differences between the King of Poland and the Teutonic Order to be settled, and also determined the itinerary of a trade route passing through Vienna. Charles Robert's successors returned to Buda, while continuing the work on Visegrád, taking up residence there as they wished. King Matthias and Queen Beatrice brought in Italian Renaissance artists who enriched the palace with fountains, decorative features and gardens. The royal couple received high-ranking guests, including the papal legate who described Visegrád as heaven on earth.

The destruction of the palace by the Turks, the use of the castle as a quarry and the passage of time caused even the very image of the palace to be forgotten. It seemed unbelievable that a palace 600m/1 968ft long by 300m/984ft wide had once stood on this site and borne witness to royal splendour. It was in 1934 that an architect, Frigyes Schulek (creator of the Fishermen's Bastion on Budapest's Castle Hill) began to uncover the site.

A place to stay

Haus Honti – *Fő u. 66.* ☎/*Fax 26/398 120. 27 rooms between €32 and €48.* A very decent *panzio* in the centre of the village.

Silvanus – *Fekete-hegy.* ☎/*Fax 26/398 311. 72 rooms between €71 and €89.* This modern hotel located just above the fortress provides a splendid view of the famous Danube Bend.

A place to eat

Jáger Csárda – ☎ *26/398 070.* This immense and tourist-oriented restaurant a few hundred metres from the fortress has several terraces overlooking the Danube. Specialises in game.

Gulyás Csárda – *Nagy Lajos kir. u. 4.* Traditional restaurant prettily decorated with strings of garlic and paprika. Hungarian specialities: raspberry soup, prawn salad, and game.

SIGHTS

Salamon-torony (King Solomon's Tower) ⌚ – Visible on arrival from the direction of Budapest. Either leave the car in the car park by the Danube, or continue for about 60m/65yd, turn left and take Salamon-torony utca. This hexagonal five-storey tower is 31m/102ft high, with walls up to 8m/26ft thick. It once served as a watchtower to keep guard over the river.

Királyi palota (Royal Palace) ⌚ – Returning from King Solomon's Tower, do not take the road along the riverbank. Rather, go in a parallel direction along Fő utca. After about 500m/550yd, at n° 27, you will come to the vestiges of the royal palace, among which are various documents and copies of architectural ornamentation that served in the reconstruction of the whole. In the 15C, with more than 300 rooms, the palace was at its most splendid. Visitors can see the main courtyard, and two fountains, the **Herkules-kút** (Hercules Fountain) decorated with coats of arms, and **Oroszlános-kút** (Lion Fountain).

★★ **Fellegvár (Castle in the Clouds)** ⌚ – *Turn left beyond the church and take a road off Fő utca. This leads to the citadel where visitors can park their cars with ease.* The citadel, built between 1240 and 1255, overlooks the river from a height of 350m/1 148ft. A small historical anecdote about the castle tells how the royal crown was kept here until 1440, when it was carried off by Elizabeth of Luxembourg who took it to Székesfehérvár where she wanted to have her son Lajos V crowned.

Climbing up to the citadel requires a little effort, but, on arrival, the view is much the same as the one admired by kings and queens in the past. Indeed, Visegrád's main attraction is without doubt the **view**★★★ from the citadel. It is here that the expression Danube Bend or Curve takes on its true meaning. As it flows out of neighbouring Slovakia, the river marks the border between the two countries for about 100km/60mi, and meanders between the Börzsöny and Pilis mountains before pursuing its course towards the Hungarian capital.

An exhibition in the middle of the castle tower traces the history of its construction. Another exhibition is devoted to the traditional activities of the people living in or near the castle: hunting, fishing etc.

In the summer, various types of entertainment (tournaments, combats, archery) are put on either in the castle or around its walls.

ZALAEGERSZEG

Zala province – Population 63 000

Michelin map 925 F 2

This county town has three interesting museums. The early 20C railway by-passed the city and Zalaegerszeg only began to develop significantly in the early 1930s when drilling for oil began.

★★ **Göcseji Falumúzeum** ⓥ – *Falumúzeum u.* Hungary's first open-air museum, the Göcsej Village Museum, is one of the most beautiful in the country. The houses and other examples of rural architecture that embellish the site have been transported from their original locations and reconstructed exactly as they were. About 30 buildings have been reconstituted, ranging from a little wooden belfry to a farm and watermill. You will discover the home life of the region's rural inhabitants, in a pleasant setting. Everything has been reconstituted, inside and outside, the interwoven wooden fencing, furniture for the various rooms, provision storehouses, barns etc. Laid out in a spacious area around stretches of water, it is a pleasant place for a peaceful picnic.

★ **Magyar Olajipari Múzeum (Hungarian Oil Industry Museum)** ⓥ – *Falumúzeum u.* This has an open-air section where machines and equipment no longer in use are exhibited. The indoor part has working models that explain and illustrate the history of underground mining operations. In this museum you can see the machines that were developed by Hungarian engineers to put out the oil-well fires set alight during the 1991 Gulf War. These are in fact jet engines, mounted on tanks to blast air at the base of the flames.

Göcseji Múzeum ⓥ – *Batthyány Lajos u. 2.* This museum is divided into three sections. The first presents the work of Zsigmond Kisfaludi Strobl (1884-1975), the creator of, among other works, the statue for the Budapest Liberation monument at the top of Mt Gellért. Originally Kisfaludi had created this sculpture in memory of István Horthy, the son of the regent who ruled over Hungary from 1920 to 1944. István Horthy was killed in an aeroplane accident in 1942. Kisfaludi, whose talents as a sculptor are significant, responded to all the concerns of his time through his work, from portraiture to social realism.

Another section is devoted to local history as well as handicrafts.

Because of its importance in local development, the third part illustrates the oil industry.

MAGYAR KÉPEK Kft

Göcsej open-air museum

ZIRC

Veszprém province – Population 8 000

Michelin map 925 E 5 – 21km/12.6mi north of Veszprém

Zirc, in the Bakony Mountains, is worth a visit for its former Cistercian abbey, built in the first half of the 18C on the site where King Béla III had established a monastery.

★THE ABBEY

The abbey, located in the town, is protected by a square planted with tall trees, and a wall that opens onto a vast courtyard. Once through the portal, you see an immense façade, bounded to the left by the towers and the entrance to the church. The rest is symmetrically aligned on either side of a central projecting part that dominates the building.

Church – The church has been renovated. Inside there are frescoes by Austrian artist Franz Anton Maulbertsch, above the main and south altars.

★**Library** – The library in the main building has a collection of 66 000 books. Some of them are of great interest: rare 14C and 15C manuscripts, a world history by Schedel, Boillon's 16C Gregorian missal, the text of Hungary's Tripartition Law, considered the source of Hungarian law, a Bible in nine languages, and the text of the French Constitution presented to Louis XVI in 1791 by the National Assembly. In one of the rooms created by Zirc joiners and cabinetmakers, you can see inlaid wood from 97 species of trees from the Bakony forests.
The vaulted and coffered ceiling is decorated with scientific symbols.

Reguly Antal Múzeum ⓥ – The ethnographic museum is in the same building. It is named after an ethnographer and linguist who was born in Zirc and was famous for research on Finno-Ugric peoples. Local fauna and flora are presented in an extremely interesting way. Numerous groups of enthusiastic children visit the museum.

Arborétum – The visit can be concluded with a stroll around the **arboretum**. Extending for 20ha/48 acres behind the abbey, it is planted with rare species of trees.

R. Palotas

Zirc Abbey

World Heritage List

In 1972, The United Nations Educational, Scientific and Cultural Organization (Unesco) adopted a Convention for the preservation of cultural and natural sites. To date, more than 150 States Parties have signed this international agreement, which has listed over 600 sites "of outstanding universal value" on the World Heritage List. Each year, a committee of representatives from 21 countries, assisted by technical organisations (ICOMOS – International Council on Monuments and Sites; IUCN – International Union for Conservation of Nature and Natural Resources; ICCROM – International Centre for the Study of the Preservation and Restoration of Cultural Property, the Rome Centre), evaluates the proposals for new sites to be included on the list, which grows longer as new nominations are accepted and more countries sign the Convention. To be considered, a site must be nominated by the country in which it is located.

The protected cultural heritage sites may be monuments (buildings, sculptures, archaeological structures etc) with unique historical, artistic or scientific features; groups of buildings (such as religious communities, ancient cities); or sites (human settlements, examples of exceptional landscapes, cultural landscapes) which are the combined works of man and nature of exceptional beauty. Natural heritage sites may be a testimony to the stages of the earth's geological history or to the development of human cultures and creative genius or represent significant ongoing ecological processes, contain superlative natural phenomena or provide a habitat for threatened species.

Signatories of the Convention pledge to cooperate to preserve and protect these sites around the world as a common heritage to be shared by all humanity, and contribute to the World Heritage Fund. The Fund serves to carry out studies, plan conservation measures, train local specialists, supply equipment for the protection of a park or the restoration of a monument, etc.

Some of the most well-known places which the World Heritage Committee has inscribed include: Australia's Great Barrier Reef (1981), the Canadian Rocky Mountain Parks (1984), The Great Wall of China (1987), the Statue of Liberty (1984), the Kremlin (1990), Mont-Saint-Michel and its Bay (France – 1979), Durham Castle and Cathedral (1986).

Unesco World Heritage sites included in this guide are:

Karst cave – Aggtelek
Budapest – the Castle District and View over the Danube
The Palóc Village of Hollókõ
The Benectine abbey of Pannonhalma
The palaeo-Christian cemetery at Pécs

Admission times and charges

Due to variations in the cost of living and constant changes in admission times for the majority of sights, the information given below is for guidance only.

This information applies to tourists travelling on their own who are not entitled to special reductions. For groups and parties, it is generally possible to obtain concessionary rates and admission times, if prior arrangements are made.

Last entry at museum ticket offices is generally 30min before closing time.

Prices are given in forints (Ft).

In the description part of the guide, visits to sights subject to special conditions are marked with the sign ⌚.

A

AGGTELEKI NEMZETI PARK

Aggtelek National Park – Summer, 8am-6pm, winter, 8am-3pm. 600Ft. ☎ 48/343 029. www.matav.hu/uzlet/anp

B

BAJA

Türr István Múzeum – Mid-Mar to mid-Nov, daily except Mon, 10am-4pm. Closed Easter and Whitsun. 80Ft. ☎ 79/324 173.

Nagy István Képtár – Mid-Mar to mid-Nov, Tue, Thu-Fri, 10am-4pm. Closed Easter and Whitsun. 80Ft. ☎ 79/324 649.

EXCURSIONS

Szekszárd: Megyeház – Apr-Sep, daily except Mon, 9am-5pm, Oct-Mar, Tue-Sat, 9am-3pm. 50Ft, free Tue. ☎ 74/312 154.

Szekszárd: Wosinsky Mór Múzeum – Apr-Sep, daily except Mon, 10am-6pm, Oct-Mar, Tue-Sat, 10am-4pm. 50Ft, free Tue. ☎ 74/316 222.

Szekszárd: Mihály Babits' birthplace – Apr-Sep, daily except Mon, 9am-5pm, Oct-Mar, Tue-Sat, 9am-3pm. 50Ft, free Tue. ☎ 74/312 154.

BALATON

i Petőfi Sándor u. 8 – ☎ 87/342 237

Balatonfüred: Jókai Múzeum – May-Sep, daily except Mon, 10am-5pm. 120Ft. ☎ 86/343 426.

Nagyvázsony: Posta Múzeum – Apr-Oct, daily except Mon, 10am-6pm. 50Ft. ☎ 88/364 300.

Szántód-puszta Majormúzeum – Mid-Mar to late Apr and early Oct to mid-Oct, Tue-Fri, 9am-2pm, May to mid-June and Sep-early Oct, 9am-6pm, mid-June to late Aug, 9am-7pm. Closed mid-Oct to mid-Mar. 300Ft. ☎ 84/343 946.

SIÓFOK

i Víztorony Pf. 75 – ☎ 84/315 355

Imre Kálmán Múzeum – Apr-Oct, 9am-5pm, Nov-Mar, 9am-4pm. ☎ 84/311 287.

Wostok Press

Lajos Kossuth's dagger – Magyar Nemzeti Múzeum

BUDAPEST

V., Sütő u. 2 – ☎ 1/317 9800

Funicular Railway (Sikló) – Daily except Mon in the second and fourth week of the month, 7.30am-10.30pm, ascent 400FT, descent 300FT, children 200FT.

Magyar Nemzeti Galéria – Daily except Mon, 10am-6pm. Closed 1 Jan. 400Ft. ☎ 1/375 8584.

Budapesti Történeti Múzeum – Mar-Oct, 10am-6pm, Nov-Feb, 10am-4pm. Closed Tue mid-Sep to mid-May, 1 Jan, 24-26 Dec. 500Ft. ☎ 1/355 8849. www.btm.hu

Ludwig Múzeum – Daily except Mon, 10am-6pm. 400Ft. ☎ 1/375 9175.

Patikamúzeum – Daily except Mon, 10.30am-5.30pm. 100Ft. ☎ 1/375 9972.

Magyar Borok Háza – Noon-8pm. Closed 1 Jan, 24-26 Dec. 300Ft. ☎ 1/212 1031. www.kernet.hu/mbh

Mátyás-templom – Mon-Fri, 9am-5pm, Sat, 9am-1pm, Sun, 1-5pm. 200Ft.

Egyháztörténeti Gyűjtemény – Daily, 9am-5pm. 400Ft with the church.

Zenetörténeti Múzeum – Apr-Oct, daily except Mon, 10am-6pm, 400Ft. ☎ 1/214 6770.

Középkori Zsidó Imaház – May-Oct, daily 10am-6pm. 200Ft. ☎ 1/355 8849.

Magyar Kereskedelmi és Vendéglátóipari Múzeum – Wed-Fri, 10am-5pm, Sat-Sun, 10am-6pm. 100Ft. ☎ 1/375 6249.

Várbarlang – Tue-Fri 10am-6pm. 300 Ft. ☎ 1/214 3121.

Budavári Labirintus – 9.30am-7.30pm. 900Ft (children 700Ft). ☎ 1/212 0207.

Telefónia Múzeum – Daily except Mon, 10am-6pm. 100Ft. ☎ 1/201 8188.

Hadtörténeti Múzeum – Apr-Sep, daily except Mon, 10am-6pm, Oct-Mar, daily except Mon, 10am-4pm. 250Ft. ☎ 1/356 9522.

Semmelweis Orvostörténeti Múzeum – Daily except Mon, 10.30am-6pm. Closed 1 Jan, 15 Mar, 25 Dec. 200Ft. ☎ 1/375 3533.

Országház – Tours on the hour. Tickets, gate n° 10, Mon-Fri, 8am-6pm, Sat, 8am-4pm, Sun, 8am-2pm. Guided tours in English, daily at 10am and 2pm. 1 700Ft.

Néprajzi Múzeum – Mar-Oct, daily except Mon, 10am-6pm, Nov-Feb, daily except Mon, 10am-5pm. Closed 1 Jan, Easter, 24-25 Dec. 500Ft. ☎ 1/473 2400. www.neprajz.hu

Coin and banknote collection – Thus 9am-2pm. Free.

Szent István Bazilika, North Tower – Daily 10am-6pm. 500Ft.

Földalatti Vasúti Múzeum – Daily except Mon, 10am-5pm. 100Ft. ☎ 1/461 6500.

Ady Endre Emlékmúzeum – Mar-Oct, daily except Mon, 10am-5.30pm, Nov-Feb, daily except Mon, 10am-4pm. Closed 1 Jan, 25-26 Dec. 100Ft. ☎ 1/337 8563.

Petőfi Irodalmi Múzeum – Daily except Mon, 10am-6pm. Closed 1 Jan, 25-26 Dec. 250Ft. ☎ 1/317 3611.

Magyar Nemzeti Múzeum – Mid-Mar to mid-Oct, daily except Mon, 10am-6pm, mid-Oct to mid-Mar, daily except Mon, 10am-5pm. Closed 1 Jan, 25-26 Dec. 400Ft. ☎ 1/317 7806. http://origo.hnm.hu

Zsidó Múzeum – Mid-April to Oct, Mon-Thu, 10am-5pm, Fri, Sun, 10am-2pm, Nov to mid-Apr, Mon-Fri, 10am-3pm, Sun, 10am-2pm. 600Ft. ☎ 1/342 8949.

Iparművészeti Múzeum – Mid-Mar to Oct, daily except Mon, 10am-6pm, Nov to mid-Mar, daily except Mon, 10am-4pm. Closed 1 Jan, 15 Mar, 25 Dec. 500Ft. ☎ 1/217 5222.

Bélyegmúzeum – Daily except Mon, 10am-6pm. Closed 1 Jan, 24-25 Dec. 100Ft. ☎ 1/341 5526.

Postamúzeum – Daily except Mon, 10am-6pm. 100Ft. Closed 2 Jan, 24-25 Dec. ☎ 1/268 1997.

Magyar Állami Operaház – Guided tours in English, daily at 3pm and 4pm. 1 200Ft (children, 600Ft). ☎ 1/332 8197.

Liszt Ferenc Emlékmúzeum – Daily except Sun, 10am-6pm, Sat, 9am-5pm. Closed 1 Jan, 15 Mar, 1-20 Aug, 23 Oct, 24-26, 31 Dec. 250Ft. ☎ 1/322 9804.

Kodály Zoltán Emlékmúzeum – Wed, 10am-4pm, Thu-Sat, 10am-6pm, Sun, 10am-2pm. Closed 1 Jan, 15 Mar, Easter, Whitsun, 2nd fortnight Aug, 23 Oct, 24-26 Dec. 150Ft. ☎ 1/352 7106.

Hopp Ferenc Kelet-Ázsiai Múzészeti Múzeum – Apr-Oct, daily except Mon, 10am-6pm, Nov-Mar, daily except Mon, 10am-4pm. 160Ft.

Ráth György Múzeum – Apr-Oct, daily except Mon, 10am-6pm, Nov-Mar, daily except Mon, 10am-4pm. 160Ft. ☎ 1/342 3916.

Szépművészeti Múzeum – Daily except Mon, 10am-7.30pm. 500Ft. ☎ 1/343 9759.

Magyar Mezőgazdasági Múzeum – Apr to mid-Nov, Tue-Sat, 10am-5pm, Sun, 10am-6pm, mid-Nov to Mar, Tue-Sat, 10am-4pm, Sun, 10am-5pm. 300Ft. ☎ 1/343 0573.

Közlekedési Múzeum – May-Sep, Tue-Fri, 10am-5pm, Sat-Sun and public holidays, 10am-6pm, Oct-Apr, Tue-Fri, 10am-4pm, Sat-Sun and public holidays, 10am-5pm. Closed 1 Jan, 25 Dec. 200Ft. ☎ 1/343 0565. www.km.iif.hu

Magyar Természettudományi Múzeum – Apr-Sep, daily except Tue, 10am-6pm, Oct-Mar, daily except Tue, 10am-5pm. Closed 24 Dec. 400Ft. ☎ 1/333 0655. www.nhmus/muzeum

Aquincum – **Ruins**: May-Sep, daily except Mon, 9am-6pm, mid-late Apr and Oct, 9am-5pm. **Museum**: May-Sep, daily except Mon, 10am-6pm, mid-late Apr and Oct, 10am-5pm. 400Ft. ☎ 1/368 8241. http//origo.hnm.hu/aquincum

Kassák Lajos Múzeum - Daily except Mon, 10am-6pm. Closed 1 Jan, 24-25 Dec. 150Ft. ☎ 1/368 7021.

Varga Imre Gyűjtemény – Daily except Mon, 10am-6pm. 200Ft. ☎ 1/250 0274.

Vasarely Múzeum – Daily except Mon, 10am-6pm. 200Ft. ☎ 1/250 1540.

Gül Baba Türbe – May-Sep and Nov, daily except Mon, 10am-6pm, Oct, daily except Mon, 10am-4pm. ☎ 1/355 8849.

Gyermekvasút – At **Hűvösvölgy**, mid-Mar to mid-Oct, Tue-Fri, 9.05am-4.05pm, Sat-Sun, 8.45am-4.15pm, mid-Oct to mid-Mar, daily except Mon, 9.05am-4.05pm. At **Széchenyi-hegy**, mid-Mar to mid-Oct, Tue-Fri, 9.45am-5.30pm, Sat-Sun, 10am-5pm, mid-Oct to mid-Mar, daily except Mon, 10am-5pm. 160Ft. ☎ 1/397 5394.

Chair-lift (Libegő) – Mid-May to mid-Sep, 9am-5pm, mid-Sep to mid-May, 9.30am-4pm. 300Ft. Closed second Mon of every month.

Pál-völgyi barlang – Daily except Mon, 10am-4pm. 400Ft. ☎ 1/325 9505.

Szemlő-hegyi barlang – Daily except Tue, 10am-3pm, Sat-Sun, 10am-4pm. Closed 1 Jan, Easter, 24 Dec. 350Ft. ☎ 1/325 6001.

Bartók Béla Emlékház – Feb-Nov, daily except Mon, 10am-5pm; Dec-Jan, daily except Mon, 10am-4pm. Closed 1 Jan, 15 Mar, Easter, Whitsun, 20 Aug, 23 Oct, 25 Dec. 300Ft. ☎ 1/394 2100.

Nagytétényi Kastélymúzeum – Mar-Apr, daily except Mon, 10am-4pm, May 10am-6pm, Jun-Aug, 10am-6pm, Sat-Sun, 10am-8pm, Sep-Oct, 10am-6pm, Nov-Dec, 10am-4pm. Closed Mon, 16 Mar, Easter, Whitsun. 300Ft. ☎ 1/226 8547.

Szoborpark – Mar-Nov, 10am-dusk. Rest of the year, Sat-Sun and public holidays at the same times. 300Ft (children, 200Ft). ☎ 1/227 7446. www.szoborpark.hu

BUGAC

Pásztormúzeum – May-Oct, daily except Mon, 10am-5pm. 100Ft. ☎ 76/372 583.

BÜKK

Bélapátfalva: Church – Mid-Mar to late Oct, daily except Mon, 10am-4pm, Nov to mid-Mar ask at Imre Kakuk's, Rózsa F. utca 42. 100Ft. ☎ 36/354 228.

Szilvásvárad: Horse Museum – Daily except Mon, 9am-noon, 1-4pm. ☎ 36/355 155.

C

CSONGRÁD

ℹ Fő u. 16 – ☎ 63/481 008

Tari László Múzeum – Tue-Fri, 1-5pm, Sat, 8am-noon, Sun, 8am-noon, 1-5pm. Closed public holidays. ☎ 63/383 103.

D

DEBRECEN

ℹ Piac u. 20 – ☎ 52/412 250

Református Teológiai Akadémia – Mon-Sat, 9am-5pm, Sun, 9am-1pm. Closed public holidays.

Déri Múzeum – Apr-Oct, daily except Mon, 10am-6pm, Nov-Mar, daily except Mon, 10am-4pm. Closed 15 Mar, Easter, 23 Oct, 24-26 Dec. 180Ft. ☎ 52/417 577.

DUNAKANYAR

Szob: Börzsöny Múzeum – Mid-Mar to Oct, daily except Mon, 10am-6pm, Nov to mid-Mar, Fri-Sun, 10am-4pm. Closed Easter, Whitsun, 25 Dec. 60Ft. ☎ 27/372 037.

E

EGER

ℹ Dobó István tér 2 – ☎ 36/321 807

Kazamaták – 9am-5pm. ☎ 36/312 744.

Dobó István Múzeum – Apr-Aug, 8am-8pm, Nov-Feb, 9am-5pm, Mar and Oct, 8am-6pm, Sep, 8am-7pm. ☎ 36/312 744.

Líceum – Jan-Mar, Sat-Sun, 9.30am-1.30pm, Apr-Sep, daily except Mon, 9.30am-3pm, Oct-Dec, Sat-Sun, 9.30am-1.30pm. Closed from 22 Dec to 16 Mar. ☎ 36/321 211.

Minorita templom – Daily except Sun, 10am-6pm, summer, Sun, 10am-5pm. ☎ 36/313 304.

Minaret – Apr-Oct, 10am-6pm. ☎ 36/410 233.

ESZTERGOM

Keresztény Múzeum – Summer, daily except Mon, 10am-5.30pm, winter, daily except Mon, 10am-4.30pm. Closed Jan-Feb, 25 Dec. 2 000Ft. ☎ 33/413 880.

Duna Múzeum – Daily except Mon, 9am-4pm. ☎ 33/550 250. www.dunamuzeum.org.hu

F

FERTŐD

Madách sétány 1 – ☎ 99/370 544

Esterházy-kastély – Mid-Apr to mid-Oct, daily except Mon, 9am-5pm, mid-Oct to mid-Apr, daily except Mon, 10am-4pm. Closed 1 Jan, Tue and Wed in Jan and Feb, Easter, 25 Dec. 800Ft. ☎ 99/370 971.

G

GÖDÖLLŐ

Tour of the royal castle – Apr-Oct, daily except Mon, 10am-6pm, Nov-Mar, daily except Mon, 10am-5pm. Closed in Jan, 24-26, 31 Dec. 600Ft. ☎ 28/410 124. www.c3.hu/~kastely

Mezőgazdasági Gépmúzeum – Daily except Mon, 10am-4pm. ☎ 28/310 200.

GORSIUM

Roman camp – May-Sep, daily except Mon, 8am-6pm. Oct-Apr, 10am-4pm, 100Ft (200Ft mid-June to Aug). ☎ 22/362 243.

GYÖNGYÖS

Fő tér 10 – ☎ 37/311 155

Mátra Múzeum – Mar-Oct, daily except Mon, 9am-5pm, Nov-Feb, daily except Mon, 10am-2pm. Closed 1 Jan, 24-25, 31 Dec. ☎ 37/311 447.

GYŐR

Árpád u. 32 – ☎ 96/311 771

Patikamúzeum – Weekdays except Wed, 7.30am-4pm. Closed Easter, Whitsun, 25 Dec. ☎ 96/320 954.

Xantus János Múzeum – Tue-Fri, 10am-6pm. Closed Easter, Whitsun, 25 Dec. 150Ft. ☎ 96/310 588.

Vastuskós-ház - Apr-Sep, daily except Mon, 10am-6pm. Closed Easter, Whitsun, 25 Dec. 120Ft. ☎ 96/310 588.

Városi Művészeti Múzeum – Mar-Oct, daily except Mon, 10am-6pm, Nov-Feb, daily except Mon, 10am-5pm. Closed 15 Mar, 20 Aug, 23 Oct. 100Ft. ☎ 96/318 141. www.home.arrabonet/cultura/muzeum/varosi/index.html

GYULA

Kossuth Lajos u. 7 – ☎ 66/463 421

Vár, Erkel Emlékház, Dürer Terem, Kohán György képtár, Ladics-ház – May-Sep, daily except Mon, 9am-5pm, Oct-Apr, daily except Mon and Tue, 10am-4pm. 100Ft. ☎ 66/361 236.

EXCURSIONS

Békéscsaba: Munkácsy Mihály Múzeum – Summer, daily except Mon, 10am-6pm, winter, daily except Mon, 10am-4pm. Closed 1 Jan, Easter, Whitsun, 24-26, 31 Dec. 100Ft. ☎ 66/323 377.

Békéscsaba: Szlovák Tájház – Oct-Mar, daily except Mon, 9am-5pm.

Békéscsaba: Meseház – Mon-Fri, 8am-4pm. 20Ft. ☎ 66/326 370.

H

HOLLÓKŐ

Postamúzeum – Apr-Oct, daily except Mon, 9am-6pm. 200Ft. ☎ 52/369 105.

HORTOBÁGY

Pásztormúzeum – ☎ 52/369 119

Hortobágyi Pásztormúzeum – Summer, 9am-6pm, winter, 10am-2pm, 200Ft. ☎ 52/369 119.

KALOCSA

Magyar Fűszerpaprika Múzeum – Mid-Apr to mid-Oct, daily except Mon, 9am-5pm. 100Ft. ☎ 78/461 819.

Viski Károly Múzeum – Mid-Mar to Oct, daily except Mon, 9am-5pm. 600Ft. ☎ 78/462 351.

Schöffer Miklós Múzeum – Daily except Mon, 9am-noon, 2-5pm. Closed public holidays. ☎ 78/362 253.

Népművészeti Tájház – See Magyar Fűszerpaprika Múzeum. http://korosnet.externet.hu/kalocsatours/

KAPOSVÁR

ℹ Fő u. 8 – ☎ 82/320 404

Rippl-Rónai József Emlékmúzeum – Apr-Oct, daily except Mon, 10am-6pm, Nov-Mar, daily except Mon, 10am-4pm. ☎ 82/422 144. www.smmi.hu/

EXCURSION

Szenna: Szabadtéri Néprajzi Gyűjtemény – Apr-Oct, daily except Mon, 10am-6pm, Nov-Mar, daily except Mon, 10am-4pm. ☎ 82/484 025.

KECSKEMÉT

ℹ Kossuth tér 1 – ☎ 76/481 065.

Cifrapalota – Feb to mid-Dec, daily except Mon, 10am-5/6pm, Sun, 1-5/6pm. Closed All Saints, Easter. ☎ 76/480 776.

Tudomány és Technika Háza – Mon-Fri, 10am-6pm. Closed public holidays. ☎ 76/487 611.

Bozsó Múzeum – Mid-Mar to mid-Dec, Fri-Sun, 10am-6pm. ☎ 76/324 625.

Leskowsky Hangszergyüjtemény – Daily except Sun, 9am-5pm. Closed public holidays. ☎ 76/486 616.

Magyar Népi Iparművészeti Múzeum – Jan to mid-Dec, Tue-Sat, 10am-5pm. 200Ft. ☎ 76/327 203.

KESZTHELY

ℹ Kossuth Lajos u. 28 – ☎ 83/314 144

Festetics-kastély – June and Sep-May, daily except Mon and day after public holidays, 9am-5pm, July-Aug, 9am-6pm. 1 400Ft (students, 700Ft). ☎ 83/312 190.

Georgikon Majormúzeum – May-Nov, daily except Mon, 10am-5pm, Sun, 10am-6pm. 150Ft. ☎ 83/311 563.

Balatoni Múzeum – May-Oct, daily except Mon, 10am-6pm, Nov-Apr, daily except Sun-Mon, 9am-5pm. Closed 1 Jan, Easter, 1 May, 20 Aug, 24-26 Dec. 200Ft. ☎ 83/312 351.

KISKUNFÉLEGYHÁZA

Kiskun Múzeum – Mid-Mar to Oct, Wed-Sun, 9am-5pm. Closed public holidays. 120Ft. ☎ 76/461 468.

KISKUNHALAS

Csipkeház – Daily, 9am-noon, 1-4pm. Closed Easter, 25-26 Dec. 100Ft. ☎ 77/421 797.

Thorma János Emlékmúzeum – Mar-Oct, Tue-Sat, 9am-5pm. 100Ft. ☎ 77/422 864.

EXCURSION

Kiskőrös: Petőfi Szülőháza – Daily except Mon, 9am-5pm. Closed Easter, 25 Dec. 100Ft. ☎ 78/312 566.

KOMÁROM

Monostori-erőd – Mid-Mar to Oct, daily except Mon, 9am-5pm. 600Ft. ☎ 34/344 0152. www.fort-monostor.hu

KŐSZEG

Jurisics Múzeum – Daily except Mon, 10am-5pm. Closed Easter, Whitsun, 25 Dec.

M

MAJKPUSZTA REMETESÉG

Tour – Apr-Oct, guided tour daily except Mon, 10am-5pm. 250Ft.

MARTONVÁSÁR

Beethoven Emlékmúzeum – Tue-Fri, 10am-noon, 2-4pm, Sat-Sun, 10am-4pm (6pm in summer). Closed 22 Dec-2 Jan. ☎ 22/569 500.

MOHÁCS

Mohácsi Történelmi Emlékhely – May-Oct, daily except Mon, 9am-5pm.

N

NAGYCENK

Széchenyi-kastély – Apr-Sep, daily except Mon, 10am-6pm, Oct-Mar, daily except Mon, 10am-2pm. Closed 1 Jan, Easter, Whitsun, 25-26, 31 Dec. 400Ft. ☎ 99/360 023.

NYÍREGYHÁZA

🅸 Országzászló tér 6 – ☎ 42/312 606

Jósa András Múzeum és Megyei Levéltár – Daily except Mon, 9am-4pm, Sun, 9am-2pm. Closed 1 Jan, Easter, Whitsun, 25, 26, 31 Dec. 100Ft. ☎ 42/315 722.

O

ÓPUSZTASZER

Panorama – Apr-Oct, 9am-6pm, Nov-Mar, daily except Mon, 9am-4pm. Closed 1 Jan, 25-26 Dec. 1 600Ft. Show every 30min. ☎ 62/275 257. www.opusztaszer.hu

Rotonda – Apr-Oct, 9am-7pm, Nov-Mar, daily except Mon, 9am-5pm. Closed 1 Jan, 25-26 Dec. 400Ft. ☎ 62/275 257.

Park – Apr-Oct, daily 10am-6.30pm. 600Ft. ☎ 62/275 257.

P

PANNONHALMA

🅸 Petőfi u. 25 – ☎ 96/471 733

Abbey – Mid-Mar to May and Oct to mid-Nov, daily except Mon, 9am-4pm, June-Sep, 9am-5pm, mid-Nov to mid-Mar, 10am-3pm. ☎ 96/570 191.

PÁPA

🅸 Fő tér 12 – ☎ 89/311 535

Késkfestő Múzeum – Apr-Oct, daily except Mon, 9am-5pm, Nov-Mar, daily except Mon, 9am-4pm. Closed 1 Jan, 25-26 Dec. 200Ft. ☎ 89/324 390.

PARÁD

Kocsimúzeum – Apr-Sep, 9am-5pm, Oct-Mar, 10am-4pm. Closed public holidays. ☎ 36/364 387.

PÉCS

🅸 Széchenyi tér 9 – ☎ 72/213 315

Ókeresztény Mauzóleum – Mid-Apr to Oct, daily except Mon, 10am-6pm. Sun, 10am-4pm, Nov to mid-Apr, daily except Mon, 10am-4pm. Closed 1 Jan, 24-26, 31 Dec. 300Ft. ☎ 72/312 719.

Csontváry Múzeum – Mid-Apr to Oct, Sun, 10am-4pm, Nov to mid-Apr, daily except Mon, 10am-6pm. 300Ft. ☎ 72/310 544.

Martyn Ferency Múzeum – Temporarily closed.

Endre Nemes Múzeum – Mid-Apr to Oct, daily except Mon, 10am-2pm. 300Ft. ☎ 72/310 172.

Modern Magyar Képtár – Mid-Apr to Oct, Sun, 10am-4pm, Nov to mid-Apr, daily except Mon, 10am-6pm. Closed 1 Jan, 24-26, 31 Dec. 150Ft. ☎ 72/324 822.

Vasarely Múzeum – Daily except Mon, 10am-6pm, Sun, 10am-4pm from mid-Apr to Oct. 300Ft. ☎ 72/324 822.

Zsolnay Múzeum – Daily except Mon, 10am-6pm, Sun, 10am-4pm from mid-Apr to Oct. Closed 1 Jan, 24-25, 31 Dec. 350Ft. ☎ 72/324 822.

Régészeti Múzeum – Mid-Apr to Oct, daily except Mon, 10am-2pm, Nov to mid-April, daily except Mon, 10am-4pm. Closed 24 Dec-1 Jan. 150Ft. ☎ 72/312 719.

S

SÁROSPATAK

Rákóczi-vár – May-Oct, daily except Mon, 10am-6pm, Nov-Feb, daily except Mon, 10am-5pm. Closed 1 Jan, 24-25 Dec. 300Ft. ☎ 47/311 083. http://origo.hnm.hu/sarospatak

SIKLÓS

Vár – Mid-Apr to mid-Oct, daily except Mon, 9am-6pm, mid-Oct to mid-Apr, daily except Mon, 9am-4pm. Closed public holidays. 90Ft. ☎ 72/351 433.

EXCURSION

Villány: Bormúzeum – Daily except Mon, 9am-5pm. Closed Easter, 25 Dec. ☎ 72/492 130.

SOPRON

ℹ Liszt Ferenc u. 1 – ☎ 99/338 892

Tűztorony Várostorony – Mid-Apr to Sep, daily except Mon, 10am-6pm. 300Ft. ☎ 99/311 327.

Storno-ház – May-Sep, daily except Mon, 10am-6pm, Oct-Apr, daily except Mon, 10am-2pm. 300Ft. ☎ 99/311 327.

Baba Múzeum, Székesfehérár

Fabricius-ház – May-Aug, daily except Mon, 10am-6pm, Sep, daily except Mon, 10am-2pm. 200Ft. ☏ 99/311 327.

Patikaház Múzeum – Daily except Mon, 9am-6pm. 150Ft. ☏ 99/311 327.

Központi Bányászati Múzeum – Daily except Mon, 10am-6pm. Closed 1 Jan, 24-26, 31 Dec. 200Ft. ☏ 99/312 667.

Lábasház – Daily except Tue, 9am-5pm. 150Ft. ☏ 99/311 327.

Zsinagóga – May-Aug, daily except Tue, 9am-5pm, Sep, daily except Tue, 10am-2pm. 200Ft. ☏ 99/311 327.

Néprajzi Gyűjtemény – May-Aug, daily except Mon, 10am-6pm. 200Ft. ☏ 99/311 327.

Pékmúzeum – May-Aug, daily except Mon, 10am-2pm. 150Ft. ☏ 99/311 327.

SZEGED

i Victor Hugo u.1 – ☏ 62/311 711

Móra Ferenc Múzeum – Daily except Mon, 10am-5pm. ☏ 62/312 033.

SZÉKESFEHÉRVÁR

i Városház tér 1 – ☏ 22/312 818

Várostörténeti Múzeum – Mar-Oct, daily except Mon, 2-6pm. Closed 15 Mar, Easter, Whitsun, 1 May. ☏ 22/315 583.

Baba Múzeum – Daily except Mon, 9am-5pm. Closed 15 Mar, Easter, Whitsun, 1 May. 200Ft. ☏ 22/315 583.

Budenz-ház – May-Sep, daily except Mon, 10am-4pm, Oct-Apr, daily except Mon, 10am-2pm. Closed Nov-Mar. 100Ft. ☏ 22/315 583.

Fekete Sas patika – Daily except Mon, 10am-6pm. Closed 24 Dec-1 Jan. 100Ft. ☏ 22/315 583.

Király István Múzeum – May-Sep, daily except Mon, 10am-4pm, Oct-Apr, daily except Mon, 10am-2pm. Closed 24 Dec-28 Feb, 15 Mar, Easter, Whitsun, 1 May. 100Ft. ☏ 22/315 583.

Palotavárosi Skanzen – Daily except Mon-Tue, 10am-4pm. Closed 24 Dec-1 Mar, 15 Mar, Easter, Whitsun, 1 May. ☏ 22/315 583.

Bory-vár – **Castle:** Sat-Sun, 10am-noon, 3-5pm. **Gardens:** Mar-Oct, 9am-5pm. Closed 1 Jan, 15 Mar, Easter, 1 May, Whitsun, 25 Dec. ☏ 22/305 570. www.fehervar.hu/kultura/boryvar

EXCURSION

Várpalota: Thury-vár – Apr-Oct, daily except Mon, 11am-5pm. Closed Easter. 70Ft. ☏ 88/472 391.

SZENTENDRE

i Dumtsa Jenő u. 22 – ☏ 26/317 965

Kmetty Múzeum – Daily, 10am-4pm. Closed first day of the week after a public holiday. 150Ft. ☏ 26/310 790.

Kovács Margit Múzeum – Mid-Mar to Oct, 10am-6pm, Nov to mid-Mar, 10am-4pm. Closed first day of the week after a public holiday. 250Ft. Guided tours in English, 3 500Ft. ☏ 26/310 790.

Nemzeti Bormúzeum – 10am-10pm. Closed 24 Dec. 100Ft, 800Ft includes tasting. ☏ 26/317 054.

Czóbel Múzeum – Mid-Mar to Oct, 10am-4pm, Nov to mid-Mar, Fri-Sun, 10am-4pm. ☏ 26/312 721.

Szerb Egyházi Múzeum – Summer, daily except Mon, 10am-6pm, winter, daily except Mon, 10am-4pm. Closed 1 Jan-28 Feb except Sat-Sun. 100Ft. ☏ 26/314 457.

Szabadtéri Néprajzi Múzeum/Skanzen – Apr to mid-Nov, daily except Mon, 9am-5pm. 500Ft. ☏ 26/502 519. www.sznm.hu

SZIGETVÁR

Zrínyi Miklós Múzeum – July-Aug, 9am-6pm, Mon, 9am-3pm, Sep-Oct and Apr-June, daily except Mon, 9am-3pm. 120Ft. ☏ 73/311 407.

SZOLNOK

🅘 Ságváry Endre krt. 4 – ☎ 56/424 803

Damjanich János Múzeum – May-Oct, daily except Mon, 9am-5pm, Nov-Apr, daily except Mon, 10am-4pm. Closed Easter, Whitsun, 25 Dec. 100Ft. ☎ 56/421 602.

EXCURSION

Cegléd: Kossuth Múzeum – Apr-Oct, daily except Mon, 10am-6pm, Nov-Mar, daily except Mon, 9am-3pm. Closed 1 Jan, Easter, Whitsun, 24-26, 31 Dec. ☎ 53/310 637.

SZOMBATHELY

Iseum – Temporarily closed. ☎ 94/312 554.

Savaria Múzeum – Mid-Apr to mid-Oct, Tue-Thu, 10am-5pm, Fri, 10am-7pm, Sat-Sun, 10am-4pm, mid-Oct to mid-Apr, Tue-Thu, 10am-5pm, Fri, 10am-7pm. Closed public holidays. 120Ft. ☎ 94/312 554.

Vasi Múzeumfalu – Apr-Oct, daily except Mon, 10am-4pm. ☎ 94/312 554.

EXCURSION

Sárvár: Nádasdy-vár – Daily except Mon, 10am-5pm. Closed public holidays.

T

TAPOLCA

🅘 Deák Ferenc u. 20 – ☎ 87/323 415

Tavas-barlang – June-Aug, 10am-6pm, Apr-May and Sep-Oct, daily except Mon, 10am-5pm. Closed Nov-Mar. 160 Ft. ☎ 87/412 579.

Iskola Múzeum – Mid-May to Aug, daily except Sun, 9am-4pm, Sep to mid-May, daily except Sun and Mon, 9am-4pm. Closed public holidays.

TATA

🅘 Ady Endre u. 9 – ☎ 34/384 806

Domokos Kuny Múzeum – Summer, daily except Mon, 10am-6pm, winter, Wed-Fri, 10am-2pm, Sat-Sun, 10am-4pm (last entry 30min before closing time). Closed 23-31 Mar, 25 Dec. 150Ft. ☎ 34/487 888.

TIHANY

🅘 Kossuth u. 20 – ☎ 87/448 804

Apátság – May-Sep, Mon-Sat, 9am-6pm, Sun, 11am-6pm, Nov-Mar, Mon-Sat, 10am-3pm, Sun, 11am-3pm, Apr and Oct, 10am-4pm. 180Ft. ☎ 87/448 405.

TISZA-TÓ

🅘 Húszöles út 21a – ☎ 59/353 000

Tiszafüred: Kis Pál Múzeum – Daily except Mon, 9am-noon, 1-5pm. Closed public holidays. ☎ 56/352 106.

TOKAJ

🅘 Serház u. 1 – ☎ 47/353 390

Tokaji Múzeum – Summer, daily except Mon, 9am-5pm, winter, daily except Mon, 10am-4pm. 200Ft. ☎ 47/352 636.

V

VÁC

🅘 Csányi körút. 45 – ☎ 27/316 160

Vácrátót: Arboretum – 8am-4pm. ☎ 28/360 122.

VESZPRÉM

🅘 Rákóczi u. 3 – ☎ 88/404 548

Gizella Múzeum – May-Oct, 9am-5pm. 100Ft. ☎ 88/426 088.

Laczkó Dezsű Múzeum – May-Sep, daily except Mon, 10am-6pm, Oct to mid-Mar, daily except Mon, noon-4pm. 120Ft. ☎ 88/426 081.

EXCURSIONS

Herend: Herendi Porcelánmúzeum – Apr-Oct, 9am-6.30pm, Nov-Mar, 9am-4.30pm. 1 000Ft (children, 300Ft). ☎ 88/261 144. www.porcelanium.com

Ajka: Bányászati Múzeum – Tue-Fri, 11am-4pm, Sat-Sun, 10am-4pm (last entry, 30min before closing time). Closed Easter, 25-26 Dec. 40Ft. ☎ 88/312 033.

VISEGRÁD

Salamon-torony – May-Sep, daily except Mon, 9am-4.30pm. 200Ft. ☎ 26/398 026.

Királyi palota – Daily except Mon, 9am-4.30pm. Closed 24-25 Dec. 120Ft. ☎ 26/398 026.

Fellegvár – July-Aug, 9am-6pm, Sep to mid-Nov and mid-Mar to June, 10am-5pm. 200Ft. ☎ 26/398 101.

Z

ZALAEGERSZEG

ℹ Kossuth Lajos u. 17-19 – ☎ 92/316 160

Göcseji Falumúzeum – July-Aug, daily except Mon, 10am-6pm, Sep-Oct and Apr-June, daily except Mon, 10am-5pm. 170Ft. ☎ 92/313 494. http://alpha.dfmk.hu/~muzeum

Magyar Olajipari Múzeum – May-Sep, daily except Mon, 10am-6pm, Apr and Oct, daily except Mon, 10am-5pm. ☎ 92/313 632.

Göcseji Múzeum – Apr-Oct, daily except Mon, 10am-6pm, Nov-Mar, daily except Sat-Sun, 10am-5pm. Closed 1 Jan, 25-26 Dec. 170Ft. ☎ 92/314 537. http://alpha.dfmk.hu

ZIRC

Reguly Antal Múzeum – May-Aug, Tue-Sat, 9am-noon, 1-5pm, Sun, 10am-noon, 2-4pm, Sep-Apr, Tue-Sat, 9am-noon, 1-4pm. Closed on public holidays. 100Ft. ☎ 88/415 422.

F. Peuriot/PIX

Waterfall in the Mátra

Index

Pécs . . . . Towns, sights and tourist regions.
Baranya . . . . Province
Kossuth (Lajos) . . . . *People, historical events and subjects*

Isolated sights (castles, abbeys, dams, passes, waterfalls etc.) are listed under their proper name.

A

B

C

D

E

F

G

H

P

R

S

T

V

W

Y

Z

MAGYAR KEPEK Kft

Notes

M. Guillou/MICHELIN

Please write to us !
Your input will help us to improve our guides.

Please send this questionnaire to the following address:
MICHELIN TRAVEL PUBLICATIONS, The Edward Hyde Building
38 Clarendon Road Watford Herts WD1 1SX

1. Is this the first time you have purchased THE GREEN GUIDE? yes ☐ no ☐

2. Which title did you buy?: ....

3. What influenced your decision to purchase this guide?

	Not important at all	Somewhat important	Important	Very important
Cover	☐	☐	☐	☐
Clear, attractive layout	☐	☐	☐	☐
Structure	☐	☐	☐	☐
Cultural information	☐	☐	☐	☐
Practical information	☐	☐	☐	☐
Maps and plans	☐	☐	☐	☐
Michelin quality	☐	☐	☐	☐
Loyalty to THE GREEN GUIDE collection	☐	☐	☐	☐

Your comments : ....

4. How would you rate the following aspects of THE GREEN GUIDE?

	Poor	Average	Good	Excellent
Maps at the beginning of the guide	☐	☐	☐	☐
Maps and plans throughout the guide	☐	☐	☐	☐
Description of the sites (style, detail...)	☐	☐	☐	☐
Depth of cultural information	☐	☐	☐	☐
Amount of practical information	☐	☐	☐	☐
Format	☐	☐	☐	☐

Please comment if you have responded poor or average on any of the above: ....

5. What do you think about the establishments provided in the guide?

HOTELS:	Not Enough	Sufficient	Too many
All categories			
"Budget"			
"Moderate"			
"Expensive"			
RESTAURANTS:	Not Enough	Sufficient	Too many
All categories			
"Budget"			
"Moderate"			
"Expensive"			

Your comments:

6. On a scale of 1-20, please rate THE GREEN GUIDE (1 being the lowest, 20 being the highest):

How would you suggest we improve these guides?

1. Maps and Plans:

2. Sights:

3. Establishments:

4. Practical Information:

5. Other:

Demographic information: (optional)

Male Female Age

Name:

Address:

Data collected may be used by Michelin Travel Publications for internal purposes only and not for resale.